VICTORIAN PRISON LIVES

English Prison Biography
1830–1914

PHILIP PRIESTLEY

With a New Introduction by the Author

PIMLICO

Published by Pimlico 1999

2 4 6 8 10 9 7 5 3 1

Copyright © Philip Priestley 1985, 1999

Philip Priestley has asserted his right
under the Copyright, Designs and Patents Act 1988
to be identified as the author of this work

First published in Great Britain by
Methuen & Co. Ltd 1985
Pimlico edition 1999

Pimlico
Random House, 20 Vauxhall Bridge Road,
London SW1V 2SA

Random House Australia (Pty) Limited
20 Alfred Street, Milsons Point, Sydney,
New South Wales 2061, Australia

Random House New Zealand Limited
18 Poland Road, Glenfield,
Auckland 10, New Zealand

Random House South Africa (Pty) Limited
Endulini, 5A Jubilee Road, Parktown 2193, South Africa

Random House UK Limited Reg. No. 954009

A CIP catalogue record for this book
is available from the British Library

ISBN 0–7126–6587–0

Papers used by Random House UK Limited are natural,
recyclable products made from wood grown in sustainable forests.
The manufacturing processes conform to the environmental
regulations of the country of origin

Printed and bound in Great Britain by
Creative Print and Design, Ebbw Vale

As one reads history, not in the expurgated editions written for schoolboys and passmen, but in the original authorities of each time, one is absolutely sickened, not by the crimes that the wicked have committed, but by the punishments that the good have inflicted.

Oscar Wilde, *The Soul of Man under Socialism*

FOR MY MOTHER AND FATHER

ESCAPING FROM THE IDEA OF PRISON

Introduction to the Pimlico Edition

What is prison for? At one level this is a naïve question. Everyone knows that prison exists to keep dangerous people under lock and key, to punish them for the crimes they have committed, to act as a warning to the rest of us, and with a bit of luck to reform some of them so they won't re-offend when they are eventually released. All entirely laudable ends, most people would say – and worth almost every penny that is spent on them.

This book begs to disagree and presents a point of view that comes from within the experience of prison in the Victorian era. It brings together the separate and dissonant voices of men and women – and occasionally children – who served sentences or worked in those places, and listens with respect as they slowly resolve into a mighty chorus of suffering – pain and misery whose origins and purpose were concealed from those who had to endure them. In fact their stories chronicle the failure of the extraordinary penitentiary experiment of the early nineteenth century.

When I first went to prison, towards the end of 1966, it was to work in one whose purpose was not at all concealed. HMP Shepton Mallet in Somerset housed an entire population of Rule Forty-Three prisoners – men segregated for their own protection from the violent attentions of their peers; mostly offenders against children, underworld informers, tobacco debt defaulters. I was intrigued by the people, and appalled by the place. It was painted half red and half yellow. It had a fully working gallows. As a key holder I soon got used to the curious, halting progressions made necessary by the locking and unlocking of gates – but I never got used to the smell of iron that clung to my hands, even into the evening. The chief officer and I shared a wash-room and he spent a lot of time in there washing his hands – after a while I found myself doing the same.

Stuart Wood is the pseudonym of a small-time crook and con-man who preyed on military families around the turn of the twentieth century. His book Shades of the Prison House *was one of the first prison biographies I read and his description of Shepton Mallet was one of the reasons I decided to gather other accounts and write this book. He writes well, and as a Christian convert in later life he also writes with engaging candour about his villainy and his life in prison.*

In my time there Shepton held some dangerous and violent offenders, all of them serving finite sentences, and all due to be released in due course. I came to two conclusions; firstly that prison in that form – in any form – was not a fit place for any human being to spend any length of time, and secondly that something constructive needed to be done with these men before they were released if they were not to repeat the behaviour that had brought them there in the first place. I approached the governor with a proposal to turn the prison into a kind of therapeutic community. He said what a good idea that was and referred me with a smile to local representatives of the Prison Officers Association. They told me, unsmilingly, to get lost. Which made the governor smile even more. I had doubts about therapeutic group-work which I thought lacking in scientific rigour. It was almost certain, I thought, to fail in practice. But in those days it was all there was.

The promoters of the great penitentiary experiment in the late eighteenth and early nineteenth centuries were faced with a similar dilemma but on a much larger scale. There was dissatisfaction with the state of unreformed prisons in Europe and North America – holding many naughty people together in free association was a recipe for corruption and contamination. The accelerating pace of industrialisation, changing sensibilities, and the heady rationalism of Enlightenment thought combined to create pressure towards fundamental change in the way that criminals and other problem groups were to be treated. A whole suite of architectural solutions was drawn up – the workhouse for the unemployed; the lunatic asylum for the mentally ill; and the penitentiary for the offender. Wonderful prison buildings were designed, palaces of order and purpose, of separation and solitary confinement, of hard work, and inward reflection. They enshrined the new legal ideas of proportion and equality and certainty that marked a shift from bodily punishment to work on the mind of the offender, and that imported mechanical analogies into social policy. 'A machine to grind rogues honest,' is what Jeremy Bentham called the prison he planned to build on the bank of the Thames where the Tate Gallery now stands.

One hundred Rule Forty-Three prisoners told me how they had been recruited to segregation status – of threats, of knives, of beatings, of boiling water, the alleged collusion in some of these events by staff at other prisons. The reasons for this rise in attacks on such men fascinated me. There were echoes, to my mind, of witchcraft accusations in earlier periods in both Europe and North America – the last judicial killing of a witch in Shepton town took place when the present prison was almost fifty years old. Mary Douglas's anthropological explanation of witch hunts is that they arise in communities with strongly demarcated boundaries and uncertain internal relations between people. The description fits the modern prison well, and my guess was that the phenomenon, being a structural one, would continue to increase. Rule Forty-Three prisoners serve a very useful function in helping prison populations define themselves. Mainstream prisoners themselves serve much the same function for the wider society. There seems to be a social need for symbols of belonging that leads to certain groups being reviled and excluded. The need will not go away; but it might be met, as we shall see, by other means.

Penitentiary buildings sprang up everywhere taking their place in a growing civic environment of schools, hospitals, lunatic asylums, town halls, libraries, museums, parks, workhouses, and sewage stations. Solitary cells replaced open wards. Silence fell across prisons throughout the land. What was happening was part of what historians of science now call a paradigm shift – a seismic re-arrangement of ideas with profound consequences for activities in the real world. But almost from the day they opened, the new prisons were manifest failures. Instead of reforming the inmates, solitary confinement appeared to drive some of them mad. Rationality had supplied a simple, utilitarian psychology for the business of reforming men's minds – an explanation of behaviour in terms of avoiding pain and pursuing pleasure. These common-sense observations still form the core of one branch of behaviourist psychology. But they fell far short of what is needed to truly change men's minds and amend their bad behaviour, and in its hour of need the fiercely rationalist enterprise of the new prison had hedged its bets and made common cause with an evangelical Christianity that promised an older mode, a surer road to salvation through repentance and good works. They were strange bedfellows and the union was not a happy one – nor was it blessed with numerous offspring in the form of converts to a crime-free way of life. And there was another reason for the failure of the penitentiary experiment. After the decline of public whipping, mutilation and execution, imprisonment became the punitive sentence of choice for many crimes. The whole focus of the new private form of punishment – and of the prison which is its epitome – remained exclusively on the person, the personality, and the conduct of the offender.

Until the end of 1968, no thought of the victims of crime had ever entered my head. Then in conversation with Chris Holtom, as we organised a round-table conference on prison after-care, an astonishing thought struck us. Daringly, as we thought, and in tune with the radical temper of the times, we had invited some former prisoners to attend. At this point we realised that the victims of crime were always left out of reckonings like ours, were missing from the criminal law, had disappeared from history, did not have a myriad organisations devoted to their welfare as did prisoners and offenders. So we also invited some victims. It changed our lives I think – it certainly changed mine. It led me to work over a number of years for the victim interest, and to show in a 1975 television programme, that victims and offenders, even in cases of extreme violence, could meet and learn from each other. Chris went on to create Victim Support which has helped millions of victims in this country and has spread to other countries. And victim-offender mediation which seemed a pipe-dream then is now a daily reality in many jurisdictions. We had stumbled upon an empty past and caught a glimpse of a different future. That future is now.

No mention of victims either in the pages of this book, or in the Victorian and Edwardian accounts on which it draws. It is one of the paradoxes of punishment that it creates a sense of victimisation in those to whom it is applied. So obsessed do prisoners become with their own suffering that they have no time to consider the suffering they may have caused to others. Victorian Prison Lives is full of these feelings. Justice itself is also a casualty of punitive policies. The consequences of conviction for a serious offence can be so dire that no rational person is likely to submit willingly to them. It is in the rational self-interest of an accused person to plead not guilty even when he or she clearly is. And it is sometimes in their interest to kill the victims of their crimes lest they live to tell the tale. So a system of justice designed to get to the truth and reduce the threat of crime can actually operate to obscure the one and increase the other.

For the past twenty-five years, with my friend James McGuire and others, I have been involved in efforts to develop and promote rational and effective alternatives to punishment and prison. One or two of our projects have shown signs of success. But recent reviews of research, based on more than two thousand separate studies, demonstrate overwhelmingly that punishment on its own either does *nothing* to stop people doing the same again, *or* makes it *more likely* that they will re-offend. On the other hand, well designed, theoretically coherent, empirically validated methods that address the person's offending behaviour in a direct and rational way, that teach thinking and problem-solving skills, that change attitudes and beliefs in a pro-social direction, and that provide alternative, positive models of behaviour can be shown to systematically reduce re-offending rates by between ten and sixty percent. These findings are finally beginning to fulfil some of the promise of the Enlightenment which aspired to use the methods of the natural sciences to tackle social ills. We are on the brink of being able to teach people who break the law how not to. English penal policy has just begun to adopt evidence-based methods that may lead in time to a world with less crime in it, and fewer victims.

When the failure of the penitentiary experiment could no longer be denied the expensive prison buildings were not abandoned along with their moral and social purposes. Instead an unlovely regime of silence and hard work and punishment for its own sake was evolved to fill the void and keep the buildings in use. There were no reformative elements at work for the later Victorian prisoner. Towards the end of the nineteenth century the futility of the regime was officially acknowledged – the writings of some of our Victorian informants, Rossa, Davitt, One-who-has endured-it, Oscar Wilde are important here – and a long process of liberalisation was started on humanitarian grounds. But there was no new vision of penal and personal reform. The Borstal experiment had its day then died.

The world of the near future may also be one with fewer prisons – indeed the prison as we know it could disappear altogether. How can I claim that? In modern societies criminal justice has to do two kinds of work – at a practical level it has to respond to crime in ways that increase public safety and diminish crime, and at a symbolic level it exists to express certain things about our society and to send messages to victims, to offenders, and to the public. Its record in the first of these domains is equivocal. Recent downturns in crime rates in the USA and the UK have been claimed as successes for zero-tolerance policing and for an increased use of imprisonment. There is no convincing evidence for causal connections between any of these factors. Prisoners as a proportion of the population in England and Wales increased enormously between 1945 and 1985, during which time there was also a continuous rise in crime rates. Crime rates were going down throughout the United States before the arrival of zero-tolerance policing, and they have declined equally in states with very different policing strategies.

On the symbolic plane, punitive justice fares even worse. As a form of communication it speaks a loud and violent language which most closely resembles that of the criminals themselves. It meets harm with harm. It operates at a level of moral development characteristic of very small children. It strikes a shoddy bargain with prisoners – you do the time and we will forget the crime. At the same time punishment ignores the needs of victims who receive only token attention in law and even less in the form of government expenditure to meet their needs. The moral space that is prison has been all but surrendered to a violent, crooked, and drug-driven prisoner society. All the problems that the reformed prison was originally designed to solve have returned with a vengeance.

It is ironic that the voices in this book raised so angrily against the cruelties of the Victorian prison, make suggestions for reform that are truly modest. If only the prison rules could be administered even handedly. If there was more concern for individual prisoners. More education. Better work. It is a reformist agenda at its most conventional. And it assumed the continuing existence of the prison more or less as it then was.

The disappearance of prison from our legal landscape may seem improbable to many people. There will always be dangerous men and women and children who must be restrained, but they are not numerous and they can be held somewhere like a hospital or a secure hotel, for our safety and not for their chastisement. For other offenders something better than prison is possible, and my suggestion is not made lightly:

1. The modern prison arrived on the scene almost overnight, historically speaking, the result of a paradigm shift in thinking about the criminal law. It could depart with equal abruptness.

2. Dissatisfaction with the reality of prison is widespread both within the system and outside it. Good work is being done by good staff in many places, but the system as a whole is not in a position to exert positive influences on most of the people it holds. Demoralisation is widespread in the face of increasing demands and tighter budgets.

3. The lunatic asylum and the workhouse, institutional contemporaries of the penitentiary, have both disappeared into historical oblivion. They sprang from the same sources within Enlightenment thought, were found not to work, and have been abandoned.
4. The outlines of a system of justice based on positive alternatives to punishment are already visible. Services for the victims of crime and a recognition of their formal status in criminal proceedings are slowly developing. Victim-offender mediation and conferencing methods that involve all the parties to an offence are being tried out. Cognitive methods have shown, even in large-scale trials, that re-offending rates can be systematically reduced. Together these changes form the basis of a new paradigm of criminal justice – one based on harm reduction, care for victims, and effective work to reclaim convicted offenders as citizens. Such a system provides better symbols for our society, and is more likely to introduce less crime.

Who would have said, when this book was first published, that Soviet Communism was about to disappear in its entirety? The comparison is not exact but the swiftness and completeness of the paradigm shift at work in human history is awesome to behold. Prison could be next.

Philip Priestley
February 1999

CONTENTS

LIST OF
ILLUSTRATIONS

The illustrations on pages 4, 7, 24, 28, 40, 53, 70, 86, 93, 109, 149, 200, 209, 216, 262, 269, and 281 are from Mayhew and Binney (1862).

The portrait of the Reverend John Clay on p. 100 is from Clay (1827).

The illustrations on pages 132, 175, 178, 272, and 285 are from Bidwell (1888); that on page 247 is from Lee (n.d.).

Those on pages 10, 13, 48, 126, 142 and 204 are reproduced by permission of the Mansell Collection.

The picture on page 161 is from A. Griffiths, *Mysteries of Police and Crime*, London, Cassell.

The illustrations on pages 245 and 250 are from Berry (1902).

PREFACE

In a long and distinguished career Sir Francis Galton made many contributions to Victorian science. One of them was finger-printing. He also devised – with the assistance of Herbert Spencer – a photographic technique which makes it possible to superimpose, one on top of the other, innumerable negatives taken of different individual faces. The resulting portraits – he called them 'generic images' – were like no likeness ever seen either by any human eye, or via the mechanical lens of the camera.

This book is conceived as a literary equivalent of that technique – an attempt to blend hundreds of personal narratives of life in the nineteenth-century English prison into a single, collective account. I have tried as far as possible in what follows to let prisoners and prison staff of the period speak for themselves. I have tried, and no doubt failed, to keep my own thoughts to myself. It is my present intention to write separately about the modern prison, and about a long and varied tradition of British political prisoners.

Meantime it is not necessary to look too hard at the details of this institutional picture to discern in them – no matter how dimly – the features of Leviathan wearing that iron grin that so reassures our rulers and yet unsettles the rest of us in ways we can't quite define.

1
INTO PRISON

On Tuesday, 27 May 1873, the Royal Mail steamer *Moselle* arrived at Plymouth from Havana. It was met by what *The Times* next day described as 'a large number of persons assembled on Milbay-pier'.[1] They were there in hopes of glimpsing Austin Bidwell, a 27-year-old American, en route to London to stand trial on charges of fraud against the Bank of England. Already in custody and similarly charged were three other Americans, including Austin's elder brother, George Bidwell. The Bidwells were, by their own accounts, the sons of religious and respectable parents; their father was a not too successful shopkeeper in and around Toledo, Ohio.[2] George especially had been an entrepreneur from an early age, buying and selling, and looking to make his fortune, at first by legitimate means, but increasingly by pitting his not inconsiderable wits against other businessmen in a succession of fraudulent enterprises. By 1872 he had graduated to international forgery on the grand scale and was enjoying a successful European trip. An accomplice, George McDonald – alias Macdonnell – had made a startling discovery in England: 'In America', he was to tell the court at his trial, 'when bills are presented at a bank for discount, when acceptances are presented, it is the custom to send the acceptances round to the persons accepting, to be what is technically called "initialed", in order that their validity and genuineness may be certified. I found that that was not the case here.'[3]

Out of this small difference between English and American financial practice was elaborated a gigantic swindle on the Bank of England. Austin Bidwell, the third principal in the conspiracy, had already opened an account under a false name at the Western branch of the bank in Burlington Gardens, with the unwitting assistance of his London tailor. Forged bills of various descriptions were made up for presentation; the cash proceeds to be transferred first to an account at the Continental Bank, and thence into untraceable US securities. The only person to 'show' himself during the whole of these proceedings was to be a 'clerk' called Edwin Noyes, summonsed from New York for the purpose, and in return for a promised 5 per cent of the gross takings.[4]

'With these simple means,' wrote George Bidwell later, 'I now proposed to enter the bomb-proof vaults of the greatest financial fortress of which history gives account.'[5] He and his colleagues entered them to such good effect that between 22 January and the end of February 1873 they had spirited no less than £100,405. 7s. 3d. from the hitherto impregnable vaults.[6] But on 1 March 1873 two bills from which the dates had been omitted were referred to Messrs Blydensteins, their supposed acceptor. They were at once declared forgeries; Noyes was arrested in the Bank, and the conspirators scattered.

Austin Bidwell was already abroad, on honeymoon in Cuba. McDonald fled via France for the United States. Following a chase through Ireland and Scotland, and some back-gardens in Edinburgh, George Bidwell was arrested by detective M'Kelvie on 10 March.[7] McDonald was seized on arrival in New York, and extradited after legal wranglings that went on until the 20th. Austin Bidwell was tracked to Havana by William Pinkerton of the celebrated agency, and put aboard the *Moselle* accompanied by four detectives.[8]

When the ship arrived at Plymouth on the afternoon of 27 May, 'So great was the crowd,' according to the *Times* correspondent, 'that it was with some difficulty that Bidwell and his escort managed to reach a cab, and were driven to the Duke of Cornwall Hotel adjoining the railway station. They left by the 7.45 mail train for London. A large crowd was present to see them off.'[9] The sensation that surrounded Bidwell's landing at Plymouth followed him to London and was to continue through the preliminary hearings at the Mansion House and at the full trial in August. Meanwhile, at the Westminster Hall, what was described by Lord Chief Justice Cockburn as 'the most remarkable trial that ever occurred in the annals of England' was entering its sixth week.[10] The man in the dock was charged with perjury, allegedly committed during civil proceedings to establish his right to substantial estates in Hampshire. He had emerged from the Australian outback in 1866, claiming to be the long-lost Sir Roger Tichborne, last heard of on board the sail-ship *Bella*, which disappeared in 1854 between Rio and Kingston. The prosecution, aided by members of the Tichborne family, sought to settle an entirely different identity on the man, who came to be known as 'The Claimant'. As Austin Bidwell made his journey towards London, a stream of prosecution witnesses entered the witness box to testify that the claimant was 'really' Arthur Orton, a butcher, and son of a butcher from Wapping.

Austin arrived in the capital early on the 28th – a 'bright spring morning', he recollects, and just as 'the mighty masses of that great Babylon were thronging in their thousands towards Epsom Downs, where on that day, the Derby,* that pivotal event in the English year was to be run.'[11] Bidwell, however, was bound for somewhat less crowded and far less convivial surroundings.

NEWGATE AND THE ENGLISH PRISON SYSTEM

'Newgate', he exclaims. 'The very name casts a chill; so too does a sight of that great granite fortress.'[12] Even to an American Newgate was notorious; it had been in use as a prison for nearly seven hundred years; William Penn and Daniel Defoe had been held there; the eighteenth-century highwayman Jack Sheppard had escaped from it into the pages of a penny literature devoted to sensational crime; other inmates were memorialized in successive editions of the Newgate Calendar. It had survived internal attack by the gaol fever, and external ones by the mobs of the Gordon Riots; it was the prison from which men and women and children had been dragged to Tyburn to be hanged; and its corrupt state had attracted the extraordinary evangelism of Mrs Fry. But Newgate was not only a monument to its own colourful past; it also did duty as the front entrance to a working prison system that was less monolithic in practice than first appearances might have suggested. In 1873 there were in fact two distinct prison systems in England and Wales. The older and more extensive of the two was the one which had been administered in the counties and the shires since the twelfth century by the justices of the peace. Beneath its spreading wings, this administration had gathered a ragged brood of prisoners and gaolers, and an ill-suited assortment of buildings in which to house them all. The most primitive of them were the 'pounds, pens and pinfolds';[13] old town lock-ups, not continuously in use, and accommodating local drunks and occasional malefactors as required. There were the Elizabethan *houses of correction*; originally intended for the discipline of unemployed and wandering labourers – the 'idle poor' – but increasingly indistinguishable from the co-existent *county gaols* in their role as depots for offenders awaiting trial; undischarged debtors waiting to be bought out; convicted men and women waiting to be hanged or transported; as well as a floating population of short-term prisoners waiting to be released after serving time for many petty offences against good order, against property, against the person, and, not least, against the laws that protected the interests of landowners and employers: the game laws and the law of master and servant.

Conditions in some of these prisons during the late eighteenth and early nineteenth centuries were marked by dirt and 'disorder' to an extent now difficult to grasp, despite the graphic descriptions of them bequeathed to us by prisoners and administrators, and by reformers intent on changing them. Squalor had been the outward order of their day, and extortion the principle on which their

* The winner was 40 to 1 outsider 'Doncaster'

Newgate: main entrance

inner economies flourished. Edward Ingall was a wardsman in Newgate – No. 24 ward on the Master's Side. In 1835 he was questioned by members of the Lords Select Committee on Gaols and Houses of Correction about his 'commercial' activities within the prison:

Have you ever procured Bread for any Prisoners while you have been there? I have sometimes. – From whom? It is brought by the Passage Man; it is brought from the Women's Side. – How does the Passage Man get it? That I cannot say. – What is the Name of the Passage Man? There have been several in my Time.[14]

Ingall sold the bread to fellow-prisoners at 'Two-pence Halfpenny and Three-pence for one of the Two Pound Loaves'.[15] 'Do you make any Profit?' he was asked. 'No,' was his reply, 'it is merely to accommodate the Men in the Yard; they are so ravenous they will eat anything almost.'[16] Between the lines of his guarded testimony, the *laisser-faire* nature of Newgate finance is clearly visible.

Alongside this 'private enterprise' local provision, a newer, smaller and – on dry land at least – an altogether more decorous prison system was adminis-tered by central government from London. It had gradually evolved out of the arrangements for transporting more serious offenders to penal colonies at the ends of the then known earth. Transportation was a substitute for death, the nominal sentence for a great range of offences until well into the nineteenth century. Some of those condemned to death were selectively – and no doubt unjustly – reprieved, and sent instead to spend the rest of their natural lives in the Americas. After the rebellion of 1775, they went to Bermuda, Gibraltar and Australia. Lesser criminals were sent out for shorter periods, and allowed after an interval to live at liberty in the penal colonies under the terms of a special licence known as 'the ticket of leave'. The government role in these events was at first restricted to gathering convicts from around the country and shipping them off to their destinations. As the distant colonies developed, largely but not entirely with the assistance of convict labour, they began to draw non-criminal immigrants of their own, and increasingly resented the continuing despatch of transports to their shores. For some time unwanted convicts were held in decommissioned naval vessels, or 'hulks', moored in the Thames estuary and on the south coast. Conditions in these craft, with their cramped and communal living quarters, were worse in some respects than places such as Newgate, and urged on by followers of John Howard, Jeremy Bentham and others, the government sanctioned the construction of a perma-nent national penitentiary in London. Millbank lay westward along the Thames from the Houses of Parliament. It was first opened in 1816, and was intended as a reformatory preparation for the subsequent banishment of con-victs. For various reasons to do with its architecture and regime Millbank was not a success. Renewed resistance from abroad and increased reformist pres-sure at home led to its replacement by the new 'model penitentiary' at Pentonville, and to the eventual creation in 1853 of a specific prison sentence to replace transportation, namely penal servitude. Prisoners were to serve these sentences in a growing number of government establishments, including the great convict stations at Portland opened in 1848, Portsmouth and Dartmoor (1850), and Chatham (1856), where a semblance of colonial labour was to be recreated on home territory.

Central government embarked on prison administration only reluctantly but, once begun, it found itself committed to a voyage that led inside a century to the complete nationalization of all the prisons in the country. On the basis of its own experience at Millbank and Pentonville, and subsequently in the run-ning of the convict prisons, the Home Office first acquired powers of inspection over the local gaols in 1835, and then promoted a succession of parliamentary measures to define and enforce the nature of the regimes which the justices were required to furnish within them. The last act in this creeping assumption of power was to be the Prisons Act of 1877, which transferred direct control of the local prisons to central government.

These encroachments did not go unresisted by the magistracy, and the battle which took place across the horizontal divide between 'national' and 'local' was compounded by a simultaneous controversy that split both systems from top to bottom. This was a fundamental and often virulent disagreement about penal theory and practice, whose course and outcome are exemplified in the careers of two men. It is not necessary to subscribe to an heroic view of social history to see the creation of a centralized prison administration in England and Wales as the handiwork of Major-General Sir Joshua Jebb and Major-General Sir Edmund DuCane. Both were soldiers, both were engineers, and both were vigorous penal administrators. But between the beginning of Jebb's work in 1839, and the end of DuCane's, in 1895, like one of the defensive ditches in the great military fortifications they both designed, lies a chasm that separates irreconcilable differences of both philosophy and method.

Jebb had made an early name for himself by advocating and designing a model penitentiary incorporating the thinking and the architectural shapes dictated by the 'separate' school of thought.[17] In essence this located prisoners in individual cells where they were held in strict solitary confinement. Reform was to be brought about by the influences of solitude, prayer, simple work, and the ministrations of sober, upright and god-fearing attendants. It was a bold conception demanding expensive new buildings and the employment of many virtuous men to make it work. The new national penitentiary at Pentonville, completed in 1842, made concrete these abstract principles but proved, alas, an expensive failure in practice, since it drove some men mad, and did not appear to reform others in numbers sufficient to redeem the original intentions of the whole experiment. A rival philosophy, that of the 'silent' system, had advocated that prisoners be kept in solitude at night but allowed to congregate during the day, in strictly enforced silence, for work and worship. A truly English compromise permitted the emergence in time of a regime which incorporated elements of both systems: separation *and* silent association. Under the later superintendence of Sir Edmund DuCane, the essentially moral purposes of both systems were discarded. Lip-service continued to be paid to the idea of reform, but its external forms were redirected towards ends of punishment and deterrence; towards the creation of a system of 'salutary terror'. This was the regime that was to become uniform throughout the prisons of England and Wales, but at the moment when Austin Bidwell was entering Newgate, it was a consummation that still lay some five years in the future.

The confused and confusing pattern of mid-Victorian prison administration is illustrated in a map which Henry Mayhew appended to his 1862 study of *The London Prisons*.[18] There were the state prisons at the Tower and the House of Commons, the former still in use for military prisoners; and there were three debtors' or civil prisons; one serving the Queen's Bench, one in Horsemonger

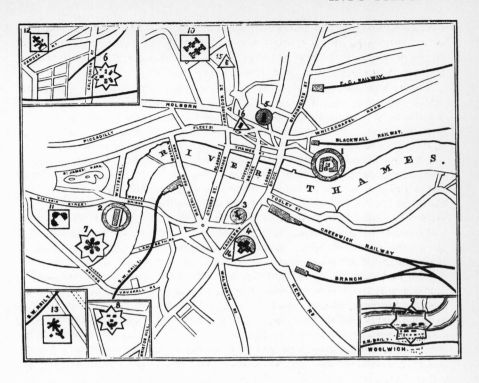

I.	II.	III.	IV.	V.
STATE PRISONS.	DEBTORS' PRISONS.	CONVICT PRISONS.	CORRECTIONAL PRISONS.	DETENTIONAL PRISONS.
Tower.	3. Queen's Bench.	6. Pentonville (Government).	10. Coldbath Fields (Middlesex).	14. Horsemonger Lane (Surrey).
2. House of Commons.	4. Horsemonger Lane (Surrey).	7. Millbank (ditto).	11. Tothill Fields (ditto).	15. House of Detention. (Middlesex).
	5. Whitecross Street (London and Middlesex).	8. Brixton (ditto).	12. Holloway (City).	16. Newgate (City).
		9. Hulks (ditto).	13. Wandsworth (Surrey).	

Map illustrative of the locality of the several prisons in the Metropolis of London

Lane, run by the Surrey county justices; and the third in Whitecross Street, run by the justices of London and Middlesex. There were three 'convict' prisons, at Millbank, Pentonville and Brixton, run by the government's commissioners of prisons, as well as some hulks on the river at Woolwich. Middlesex magistrates had two prisons for convicted criminals, at Coldbath Fields and at Tothill Fields, and one remand prison, the House of Detention at Clerkenwell. The Surrey justices were in charge of Wandsworth for convicted men and women, and Horsemonger Lane for the unconvicted. Finally the Court of Aldermen of the City of London reserved Holloway for convicts, and Newgate for prisoners awaiting trial.

POLICE CELLS

The Bidwells and their co-accused were kept at Newgate because of its proximity to the Central Criminal Court – the Old Bailey – where major trials were held. But for many other prisoners, both in London and elsewhere, captivity began in the rather less imposing and even more unpleasant surroundings of the police cells. The reception they received there could be rough and ready; the earlier in the century they were arrested, the rougher it was, and the readier. Thomas Cooper was a Chartist agitator whose fiery oratory sparked off the so-called Pottery Riot of 1842. He was taken to the 'lock-up' at Hanley, where, he says, 'a large, coarse fellow who was set to watch over me, put huge iron bolts on my ancles, so that I could not sleep as I lay in my clothes on a board.'[19]

Chartist leader William Lovett had not been chained, but was 'locked up' at the Marlborough Street police office 'in a dark cell, about nine feet square, the only air admitted into it being through a small grating over the door, and in one corner of it was a pailful of filth left by the last occupants, the smell of which was almost overpowering.'[20] It was a smell that was to get up the noses of political prisoners for a long time to come. Almost seventy years later, Lady Rhondda was arrested for damaging property during the campaign to secure votes for women. She was admitted to a police cell in Newport in which 'someone had been sick down one of the walls. It was a dark and a very dirty cell,' she says, 'and it smelt like a urinal.'[21] A similar thought struck Lady Constance Lytton, active in the same cause. The whole aspect of the remand cells at Bow Street police station, where she visited Mrs Pankhurst, 'more nearly resembled the "Ladies" at Waterloo than any known thing' she could recall.[22] In due course, Lady Constance found herself locked in one of these cubicles together with several companions in the struggle. 'Knowing that we had yet a long day before us, we in turns took advantage of the lavatory end of the cell, the others mounting guard in a group round the grating to ensure privacy. This was my first experience of the publicity attending this process throughout prison life. It is, without doubt, one of the greatest trials to the better-educated prisoner.'[23]

BLACK MARIA

For many hitherto 'respectable' men and women this abrupt decline into the company of the lower orders took place, not in the cells below the police offices, but in the van that plied between these places, the court-houses and the prisons. The van belonged to the local prison, and was more familiarly known as 'the black maria' or 'prison omnibus'.[24] In a ruder era the interior of these conveyances had reproduced in miniature the conditions of the unreformed prison. The inspectors for the Home District, appointed under the Prisons Act of 1835, could barely conceal their indignation at what went on in them:

They are 8ft. 4in. long, 4ft. 5in. wide, and 5ft. $5\frac{1}{2}$in. high, and will each conveniently accommodate about twenty prisoners, but upwards of thirty are occasionally conveyed. No officer, either male or female, is inside the van. It can excite no surprise that, under such circumstances, scenes of gross indecency constantly occur. We have ourselves been frequently present when the van has reached the prison and seen profligate characters, of both sexes, after being thus mingled together, descend from that carriage with clothing not sufficient to cover their nakedness.[25]

Little wonder then, that alongside his early drawings for a model gaol at Pentonville, *Captain* Jebb, as he then was, produced five pages of minutely detailed drawings for what amounted to a 'model' prison van.[26]

Externally the new van 'looked like a sort of hearse with elephantiasis',[27] but inside it conformed to the principles of separate confinement adopted for the penitentiary. One-who-has-endured-it was an anonymous Victorian gentleman – one of a number – who wrote about his *Five Years Penal Servitude*. His real name was Edward Callow, and the restrained intelligence of his best-selling book makes it the classic account of later Victorian prison life.[28] When he first climbed up into the maria for the trip to Newgate he entered a 'passage running up the centre from end to end of the "bus" with a number of doors on each side, through one of which', he says, 'I was gently pushed. I found myself shut up in a close box, with seat, not too well ventilated nor too clean, and out of the gratings of which I vainly endeavoured to catch a glimpse of the world I was leaving.'[29] Each cellule – 'a mere pigeon-hole or cattle compartment' – was so small that another gentleman prisoner's top hat 'fared badly',[30] and 'so shallow', according to a woman passenger, that 'it was impossible to sit properly on the narrow ledge provided. You had to sit sideways and you could not stand up, as the ceiling was too low. All you could do was shift about in a near-crouching position. When one side grew numb you changed on to the other.'[31] Very large prisoners could not be accommodated at all, as the Tichborne Claimant discovered: 'Owing to my immense bulk, and my weight being then about 25 st., the warders found they could not possibly squeeze me into one of the cells of the prison van.'[32] He was allowed instead to occupy a chair placed in the central corridor. Smaller mortals had no choice but to endure the worst that the construction of the vehicle had to offer: 'What with the darkness, the heat, the smell, and the jolting over the stones, it was more like being in the hold of some small coasting-steamer than anything else.'[33]

And to its physical discomforts, there was sometimes an element of mental anguish to be added. When Emmeline Pethick-Lawrence saw the size of the compartment she was to enter, 'my heart', she says, 'died within me. I climbed into the van, my heart beating wildly. I shut my eyes and prayed that I might not lose self control.'[34] 'There is a sensation almost of suffocation', agrees Jabez Balfour, 'in the tiny closet in which one is confined, and to a man of refinement' (in which category he placed himself, having been Member of Parliament for Tamworth and for Burnley, and chairman of the Liberator group of

The black maria

companies) 'the sudden association on terms of equality, for the first time in his life, with the noisy and ribald dregs of criminal and outcast London is an experience calculated to beget despair in the most sanguine mind. I have been through many more troubles since, but I shall never forget that disgusting ride.'[35] Part of the disgust was occasioned by the language of his fellow passengers; their 'oaths and obscenities' were 'stamped indelibly' on his brain.[36] Sylvia Pankhurst's female companions, 'some women taken up from another police court, were shrieking strange words I had never before heard, their voices in the inky blackness lending a horrible misery to the experience.'[37] That was the impact of low language on the virgin ears of gentlefolk fallen among thieves for the first time in their lives, but to the thieves themselves the van was a familiar environment. 'Spirits ran high' in the one that ferried journalist John Dawson from the court-house. 'The very natural excitement caused by being brought before the magistrate and the subsequent chatter and cracking of jokes in the police cells had not died out, hence what are termed "peckers" were kept wonderfully well "up," and one might have thought, judging by the geniality of the conversation, that we were now bound on a pleasure excursion rather than for a prison.'[38] In due course, they reached their destination, the House of Detention at Clerkenwell, where they 'were received by several breezy gentlemen in uniform, one of whom anon proceeded to call the roll. From some papers which he held in his hands he shouted out our names, and we had each to say what offence we were charged with. This was done in order to make sure no person had come here who should have been sent to some other prison.'[39]

IDENTIFICATION

For the greater part of the nineteenth century it was not possible to fix the identities of newly arrived prisoners with any certainty. 'Oh! So yer name's James Thompson now is it?' remarked the receiving officer at Clerkenwell to one of the men – 'a pickpocket to his fingertips'. 'It was "John Smith" the last time yer was 'ere.'[40] It was a ruse so often resorted to that Governor Chesterton of Cold Bath Fields felt moved to comment on 'the inexhaustible name of "Smith," a name, indeed, that perplexed us not a little, so very numerous were its bearers.'[41] There were good reasons why new prisoners should wish to shelter behind false names. One was to avoid being charged with additional offences they might have committed, and another was to escape the severe sentences that were awarded to those with proven previous convictions.

For their part, the authorities employed a variety of devices to make more certain the identification of the prisoners they held. They relied initially on a good eye and a retentive memory:

About a fortnight before the assizes Mr— opened my cell door, and a tall man with a very searching glance confronted me. He told me to look him in the face, and I stood staring at him in wondering amazement. He then turned to the warder and said something about me being a 'green hand'. I was afterwards told that he was the chief warder of Walton Gaol, in search of old hands, and on this occasion he renewed acquaintance with a good many old faces.[42]

More often this scrutiny took place out of doors. The prisoners were 'ranged shoulder to shoulder round the walls' of the exercise yard, and inspected by 'a long string of men in single file – the detectives some seventy or eighty in number, bent on a mission of recognition'.[43] John Dawson says there were paid officials called 'recognising officers – usually described in the newspapers as "sessions warders," ' and dressed in uniform. [44] The job of the detectives and the 'recognising officers' was to 'see if they could detect among the "new chums" any old offenders'. In George Bidwell's experience they 'seldom failed to call out several'.[45] But there was in this, and in similar scenes elsewhere, an unlooked for consequence which was spotted by John Dawson; namely that 'as matters at present stand, the detectives of London are better known to the criminals than the criminals are to the detectives.'[46]

Prison staff too took physical descriptions of newly arrived prisoners, for inclusion in the official records. To Lady Constance Lytton 'it was a comic moment when the wardress looked up with her head on one side, as any portrait painter might do, to investigate the colour of one's hair and eyes.'[47] In the case of Josh Poole – a drunken public-house fiddler – the examination was more intimate, and it was the examiner who appeared to find a kind of humour in it: 'every mark on my body was carefully set down in a book. On completing the survey, the officer, astonished at my leanness, said, "You would bring a poor price if you were sold as a nigger." '[48]

Detailed instructions were given in the Convict Prison Standing Orders of 1902 for measuring convicts and recording their 'bodily marks'. Specific items were listed for each area of the body: head and face, throat and neck, chest; e.g.: 'Back and loins (tattoo marks, hump-back or crooked spine, miners' marks, marks of corporal punishment, moles or birth marks, cupping marks on loins or between shoulder blades), etc. etc.'[49] Arms and hands and legs and feet merited separate entries of their own but Standing Order 28 insists that where female convicts are received 'in all cases the foot length, as well as the complexion, hair, eyes and distinctive marks, will be taken by a female officer'.[50]

But with or without such descriptions, recognition remained an essentially fallible business. A more inescapable justice had to wait on the contributions that science could make to forensic technique. Among the first of its products to be pressed into service were the newly popular arts of portrait photography. Governor Gardner of Bristol claimed to be the pioneer in this field: 'I introduced some years ago (indeed I was the first who introduced them) the daguerrotype portraits of prisoners, and from having succeeded in one or two cases, we introduced it more freely.'[51] It is perhaps fortunate for prisoners of the period that M. Daguerre made his invention when he did because other witnesses to the

At the prison gate

1863 Committee on Prison Discipline were in favour of more drastic means of identification. Governor Shepherd of Huntingdon saw no objection to 'marking' prisoners 'the same as a deserter is marked'. 'Would that be by means of gunpowder?' he was asked. 'I think that or Indian ink produces the most lasting impression,' he replied; 'it could be taken out but it would leave a scar.' He thought the best place for such a mark might be 'under the arm', 'in such a place as scars are rarely to be found, in some soft part of the flesh.' He did not have 'much faith' in the system of photography.[52]

Despite such doubts, it became a matter of routine to take photographs of prisoners just after their arrival in custody, and just before their departure. Precise instructions for the placing and focusing of the camera were accompanied in Standing Orders by advice to the photographer that 'the sitter should slightly moisten his lips before the portrait is taken to avoid an unnatural expression of the mouth.'[53] Not all prisoners submitted willingly to this exposure and some would not assist in even the most basic ways, let alone agreeing to lick their lips in the officially approved fashion. Eddie Guerin, a French–Irish–American gangster, was one of them: 'a couple of men took me away and informed me that I would be photographed whether I liked it or not. But for all the good it did them they might just as well have saved themselves the trouble. At the time they took it I was wearing a couple of months' beard. Also, on my way to the photographer I picked up a couple of pebbles, put them in my mouth, and screwed up my face until even my own mother would not have recognized me.'[54]

Although these tactics did not altogether destroy the utility of the likenesses, the absolutely certain identification of the criminal awaited yet another development. Shortly before Lord William Nevill left Parkhurst in 1901, 'the system of taking and registering impressions of the thumbs and fingers was introduced, a sort of Berthillon method . . . supposed to be an absolutely infallible means of identification', although that was, he thought, 'open to doubt'.[55] As with photographs, the consent of the subject was a prerequisite of good results. Mary Richardson adopted the suffragette policy of total non-cooperation with the prison authorities and was 'thrust into a chair while two wardresses pulled and twisted my fingers until the joints were so painful resistance became impossible. A series of blurs on the paper was all they got.'[56]

REMAND

Once ensconced in Newgate, Austin Bidwell 'took it for granted – since the law regarded us as innocent until we were tried and convicted – that we could have any reasonable favor granted us there which was consistent with our safe keeping. But no. The system of the convict prison was enforced here, and with the same iron rigor. Strict silence was the rule along with the absolute exclusion of newspapers and all news of the outside world.'[57] Other rules obliged the 'innocent' remand prisoner to 'polish his floor, keep up the lustre of his brass basin, scrub the table, and fold up his hammock and bedclothes, and arrange the smallest articles of his cell furniture in one precise way.'[58] Nor was he 'allowed knife or fork, and must tear the coarse food provided with teeth and fingers.'[59] At Leicester Prison, as a Royal Commission of 1853 learned, untried prisoners suffered 'stoppages of food for such offences as the following: – "Coughing to each other in the airing yard;" "attempting to communicate;" "attempting to look over the stall in chapel;" and "repeatedly turning round in chapel." '[60]

'It is a curious fact,' wrote Sir Edmund DuCane, looking back at the progress of the system in which he had personally played no small part, 'that amidst all the improvements and ameliorations in the lot of prisoners, which previous discussion had brought about, little or no attention had been paid to the unconvicted prisoner.' To his mind, the omission was put right by the Prison Act 1877, which 'requires the Secretary of State to make rules for the treatment of this class of prisoner, under which a clear difference should be made between the convicted prisoner and one who is presumably innocent'.[61]

The difference continued to be one that was more or less clear according to the private means at the prisoner's disposal. Those who were well off, like Jabez Balfour, were able to hire their own rooms, and even a servant:

> The windows of the room which I rented were heavily barred, the room itself was barely, but not uncomfortably furnished. There are, I dare say, many worse at fashionable watering places. I had a decent bed, and was allowed to pay a prisoner, who was detained for debt, sixpence a day, which he was very glad to earn, to clean out my room and make my bed.[62]

The privilege of feeding themselves was also vouchsafed to remand prisoners. They need not be rich to do this; Mark Jeffrey's mother worked as a servant, but she arrived to 'take him off the country' as he awaited trial in Cambridge prison on charges of burglary, for which he was subsequently convicted and transported. What this meant was that she agreed to supply him with 'special food at her own expense'.[63] Prisoners without relatives in the vicinity, however, were 'completely at the mercy of the shopkeepers, who are thus enabled to ask any price they like for most indifferent food, and in many places bribe the warders to bring them the prison custom'.[64] The advice of a gentleman prisoner who escaped this experience was 'to stick to the prison fare, and carefully to avoid the refreshments supplied from the cat's meat houses in the neighbourhood'.[65]

The perils of the 'cat's meat' affected only the affluent, but the more general point of equity claimed the attention of another pseudonymous gentleman, One-who-has-tried-them: 'It is all very well to say that a man can buy his own food and live like a fighting cock if he likes, but this looks suspiciously like one law for the rich and another for the poor'.[66] Another 'privilege' allowed the unconvicted prisoner was that 'any man who is wearing decent clothes is allowed to retain them while on remand if he wishes to do so; but no option is given to prisoners whose clothing is either ragged or dirty'.[67]

All of these discriminations, irritating though they might be, were as nothing compared with the difficulties placed in the way of the prisoner 'whose whole future welfare may depend on the arrangements he may make for his defence.'[68] Following his arrest, a middle-class prisoner, to his 'utter astonishment and dismay, was prohibited for nine or ten days to have any communication' with his friends.[69] The rules *after* nationalization in 1877 were admittedly generous as to letter-writing:

A prisoner on remand or awaiting trial may write one letter a day every day that Government will pay the postage of, and he may send as many more as he likes provided that he either pays the postage himself or is willing for them to be posted unstamped. There is no restriction on the number of letters he may receive.

But it was a mixed blessing since 'every letter, whether going out or coming in, is read by the prison authorities, and in many cases copies of them are taken and supplied to the prosecution'. According to Frederic Martyn: 'This was done in my case, and it appeared to me to be a glaringly unfair proceeding, because the police were thereby made acquainted with every step I was taking in my defence, and the not over-scrupulous detectives were able, in two cases at least, to influence people whom I had asked to give evidence in my behalf to give evidence against me.'[70]

Lawyers were another hazard. John Hay had worked as a solicitor's clerk before himself being sentenced to seven years' penal servitude. He confirmed the suspicions harboured by many prisoners about their legal representatives. 'What tales could be told of the villainies of solicitors or their clerks, who receive fees from poor, unhappy wretches who expect to be properly defended, but find themselves left in the lurch!' And the damage did not end there since he had 'known wives and friends to pawn watches, jewellery, and other articles to find the money for the defence of those dear to them.'[71]

Nor were solicitors alone in their pursuit of profit at the expense of the helpless remand prisoner. Frederic Martyn found himself besieged from every quarter:

Everybody who is brought into contact with a prisoner during the police court stage of his case is on the make . . . the detective who arrests him expects something; the gaoler at the court will ask him if he wants the change out of the half-crown he has given to the officer to purchase food; the warders at Brixton hover round him with solicitous attentions if he looks as if he has money or moneyed friends. . . . One of the warders at Brixton even asked me to give him my dirty underclothing, and got it too.[72]

TRIAL AND SENTENCE

The trial itself was often as much of an ordeal as the period of waiting that preceded it. 'The misery of those eight days!' sighs Austin Bidwell. 'No language can describe it, nor would I undergo it again for the wealth of the world.'[73] Despite a dignified and eloquent plea from McDonald, and a statement from George that Austin and the fourth partner Edwin Noyes were, if not entirely innocent, then certainly less culpable in the matter, all four were duly

found guilty by the jury on 26 August 1873. Mr Justice Archibald then proceeded to sentence: 'I can see no palliating or mitigating circumstances in your
offence', he told the prisoners at the bar:

> You were persons of education, so far, indeed, as I can apply that term to
> persons of mere intellectual training without any corresponding develop-
> ment of the moral sense. You, who now ask for mercy, and who are not
> restrained by respect for law and honesty, must be met with a terrible
> retribution; and it should be well known that persons who commit crimes
> which only persons of education sometimes commit will be sure to meet
> with a very heavy punishment. The sentence is that each and all of you be
> kept in penal servitude for life; and, in addition to that sentence, I order
> that each one of you shall pay one-fourth of the costs of the prosecution.[74]

George Bidwell, 'strange as it might appear, felt an immediate relief from the
terrible strain of the previous five months. The worst now being known, a great
load seemed removed, for the matter was settled – my career on earth
finished.'[75]

'Ordinary words', says Jabez Balfour, 'cannot describe the feelings of a man
in my position. It seemed then the end of everything. One's whole life flashes
across one's brain in a second – childhood, youth, earliest ambition, family
life, children, success, failure, ruin and – fourteen years penal servitude! The
sentence was so colossal that I quite failed to realize it, and at one moment my
brain seemed to regard it almost as a gigantic and absurd joke.'[76]

Lord William Nevill, found guilty of fraud, denied a newspaper report that
he 'seemed utterly stunned' by his sentence of five years' penal servitude. 'I had
come to regard myself as someone else, with whom I could sympathize, but in
whose feelings I had only a secondary interest.'[77] This state of detachment no
doubt helped him run the gauntlet of 'the huge crowd in the street' which had
greeted his arrival for trial at the Old Bailey. After receiving his sentence he was
kept in a cell 'until three or four o'clock, the authorities not thinking it advisable
for me to be taken out until the crowd had dispersed'. He was then handcuffed
and 'driven off in a four wheeler. There were still a great many people about,
and on the way I constantly saw my name in big type on the posters, with the
verdict underneath.'[78] In Lord William's case, the crowd was neutral; merely
intrigued to see a member of the aristocracy in such unaccustomed circumstances. Austin Bidwell had been accorded almost a hero's welcome at
Plymouth. In other cases the function of the law as public spectacle spilled out
on the streets and aroused conflicting passions. At Liverpool, where another
American citizen, Mrs Florence Maybrick, was sentenced to death for poisoning her well-to-do husband: 'the mob, before they had heard or read a word
of the defense had hissed me when I entered the court; and now, that they had
heard or read the evidence, cheered me as I drove away in the prison-van, and
hissed and hooted the judge, who with difficulty gained his carriage'.[79]

RECEPTION

Prisoners newly arrived at the Middlesex County Gaol – Cold Bath Fields –
were ushered into the 'Reception Room'. 'Can any name', asks Captain
D— S—, 'be more suggestive of satire, except perhaps "Mount Pleasant", the
hill so called on which the prison stands. The reception we received in the
Reception Room was far from a cordial; it was, indeed, as cold as the weather
outside. The Reception Room is octagon shape, with benches arranged over the
entire floor; on these we were directed to sit down, about a yard apart. In front
was a large desk and a high stool, on which a turnkey was perched, whose sole
duty was to prevent the least intercourse between the prisoners; in fact, the
entire room and its fittings conveyed the impression of being connected with a
charity school for mutes.' In these cheerless surroundings, and in similar places
the length and breadth of Victoria's realm, men and women began the process
of becoming convicts; here that, as the captain puts it, 'the prisoner is transformed into the Queen's livery.'[80]

The first step in this transformation was the surrender of personal property.
'Goodbye to pipe, watch, chain, collar, tie, matches, fountain-pen, purse, and
the money in it. With great sorrow we come when we are called, to lay these on
a desk where a warder enters them in the Property Book.'[81] These preliminaries
did not long detain people like 'the sickly pale faced consumptive youth' who
had 'only three buttons to declare'.[82] Even minor articles of personal toilet were
forbidden entry with the new prisoner. George Bidwell had been allowed to
leave Newgate with 'two serviceable silk handkerchiefs, a tooth and a nail
brush'. On arrival at Pentonville, an officer 'took away the handkerchiefs, and
ordered me to stamp upon the brushes and break them.'[83] 'If you are particular
about your teeth, my man,' the chief officer of Millbank told One-who-has-
endured-it, 'use a corner of your towel.'[84]

Prisoners were next required to remove their clothes, so that they might be
searched, and to prepare them for the bath – the universal institutional
baptism.

THE BATH

One-who-has-endured-it thought the bathing arrangements at Newgate 'very
similar in every way to ordinary second-class baths at the various public establishments in London. All,' he says, 'was clean – water, towel and bathroom.'[85]
Frederic Martyn, who described his stay at Brixton as A Holiday in Gaol,
reported 'luxurious porcelain baths' there.[86] But at Leicester there was a 'leaden
bath'.[87] The prison bath-house patronized by yet another pseudonymous
author, One-who-has-suffered, was 'a long, low whitewashed shed, scantily
lighted by a few small windows in the roof, and having on either side a series of

closets, about 26 inches wide by 35 inches from front to back; the depth from floor level to bottom of bathing place was about 20 inches. These so called "baths" were separated by walls of corrugated iron, about 7 feet high; the doors or wickets to each bathing place did not reach lower than about 12 inches, so affording a full view of the occupant to the individual in the opposite bathing place. Holes large enough to distinctly see the bather in the adjoining cells were very frequent in the corrugated walls or divisions. The lower part of this "bath" was coated with cement and a curious dark, greasy slime which caused an uneasy shudder to the bather when touched by the naked body.'[88] It was not only the slimy cement that caused prisoners to shudder.'The first time I saw my bath', says one, 'I was thoroughly disgusted, as the water was not unlike mutton broth.'[89] In some establishments the state of the water was due to the design of the baths. 'The bath-room is a dark dingy room, with a narrow strip of water on each side, divided into compartments, but not dividing the water; and it is not a very pleasant thing for a man to have to bathe in the same water along with men suffering from every variety of skin disease and cutaneous eruptions.'[90] Nor were women excused 'the filthy horrors of reception, when all wash from one tank, and wipe on one towel'.[91] So much then for the bath, which as Captain D— S— remarks, 'admirably fulfils its twofold function; it insures a thorough wash, and removes the last trace of one's former self.'[92]

THE PRISON DRESS

It was at this point that newly convicted prisoners took leave of their 'citizen's apparel'.[93] 'Do you identify these as your clothes?' One-who-has-endured-it was asked at Millbank as he began his five years of penal servitude. 'Yes, I did.' 'They were ruthlessly cast aside into a corner where plenty of other bundles were lying.'[94] 'I had been previously told that whatever clothes I wore or had when convicted would be forfeited; I took care therefore not to wear too good a suit and all the extra clothes I had in the prison for change I had sent away previously.'[95] Balfour, the former MP, was not so ready for the loss of his clothes; 'Even though I had grown accustomed to "the slings and arrows of outrageous fortune" and was prepared for this experience, this breaking with the old life by the casting away of its garments proved a greater trial than I anticipated.'[96] A different sense of loss was felt by John Hay. 'I had to doff a suit of good clothes that had cost me £5, and these I never saw again.'[97] And when he had finished grieving at the symbolic passing of his former self, the financier in Balfour brought him to the same subject. As he understood it, a contractor paid the government 'two and sixpence a suit for good and bad alike. It appears that the Government actually appropriated this half-crown – a proceeding, of course little short of theft.'[98]

The lack of uniformity in the administration of English local gaols showed most noticeably in the different kinds of dress they required their inmates to wear in place of their own clothes. They did not quite embrace all of the colours of the rainbow, but they accounted for quite a part of the spectrum. One-who-has-tried-them saw men 'clad in a combination of bright scarlet and grey' at one prison, and in 'dark chocolate and the brightest canary yellow' at another; the colours at both places 'arranged in alternate patches'.[99] These displays were not without their critics. Frederic Hill was an inspector of Scottish prisons, then inspector of northern prisons in England, and he thought 'the use of party-coloured clothing' to be 'opposed to that feeling of self-respect which, in the process of reformation, it is so important to create and preserve'.[100] It was a view that prevailed and subdued colours became the height of prison fashion. A prisoner at Kirkdale in Lancashire was issued with 'articles as would have been an appropriate costume for the "artful dodger" – a coat of dirty brown shoddy, full of patches, a pair of trousers, and vest of same material.'[101] The suit at Holloway consisted of 'blue serge jacket and trowsers'.[102] A prisoner at Leicester was supplied with 'a bran new suit . . . the colour of a blue bag'.[103] And Captain D— S— was handed a bundle containing 'a pair of blue worsted socks, a blue striped shirt, a blue pocket handkerchief the thickness of a tile, a towel as coarse as a nutmeg grater, and a suit of clothes.'[104]

Even more distinctive was the dress designed for men serving sentences of penal servitude:

> Each man was dressed in a short, loose jacket and vest, and baggy knickerbockers of drab tweed with black stripes, one and a half inches broad. The lower part of their legs were encased in blue worsted stockings with bright red rings round them; low shoes and a bright grey and red worsted cap, which each man wore in accordance to his own taste, completed the costume. One thing spoiled it. All over the whole clothing were hideous black impressions of the Broad Arrow, the 'crow's foot' denoting the articles belonged to Her Majesty.[105]

'The broad arrow', according to one prison officer, 'is the mark of the Board of Ordnance, which is placed on all descriptions of property belonging to the board. We find this mark on soldier's great coats, not only for regiments of the line but the artillery; and it is placed on these garments to deter soldiers from selling them.'[106] The appearance of this 'hideous dress', described by Jabez Balfour as 'the most extraordinary garb I had ever seen outside a panto-mime',[107] was made worse by the fact that, to begin with at least, 'no one article had the slightest semblance of fitting'.[108] 'As the height of the convicts was from four feet six inches to six feet, and the bundles were thrown down to each convict indiscriminately, the grotesque figures presented by these miserable wretches when the order was given to "pace to the front" and "come out of your baths" was ludicrous in the extreme.'[109] No attempt was made to put the Tichborne Claimant in standard-issue dress – 'they had not got any clothes big enough to put me in' – and special ones were made to accommodate his great girth.[110]

Until quite late in the nineteenth century there was also a notable omission

from the wardrobe. Jeremiah O'Donovan Rossa was a Fenian, convicted of
'treason felony', who arrived at Pentonville on a cold Christmas Eve in 1865.
'The first thing I looked for,' he recalls, 'were the flannels, but I looked for them
in vain. I asked where was the inside clothing, and was told there was none.
This was the most cruel treatment, for it was mid-winter, and the snow was
covering the ground.'[111] Women fared no better in the dress department. The
outfit provided at Tothill Fields for Mrs Susan Willis Fletcher consisted of
'brown serge prison-dress . . . with a not unbecoming white hat. The stockings
are blue with a red stripe, and very coarse. There is one white flannel skirt, and
a flannel under vest if the prisoner is wearing one at the time of admission; but
there are no drawers (and this slight addition would prevent much suffering), a
brown serge petticoat, skirt and jacket, and blue check handkerchief to wear
under the jacket, and another for the pocket (very coarse and rough) and a
white cotton cap.'[112] The rules were later amended so that 'If you have flannels
and drawers on, they give them to you,'[113] and these consisted of 'a flannel shirt
and drawers, having at intervals a red line wove in the material'.[114] But to avoid
any charge of pandering to the luxury of the convict, 'underclothing was only
made of one size', when One-who-has-endured-it worked in the tailor's shop at
Dartmoor. 'What will fit a big man there is no difficulty in a little one getting
into.'[115] And eventually drawers were issued to women as well, although these
sometimes proved to be less than welcome. Mrs Pankhurst, for instance,
'shivered' herself 'into some frightful underclothing, old and patched and
stained'.[116] The ones issued to Constance Lytton looked 'as if they had been
washed in cold water by a child'.[117] Sylvia Pankhurst also had difficulties over
an item of underclothing which she did *not* wish to wear, 'a curious sort of
corset reaching from neck to knees'. ' "You have not put on your stays!" the
wardress screamed at me, with indignant scorn. "I don't wear them." "Unless
you were not wearing stays when you came in, you must put them on at once!"
"Did she bring any stays in with her?" A long discussion ensued.'[118]

The distribution of shoes to both sexes was organized on principles consistent
with those adopted for the clothing. At Cold Bath Fields 'a warder, accompanied by two prisoners carrying sacks, made their appearance. The contents
of these, being thrown on the floor, were discovered to be boots, not new ones,
or even pairs, but very old and dirty, mended and patched with lumps of
leather on the soles, on the heels, and, in fact, anywhere. We were now invited
to "fit" ourselves, and a scramble ensued amongst a section of the prisoners.'[119]
Mrs Fletcher's shoes were 'made very low, with very thick soles' and apparently
designed to 'fit as may happen'.[120] At the convict public-works prisons men
were issued with working boots which almost defied even the descriptive
abilities of one so fluent with the pen as Jeremiah O'Donovan Rossa:

But weren't they boots? Fully fourteen pounds in weight. I put them on
and the weight of them seemed to fasten me to the ground. It was not that
alone, but the sight of the impression they left on the gutter as you looked
at the footprints of those who walked before you, struck terror to your

heart. There was the felon's brand of the 'broad arrow' impressed on the soil by every footstep . . . the nails in the soles of your boots and shoes were hammered in an arrow shape, so that whatever ground you trod you left traces that Government property had traveled over it.[121]

MEDICAL EXAMINATION

Either before or after or during the fitting of the prison dress, it was customary to subject the prisoner to a medical examination. This might consist simply of weighing and measuring. 'My weight', says Mrs Maybrick, 'was one hundred and twelve pounds, and my height five foot three inches.'[122] Or it might mean a perfunctory physical inspection: 'told to let down my trousers and pull up my shirt to be examined.'[123] Sylvia Pankhurst and her companions trooped past the doctor fully clothed. ' "Are you allright?" "Are you allright?" he asked mechanically, not waiting a reply, touching us lightly with his stethoscope, but not pausing to apply his ear to it.'[124] One-who-has-suffered claims to have been medically examined whilst standing in a 'dirty coalyard' in 'cold drizzling rain'.[125] But Lord William Nevill's medical examination was far from a formality. 'I was next examined by the doctor, who at once ordered me to be admitted to the hospital, as I was already beginning to suffer from a painful and troublesome internal complaint, which very nearly necessitated an operation.'[126] Part of the doctor's duty at this juncture, more disciplinary than medical, was to pronounce prisoners 'fit for hard labour, or light labour, or the hospital, or the observation cell, according to his rapid judgment.'[127] Many of the prisoners would of course have had little previous knowledge of being medically examined for any purpose, but for someone like Lady Lytton, 'It was a new and strange experience to be so closely examined by a doctor and not to learn anything of his verdict.'[128]

HAIR

By now the appearance of the new convict was almost complete, save for a finishing touch which some prisoners found the most cruel of all; for example Mrs Maybrick: 'The warder then stepped quickly forward, and with a pair of scissors cut off my hair to the nape of my neck. This act seemed, above all others, to bring me to a sense of my degradation, my utter helplessness; and the iron of the awful tragedy, of which I was the innocent victim, entered my soul'.[129] 'I knew this must come', says One-who-has-endured-it, 'but dreaded it greatly.'[130] 'As close as the scissors can go: them's the governors's orders', said the convict-barber to One-who-has-tried-them.[131] 'No combs are used in cutting convict's hair,' according to One-who-has-suffered: 'the scissors are laid flat on the head and cut away all hair until the officer can feel the scalp; the beard the same'.[132] And poor Balfour did not 'know to what extent it had taken place till I put my hand to my head when the process was half finished, and felt that my head was already almost as smooth as a billiard ball.'[133]

The effect of these procedures on new entrants to the prison system was profound: as *The Times* reported concerning George and Austin Bidwell, George McDonald and Edwin Noyes, 'Before they left Newgate, they were shorn of their beards and whiskers, and clad in prison garb, and no one, it is said, could have recognized them after this change in their appearance had been effected.'[134]

One last act of dispossession remained before the convict could be led away to begin his new life. It came disguised as a gift – 'your number, which takes the place of your name, is marked upon an iron plate worn upon the right breast of the jacket, and the number of your cell in calico upon your back.'[135] A more temporary expedient at one prison was 'a huge chalk mark on our backs', [136] but the usual insignia given to the prisoner was a cloth disk 'bearing the number and location of the cell he was to occupy. He was told to hang this label on the top button of his coat.'[137] The number given to Jeremiah O'Donovan Rossa was '26'. 'This 26 was the number of my cell, and it was to be my name in prison. I was newly christened, and the name of Rossa was to be heard no more. 'Twas 26 here and 26 there and 26 everywhere.'[138]

THE RULES

As the reception procedures came near to completion it was customary to introduce the newly made convicts to the rules and regulations that would govern their lives, in some cases for years to come:

> After our bath, one of the principal warders read over the whole of the rules and regulations to us, strongly impressing on us the necessity of observing every one of them, if we wished to avoid punishment. As it took him about three quarters of an hour to read them, by the time he had got to the last rule I had forgotton all the others, with the exception that whilst almost every rule contained a punishment clause, I could not remember one that referred to a reward.[139]

The sole regulation which 'stuck' in one man's memory was 'Salute the Governor when yer see him.'[140]

At long last the process was completed, the first day in prison drew towards its end – a day full of incident, but also one, as Constance Lytton puts it, 'of longer waiting than I had ever thought a single day could contain. Already one began to taste that peculiar feature, most markedly characteristic of the whole of prison life, that of being in ignorance of what is going on outside your cell, of

why you are being kept there, and of what will happen to you when the keys
jangle, bolts rattle, the door is thrown open, and you are ordered out.'[141] It only
remained to show the new prisoners, 'fairly installed in convict dress, washed
like babies, cropped like cocoa-nuts', to their living quarters.[142]

Before its final demolition in 1902, Newgate was only used for some years,
when sessions were in progress at the Old Bailey. W.T. Stead was one of those
whose first taste of prison took place in this strange environment: 'Newgate is a
deserted gaol. The long corridors, like combs of empty cells, stand silent as the
grave. As we were marched down passages and through one iron gate after
another, I experienced my first feel of gaol. It is a feel of stone and iron, hard
and cold, and, when, as in Newgate, the prison is empty, there is added the
chill and silence of the grave. Overhead the tiers of cells, with their iron balus-
trades and iron stairs, rose story after story. It was as if you were walking at the
bottom of the hold of some great petrified ship, looking up at the deserted
decks.'[143] Millbank was even more of a labyrinth than Newgate; we will follow
One-who-has-endured-it from the reception area to his cell:

> When fully equipped, and feeling very uncomfortable, I was marched off
> down a passage and through a door at the foot of a winding spiral stone
> staircase into the Pentagon yard – across this and through a gate or two in
> the dividing railings and into a similar door – up a spiral stone staircase
> like the first one I had passed – one flight – two flights – three
> flights – to the very top where I was transferred by the warder who had
> conducted me so far to the care of another warder, and he at once pointed
> out the way along the passage to a cell, the door of which he opened and
> introduced me to my first lodging under Her Majesty's roof. The little
> ticket with my number on he took from me, placed it in a rack over the
> doorway, and shut me in.[144]

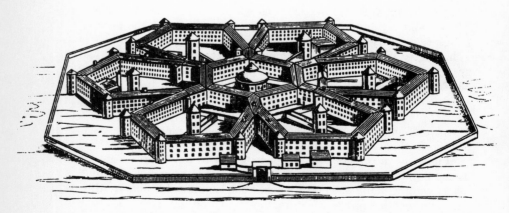

Bird's-eye view of Millbank Prison (copied from a model by the Clerk of the Works)

NOTES

1. *The Times*, 28 May 1873.
2. G. Bidwell, 27.
3. Dilnot, 251.
4. G. Bidwell, 195.
5. Ibid., 201.
6. Dilnot, 53.
7. G. Bidwell, 247.
8. A. Bidwell, 375.
9. *The Times*, 28 May 1873.
10. Woodruff, 370.
11. A. Bidwell, 379.
12. Ibid., 379.
13. Wilmott Dobbie, 3.
14. Select Committee on Gaols (1835), 1st report, 310.
15. Ibid., 310.
16. Ibid., 312.
17. Report of the Surveyor General (1844), 171.
18. Mayhew, 276.
19. Cooper, 212.
20. Lovett, 81.
21. Rhondda, 154.
22. B. Balfour, 143.
23. Ibid., 60.
24. G. Bidwell, 402.
25. Second Report of the Inspectors. (1837), I, 18.
26. Third Report of the Inspectors. (1838), I, 155.
27. Lytton, 63.
28. Halkett and Laing, 107.
29. One-who-has-endured-it, 3.
30. *Pentonville Prison from Within*, 19.
31. Richardson, 14.
32. Orton, 29.
33. One-who-has-tried-them, I, 128.
34. Pethick-Lawrence, 168.
35. J. Balfour, 14.
36. Ibid., 14.
37. S. Pankhurst, 230.
38. Dawson, 72.
39. Ibid., 77.
40. Ibid., 77.
41. Chesterton (1856), I, 120.
42. *Kirkdale*, 17.
43. D— S—, 63.
44. Dawson, 110.
45. G. Bidwell, 264.
46. Dawson, 112.
47. Lytton, 75.
48. Poole, 67.
49. Standing Orders (1902), 292.
50. Standing Orders (1902), 6.
51. Carnarvon Committee (1863), 336.
52. Ibid., 290.
53. Standing Orders (1902), 322.
54. Guerin, 88–9.
55. WBN, 47.
56. Richardson, 153.
57. A. Bidwell, 380.
58. Letter, 493.
59. One-who-has-suffered-it, 583.
60. Leicester Inquiry (1854), x.
61. DuCane (1885), 73.
62. J. Balfour, 17.
63. Hiener, 49.
64. One-who-has-tried-them, I, 158.
65. D— S—, 17.
66. One-who-has-tried-them, I, 155.
67. Martyn, 53.
68. Letter, 491.
69. Henderson, 12.
70. Martyn, 91.
71. Hay, 3.
72. Martyn, 49.
73. A. Bidwell, 386.
74. Dilnot, 273.
75. G. Bidwell, 399.
76. J. Balfour, 27.
77. WBN, 19.
78. Ibid., 24–5.
79. Maybrick, 57.
80. D— S—, 139.
81. *Pentonville Prison from Within*, 21.
82. Brocklehurst, 3.
83. G. Bidwell, 403.
84. One-who-has-endured-it, 73.
85. Ibid., 7.
86. Martyn, 153.
87. Barrow, 6.
88. One-who-has-suffered, 3.
89. Kirkdale, 14.

90. Sykes, 188.
91. Fletcher, 320.
92. D—S—, 142.
93. G. Bidwell, 401.
94. One-who-has-endured-it, 72.
95. Ibid., 41.
96. J. Balfour, 38.
97. Hay, 30.
98. J. Balfour, 38.
99. One-who-has-tried-them, I, 195.
100. Hill (1894), 261.
101. *Kirkdale*, 3.
102. One-who-has-just-left-prison, 25.
103. Barrow, 6.
104. D—S—, 141.
105. One-who-has-endured-it, 68.
106. Such, 11.
107. J. Balfour, 36.
108. WBN, 25.
109. One-who-has-suffered, 4.
110. Orton, 29.
111. Rossa, 84.
112. Fletcher, 321.
113. One-who-was-there, 12.
114. One-who-has-suffered, 3.
115. One-who-has-endured-it, 307.
116. E. Pankhurst, 100.
117. Lytton, 85.
118. S. Pankhurst, 231.
119. D—S—, 140.
120. Fletcher, 321.
121. Rossa, 127.
122. Maybrick, 64.
123. Barrow, 6.
124. S. Pankhurst, 230.
125. One-who-has-suffered, 2.
126. WBN, 25.
127. *Pentonville Prison from Within*, 23.
128. Lytton, 74.
129. Maybrick, 63.
130. One-who-has-endured-it, 48.
131. One-who-has-tried-them, I, 201.
132. One-who-has-suffered, 5.
133. J. Balfour, 37.
134. *The Times*, 2 September 1873.
135. One-who-has-just-left-prison, 25.
136. D—S—, 159.
137. Martyn, 60.
138. Rossa, 97.
139. Sykes, 137.
140. Brocklehurst, 4.
141. Lytton, 59.
142. Fannan, 93.
143. Stead, 3.
144. One-who-has-endured-it, 74.

2
THE CELL

'Alone with God and a wounded conscience.'

The cell was to be the physical hub of the new prisoner's unfamiliar future. Its size and shape and purposes were the products of a bitter historical battle between two ideas: between separate confinement and silent association, from which the advocates of separation had at first emerged victorious during the 1830s. Their victory was celebrated in the construction of a government penitentiary at Pentonville in 1842, and in the rash of imitative building that spread across the country in the years that followed.

To the prisoner who knew nothing of this history, the cell was no more than a special kind of room. 'Imagine to yourself,' we are invited by Frederick Brocklehurst, 'a whitewashed cube 7 feet by 13, with a barred window of ground glass at one end, and a black painted door at the other, and you can form some idea of the dimensions and appearance of a prison cell.'[1]

Brocklehurst belonged to the recently formed Independent Labour Party. Its Manchester members insisted on exercising rights of assembly and free speech on the Boggart Clough, an historic open space and popular meeting place in Manchester. For defying a local order banning meetings on the Clough, Brocklehurst, together with a colleague, Leonard Hall, was committed to the borough gaol for one calendar month in 1896. Strangeways was a local prison, in whose construction 'the model of Pentonville' was 'pretty closely adhered to

Corridor at Pentonville Prison
(from a drawing in The Report of the Surveyor-General of Prisons)

. . . Colonel Jebb having had the approval of all the designs'.[2] The intention, as in all these designs, was to create what a penitentiary chaplain called 'a noble building – the very reverse of gloomy' and such as to show at once to a man that he was entering 'a prison of instruction and of probation rather than a gaol of oppressive punishment'.[3]

A quite different message was spelled out by the cellular arrangements at Chatham, Dartmoor, Portland and Portsmouth, where men were sent to complete their sentences of penal servitude labouring on large-scale public works projects. Jabez Balfour's cell at Portland was 'nothing but a small corrugated iron kennel with a stone or slate floor . . . seven feet long, seven feet high, and four feet broad'.[4] It reminded one gentleman of 'a small second-class state room on board an emigrant ship'.[5] Convict 77, a person of humbler station in life, thought his 'smaller than the third class compartment of a railway carriage'.[6] But whatever their social origins, many convicts saw the cell as a dismal terminus. 'Oh, don't put me in there,' cried Mrs Maybrick, 'I cannot bear it.'[7] Her cry was one that echoed and re-echoed around the stone walls of the prison house. Helen Gordon heard it years later at Strangeways: 'a scream of horror – re-iterated, imploring – rising in notes of entreaty – "Don't put me in there," over and over again, until the voice changes from entreaty to impotent anger till the limit is reached – there is terror of the thing feared, and the terror of lost self-control'.[8] Mrs Maybrick's entreaty fell on deaf ears. 'For answer', she says, 'the warder took me roughly by the shoulder, gave me a push and shut the door.'[9]

Inside the locked cell, the first impression was one of darkness; the gloom in Mrs Maybrick's was relieved only 'by the dim light of a window that was never cleaned'.[10] 'Outside, the day may be blue and gold,' said Oscar Wilde, 'but the light that creeps down through the thickly-muffled glass of the small iron-barred window beneath which one sits is grey and niggard. It is always twilight in one's cell, as it is always midnight in one's heart.'[11] Reading, where Wilde was held, was a local gaol reserved for not so serious offenders: even less light penetrated to the penal servitude prisoners. 'Daylight never entered' Convict 77's cell at Portland, 'except through the aperture under the door,'[12] and at Dartmoor the limited illumination came via a 'narrow window of thick rough plate glass' which gave onto the *interior* of the prison. Only 'immediately close to the window' was there 'light enough to see anything distinctly'.[13] Until quite a late date the Dartmoor cells were lit at night by candles, but at Millbank the standard equipment was a 'small gas-jet protruding from the wall about 4 feet from the ground'.[14] The unauthorized use of the gas for self-asphyxiation, and of the jet itself for suspending nooses, led to its reinstallation behind a 'tiny thick ribbed glass window, inserted in the wall outside'.[15]

But if light was supplied through these openings – 'as grudgingly as food',[16] – there were others through which generous measures of supervision were possible: 'alongside the door was a loophole similar to those usually seen in old castles for arrow slits, and in fortified outworks for musketry firing. . . .

Anyone walking along the corridor could see at once the inmate of the cell and what he was doing, and had a full view of him both when at work or in bed.'[17] Another singular device for keeping watch on prisoners was 'the eye that never slept'.[18] This was a 'cunningly contrived spy hole'[19] in the centre of the cell door, sometimes made to resemble a human eye, 'complete in every detail, pupil, iris, eyelashes, eyebrow, etc. It was not only painted but carved, to add to the realism of the thing.' 'No matter how you would place yourself in your cell, standing, sitting, or lying down, that cursed eye seemed to follow you'.[20] Below the spy-hole, in some cells but not all, there was 'a trap door, eighteen inches by twelve, cut in the door itself',[21] which could be opened only from the outside, and used both for passing things through and for inspection.

The slits and spy-holes were meant to be looked through in one direction only, and in a way that robbed the observed prisoner of privacy, but other contrivances were provided which allowed him or her to communicate with staff in the main body of the building. In some cells there was to be found 'a thin lath of wood, 3 foot long, $2\frac{1}{2}$ inches wide, and ¼ inch thick; one half painted on both sides black, and the other bright red.' One-who-has-endured-it 'was at a loss' to understand the purpose of this 'mysterious wand' until an officer explained, 'When I wished to speak to a warder for any purposes, I was to put out the red end from the inspection aperture, to cause him to come to me.'[22]

More mechanically advanced was the 'gong in the corridor, the handle of which is just inside, and to the right of the door';[23] 'when the gong is rung, a wooden slip attached to the handle just outside the door, is projected into the corridor, having on it the number of the cell in bold characters, and should the warder happen to be aside when the gong sounds, his attention is called to the sign directly he enters the corridor'.[24]

Two kinds of distress most commonly prompted recourse to these signals: sickness of all sorts, and an urgent need to use the closets. If the prisoner was fortunate, his 'signal was immediately attended to, and he was carefully let out'.[25] On this point, the members of the 1879 Penal Servitude Commission were assured by 'officers that ample facilities are given' for men wishing to go to the closets. But after 'personal inquiries made of some prisoners at Pentonville' they came to the conclusion that they were 'not quite satisfied that there is no ground' – note the delicate double negative – 'for complaint in this respect'.[26]

THE 'BEAK'

So long as prisoners remained in their individual cells, communication – and contamination – could be reduced and kept to a minimum. But on those occasions when prisoners had to be moved about the building, to go to the closets or the bath-house or the yards, or to see the governor or the doctor, then problems arose. In the early days of the penitentiary, administrators sought to

extend the anonymity of separation into situations where prisoners were associated together. Their chosen instrument was the mask or 'beak': 'every one
wears a peculiar brown cloth cap, and the peak of this (which is also of cloth)
hangs so low down as to cover the face like a mask, the eyes alone of the
individual appearing through the two holes cut in the front, and seeming
almost like phosphoric lights shining through the sockets of a skull. This gives to
the prisoners a half-spectral look.'[27]

Critics of the mask insisted that it did not work. 'In passing along the corridors, the men see each other's forms, motions, and as much of the face as they
wish, in spite of the hood-beak – one of the paltriest expedients for self-
deception ever invented.'[28] And eventually Joshua Jebb himself came to the
view that 'the mask or peak does not prevent prisoners from recognising each
other in the prison; moreover that as prisoners see each other before they are
brought to the prison, come in considerable bodies, and are assembled together
when they leave the prison, it would be desirable to discontinue it, since the use
of it appears calculated to depress the spirits of the men, without obtaining any
corresponding advantage.'[29]

The mask came off therefore, but a shadow of its intention lingered on. In
Newgate it took the form of 'a lively and instructive regulation . . . that if a
prisoner is passing from one portion of the prison to another, and he meets
anyone on his journey, he has to halt, put his hands behind his back, and stand
with his face to the wall, like a schoolboy in disgrace, until the individual in
question has passed him.'[30]

FURNITURE

In the cell itself, the largest, and arguably the most important, item of furniture was the bed, or what passed for it. 'The first thing' noticed by Arthur
Harding, an East End criminal, was that he had 'no bed to sleep on. Some
eminent Christian with the love of Christ in his heart had ordained that we
were to sleep on a plank of wood.'[31] The 'eminent Christian' was H.H.G.
Herbert, the fourth Lord Carnarvon, and chairman of the 1863 Lords Select
Committee on Prison Discipline. His report turned out to be a signpost in
nineteenth-century penal history, pointing the system away from what were
seen as the failures of the penitential and reformatory ideal, and increasingly in
the direction of punishment and deterrence. One of the committee's recommendations was that 'during short sentences, or the earlier stages of a long
confinement, the prisoners should be made to dispense with the use of a
mattress, and should sleep upon planks.'[32]

In fact many of them did *not* sleep, for as Oscar Wilde observed, 'the object
of the plank bed is to produce insomnia. There is no other object in it, and it
invariably succeeds. . . . It is a revolting and ignorant punishment.'[33] One-
who-has-tried-them, when he first tried one of them, 'was as sore all over' as if he

had been 'beaten with a good thick stick'.[34] And for the first few weeks, Austin Bidwell's made his 'bones ache'. But the answer, he found, lay not so much in the material properties of the bedding as in men's minds:

> Most men have little patience and small fortitude, and this bed kills many of the prisoners. I mean breaks their hearts, simply because they do not have the wit to accept the matter philosophically and realise that they can soon become used to any hardship. It took six months for my bones to become used to the hard bed, but for the next nineteen years I used to sleep as sweetly on that oak board as I ever did or now do in a bed of down.[35]

The officially issued pillows were made in the same mould as the mattresses; the one on which rationalist missionary George Jacob Holyoake laid his head was of 'coarse sacking stuffed with cocoa-nut fibre, so hard that it flattened and elongated my ears beyond the length which my adversaries expected to find in a person of my way of thinking.'[36]

Over the boards, or the mattress, went the bed-clothes. 'The old filthy blankets' issued to Chartist William Lovett 'stank so abominably' that he and his companion were obliged to 'shake them up and down for upward of an hour before we could bear to lie down in them.'[37] Other complaints were of 'a fetid, greasy scum' that remained on the prisoner's body after contact,[38] and of 'bedclothes soiled with human soil'.[39]

The enemies of sound sleep had another ally, and that was the hammock – a legacy of the hulks, and widely but not uniformly used in both local and convict prisons. It lingered on until well into the twentieth century, and was not without drawbacks. It was normally equipped with 'straps of leather to stretch it across the cell' and these were prone to break in the middle of the night. Balfour 'experienced this fate two or three times. Shivering and bewildered, the victim has to gather up his bed clothes, summon the patrol, and receive from him another strap. Then the bed has to be made up again as best it might. All this had to be done in the dark by a man wearing no other garment than a cotton shirt, and pattering about the stone floor with bare feet', the whole proceedings being enlivened 'by the curses of the men near him whom the accident had disturbed.'[40] Despite all that, One-who-has-endured-it retained an admiration for the hammock, with its 'two good blankets (three in winter), a capital rug, and two stout, coarse linen sheets, with a wool or hair pillow. A great many of prisoners', he surmises, 'never slept in such good beds when free men.'[41]

The rest of the contents of the typical cell take up as little space on the page as they did in their original surroundings. 'A wooden platter and spoon, a wooden salt-box, two tin pint-mugs, a bright pewter chamber utensil, an ordinary school slate, a large wooden bucket or pail, with wooden flat hoops, and fitted with a close-fitting lid, a short-handled hair-broom or brush', was the full list at Millbank.[42] There were also some minor but necessary items of toilet: 'a coarse towel which hangs on a nail or hook, on the door, and a piece of soap, which rests on a few little squares of soft brown paper'.[43]

Earlier versions of the penitential cell, designed for absolute separation, were furnished with their own lavatory arrangements. They did not long survive the abuses of those untutored in their use but examples survived into the 1870s in places such as Newgate, where the cells had 'a water closet seat in one corner', and 'a bright copper wash basin, burnished like gold, fastened to the wall, with a water tap over it'.[44] They proved to be mixed blessings. Dr McCook Weir had one in his cell, but 'the flushing was contemptible and was carried on through the discharge pipe of the wash hand basin in proximity thereto.'[45]

Lastly, all cells, except those reserved for prisoners undergoing punishment, contained a standard issue of printed materials: 'A Bible, Prayer Book, and Hymns Ancient and Modern were arranged upon the table, and above it were hung a copy of the rules and dietary.'[46] 'The cell with its paraphernalia,' by one contemptuous estimate, 'would be a dear bargain at £10.'[47] 'Scantier appointments were impossible,' thought another prisoner, and yet, to his surprise, 'an officer came in one day with an inventory, to see if anything was missing.'[48]

SILENCE AND SOLITARY: THEORY AND PRACTICE

No merely physical description of the cell and its contents, no matter how minute or detailed, yields any real clue to the spiritual and moral purposes for which it was designed. In order to understand why so many Victorian prisoners were locked up in these gloomy rooms and forced to endure absolutely solitary confinement that might last anything from a few days to eighteen months, and for many hours of each day thereafter, it is necessary to look back at what went on in the unreformed prisons of the late eighteenth and early nineteenth centuries. Cold Bath Fields prison in 1827, at the beginning of George Laval Chesterton's governorship, is as good a place to begin as any. 'As the yard was approached', he says, 'the ear was assailed with a discordant buzz of voices, occasional singing and whistling, and ever and anon an interjectional shriek.'[49] For such a confirmed disciplinarian, the *sounds* of the yard at a distance were no more than a prelude to the distress he was to feel at the *sight* of its denizens. 'Some were wholly clothed in the prison garb, others wore a portion only of that attire, while, perhaps, one-half of the division retained their own clothes, however tattered or unseemly they might be.'[50]

The 1835 Select Committee on Gaols and Houses of Correction closely questioned the governor of neighbouring Newgate about stories that 'there was gambling carried on all Day long; Card-playing. Pitch and Toss and Chuck Farthing', and that some prisoners were 'boasting of their former Robberies, some cursing and swearing, telling of obscene stories, and some singing vile Songs'.[51] Members of the committee also examined a number of convicts at

Millbank about their experience in local prisons in different parts of the country, and, although there were exceptions, the picture they painted generally confirmed the Newgate evidence. Here and there, these ribaldries were lubricated with quantities of beer; supplied in Newgate by the ubiquitous Edward Ingall. In theory he was allowed to serve only two pints per man per day. Was it possible, he was asked, that some prisoners asked others to purchase beer for them over this limit? 'No, I do not think it; that may be the Case; I think it is very likely but it has not come under my Recollection.'[52] Thomas Dexter, also a Newgate prisoner – but not a wardsman – had a clearer recollection of the quantities allowed:

> I never knew any Limit; as much as you could obtain Money for. . . . I have known several purchase as much as Eight Pints; and it was a common thing to fill Two or Three Buckets, and carry them up into the Ward. Always, the Night previous to the Sessions commencing, it was the Rule, and had been for Years, as I was informed, to have what is called a Free and Easy, when any Person that would not sing was compelled to undergo some little Punishment.[53]

So what with the language, and the beer, and the lack of supervision, and the overcrowding they had heard of, their lordships clearly suspected that one thing might lead to another between the prisoners. 'Do you not conceive it possible,' Ingall was asked, 'from the manner in which they sleep together that Offences of a very disgusting Description may take place?' Edward the innocent, his recollection clouded no doubt by his daily two pints ration, had 'never heard of any thing of the Kind being attempted'.[54] The next witness, principal Turnkey Mr Matthew Newman, was more forthright when asked if *he* had ever heard of such goings-on. 'I have', was his reply.[55]

The tenor of the committee's questioning indicated the general conclusion they were eventually to reach, namely that imprisonment in Newgate, and in other places where conditions were the same, 'must have the effect of corrupting the Morals of their Inmates, and manifestly tend to the Extension rather than to the Suppression of Crime'.[56]

It was a desire to remove these sources of corruption that led the 1835 committee to propose fundamental changes in the English prison system. Their views were not in the least revolutionary; their origins can be located in a tradition of reformism that predated the work even of John Howard. And in the fifty-eight years that had elapsed since the first appearance of his book, *The State of the Prisons*, the perils of 'promiscuous mingling' had been widely advertised by many other labourers in the same vineyard: clergy, politicians, philanthropists and lady visitors. Condemnation of these evils was so widespread as to constitute an almost unanimous expression of enlightened opinion in the early part of the nineteenth century. All the more surprising therefore to discover with what violence this degree of agreement was torn apart when it came to deciding how best to put the situation right.

The recommendations of the Select Committee started with the proposition that 'One uniform System of Prison Discipline be established in every Gaol and House of Correction in England and Wales.' More importantly for the future development of imprisonment in England and Wales, they suggested a means by which this uniformity might be achieved, namely that 'Inspectors of Prisons be appointed to visit the Prisons from Time to Time, and to report to the Secretary of State'.[57] As to the nature of the 'uniform System' the committee wished to see established, the intellectual climate of the time presented them with 'two principal plans between which a choice must some day be made . . . the silent and the separate'.[58] Given the virulence with which individuals attached themselves to one or the other of these two positions, it is curious that the terminology sometimes gave rise to confusion. 'The term Silent or Silence', according to the Reverend Daniel Nihill (who was also governor at Millbank from 1837 to 1843, a unique permanent post for a clergyman), 'fails to mark the distinction, and these systems are in consequence generally confounded. Silence is no more the attribute of the one than of the other, being, in fact, equally characteristic of both. The main difference is this: under the Silent System the prisoners are collected in masses for work and other purposes, but are forbidden to speak or hold any intercourse: under the Separate System they are precluded from intercourse, by being kept not only in silence, but separation at all times.'[59] The 1835 Committee came down firmly on the side of 'silence', recommending

> That entire Separation, except during the Hours of Labour and of Religious Worship and Instruction, is absolutely necessary for preventing Contamination, and for securing a proper System of Prison Discipline [and] That Silence be enforced, so as to prevent all Communication between Prisoners both before and after Trial.[60]

Prisons had already begun to adopt 'silent regimes'; among the first being the county gaol at Wakefield. The event is recorded in the governor's cryptic journal entry:

> 18 March, 1834. Four extra Assistants as Superintendents were appointed to carry out American system of silence, they acted as overlookers of the wardsmen who were appointed in every workshop.

By 9 May 1834 he was able to report the 'conduct of wardsmen satisfactory; they are vigilant and anxious to retain their stations,' but the remainder of the prisoners were more restless: 'Silence was very irksome to the men. 533 deprived of their food.'[61] There was no such resistance from prisoners when, shortly afterwards, Governor Chesterton imposed silence on the noisome yard at Cold Bath Fields:

> On the 29th December, 1834, a population of 914 prisoners were suddenly apprized that all intercommunication by word, gesture or sign,

was prohibited; and without a murmur, or the least symptom of overt opposition, the silent system became the established rule of the prison.[62]

Chesterton's commitment to the rule of silence was passionate but it was not shared by powerful figures in the emerging Inspectorate established by the Prisons Act of 1835. William Crawford had been a leading light in the Prison Discipline Society before his appointment as one of the first inspectors. The Reverend Whitworth Russell had been chaplain at Millbank. Both were committed, with a passion that equalled Chesterton's, to the rival system of 'separation'. There were home-grown precedents for both the idea and the practice of solitary confinement as the basis of a penitentiary regime. Gloucestershire magistrate Sir George Onesiphorous Paul had built and run a number of prisons in the county along these lines around the turn of the eighteenth century. Millbank itself had attempted something similar but failed. For fresh inspiration penal reformers of the 1820s and 1830s looked across the Atlantic, where working examples of the 'separate' and 'silent' systems were to be seen at Walnut Street, Philadelphia, and Auburn, New York, respectively. Crawford had paid a visit to Philadelphia and, together with Whitworth Russell, made use of the annual Inspector's reports to make propaganda for the 'separate' cause. Their persistence was rewarded with a decision to construct a new national penitentiary at Pentonville along 'separate' lines, much to the chagrin of Chesterton who thought they had been unfair to his 'silent' experiment at Cold Bath Fields. 'The separate system', he complained, 'was panegyrised in a tone of magniloquent exultation and the silent system was derided, and assailed with every vituperative term that verbose hostility could supply.'[63]

The design of the new penitentiary was entrusted to Captain Joshua Jebb of the Royal Engineers, who had no doubts about his preferences. 'The silent system of discipline has its advocates, but the arguments in support of the advantages of association, however strictly regulated it may be, leave so much obvious evil untouched, that there can be no question as to its being wrong in theory, and if so, it will be difficult to prove it right in practice. We will therefore dismiss the silent system with faint praise, and advert to the details of the separate system.'[64] In his eyes, the virtue of the separate system was that 'in depriving a prisoner of the contaminating influences arising from being associated with his fellow prisoners, all the good influences which can be brought to bear upon his character are substituted for them; and that scarcely an hour in the day will pass without his seeing one or other of the prison officers, and that he is required to have constant employment or labour.'[65] The plan at Pentonville was to test the theory under near-ideal conditions, holding selected prisoners in solitary confinement for eighteen months, prior to their being transported to Australia. Jebb clearly saw what he was doing as a model for the future: 'with reference to prison discipline we are evidently on the eve of reform. The subject is under anxious consideration from one end of Europe to the other; and there appears every reason to believe that the separate system of discipline will, by its own merits, eventually bear down all opposition'.[66] He was right. Local magistrates up and down the land did not wait to see what the results of the experiment would be; they began at once to build new prisons and adapt existing ones after the fashion of Pentonville.

One of the reasons for the immediate success of the 'separate' system was its capacity to appeal simultaneously to different and often conflicting constituencies of interest. It appealed, at one level, on purely punitive grounds. General Dyott argued with his fellow magistrates in Stafford for the new cells to be arranged in 'such a manner that they should be a terror to the inmates by making them truly solitary, lonely, and as inconvenient and irksome as the human mind could bear'.[67] Its appeal to divines and reformers was on quite different grounds. Of all the voices raised in favour of 'separation' none was more persistent, or listened to, than that of the Reverend John Clay, chaplain to the Lancashire County Gaol at Preston between 1821 and 1857. For him the choice of method was dependent on 'whether to *punish* for the crime already committed, to *deter* from the repetition of it, or to *reform the culprit*, should be the main object. It is scarcely necessary for me to add, that I consider the *reformation* of criminals a paramount object in their discipline.'[68]

Two types of metaphor flourished in the discourse of those who supported these reformatory ambitions; the medical and the mechanical. The chaplain at Wakefield saw 'a close and obvious analogy between the physical and spiritual parts of man. The diseases of the body have their counterparts in the soul. . . . If the one has its malignant fever, the other has its ungoverned passions – if the one has its odious leprosy, the other is covered with "the wounds and bruises and putrefying sores" of lust, pride, avarice, envy, and ambition.'[69]

The nature of this diagnosis led inevitably to the formulation of pseudo-medical remedies for crime:

> Some argue that it is very unnatural to isolate men and seclude them in separate cells; but it is not more unkind, than to isolate an individual with the plague, and keep him under medical treatment, until the contagion shall have been removed, and the individual be fit to resume the duties of life.[70]

In this isolated state, so the theory continued, in 'the solitude of the cell . . . alone with God and a wounded conscience, the unhappy man is forced to exercise his powers of reflection, and thus acquires a command over his sensual impulses which will probably exert a permanent influence.'[71] For the Reverend J. Kingsmill, a further, but rather different attraction of 'solitary' was the nicety with which it was 'calculated to strike more terror into the minds of the lowest and vilest class of criminals than any other hitherto devised, whilst those who have not fallen so low, feel more than compensated for its peculiar pressure, by the protection and privacy which it affords, and most of all the penitent.'[72] Such a system, was, in Clay's words, 'adapted to reform the one, and deter the other. It may be said, indeed to possess, as regards the characters of the confined, a *self-adjusting principle.'*[73] It possessed, in other words, something of the quality of a machine. If machines could help men acquire mastery over the material world, and the evidence that they could was everywhere to be seen in the early Victorian era, then might they not prove to have equally dramatic applications in the moral sphere as well?

Nevertheless, not everyone connected with the penal enterprise agreed that machines were necessarily the proper thing for human beings. When the penitentiary crossed from England to Ireland it drew sharp criticism from the chaplain of Spike Island Prison in Cork harbour. He described the first governor of Mountjoy as 'somewhat in the position of a boy who had been made a present of a new mousetrap, full of curious little chambers, and worked by a multiplicity of springs, of whose operation he was ignorant. Not wishing to injure his fingers, he went to London to take lessons from the Governor of Pentonville, on the proper working of the new trap.'[74] But although his simile turned to toys, the Reverend Charles Gibson did not think the penitentiary a mere plaything. On the contrary. 'A cellular prison is a delicate piece of machinery,' he warned, 'which no unskilful hand should touch. A few more turns of the screw, and you injure both the body and mind of the prisoners.'[75] And so it proved in practice at Pentonville.

To begin with, the annual reports of its commissioners reflected an urbane optimism about the splendours of the separate system. But by their sixth report, that of 1848, there is talk of 'some instances of partial aberration of mind not amounting to insanity,' and, more worryingly, 'the occurrence of hysterical convulsions in some of the convicts on their first being embarked for transportation'.[76] Governor Chesterton, still smarting at the summary dismissal of his 'silent' regime by Messrs Crawford and Russell, was pleased to dilate on the effects wrought by eighteen months' solitary confinement on a batch of Pentonville convicts: 'At the expiration of that time, they were transferred to Millbank Prison, where their attenuated condition, and mental disturbance, created a marked sensation in the mind of the then governor, Captain Groves, who could not repress his condemnation of separation to so fatal an extent'.[77] Even Elizabeth Fry, whose vision of prison discipline for both men and women was far from sentimental, became an implacable opponent of separation and of its supporters. 'They may be building,' she confided in her journal, 'though they little think it, dungeons for their children and their children's children, if times of religious persecution or political disturbance should return.'[78]

As the tide of experience and opinion turned against his pet scheme, John Clay mounted a rearguard action in defence of separation: 'after an eight years' trial of our plan . . . I may now state, that *not one case of insanity has ever resulted from it.'* Some individuals, he even insisted, had 'decidedly improved during their imprisonment'.[79] However, he felt compelled to acknowledge that solitary confinement 'should be for short periods',[80] for 'at a certain point the cell loses much, if not all, of its penal character. In proportion to the prisoner's mental and spiritual improvement, the sense of punishment passes away. He declares that he is "very contented", that his prayers have procured for him peace of mind, and that, were the choice in his power, he would choose to be alone in his cell, with his books and his work, in preference to association with other prisoners.'[81] Clay may have seen this as a tactical withdrawal in the face of hostile evidence; an attempt to re-muster what was left of the theory around some defensible if undefined period of optimum effectiveness, but it was a losing battle against critics like Chesterton armed with the facts about Pentonville: 'The public may now contemplate the very insufficient grounds upon which the separate system was ushered into England,' he declaimed. 'It rested upon conclusions, seized upon and held fast, equally against facts and sound deductions.'[82] And now that he thought victory over the separate system was in sight, he permitted himself a little dance on its grave:

That the engaging aspect of the buildings, the unbroken quietude prevailing, and the subdued demeanour and copious tears of the inmates, should lead captive the minds of philosophical inquirers, is to me a subject of deep wonderment; but that it should evoke the admiration and enthusiasm of Christian hearts, is a matter of still graver astonishment.[83]

He would have done better to curb his natural exultation, because the result of the contest turned out to be neither a win for the 'silent' system he preferred, nor a defeat for the 'separate' one, but a draw. What emerged from the débâcle was a distinct child of neither system but the bastard of both; what William Hepworth Dixon described as 'an imperfect amalgam of the two rival disciplines, the best element of the social, or silent, system, the labour in common, being left out.'[84]

Following the Pentonville fiasco, the period of solitary confinement that preceded transportation, or transfer to one of the convict public-works establishments, was progressively reduced from eighteen months to twelve months (1848), and then to nine months (1853)[85] and, after a longer interval, to six months (1899).[86] So for most of the second half of the nineteenth century the 'normal' period of solitary confinement for the convict was nine months. For men and women in the local gaols the practice of separation varied until the 1877 Prison Act imposed a centralized uniformity upon them. Thereafter, all those sentenced to hard labour served the first twenty-eight days in solitary confinement, which in the case of short sentences meant the whole of them. The thread that held together this patchwork of times and places was the subjective experience of the men and women and children who suffered solitary confinement.

After the excitement and tensions of the trial; the clamour of the crowd in some cases; the nightmare ride in the van; the rude shocks of reception; an awed first glance at the iron galleries of the prison hall – after all that, the separate cell must have seemed like a promise of relief to prisoners, and yet there was in the first closing of the door behind them a finality that betokened a dreadful new beginning. Austin Bidwell examined his 'little box with a mixture of curiosity and consternation for the thought smote me with blinding force

Separate cell in the old part
of the prison at Brixton

Separate sleeping cell in one
of the new wings of the female
convict prison at Brixton

that for long years that little box – eight feet six inches in length, seven feet in height and five feet in width, with its floor and roof of stone – would be my only home – would be! must be! and no power could avert my fate.'[87] Not all prisoners were able to control their emotions when this realization was borne in on them. 'I sank to my knees,' says Mrs Maybrick, 'I felt suffocated. I sprang to my feet and beat wildly with my hands against the door. "For God's sake let me out! Let me out!" '[88]

These were immediate reactions to being locked up, but the longer prospect was of a solitude for which nothing in the previous life of first-time prisoners could possibly have prepared them. 'Unless one has experienced it,' says One-who-has-tried-them, 'one can have no conception of the effect of close confinement upon the nervous system. People who have not tried it are apt to say, "Well, it's only for twenty-eight days;" but if they were to try what it was like having nothing but white-washed walls to stare at day after day, and neither book nor employment to take one's thoughts, as it were, out of one's self, I don't think they would say anything more about it's being "only twenty-eight days."[89] Frederick Brocklehurst did spend 'only twenty-eight days' in prison, all of them in solitary confinement, and the sensation of it was fresher in his recollection than it would be for anyone released after serving a longer sentence.

> Imagine a blind man denied human intercourse, with power of motion only in a space 14 feet by 7, whose only contact with a limited outside world comes through ceiling, walls and iron door, and you can form a faint idea of what life in a prison must be. A prisoner sees nothing beyond the limits of his cell; feels only its discomforts; tastes the prescribed prison fare; hears the limited sounds of his strange environment; and smells little beyond the scent of the creosote as it exhales from the oakum.[90]

At this point, the official view as expounded by Sir Edmund DuCane was that 'the prisoner's mind is thrown in upon itself,' and 'he becomes open to lessons of admonition and warning; religious influences have full opportunity of obtaining access to him; he is put in that condition when he is likely to feel sorrow for the past and to welcome the words of those who show him how to avoid evil for the future.'[91] The theory supposed, in other words, that men and women would use their period of seclusion to think on their misdeeds and repent of them, and there were some individuals who did indeed do so. 'I rather liked it,' says one, 'I wanted to be alone with myself. I wanted to think. I did not want to hear the voices of the other men and the language they use among themselves.'[92] 'Was never more composed in my life,' says another, 'away from others; had time to enter into myself, and soon learnt the sources of my weakness and of my strength.'[93]

On the other hand, says Ticket-of-leave-man, who glimpsed a better future for himself in the dregs of his suffering, 'it is argued that solitude renders men dull and morose. Well, men cannot be overcome with remorse for an ill-spent life, and feel at the same time particularly jolly.'[94] Not that they often did feel 'particularly jolly', especially when, into the silence and solitude of the cell, there came 'unbidden and unwished for, the pale spectres of the past'.[95] O'Donovan Rossa could not prevent himself 'from counting over the memories of the past, the friends and the friends' meetings of bygone days'.[96] George Bidwell's thoughts would 'surge tumultuously as some picture of the happy past flashed across the mental vision and plunged the writhing soul into an agony of remorse.'[97] And when these feelings were projected forwards by prisoners with a long time to serve they became almost intolerable. Mrs Maybrick was convinced that solitary confinement was 'by far the most cruel feature of English penal servitude. It inflicts upon the prisoner at the commencement of her sentence, when most sensitive to the horrors which prison punishment entails, the voiceless solitude, the hopeless monotony, the long vista of tomorrow, tomorrow, tomorrow stretching before her, all filled with desolation and despair'.[98] The vista that faced Jabez Balfour was almost too much for him: 'When I looked up at that appalling wall of 3,833 days, it seemed that I should never surmount it. . . I had not sufficient mastery of my thoughts at that time to keep my mind from the interminable reflections that haunt a ruined man. My fear was that I should be overtaken by madness.'[99]

Balfour was not alone. His feelings were shared by many convicts; the most distinguished member of the whole fearful company being Oscar Wilde. 'His chief danger,' he wrote of himself in a petition to the Home Secretary, 'is that of madness, his chief terror that of madness. He is conscious that his mind, shut out artificially from all rational and intellectual interests, does nothing and can do nothing, but brood on those forms of sexual perversity, those loathsome modes of erotomania, that have brought him from high place and noble distinction to the convict's cell and the common gaol.'[100]

To ward off thoughts of this sort, and to keep creeping insanity at bay, English convicts developed a number of stratagems; One-who-has-tried-them 'suffered to such an intense degree' with a 'craving to shout out aloud' that he was obliged to force his handkerchief into his mouth to prevent himself 'yielding to the temptation'.[101] A different form of physical activity, widely understood as a symbol of captivity, was perceived by Brocklehurst in the 'tramp of numberless feet, as my companions moved to and fro in their narrow compass. Tramp, tramp, tramp they went for hours, speaking of a vacuity of mind, and wretchedness of spirit in tones more eloquent than words.'[102] It was in fact a major flaw in the penitentiary design that the human material on which it was inflicted could not live up to its high ideals. Hepworth Dixon thought that 'few of the really criminal order can be left in worse company than that of their own thoughts.'[103] Left to themselves indeed the thoughts of some such men turned neither towards repentance nor to insanity, as one witness to the Gladstone Committee of 1895 admitted: 'I remembered some houses that I knew at my own home in Devonshire, and I really formed plots in my head how I would go to those houses and commit a burglary in those houses, because I knew them so well.'[104] The non-criminally minded, by way of contrast, sought to obliterate the past; Mrs Maybrick did it by compressing her thoughts 'to the smallest compass of mental existence, and no sooner did worldly visions or memories intrude themselves, than I immediately and resolutely shut them out as one draws the blind to exclude the light.'[105] A variation on this tactic occurred to O'Donovan Rossa as he tried to come to terms with a life sentence imposed for treason-felony: 'The thoughts that troubled me during the day, I tried to count out of my head by counting the stitches I put into the clothes I was making.'[106] Fellow life-sentence prisoner George Bidwell did likewise: 'I adopted the device of counting,' he says, 'and this I found necessary to do during every waking moment when I could not see to study.'[107]

On the first night of her solitary confinement, Florence Maybrick 'prayed for sleep' that she might lose consciousness of her 'intolerable anguish'.[108] Her prayer was shared by many of her fellow-prisoners, 'for a prison day is a very long day, a very weary day, and one longs for sleep, with its sweet oblivion of all the petty trials and annoyances that are of daily occurrence in a prisoner's life.'[109] But sleep, 'that gentle nurse of the sad and suffering, came not' to Mrs Maybrick. 'What a night'.[110]

Carnarvon's committee of 1863 considered the question of sleep for prisoners at some length, and having observed that '$9\frac{1}{2}$ to 10 hours is the proportion of time' devoted to it, came to the conclusion that 'this exceeds the fair allowance due to health, and is injurious both to the prisoners and the prison discipline.'[111] But the committee, keen as it was to turn the screw a little tighter wherever it could, might have regretted its recommendation for a reduction had it heard at least one prisoner's view of 'the "reforming" influence of thirteen or fourteen hours of darkness. Oh, the torture of those fearful nights wherein the hellish beleaguering of insanity must be strenuously repelled!'[112]

For some prisoners, the first sleepless night set a pattern for what was to follow. 'During all the fifteen years of my imprisonment, insomnia was (and, alas! is still) my constant companion,' laments Mrs Maybrick.[113] O'Donovan Rossa did not have 'one hour of calm, easy sleep during these years.'[114] Balfour 'rarely slept much more than some two hours a night during the whole of . . . twelve years' imprisonment', and 'many nights . . . did not sleep at all'.[115]

There were many reasons for sleeplessness besides hard beds and the working of guilty minds. To begin with, in spite of the silence rule and the segregation of prisoners in separate cells, prisons were often noisy places. Mary Richardson describes 'that horrid hush we always knew at night, a vacant, chilly hush that was broken so often by the sobbing of the prisoners. I always slept badly and these sobs were sometimes almost more than I could bear. Some people imagine that prisoners do not suffer in prison. I wish all who think so would spend a night in Holloway'.[116]

At Wormwood Scrubs 'it was a gruesome and not uncommon experience to hear the shrieking of some half-demented or conscience-stricken creature in a nightmare.'[117] And, 'in the adjoining cell' to Mrs Maybrick, 'an insane woman was raving and weeping throughout the night.'[118] On a different note, One-who-has-endured-it once had to endure a neighbour who was undergoing punishment in chains 'and every time he moved in bed they clanked and rattled; and sometimes in turning round they would strike against the corrugated iron partition of the cell; not a very cheering sound to hear in the dead hours of the night.'[119] In Millbank, the nightly ordeal was made worse by the adjacent noises of the metropolis, and in particular 'the voice of Big Ben, telling the listening inmates of the penitentiary that another fifteen minutes of their sentences have gone by!'[120]

Then there was the spy in the door; Jabez Balfour 'could hear the warders in their "sneaks" moving about, and now and again . . . endured the misery of knowing that the shield of the spy-hole was raised' and that he was being 'carefully watched'.[121] Where the cell door was equipped with a 'heavy iron trap-door' it made 'a noise something like a small cannon being fired' when the officer banged it up.[122]

Disturbed by these noises and intrusions from outside the cell, and prompted by inner fears that they might become demented, convicts engaged in a sometimes despairing search for ways of getting off to sleep. George Bidwell resumed his daytime 'counting'[123] and a Female Debtor 'preached a little sermon' to herself.[124] But Stuart Wood, a petty criminal, in and out of prison during the first years of the twentieth century, 'became that pitiful thing – the habitual masturbate. This horrible, loathsome practice was the inevitable consequence of segregation and the intense petrifying monotony of prison life as I first knew it.' In his own case, he says, 'it was not lust, but sleeplessness that first led to the formation of the habit. One lay awake at night, not one night but every night, especially when one has slept for an hour or two before midnight; lying awake hour after hour, a prey to all sorts of thoughts and imaginings, one finally yields to temptation in the hope of inducing sleep.'[125]

The extent of these torments can not have been too apparent to some of the senior officials in the prisons where they took place. Basil Thomson, governor of Dartmoor in 1896, thought that 'at the end of the day a convict is dog-tired and sleeps a dreamless sleep,'[126] and Chaplain Clifford Rickards shared his view: 'All these criminals,' he declares, 'sleep the sleep of the innocent, and there is neither nightmare nor groans nor snores to be heard through the long hours of the night. All are sleeping the sleep of a little child and no ill dreams appear to disturb their rest.'[127]

COLD

In the real world of the cell, one of the most pervasive causes both of sleeplessness and of bodily suffering in general was the cold. 'Oh, Rossa', a Fenian comrade groaned to him one day, 'the cold is killing me.'[128] Rossa was already only too familiar with 'the horrible sensation of cold in the morning in those cheerless Pentonville cells. It was not so much the intensity of the cold, for probably the cold was not so intense, as the abominable feeling of always waking cold, and the hopeless and helpless feeling that there was no prospect of going to sleep again, and no possible way of getting warm till the bell rang and you were allowed to get up and put on your clothes.'[129] 'For two months' George Jacob Holyoake 'was never warm'.[130] William Barrow spent the night 'shivering in bed'.[131] And so did anarchist David Nicoll, because whereas the 'plank beds at Pentonville are solid, the planks nailed closely together; at some jails there is a space of an inch between every plank through which the cold air can creep.'[132]

Elsewhere, 'any water spilt took days to dry up',[133] or 'frequently froze . . . overnight';[134] 'hands and feet were covered with chilblains';[135] fingers 'had large cracks in them'.[136] Helen Gordon, a suffragette, suffered from a coldness that was 'gradually penetrating – every afternoon the prisoner knows that an hour after exercise her body will become gradually petrified.'[137] And at Portland 'it was so cold in winter that the very warders of the night patrol used to make their rounds of the peep-holes with blankets wrapped about their heads and shoulders. But if *they* suffered from the cold,' asks Balfour, 'what was it to us prisoners?'[138]

Complaints about the cold at Pentonville were ironic in view of the efforts that had been made in its design and construction to avoid extremes of temperature. The first report of the commissioners for the prison, published in 1843, was less than two pages long, but room was found in it to boast that 'The perfect ventilation of the cells, and the means of maintaining an equable and proper temperature, have been successfully accomplished, and cannot fail to have a beneficial effect on the health of the prisoners,' and all 'at a cost of less than one half-penny per cell for 24 hours . . . in the coldest weather of the current winter'.[139] Hepworth Dixon was predictably moved to criticize 'the costly extravagances of the model cell, with its scientific ventilation – its elaborately adjusted temperature, kept at the nicest point of comfort by means of valves, which let in warm air or cool air as the case may require.'[140]

Many prisoners from 1849 onwards were confined, however, not in 'model' cells but in the corrugated iron 'kennels' of the convict establishments. Ticket-of-leave-man for instance had a 'vagabond' next to him who was 'not only a moral but a physical nuisance; the effluvium which was exhaled from his body . . . found its way through the chinks of my cells and disgusted me'.[141] And if men were obliged to make use of their pots in the night, the results were equally offensive: 'when an occurrence of this kind happens, which, owing to the nature of the food, it does very frequently, the fact is made known by a nasal telegram, almost over the whole ward, announcing an addition to the already over-tainted atmosphere.'[142] 'You grow gradually sensible,' wrote the writer of *A Letter From a Convict*, 'as the morning draws on, that you are in the midst of a great cesspool. I speak strongly, but with truth.'[143] It was a general complaint, due to the fact that 'there was no adequate means of escape for the foul air that collected in the central hall of the prison, and the smell there of a morning was enough to knock you down'.[144] 'It is no uncommon thing', claims Oscar Wilde, 'for warders, when they come in the morning out of the fresh air and open and inspect each cell, to be violently sick.'[145] At Liverpool, the stench was 'unbearable, especially in the morning. To keep down putrid fevers – indeed to render the corridors at all passable – it is found necessary to burn chloride of lime in them incessantly, as well as in the day-rooms and eating rooms.'[146]

COMMUNICATION

Besides the cold and the smells, the killing thing about solitary was, of course, the absence of ordinary human contact. The 'scattered words' spoken by Fenian Michael Davitt during his first ten months at Millbank 'would not occupy twenty minutes to repeat'.[147] Stuart Wood 'craved for human companionship . . . for the sound of a human voice not raised to threaten, but just to utter the most absurd commonplace; to catch and respond to the twisted, frightened smile of understanding that springs from suffering endured in common'.[148]

In the absence of verbal contact, other means were tried. 'A soldier waiting trial next door' to Dr McCook Weir 'kept knocking all day, and frequently far into the night. In fact, he and his next door neighbour kept up a dumb conversation in this manner, and a double rap for "goodnight" was almost as distinct and impressive as the words themselves'.[149] The noise of these knockings could be heard all over the prison: 'the rappings, and the mysterious code by which the prisoners communicate, sound through the building like an imprisoned woodpecker tapping to be free'.[150]

It was in fact possible for 'telegraphing' to be 'carried on between two prisoners though four or five cells might intervene – that is, provided the fellow receiving the message pressed his ear against the wall, making, as it were an air-tight connection.'[151] Also, there was a time when 'the W.C. system used to be the favourite avenue of communication. Emptying the bowl of its water, they converted the refuse pipes into speaking tubes. By this morally disgusting and physically dangerous means a prisoner used to carry on regular conversations with any one or all of the other seven prisoners connected with the drainpipe of his cell.' 'Under the pail system', says Brocklehurst with relief, 'this is done away with now.'[152]

In the penal servitude prisons at Chatham, Portland and Dartmoor none of these ingenious expedients was necessary; the fabrication of the compartments out of thin corrugated iron made cell-to-cell conversation a simple matter of convenience: 'a man with good ears can listen to his neighbour's yarns even without the aid of a "chat-hole". It is the custom however, for prisoners to bore a small hole through the partition, near to the ground, through which the chat takes place. The one prisoner lies down on the ground and talks and listens, with his mouth or ear to the chat-hole; his neighbour sits at the window, which opens onto the landing along which the officer in charge walks. If he approaches, a knock from the watcher causes the chat to be suspended until he has passed, when it commences again.'[153]

An alternative mode of communication, albeit a slow and non-reciprocal one, was to scratch messages on the cell tins. The meal tins in which food was brought to the cells provided a mobile medium of communication because they were not personal to each prisoner but part of a common stock which circulated daily. Some men simply scratched their names on them; 'Black Prince, King Theodore, Swansea Pet, Black Jim, Poor Bill from George Street'.[154] Some of the specimens collected by Brocklehurst from tins at Strangeways reflected essentially corporeal concerns: 'Wouldn't you like a pork pie?' 'Plenty of beef and beer for the brothers Loney on the 29th of August.'[155] Most often though, the messages in this genre consisted of simple but cheerful exhortation. O'Donovan Rossa 'came to read "cheer up" – "cheer up", so often' that he felt himself 'growing sympathetic towards the writers'.[156] 'It is perhaps', concludes Brocklehurst, 'the strangest postal system extant. The warders are the postmen, and, instead of postage stamps, the "broad arrow" is the only sign of Her Majesty's approval.'[157]

PETS

Denied proper human intercourse, there were prisoners who sought solace instead from an unlikely quarter – the indigenous fauna of the prison cell. Chicago May made overtures to some flies, and 'tried to make friends with a couple of these insects, which ventured into my prison. If only I could have had some sort of an animal to care for and love, it would have been of the greatest help in keeping my mind occupied.'[158] George Bidwell 'never destroyed any kind of insect' which found its way into his cell – 'even when mosquitoes lit on my face I always let them have their fill undisturbed, and felt well repaid by getting a glimpse of them as they flew, and with the music of their buzzing.'[159] Manchester Merchant, on the other hand, had befriended 'a tremendous spider' which he kept in his soap box; 'I then made a raid upon the other occupants of my cell (the flies), which as I caught I deposited in the soap box. Such was the manner in which I relieved my distressed condition for some days, until fly hunting became monotonous.'[160]

Prisoners did have more acceptable pets. Michael Davitt had a blackbird at Portland, 'through the kindness of the governor'. 'He would stand upon my breast as I lay in bed in the morning and awaken me from sleep. He would perch on my plate and share my porridge. Towards evening he would resort to his perch, the post of the iron bedstead, and there remain, silent and still, till the dawning of another day.'[161] Davitt's blackbird was also the occasion of his prison writing. 'One evening as "Joe" sat upon his perch, it occurred to me to constitute him chairman and audience of a course of lectures: and with him constantly before me as the representative of my fellow creatures, I jotted down

THE PRISONER AND HIS FAVOURITE BIRDS

Prisoners' friends

what I have substantially reproduced in the following pages.'[162] Perhaps appro-
priately, George Bidwell had a rat 'that was easily taught', and he trained it 'to
stand upright on his feet, with his head up like a soldier'.[163] So pleased was
George with his account of this friendly and talented rodent, that he persuaded
brother Austin to include it in *his* memoirs as well – word for word the same,
and unacknowledged.[164] But these objects of affection also created possibilities
for the display of other and less attractive human emotions. A prisoner at
Portland 'was greatly wrapped up in a mouse that nestled in his breast by day,
and careered about his cell by night. Happening one day to leave it behind him
in his cell as he went out to work, the warder, with stupid cruelty, drowned the
mouse. Its master was heart-broken, sat moodily in his cell and refused to do a
stroke of work. The governor himself tried to soothe him, but he was incon-
solable, and gave warning that if he ever met that warder he would murder
him!'[165] Basil Thomson says that 'although it is contrary to the rules for pets to
be kept, the warders used to look the other way when mice were in question. I
had long observed that pet birds and mice kept violent men out of mischief.'[166]

   All of these methods for combating the ordeal of solitary confinement were at
best partial ones. In order to cope more effectively with their sentences, in
order 'to get through with the minimum of mental and physical injury,'

prisoners had to turn in on themselves to find the resources they required. One well-used route to survival lay through a straightforward acceptance of the situation. 'Satisfied, after a time, that what is cannot be helped, that no anxiety on their part can undo the past or affect the future, they put aside all thought both of past and future, and live only for the present, making the best of everything. . . . This power of living for the present seems to be possessed by all alike.'[167] It was certainly possessed by Mrs Maybrick; she called it 'the opiate of acquiescence . . . the keeping of my sensibilities dulled as near as possible to the level of the mere animal state which the Penal Code, whether intentionally or otherwise, inevitably brings about.'[168] But beneath these outward shows of conformity there was usually concealed a mixture of private responses. 'As he grows accustomed to imprisonment,' says an anonymous convict, 'much as a woman may become accustomed to being kicked, a quiet, immeasurable contempt for legality and "authorities" and "regulations" and "discipline" dominates and never leaves him.'[169]

Political prisoners were more likely to be sustained, not by personal hatred, but by their political convictions; a feeling that they suffered in a noble cause; and a sense of distance from the common criminals amongst whom they were condemned to pass so many years of their lives. 'I kept myself a free man in prisons,' insists O'Donovan Rossa; 'while they had my body bound in chains, I felt that I owed them no allegiance, that I held my mind unfettered – that I was *not* their slave.'[170]

There was also for long-sentence and repeated offenders, a process of habituation which softened and made the privations of imprisonment seem, if not more acceptable, then at least less intolerable. Stuart Wood says: 'I wept in the shadows of my cell and longed to die; but as the weeks crept on I wept less and less; the process of hardening had set in.'[171]

NOTES

1. Brocklehurst, 6.
2. Hepworth Dixon, 304.
3. Kingsmill (1854), 121.
4. J. Balfour, 73.
5. One-who-has-endured it, 162.
6. Convict 77, 21.
7. Maybrick, 67.
8. H. Gordon, 4.
9. Maybrick, 67.
10. Ibid., 67.
11. Hart-Davis, 186.
12. Convict 77, 22.
13. One-who-has-endured it, 162.
14. Ibid., 79.
15. Convict 77, 22.
16. J. Balfour, 183.
17. One-who-has-endured it, 179.
18. Sharpe, 186.
19. One-who-has-endured-it, 110.
20. Sharpe, 186.
21. One-who-has-endured-it, 11.
22. Ibid., 79–82.
23. McCook Weir, 60.
24. Ibid., 191.
25. Cozens, 70.
26. Penal Servitude Commission (1879), xliv.
27. Mayhew, 141.

28. Hepworth Dixon, 157.
29. Convict Prisons Report (1853), 11.
30. Sykes, 110.
31. Samuel, 72.
32. Carnarvon Committee (1863), xi.
33. Hart-Davis, 336.
34. One-who-has-tried-them, II, 69.
35. A. Bidwell, 403.
36. Holyoake (1893), I, 174.
37. Lovett, 230.
38. One-who-has-suffered-it, 583.
39. Penal Servitude Commission (1879), 519.
40. J. Balfour, 73.
41. One-who-has-endured-it, 169.
42. Ibid., 79.
43. McCook Weir, 59.
44. One-who-has-endured-it, 9.
45. McCook Weir, 139.
46. One-who-has-tried-them, I, 169.
47. One-who-has-suffered-it, 585.
48. Foote, 126.
49. Chesterton (1856), I, 56.
50. Ibid., 57.
51. Select Committee on Gaols (1835), 1st report, 307.
52. Ibid., 1st report, 312.
53. Ibid., 2nd report, 318.
54. Ibid., 1st report, 313.
55. Ibid., 1st report, 313.
56. Ibid., 1st report, iii.
57. Ibid., 1st report, iv.
58. W.L. Clay, 139.
59. Nihill, 38.
60. Select Committee on Gaols (1835), 2nd report, iv.
61. Turner, 188.
62. Chesterton (1856), I, 303.
63. Chesterton (1856), I, 320.
64. Jebb, 8–9.
65. Ibid., 10.
66. Ibid., 10.
67. Dyott's Diary, 4 October 1828, 32.
68. W.L. Clay, 146.
69. Reynolds, 1.
70. Ibid., 84.
71. Ritchie, 4.
72. Kingsmill (1854), 116.
73. W.L. Clay, 140.
74. Gibson, 53.
75. Ibid., 52.
76. Pentonville Commissioners, 6th report (1848), 6.
77. Chesterton (1856), I, 336.
78. E. Fry (1847), II, 254.
79. W.L. Clay, 313.
80. Ibid., 145.
81. Ibid., 297.
82. Chesterton (1856), I, 337.
83. Ibid., II, 10.
84. Hepworth Dixon, 370.
85. Gladstone Committee (1895), 27.
86. Hobhouse and Brockway, 319.
87. A. Bidwell, 397.
88. Maybrick, 67.
89. One-who-has-tried-them, I, 264.
90. Brocklehurst, 29.
91. DuCane (1885), 157.
92. B. Thomson (1925), 38.
93. Letter, 204.
94. Ticket-of-leave-man, 202.
95. One-who-has-tried-them, II, 83.
96. Rossa, 119.
97. G. Bidwell, 504.
98. Maybrick, 75.
99. J. Balfour, 48.
100. Hart-Davis, 143.
101. One-who-has-tried-them, I, 218.
102. Brocklehurst, 31.
103. Hepworth Dixon, 409.
104. Gladstone Committee (1895), 285.
105. Maybrick, 105.
106. Rossa, 119.
107. G. Bidwell, 405.
108. Maybrick, 64.
109. One-who-has-tried-them, II, 154.
110. Maybrick, 64.
111. Carnarvon Committee (1863), xi.
112. One-who-has-suffered-it, 587.
113. Maybrick, 86.
114. Rossa, 95.
115. J. Balfour, 43.
116. Richardson, 69.
117. J. Balfour, 44.
118. Maybrick, 65.
119. One-who-has-endured-it, 166.
120. Davitt (1885), I, 172.
121. J. Balfour, 43.
122. T. Clarke, 8.
123. G. Bidwell, 403.

124. Female Debtor, 9.
125. Wood, 61.
126. Thomson (1925), 95.
127. Rickards, 64.
128. Rossa, 117.
129. Ibid., 86.
130. Holyoake (1893), I, 174.
131. Barrow, 8.
132. Nicoll, 5.
133. Blagg, 12.
134. Maybrick, 123.
135. Ibid., 85.
136. *Kirkdale*, 63.
137. H. Gordon, 35.
138. J. Balfour, 74.
139. Pentonville Commissioners, 1st report (1843), 3–4.
140. Hepworth Dixon, 10.
141. Ticket-of-leave-man, 162.
142. Davitt (1886), 16.
143. Letter, 499.
144. One-who-has-tried-them, II, 39.
145. Hart-Davis, 336.
146. Hepworth Dixon, 333.
147. Davitt (1886), 10.
148. Wood, 67.
149. McCook Weir, 193.
150. Graham, 92.
151. T. Clarke, 71.
152. Brocklehurst, 103.
153. Ticket-of-leave-man, 161.
154. One-who-has-suffered, 4.
155. Brocklehurst, 111.
156. Rossa, 91.
157. Brocklehurst, 116.
158. Sharpe, 177.
159. G. Bidwell, 509.
160. *Kirkdale*, 13.
161. Davitt (1885), I, vii.
162. Ibid., I, viii.
163. G. Bidwell, 505.
164. A. Bidwell, 410.
165. Fannan, 107.
166. B. Thomson (1925), 81.
167. 'Convict's view', 722.
168. Maybrick, 104.
169. One-who-has-suffered-it, 589.
170. Rossa, 212.
171. Wood, 33.

3
PRISONERS

Between 1837, when Victoria came to the throne, and 1901 when she died, there were more than 15 million receptions into the prisons of England and Wales. Some of those received were on remand and never returned after trial; some were convicted of criminal offences – and some of misdemeanours; some were committed in default of payment of fines. Some of them made the journey more than once, and most of them stayed inside for only a few days – four out of five sentences were for less than one calendar month.

Who were the people who served in the ranks of this enormous army as it marched through the anonymous columns of the nineteenth century's criminal statistics? Who were the men and women and children who acted as unwilling subjects in the extraordinary experiment of the penitentiary – as the raw materials that were fed into the 'machines for grinding rogues honest?' The pages of the period's biographies put names and faces to these otherwise unknown batallions – a mass of individual portraits that re-merge into patterns of a different complexion from the ones presented by the bland totals of the official figures.

In theory the penitentiary was a private version of hell; a place of perfect silence and separation. In practice the later Victorian prison was peopled by a 'mixed multitude' of sinners with whom human contact became increasingly possible through the chinks and cracks that appeared in the structures designed to keep them apart. One of the first things that George Bidwell learned from conversations with his companions filled his mind with 'amazement'. 'During fifteen years in English prisons I never found a man who was guilty, all being innocent in their own opinions.'[1] It was an opinion shared by many others. 'The majority of prisoners' with whom John Dawson talked 'declared they were innocent'.[2] Governor Chesterton saw 'something perfectly ludicrous in the all but universal claim to innocence', and tended to greet such protestations

Male convict at Pentonville and female convict at Millbank

with scepticism: 'You are not guilty! Well, I know that full well. I have long since discovered that the prison was built purposely to receive innocent people. It's always full of them.'[3]

In fact, an imperfect nineteenth-century justice – defendants could not give evidence in their own behalf until 1898, and there was no proper appeal court until 1907 – delivered numbers of clearly innocent men and women into custody. One of them was 18-years-old William Dawson, committed to Chester Castle 'for robbing an old fish-man on the highway' and 'sentenced to ten years transportation'. 'He always declared his innocency of the charge, and very frequently burst into tears when telling the tale.' His claim to have been ballad-singing in a nearby village at the time of the robbery in question was investigated by the prison chaplain, who found it to be true. He hastened to tell the judge in the case and Dawson was then released;[4] as was a soldier condemned to death for 'murdering' his wife on a day when he was actually confined in Cardiff gaol. When asked why he had not put forward this defence at his trial, he said, 'Because I wasn't asked, nor allowed to say anything.'[5] These men were fortunate. Their stories were proved to be true, and the errors of justice were corrected, but Bill Sykes's 'next door captive . . . a young country lad, one of the handsomest youths I ever saw in my life', was less lucky. He was doing five years for 'an imaginary case of robbery', which had been got up against him by associates of his rival for the favours of 'a very pretty girl, who worked on the same farm'. 'He had no friends to take any interest in his case, or put the facts before the Home Secretary, or else', declares Sykes, 'I am confident he would have got his release in a week.'[6]

In some cases, prisoners' assertions of innocence served quite different purposes: 'what they mean', says Basil Thomson, 'is that another man who received a lighter sentence than they was the more guilty, or that they were the tools of a man who got off altogether'.[7] Propositions of this nature were developed by George Bidwell into a theory of criminal 'self-justification':

> Many a professional thief has said to me: 'The whole world is dishonest. The grocer sands his sugar; the stock exchanges, the bankers and the merchants have their tricks of trade. The point is that those who cheat legally, keeping within the letter of the law, are more cowardly, while we are brave enough to act out the same moral principles and dare the law. . . . Of course, we don't blame them for their methods, only that they find fault with and punish us because our circumstances prohibit us from getting money in the way they do.'[8]

In his time, George had himself been a most professional thief who 'never felt a twinge of conscience' until 'that first night in Newgate after the sentence'. He then came to the realization that he had landed in prison, facing a life sentence under conditions of penal servitude, 'by a series of acts, each leaving the mind on a lower level, not realizing any departure from its original high moral tone, each taken without any feeling of guilt.'[9] Similar denials appear in what a number of authors choose to reveal or conceal concerning their own offences, particularly those related to peculation. 'Suffice it to say,' says One-who-has-endured-it, at the beginning of his book, 'I found myself drawn into the meshes of a man who was too clever for me and for the law, and who, crossing the seas to a place of safety, left me to meet a charge to which in his absence I had really no defence.'[10] Convict *No. 7* took two gold sovereigns belonging to his employer, with the 'intention of paying it into the firm before a month should elapse'.[11] Frederick Martyn was unable to repay a loan – 'due to the defection of a firm associated with me'[12] – and was charged with false pretences. The largest amounts of money in any of the cases involving our authors were those debited to Jabez Balfour, the former Liberal Member of Parliament for Tamworth. His account of the events that led to his conviction is one of successful financial operations fallen on hard times; of 'general mistrust', and of an 'abrupt and almost total stoppage of . . . investment income'. In his efforts to save the companies and their assets he 'was rebuffed and thwarted at every turn by the predatory hosts who were determined to drive the companies into liquidation to slaughter their assets, and to batten on the costs'. 'I would like to state here', he concludes in his own defence, 'that I never withdrew one farthing from any of the companies.' 'My side of the case has never been made public.'[13] Significantly perhaps, he fails to repair the omission in his lengthy memoirs of prison life.

CHILDREN

A different kind of innocence surrounded another whole class of Victorian prisoners. A halo was bestowed on children by an adult world that grew progressively conscious of the need to shield them from the harshness of prison life. The prize in a close-run race for the youngest prisoner of the century has to be awarded to William Hepworth Dixon for a case he came across in which 'an infant of three years was imprisoned for contempt of court, in a process before the Chancery of the duchy of Lancaster'.[14] Second place could have been claimed by Canon Horsley in his report for 1878. 'Obviously nothing can be said in favour of a boy of six years being remanded here and kept in silent and solitary confinement on a charge of vagrancy, nor for a girl of seven being sent here for running an errand for her mother with a bad fourpenny bit.'[15] In the same age range, an old warder at Millbank remembered 'a little boy six years and a half old sentenced to transportation; and the sentence carried into effect, too, though the poor child couldn't speak plain.'[16]

At least the children convicted later in the century were spared transportation, or the sorts of sentence that so appalled the Newgate Schoolmaster:

Nothing can be more absurd than the practice of passing sentence of death on boys under fourteen years of age for petty offences. I have had five in one session in this awful situation; one for stealing a comb almost valueless, two for a child's sixpenny story-book, another for a man's stock, and the fifth for pawning his mother's shawl.[17]

The death sentence for offences against property disappeared, in due course, for offenders of all ages, but the committal of children to prison for the pettiest of crimes continued. Stafford Gaol received children convicted of stealing 'gooseberries, apples and the like, and trespassing in fields in pursuit of birds' nests. It was all very annoying to the complaining party,' agrees the governor, 'but when it involves the result of sending boys of eight and nine years of age to prison for a month, or indeed, three months, as has happened here, it is monstrous'.[18]

Children of any age could be bewildered by their induction into the strange world of the prison; a suffragette recently arrested with colleagues 'remembers how the outer door opens as they sat and waited and a little shawled figure is brought in by a policeman, a little, dark, wistful face; it must have been a girl of 16. It is evidently her first experience, and as the matron asks her name and questions her she begins to cry – such a pathetic, frightened sound of the trapped animal.'[19] Oscar Wilde, too, saw a child at Reading whose 'face was like a white wedge of sheer terror. There was in his eyes the terror of a hunted animal. The next morning I heard him at breakfast-time crying, and calling to be let out.'[20] 'Sometimes,' said one chaplain, 'they would neither eat nor sleep, but wept continuously for three or four days till the gaolers were at their wits' end.'[21] But a less sympathetic cleric reassured his readers that 'as a rule within three days they have cried themselves quiet, and are ready for something to eat.'[22] As staff perceptions differed, so did the treatment they meted out to their child prisoners. The Reverend Henry Ryder 'often sat with one of these big fellows on my knee, trying to coax him to be less wretched, and to take some food for his mother's sake, whom I would promise to visit, etc.'[23] Major Fulford told the Carnarvon Committee 'I have had them really so small and so tender that I have been obliged to put them in the female hospital to play with the kitten; that is an absolute fact . . . and I have had three or four boys in whose cases we have been obliged to light their gas, and leave the door of their cells open by night'.[24] Not so considerately, reports Stuart Wood, 'the pitiful cries' of 'boys who were little more than children' were 'often suppressed by blows'.[25]

Apart from these brutalities, which were not intended in the grand penal design, the great concern of contemporary observers was with the possibility that simply being in prison could act as an agency of corruption, especially when young minds were repeatedly exposed to it. The process of corruption began – was at its worst, some might have said – during periods of remand, especially in the era of the unreformed prison, when little or no effort was made by the authorities to separate the young from the old; the more confirmed offenders from the novice in crime. 'Throughout the whole day, these boys were associated with men who had been in nearly every prison in London. The offences for which these boys were arrested were in all cases of a comparatively light nature.' And what appeared to the Reverend J. Kingsmill to 'aggravate the evils induced by this vicious system was, that two thirds of the boys, when brought up for examination a second time, were acquitted. Here, then, we see a number of boys condemned to association for four or five days with those whose whole lives have been spent in a course of crime; here they listen to their relations of feats, the cleverness of which they can readily perceive, whilst their minds are not sufficiently cultivated to feel the immorality; nay, they are even trained in such places to that manual dexterity which characterises an accomplished thief.'[26]

'They might come in "flats" ', says David Fannan in the more colloquial tones of a two-time penal-servitude man, 'but they were sure to go out "sharps".'[27] Oscar Wilde accepted that a child could be 'utterly contaminated' in prison but contended, somewhat idiosyncratically, that 'the contaminating influence is not that of the prisoners. It is that of the whole prison system – of the governor, the chaplain, the warders, the lonely cell, the isolation, the revolting food, the rules of the Prison Commissioners, the mode of discipline, as it is termed, of the life'.[28]

'THE DANGEROUS AND PERISHING CLASSES'

Children made up a small but distressing minority amongst prisoners. Reformers like Mary Carpenter of Bristol wished to remove them entirely from the harmful environment of prison, and in 1851 she published a book proposing *Reformatory Schools for the Children of the Dangerous and Perishing Classes*. The 'dangerous and perishing classes' of her title were the parents of the children in question. They were 'perishing' because they were too poor to live properly, and they were 'dangerous' because, having nothing to lose, they could not be safely incorporated into the increasingly disciplined mechanism of an industrial society. They found their way into prison in disproportionate numbers, but they did not form, any more than did the members of other social classes, an homogeneous group.

Some of them belonged to a large and constantly changing population of itinerants and vagrants who had been detached from their peasant roots in the land but were not yet integrated into settled patterns of town life and factory work.

The visibility of vagrants had always served as a crude barometer of economic conditions, and providing for them was an important impulse in the development of English penal and social policy. The houses of correction were memorials to the passing of a previous wave of vagrants over the Elizabethan countryside, and testified besides to an indelible connection in the official mind between work, punishment and public relief. Mark Jeffrey took to the road at the age of 15, along with his 12-year-old brother, and made his way successfully enough in the world as a hawker to *pay* for their accommodation at nights. At Mrs Langford's in Ely they stayed in what he calls a 'padding ken' where 'the heterogeneous mass of the lame, the halt and the blind of both sexes congregated and slept without any partitions or regard to decency.'[29]

The viability of this way of life for Mark Jeffrey, and for thousands like him, made it possible to take a romantic view of vagrancy: 'There must be great charm in a wandering life, for you can seldom make any one, who has tasted of its sweets, forgo it.'[30] But women in the Blackfriars Bridewell 'declared' to lady visitors 'that they had passed several nights together in the streets – that they had been refused admittance into a workhouse, or any relief for their pressing wants – and then, not knowing where to turn, they followed the example of others in the same circumstances, and by breaking a window, or committing some trifling act of insubordination, secured in Bridewell what they had failed to find elsewhere – a shelter.'[31] In Yorkshire this phenomenon was seasonal: 'They prefer being in gaol in the winter season, especially in severe weather, for whenever the weather becomes stormy, vagrants are brought from all parts of the Riding . . . and some, who knew the rules well, have committed felony for the purpose of getting a better diet than that allowed for vagrants.'[32]

A large contingent of the itinerant and the unemployed were not of course native-born English, but fugitives from the Celtic fringe of the British Isles. Of these, the most noticeable were the Irish, driven from their homes by hunger and poverty; by disease and political dispossession. Many of them flocked to the industrial centres of the north. John Clay reported to his visiting magistrates in 1849 that 'natives of Ireland are more numerous than natives of our own division of Lancashire' amounting to 140 out of 'the whole complement of 347.'[33] And of the 187 people confined in a Yorkshire prison, 'Thirty-four only belong to the Riding, the rest are strangers, many Irish, and of Irish parents.'[34]

The presence of the Irish in prison was unmistakable but, Fenian that he was and patriot that he was, Jeremiah O'Donovan Rossa had to struggle with an inner reluctance before he would acknowledge it on the pumping party at Millbank: 'Thirty of us were in the gang, and fifteen of us stood at each side of the crank, facing each other.' 'Will I say it? Yes. Nearly half these men were of Irish parents, and their crimes were traceable to poverty and whisky – two things which the Irish people could well afford to get rid of, and which are a curse to any people they afflict.'[35] Far from hesitating in the face of figures like these, the Reverend Joseph Kingsmill, however, could not bring himself to pass them by without loosing off yet another pot-shot at one of his many pet hates: 'The crimes of Ireland indicate a country emerging from barbarism, or relapsing into that state. . . . As Popery declines in Ireland, so will her crimes.'[36]

THE WORKING CLASSES

A more settled portion of the English population formed the major recruiting ground for Victorian prisons. In his *Chapters on Prisons and Prisoners* Kingsmill reproduces 'the means of living' of the first one thousand men to be received at Pentonville: '67 had been employed in office of trust, 71 as in-door and out-door servants, 388 were tradesmen and mechanics, 50 weavers and factory labourers, 100 farm labourers, 25 colliers, 15 boatmen, 10 common sailors, 18 in the army and navy, and 256 general labourers and hawkers.'[37] 'One is astonished', he says, 'at finding in that return so small a proportion of the most ignorant and neglected part of the whole community – factory labourers, colliers, and boatmen. . . . the causes of the small proportion of criminals in those classes being, rather that their wants are few; that they are accustomed from their childhood to the hardest toil, and that, worn out by overwork, they have little energy left for good or evil.'[38]

When it first opened, Pentonville accepted only convicts sentenced to transportation, so their convictions were for 'more serious' offences. A different occupational picture presented itself at the county gaols. The daily 'male' reception at Northampton amounted to 'six or seven, most of them drunken shoe hands, poachers or tramps';[39] and at Cardiff 'The population of the prison consisted largely of miners and sailors.'[40] 'The great mass of the prisoners' at Stafford were 'taken from among the colliers, boatmen, potters, and the iron-work men and tin-plate workers – people who are brought up in the roughest and most miserable manner as to morals, who are rarely or never accustomed to come in contact with any educated people, whose knowledge of right and wrong is of the most limited kind, and whose value of human life, from the perilous trades many of them pursue, amounts to nothing. They come in here perfect savages.'[41] These 'savages' were actually working-class men who worked in the new heavy industries, and who lived in the fast-growing industrial towns. But many of them remained psychologically rooted in a countryside that was never very far away geographically either. It was also a theatre in which scenes from a continuing drama of class war were acted out.

The Reverend John Clay once accompanied a group of justices on an inspection of Preston prison.

I had occasion to point out to them some sleeping cells so damp that the water lodged on the floors, when one of the inspectors observed, 'Oh, they're good enough for poachers.' This was the first intimation I had of the light in which the poacher is viewed by a large portion of the country magistrates. In their eyes he is the worst of criminals, and to put him down the law may be strained a little beyond its equitable limits.

This was done, in Lancashire at any rate, by sentencing men to terms of imprisonment for poaching and, when they were released, putting them in front of a commissioner of taxes for 'taking game without a licence'. They were then recommitted to prison as being unable to pay a monetary penalty. Clay protested to the Home Secretary, Sir James Graham, who put a stop to it; but under Lord Palmerston, his successor at the Home Office, he says, 'the practice has revived of discharging both (legal) barrels at the poaching offender.'[42] It was not only 'legal' barrels that were discharged in this rural warfare. Clay 'found in the hospital two poachers in very severe pain, from having in the late affray with Mr F—'s gamekeepers, been shot in the legs. I was sorry to observe that the wounds were not made by round pellets, but by angular pieces of lead about the size of shot.'[43]

The intimate relation between crime and the countryside is underlined by the testimony given to the Royal Commission which in 1854 enquired into discipline at Leicester County Gaol. A series of prisoners and former prisoners was asked why they were in prison: William Burton – 'I went from Croxton Park races for gambling. I won a sovereign. They took me up, and I had a month in half an hour';[44] William Pratt – 'Getting turnip tops. . . . Two calendar months';[45] Isaac Weston – 'for shooting at a stuffed pheasant' 'Three months';[46] Frederick Holyoake – 'For standing by and seeing a dog fight.' 'Three months'.[47] This list of trivial offences, and the trivial sentences they were thought to merit, typify one aspect of petty crime in the mid-century Midlands. But the altercation that subsequently developed between Frederick Holyoake and his inquisitors typifies another:

> Have you ever been in trouble before? – Many a time. . . . Let me see if I can give you a list. . . . September 18th, you were charged with rescuing a prisoner from the police, and fined, 1 *l* or one month's imprisonment again? – So would you for your own brother. I would not see him taken. . . . August 15th, 1844, again taken before the magistrates for assaulting the police. Fined 10s. or three weeks' imprisonment? – You have got it all down. . . . February 3d, 1845, you were again taken before the magistrates for fighting, and ordered to find sureties to keep the peace? – I did not break it; I kept the peace. . . . But you were taken before the magistrates? – Do not you put it on so thick, it is not of any use.[48]

Frederick Holyoake's testimony breathes truculence in every line; he is not intimidated by the Royal Commissioners, or their proceedings, and is determined to give as good as he gets. From the evidence of his criminal record it was an attitude he carried onto the streets and into his dealings with the humbler functionaries of the newly formed police force. His disrespect for their persons, and for the older 'legality' they represented, was not however universally shared by members of the lower orders. When George Jacob Holyoake – no relation – was awaiting his turn to be tried at Gloucester, he saw 'a man sentenced to transportation for life to Norfolk Island. His offence had arisen in ignorant and depraving circumstances, yet, when he heard the ferocious sentence, in genuine and awkward humbleness he made a rustic bow to the

Bench, saying "Thank you, my Lord." Ignorance had never appeared to me before so frightful, slavish and blind. Unable to distinguish a deadly sentence passed upon him from a service done to him, he had been taught to bow to his pastors and masters, and he bowed alike when cursed as blessed.'[49]

THE CRIMINAL CLASSES

Frederick Holyoake and his cronies were rude and unruly members of Leicestershire civil society, but their offences against it were no more than by-products of the gaming, drinking and fighting that characterized their own traditional, semi-rural ways of life. As the countryside was invaded by a more densely settled townscape and as city slums flourished, these habits and attitudes began to cross the boundaries surrounding an area of society in which individuals made their entire *livings* by thieving and cheating. These were inhabited by the criminal classes, within which there existed a recognizable hierarchy of technical skill, of 'moral' commitment and mutual regard. At the bottom end of the ladder were men not too dissimilar in character from the Leicester roughs, but with a more predatory turn of mind that led them to pursue careers as footpads. A street robber describes his last offence:

> I had a bit of luck and had plenty on me, had been to see my mother and had given her some money and was on my way to my own place, when a young lady that looked like a school teacher girl passed me with a watch hanging outside her dress; I said to myself, 'I've got enough. I will let her off,' so let her go by. I hadn't gone 200 yards before a feeling came over me, 'I must have that ticker', so I turned round, followed her up, knocked her down, collared her watch and rings and made off.[50]

Equally rough characters could be culled from every prison register. There was a Lancashire man called Braithwaite, who had, 'it was said, a head that was as hard as iron, and would, for a quart of ale, undertake to break with it any mantelpiece before which he was placed'.[51] Also in Lancashire was a prisoner in the Salford New Bailey who 'had been a prize-fighter, he had fought more than 20 pitched battles, and he was generally backed by the publicans to fight'. He told the Reverend Bagshaw he 'had been for many years so employed, that he would fight for 20*l*. a battle; that he had fought 150 rounds on one occasion'.[52] The face of a man known to Dr Quinton told a similar story: he had 'a broken nose, rupture of one tympanic membrane, and a generally battered look about his face, but he had, further, dozens of tiny cicatrices like the pitting of small-pox, only more irregular, on both cheeks. These were caused by killing rats with his teeth against time, an occupation which he had recourse to in his declining years, and out of which he made "a good bit".'[53]

PICKPOCKETS

Alongside these crude operators at the bottom of the criminal ladder were the sneak-thieves, amateur pickpockets, and snatch-purses; some of them mere children like 'Elizabeth P., aged eleven . . . committed for pocket picking':

> The first time I ever took money was in Byrom Street; there was a fire in that street, and I saw a lady with three sovereigns in a purse. I went up to her and said, aye? do you see that woman on fire? I then put my hand in her pocket and took out her money, and ran off with it.[54]

Proper pickpockets considered themselves a cut above the snatch-thieves and crude footpads; they saw themselves as skilled craftsmen, and often operated with one or more accomplices. Some such men could not resist an opportunity to demonstrate their skills in prison. When Major Blake was in training at Chelmsford Prison, the then governor, Captain Conor, 'was the possessor of a very valuable gold watch and chain which he was in the habit of wearing, and which he very highly prized. When he came to look at the time one morning after inspecting the prison he found that he was not wearing his watch. He could not find it anywhere until a prisoner was brought in at his own request.' 'The first thing he did was to hand the Governor the missing timepiece, complete with chain. "I 'ope you won't be angry with me sir," he said apologetically. "I never meant to keep it. But you were wearing it as you were going your rounds and – well – I just wanted to keep my hand in".'[55]

Professional pickpockets not only had to keep their 'hand in'; One-who-has-endured-it for instance, asked 'a man who had the reputation of being a most expert hand at "slinging his hook," . . . if the hard work of prison did not spoil his hands for delicate manipulations. "Oh, bless you, no!" he replied, "a few bread and water poultices followed by wearing well greased gloves will set all that to rights. In a week or two a man can bring his hooks and feelers into full working trim again and no mistake." '[56] 'Trained thieves and pick-pockets', says the Reverend John Clay, 'differ from the mere tramps, both as requiring a far greater amount of plunder to support them, and as more constantly and actively seeking it. While the tramps are always pedestrian, and are content to herd in the most sordid lodging houses; the professional thieves resort to alehouses and taverns, travel by rail, and altogether maintain a style of living unattainable by meaner rogues. They differ again from the "resident bad characters", inasmuch as they *never* work; but live entirely upon the fruits of their daily villainy.'[57]

Almost at the top of the criminal tree were the men who undertook audacious robberies and burglaries requiring degrees of planning and daring, of the sort displayed by a 'professional "cracksman" ' who was met by 'Merchant' – another pseudonymous gentleman prisoner: 'He was a man of fair education, good appearance, and considerable natural ability; much above the average of his professional brethren. He had been living luxuriously in London, on the fruits of his professional industry and skill.'[58] Another of Merchant's prison acquaintances engaged in the same trade when at liberty:

My brother and I and another bloke went out 'chance screwing', one winter, and we averaged three pounds a night each. My brother had a spring cart and a fast trotting horse, so when it began to grow dark, off we set to the outskirts of London. I did the screwing in this way. Wherever I saw a lobby lighted with gas, I looked in at the key-hole. If I saw anything worth lifting I 'screwed' the door – I'll teach you how to do it – seized the things, into the cart with them, and off to the next place.[59]

One of the marks of the truly professional criminal was a determination to foil the efforts of the law, at almost any cost. Two men had effected an entrance to a house in Bedford Square, but were discovered and apprehended. Both were removed to the nearest police office. ' "On me", said one of the pair, "nothing was found", but from his pockets some money and articles were removed. To this he offered no opposition, but he steadily refused to open one of his hands, which he kept firmly clenched in spite of every attempt that was made to relax it. It was struck with a baton, trodden on the ground by an iron heel until the blood was streaming, yet not for a moment did he loosen his grip. He succeeded in keeping it, but his disappointment was extreme when he discovered afterwards, from his knowledge of *stones*, that his firmness had been exerted in preserving a paltry counterfeit.'[60]

FRAUDS

Counterfeiting was itself a multi-faceted criminal activity within which there was a hierarchy of skill and respect parallel to that for straight theft. At its base were the 'snyde pitchers' or dealers in bad coin.

Suppose you start in the morning with a good sovereign and a *'snyde'* half-sovereign in your pocket; you go into some place or other, and ask for change of the sovereign, or you order some beer and give the sovereign in payment; it's likely you will get half-a-sovereign and silver back in change. Then is the time to 'twine'. You change your mind after you have 'rung' your snyde half 'quid' with the good one, and throwing down the 'snyde' half, say you prefer silver; the landlord or landlady, or whoever it is, will pick up the snyde half-quid, thinking of course it is the same one they had given you.[61]

Simpler still, in that it required no capital outlay, but at the same time more demanding of criminal nerve and skill, was 'telling the tale'. Stuart Wood was a self-confessed adept at it. 'The theft of money is wrong,' he admits, 'but it is a clean act compared with the theft of human faith in one's fellows.' He was court-martialled out of the navy in 1908 for stealing, and had no job or means of supporting himself. At first, he says, 'I told the people I approached for help quite frankly that I had been in trouble and had been kicked out of the navy; but the result was not offers of help if I would promise to go straight, but refusals and threats to put the police on my track.' [62] His strategy after that was to track down people who had military connections, to pass himself off as an Engineer Sub-Lieutenant down on his luck and to ask for assistance. 'I was fairly well educated and, what was far more important, had the accent and bearing of one born in a much higher station of life.' [63] 'My greatest personal assets as a young man were a good accent and address, a frank, open countenance, the habit of looking people straight in the eyes, and a shy diffident manner which disarmed the suspicion of being too facile in telling my tale.' His first victim was the 'Hon Mrs.—, wife of the General in Command of the military forces at Portsmouth'. 'I looked her up in *Who's Who* and went to her house in the character of a young naval officer who had got into a scrape and was stranded. I told her my father was an Army officer serving in Ireland, and she pressed me to go to him and get squared up with him, lending me the money for fare and expenses. It was the act of a scoundrel.' [64]

All of these depredations pale into insignificance when placed alongside those of big league operators like the Bidwell brothers and their two accomplices, 'Mac' McDonald and Edwin Noyes. Their preparations for the assault on the Bank of England were minute, prolonged and expensive. 'While in Germany,' says George Bidwell, 'I had purchased every variety of ink on sale at the stationers, so that in case of need I could have not only any written documents imitated, but also written with like ink. I had also, out of curiosity, purchased a great variety of blank bills of exchange, printed in French, German, Dutch, Italian, Russian, Turkish and Arabic.' [65] He next required 'some small wood engravings – fac-similes of the various bank and private endorsement stamps'. McDonald failed to procure the necessary stamps in Paris, so George, with, he says, the feeling that he was committing 'a grave error', proceeded to make 'a list of all the wood engravers in London'. He then spent 'two or three days driving about in a cab, selecting five out of the forty or fifty with whom I conversed, to do the work, judging them to possess simple, unsuspicious natures.' [66]

While this work was proceeding, Austin Bidwell busied himself establishing his *bona fides* as an American entrepreneur with large interests in railroads. This entailed frequent trips to Paris and other European financial centres where he purchased genuine bills of exchange. These were first copied, then deposited in the Bank of England, and discounted for cash with which even more foreign paper could be purchased. 'Again and again I went to the Continent, repeating the operation, until at last my credit at the bank was firm as a rock, and we were ready to reap our harvest. But these operations, simple as they seem, lasted over a period of six months, and had been made at heavy cost.

Our ordinary living expenses were not less than $25 a day for the three, while our extraordinary expenses were enormous. I probably travelled 10,000 miles over the Continent in my bill-buying expeditions to Paris, Amsterdam, Frankfort and Vienna.'[67] These costly preparations nearly paid off. The two Bidwells and their co-conspirators played for high stakes and lost. They not only forgot to put dates on two of the later bills they presented, but McDonald, 'the man who actually forged the notes, left his lodgings in such a hurry when the plot was uncovered that he failed to destroy a piece of blotting paper which was spotted by one of the investigating detectives. He ironed it flat, and then saw that there was blotted on it the contents of a Forged Note!' Three of the four also had 'mistresses' – tastefully absent from the pages of the Bidwell memoirs – who told the authorities 'everything that was material for the prosecution'.[68] For these failings in their almost perfect scheme, they were all obliged to pay the highest price that could be exacted from them under the English law . . . and that was a life sentence apiece.

GENTLEMEN PRISONERS

Because they were American, the Bidwells could not be placed with any accuracy in an English social hierarchy. Part of Stuart Wood's offence against polite society lay in the ease with which he cultivated the outward signs of gentility and concealed his own humble origins. But as he clambered up the social ladder in search of victims, and as he laid up in prison between offences, he met genuinely gentle folk on their way down, doubly condemned for breaking the law *and* for breaching the unwritten codes of conduct to which they had been born. They were not immediately obvious in prison, where the dress and the crop were great levellers of appearance. But they could not help revealing themselves when they spoke. 'It was in Northampton Prison,' says Basil Thomson.

> One afternoon a slouching-looking tramp who was waiting his turn for the bath answered my question in an educated voice, and when I pressed him for an account of his life he told me that he had been through public school and a certain university. At that critical time when a boy has to choose a profession and go through the mill of its lower grades his courage or his enterprise had failed him. I determined to make a strong effort to redeem this vagrant, if only as an experiment.

He procured money from one of the man's brothers and from an Aid Society 'to send him to South Africa to enlist in one of the regular forces that were mobilized for the Boer War'. He heard from him later that he was 'a new man'.[69]
    In the early part of Eustace Jervis's prison ministry 'it was the rarest thing' to have public-school men in prison, but later on he had them from 'Eton,

Harrow, Rugby, Marlborough, Clifton, Malvern, Cheltenham, Tonbridge, Dover, Wellington, Radley, Kingswood, and Kelly College, Tavistock.'[70] As well as the schools, all the professions were represented in the prison population. 'At Chatham the organist was a clergyman undergoing a severe sentence for bigamy.'[71] There were several Anglican and former Dissenting ministers at Parkhurst in Lord William Nevill's time, but never 'a single ex-Catholic priest. Whatever may be the merits or demerits of the Catholic clergy, they have the knack of keeping outside of convict prisons, except when engaged in their religious duties.' He also remembers amongst his fellow prisoners 'ex-doctors, ex-solicitors – these in overwhelming proportion to the others – soldiers, sailors, school-masters, bank managers, and for a time one ex-M.P. I do not remember any ex-barristers.'[72]

Imprisonment was undoubtedly more difficult for middle-class prisoners in many ways; their standard of living suffered a more abrupt decline; they were more likely to be racked with remorse and visions of social ruin, both for themselves and their families; they were unused to hard physical toil; and their prospects after release were far worse than those of the casual labourer or professional criminal, to whom having been in prison was not that much of a handicap. And yet, according to Dr John Campbell, 'The educated and better class of prisoners accustomed to the comforts and luxuries of life, generally adapt themselves more readily to their painful position than others less favourably circumstanced.' 'They rarely give trouble to the authorities, and are always ready to perform the work required of them.'[73] Although he thinks it 'would perhaps be unjust to make a difference between prisoners who had been in a good position and those of low degree, still it is painful to see such men associating by necessity with the worst description of prisoners.'[74]

CELEBRATED PRISONERS

Like any other place full of people, prison had its celebrities. The Victorian era had its share of convicted heroes. Some of them enjoyed a transient notoriety only – who now remembers the Penge Murder, or the Gold Dust Robbery, or the Great Turf Fraud? Others have passed into a pantheon of criminal immortals – George Joseph Smith, and Charles Peace, both of them executed.

But looming larger than any of them – in the flesh as well as in the prison writing of the time – is the man who is remembered as the Tichborne Claimant. Despite prolonged civil proceedings and the longest criminal trial in the history of the English Bar up to 1872, it is still not possible to say with certainty who the man was who emerged from the Australian bush claiming to be the long-lost Sir Roger Tichborne.[75] The jury at his perjury trial brought in a verdict which endorsed the prosecution's contention that he was 'really' Arthur Orton, son of a Wapping butcher, and the judge sentenced him to a total of fourteen years' penal servitude. The Claimant himself, following his release from prison, wrote a 'Confession' for the *People* newspaper, in which he confessed that he was Arthur Orton after all – although it was more likely to have been done for the money than in the interests of eternal truth. The confession was riddled with anomalies and the doubt about his true identity remains.

Michael Davitt saw the man at Dartmoor. 'His arrival . . . created unusual excitement among both warders and prisoners, but particularly among the latter. "Sir Roger" soon became the lion of the place. To fall into exercising file with him on Sunday was esteemed an event to be talked of for a week afterwards for the fortunate convict, who had, for once in his life, rubbed his skirts against one of England's proud aristocracy.'[76] Arthur Griffiths had charge of him at Millbank. 'He was very soft-spoken, very mild-mannered, apologetic rather than deferential, excessively anxious to be polite, but with the air of one who wished to convey that he knew what was due to himself. . . Many of our warders firmly believed in him, and quite expected as he wasted away, that he would some day resolve into the slim, pensive youth in the straw hat and yachting suit of the well-known photograph that was given out as the true presentment of the rightful heir who went down in the *Bella*.'[77]

Taking sides in the Tichborne case was a popular national pastime from which prisoners were not exempt. Michael Davitt says, 'he exhibited, while under my observation, an individuality and a bearing, in marked contrast to the ordinary impostors and criminals with whom he was associated.'[78] But Ticket-of-leave-man had a different impression: 'It was generally admitted by

Michael Davitt

the more intelligent prisoners who came in contact with him that his habits and manners were vulgar.'[79]

Political prisoners like Davitt were frequently looked on as notabilities in their own right, by other prisoners at any rate. 'Some of the Fenian prisoners were pointed out as great heroes' to One-who-has-endured-it on his first circuit of the exercise yard at Dartmoor.[80] Balfour's 'near neighbours' at Portland 'were Irish Fenian prisoners, some of whom had been engaged in the attempts to blow up the House of Commons and the Mansion House, and in what were known in those days as the dynamite outrages.' 'They were extremely well behaved and as far as one could judge quiet and pleasant fellows. They were perfectly honest fanatics.' 'The besetting sin of these Fenians struck me as being vanity tempered with an amazing degree of levity, and I can conceive of no more drastic remedy for that than Portland.'[81]

From the point of view of English officialdom, the Irish were troublesome prisoners; principled in their opposition to the terms of their captivity, persistent in their efforts to undermine the discipline of the places where they were held, and skilful at manipulating a vociferous Irish and pro-Irish lobby in the outside world. The success of their efforts can be counted in the number of commissions of inquiry which sat on their complaints.

George William Foote was a minor political prisoner convicted of blasphemy, and a fleeting *cause célèbre* in free-thinking circles. Whilst at Newgate, the very cell in which George Bidwell had awaited trial was pointed out to him. 'This information was communicated to me with an air of solemnity, as though so eminent a criminal had left behind him the flavor of his greatness, and had in some measure consecrated the spot.'[82] Most prisoners, however, needed no bidding to treat the Bidwells with respect, as George modestly admits. 'Being one of themselves, and on account of the colossal fraud in which I had been implicated, I was in their eyes a prison aristocrat, and one whose notice was esteemed a high honor. Indeed, many a man took the risk of three days in the solitary cell on bread and water to speak to me so that he could brag among his fellows, "Bidwell told me so and so." '[83] Ticket-of-leave-man did not count himself a member of this admiring *galère*. 'He has had any amount of bread-and-water punishment, and has thoroughly deserved it, for in addition to his laziness and obstinacy, and imposture, his habits are of the most filthy and disgusting character.'[84] Ernest Terah Hooley, not so celebrated as the Bidwells, but far better off from his fraudulent enterprises, was well received in prison when he began a twelve-month sentence in 1912: 'Never before in the history of Wormwood Scrubs had an ex-millionaire been received there. Everybody treated me deferentially, and expressed a sympathy which went a long way towards consoling me in my sorrow and humiliation.'[85]

If 'Sir Roger Tichborne' was *the* celebrated prisoner of the third quarter of the nineteenth century, his heir to that position at the beginning of the twentieth was Steinie or Stinie Morrison. Basil Thomson knew him under another but not dissimilar name. 'Morris Stein was a Russian Jew, tall, well-built, and athletic-looking, with features that might have been called comely.'[86] Morrison lived, when at liberty, in London's East End and moved in circles that over-lapped with *émigré* anarchist groups. He was arrested and tried in 1911 for shooting and killing, on Clapham Common, a well-known 'fence' called Behrens. He pleaded not guilty, but following his conviction was sentenced to death. This was later commuted to life imprisonment, which suggests some degree of official doubt about the case. Morrison continued to protest his innocence whilst in prison and eventually starved himself to death during a hunger strike. Thomson had met him on a previous sentence: 'I saw Stinie Morrison in every mood – defiant and wheedling, sarcastic and murderous – and though we contrived to manage him and keep him clear of open mutiny, I always expected him to commit some act of violence in the prison that would add many years to his sentence.'[87]

Thomson's position as governor of Dartmoor brought him into contact with many well-known prisoners; the one who made the most dazzling impression on him was 'Monte Carlo' Wells. 'In the frigid language of the law he defrauded investors by false representations. Of course he did: if when I met him he had been a free man and I had money to invest and he had held me with his glittering eye and discoursed fluently on his latest project for making money, he would have defrauded even me, who have a fairly wide acquain-tance among fraudulent company promoters, so great is the persuasive power of the man who believes in himself.'[88]

Another of his briefly celebrated prisoners was 'the Dartmoor Shepherd', alias David Davies, a recurring offertory-box thief whose job when at Dartmoor was to tend the sheep: 'He was the only English shepherd I knew whose sheep followed him in oriental fashion, and sometimes when a lamb had broken away and refused to be driven by the dogs, I have seen him come down from the farm and bring it in by calling it by name.'[89] Thomson had mentioned him in an earlier book on Dartmoor prison. 'Someone called Mr. Churchill's attention to this passage, and he asked for further particulars, and learnt that the shepherd was a Welshman.' 'Not long after this he visited Dartmoor in company with Mr. Lloyd George, and the shepherd was called before them and conversed with Mr. Lloyd George in Welsh. He was always a pathetic figure in an interview, and I was not at all surprised when it was announced that Mr. Churchill had decided to give him another chance by allowing him out on remission.'[90] 'He did not of course last long.'[91]

WOMEN

Prison was a man's world; made for men, by men. Women in prison were seen as somehow anomalous: not foreseen and therefore not legislated for. They were provided with separate quarters and female staff for reasons of modesty and good order – but not otherwise dealt with all that differently. There were, it is true, fewer of them in prison than men, but there were still enough of them to have warranted more attention from penal theorists and administrators than they ever received in the nineteenth century. For the most part, and in the absence of any positive policy to the contrary, they were treated rather like rather difficult men – although protected to some extent by their sex from overly physical measures of repression. *Or* they were treated like the lunatics they were thought by some governors to resemble.

One of the difficulties women prisoners presented to prison administrators, more of a practical nuisance than a problem of discipline, was that of caring for

The convict nursery at Brixton

the babies they sometimes brought with them, or gave birth to whilst in prison. At Liverpool, in Basil Thomson's time, there was 'a creche, with a daily average of from fourteen to twenty babies. The rule was that babies could not be kept in the prison after they were a year old. In rare cases the mother's sentence exceeded a year, and then, if there was no good home for the child to go to, it was kept until the mother's discharge. . . . A baby disorganizes the entire female prison, from the matron downwards. Everyone wants to play with it, and, as sunshine is followed by storm, so the baby causes jealousy and uncharitableness to divide the oldest friends. The landing cleaners who work outside their cells used to compete with one another for the privilege of holding the baby for a moment, and the only person who seemed never to get a "look in" was the mother.'[92]

Women, even without babies, were still thought of as troublesome. In its mildest manifestation – expressed by Dr Quinton, for example – this official attitude took the form of contempt:

The woman who will curl her hair with the pages of a library, or even a devotional book, is not a hopeful subject for intellectual improvement.[93]
The general ideas and talk of many of these young female prisoners are so inconceivably vapid and silly, as to give one the impression that their opportunities for talking with sensible people have been very limited. . . . Tawdry finery is very generally their chief aspiration, as well as the cause of their downfall.[94]

There were other women in prison, however, who would never have permitted such faint-hearted antipathy to settle in the minds of the male officials who had anything to do with them. Basil Thomson took Sir Evelyn Ruggles-Brise, only recently appointed to the chairmanship of the Prison Commission, on a conducted tour of his prison. 'I remember taking a wicked delight in showing him the Liverpool women as a sample of the material for which he had to legislate. I thought that I detected a faint blanching of his cheek as he emerged from the female wing.'[95]

Male governors saw mainly trouble in their women prisoners; suffragettes looked at them with fresh eyes, with curiosity and pity, and recognized in them sisters. Sylvia Pankhurst, who had been so shocked by the language she heard in the black maria, felt a deeper sympathy than most; a feeling first excited by the sight of the congregation in morning chapel, where women wept openly: 'I wept with those poor souls; and when the cell door closed on me again, the shrunken forms of frail old grannies, with their scant white hair, their shaking hands and piteous, withered faces, and the tense, white looks and burning eyes of the younger women haunted me.'[96] Some of them were brought to scrub out her cell: 'old women; pale women; a bright young girl who smiled at me whenever she raised her eyes from the floor; a poor ugly creature without a nose, awful to look upon.'[97] Mary Richardson saw 'one girl of only eighteen, the youth in her face crushed as one might crush a flower.'[98] And Lady Constance describes a woman who 'was young, her skin was remarkably smooth and devoid of expressive lines, but yellow as if she had jaundice. Her appearance illustrated to me the meaning of despair more clearly than I have seen it hitherto in any living being. She was entirely passive and unresentful, but if hope had tried to enter into her mind it would find no lodging there. It seemed to me that neither life nor death had anything to offer her, nor was there anything she possessed of which they could rob her.'[99] On another occasion, she records:

> Suddenly I felt awed, a feeling of supremest pity almost took my breath away. Passing in front of me into the larger hall was a woman of great beauty, her features were intensely refined, and in every part of her there seemed to be some great determination, not in respect of the prison she was in now, that was only part of it, but with regard to her life of shame that went before; the whole face and figure were virtuous and good.[100]

The prostitute was *the* typical woman prisoner of the later nineteenth century, committed to prison in such numbers as to make possible a remarkable survey of 16,000 'fallen women'. It was conducted by the Reverend G.P. Merrick, MA, MB, chaplain of HM Prison, Millbank, and presented in a paper read before the ruri-decanal chapter of St Margaret's and St John's, Westminster – in the Jerusalem chamber – on Thursday, 17 July 1890. He clearly had to choose his words carefully when reporting such a subject to such an audience. The archdeacon points out in his introduction to the published version of the paper that the chaplain has managed to express himself 'with extreme delicacy and singular moderation'. And so he has, except that he contrives to mention within the first five pages that one of the 'victims of the Whitechapel murderer' (better known as Jack-the-ripper) had been released from Millbank and 'received a gift of clothes from me within twenty-four hours of her murder'.[101]

Almost 6000 of the women he surveyed had worked as domestic servants, 779 had been barmaids and waitresses and 191 claimed to have been ballet dancers.[102] They had not, however, been convicted of prostitution – which was not in itself an offence; most – almost 10,000 of them – were in prison for drunkenness offences. Merrick sees the relationship between drink and 'the life' as a consequence rather than a cause.

> I say I have not met a hundred women – perhaps out of a hundred thousand – who have said that they like their wicked and wretched mode of life. They loathe it, and their repugnance to it can only be stifled when they are more or less under the influence of intoxicating drinks. We must not forget that modesty is particularly a woman's natural possession, and it is only when she is impelled to do so by drink, or necessity or by her utilized affections that she allows it to leave her.[103]

He also notices that in many cases 'the "street" is resorted to only during the time that more reputable work fails, and the women cannot pay their rent. When their trade revives they gladly forsake the streets, and as they say, "Keep within doors." '[104]

Mary Gordon, the first woman inspector of prisons, was sympathetic to the plight of the common prostitute. 'Once branded with the name, the girl's chances of a respected life or honest employment are often over. She is practically, to use a common phrase, "ruined," and bankrupt of all character.'[105] But Joseph Kingsmill, writing at a time of sterner morality, thought of the fallen woman more in terms of the further damage she might do to innocent men.

> Take, for instance, the case of a libertine in the higher ranks, or in any class, who has brought one woman to ruin. That ruined individual descends into a lower deep, becomes in turn the seducer of virtue, not in one, but hundreds of young men; robs them of their strength, their money, their character; and then confederates them in those bands of midnight robbers, and those hordes of swindlers and gamblers, which make necessary an army of police for the protection of property and life; and innumerable prisons to punish, correct, and lead them, if it be possible, back to virtue.[106]

SUICIDES

Between 1868 and 1877 more than 2000 people accused of the criminal offence of attempted suicide were committed to the House of Detention at Clerkenwell. They were 'remanded to receive the advice of the prison chaplain', who happened to be Canon J.W. Horsley.[107] In his *Jottings from Jail*, he recites some facts and figures about 300 of these individuals – 'not picked cases . . . but simply taken as they come.'[108] Out of this total, '117 were males, and 183 females.' The disproportion, he thinks, may be due to the fact 'that a man often has more force, both physical and mental, and therefore his attempt is more frequently successful; and again, the sham attempts of silly girls may help to swell the record against their sex.'[109] Most of the women were aged under 30 and had been arrested for making public suicide attempts; the most favoured method being that of attempted drowning. The next most popular method was poison, followed by hanging, followed by cutting the throat; 'It may be noted also that women have an aversion to shed blood, very rarely cutting their throat.'[110] He claims that more than half of the suicide bids were made under the influence of alcohol, and in some cases during attacks of the *delirium tremens*.

Some examples:

> Girl, 16, sexual and suicidal, often apprehended for threatening suicide,
> also for being drunk, illiterate, not responsible at times for her actions;
> living with her parents but not brought up by them. . . .
> Girl, 17, confirmed drunkard: father drinks; dishonest and rebellious:
> into canal because shut out from home for bad conduct. . . .
> Girl, 14, into the Serpentine: shut out from her lodgings because drunk;
> elder sister immoral. . . .
> Girl, 17, work-house-reared; has been in prison for theft and drink; into
> the fountains in Trafalgar Square because miserable on the streets and
> mother would not have her home.[111]

In addition to drink, Canon Horsley had discerned at least one other possible
cause of suicide: 'I distinctly assert my belief that the poem of T. Hood, "The
Bridge of Sighs," written with the sole object of evoking charity for the
despised, has yet, with a certain class, tinged suicide with a halo of romance,
and afforded a justification of cowardice and crime to the unreasoning and
hysterical.'[112]

The Bridge of Sighs

. . .

Touch her not scornfully;
Think of her mournfully,
Gently and humanly;
Not of the stains of her,
All that remains of her
Now is pure womanly.[113]

. . .

Canon Horsley does not say what sentences were awarded to the
'unreasoning and hysterical' cases after they had been remanded to receive his
'advice', but some at least were imprisoned:

> She came to my notice first under a punishment of two months, in default
> of bail, for attempting suicide (the third time). On discharge she soon
> attempted twice again, and was remanded to Horsemonger Lane Prison.
> In a month or so she reappeared here for attempts in a canal and in the
> police-cell, and got six months. She attempted to strangle herself a few
> days after entrance . . . and finally, on the day before her discharge.
> Two days after, she got a month's hard labour for being drunk and
> attempting suicide, and thence came to us for six months. . . . I knew of
> her attempting her life twenty-eight times in two years; every means had
> been tried with her, but no doctor would, or could, ever certify that she
> was insane, in the legal sense of the word.[114]

Nevertheless, 'she spent nearly three years in an asylum . . . and then was sent to the workhouse as insane.' The sufferings of this woman, and of others like her, elicit no sympathy from Horsley. 'I firmly believe that if it became the exception instead of the rule for such offences to escape a period of hard labour, the numbers of attempts would at once, and to a remarkable extent, diminish.'[115]

THE CAUSES OF CRIME

There was an evident fascination in prison writing, no matter who wrote it, with the nature of the individuals who ended up as prisoners. It was linked with a desire to track down the causes of crime to one or other of whatever were the theoretically fashionable sources of the time. To this end, offenders were often invited to testify from their own experience. Children, when asked, tended to give pathetic life stories:

My mother is dead: I do not remember her. My father often got drunk: he used to lick us with a rope: he used to bring women into the house – drinking – on Saturday nights. My father married again about two years ago: he sold all the furniture and left us.[116]

The detail in such a life is clearly real, but it was collected in support of the idea that much if not most of the blame for juvenile crime could be laid at the door of bad parents. In his report for 1839, the governor of Parkhurst made a list of boys in the prison together with some 'remarks' about each:

Bad company; not corrected by parents; stubborn temper.
Parents both drunkards; cruelly used by them.
Bad company; placed by mother in a workhouse.
Sent out to beg and steal by mother; forced into crime.
Prosecuted by mother for robbing her; ignorance and low associates.[117]

No doubt where the blame was being cast in these cases. The chaplain at Wakefield, the Reverend R.V. Reynolds, entertained a similar certainty: 'From his intercourse with 1224 criminals, the Writer has come to the conclusion, that, in *nearly* all cases of crime, the cause is to be traced, *primarily*, to the Parents, or Guardians, in having neglected to infuse religious principles, or having neutralised those principles by evil example.'[118]

On a less serious note, although evidently sincerely held, was the belief of the ever inventive Canon Horsley that 'the perverted taste for lollipops caused chiefly (because not prevented) by mothers, is a large – very large – cause of juvenile crime.'[119]

A different addiction was more commonly held to lie behind much adult crime. 'The liquor traffic', according to Henry Holloway, a prisoner who eventually escaped from its clutches, 'is the devil's express train, whose crowded freight of maddened souls start from rum and brandy on the line of dissipation. The engine-driver is folly'.[120] Prison chaplains used the same kind of language: 'intemperance' was 'like a destroying pestilence . . . sapping the very foundations of society'. It was 'a monster evil in the land . . . a plague in the midst of us, more fatal than any malady which ever visited our shores'.[121]

There was no shortage of evidence about the prevalence of drinking amongst the working classes. John Clay, a keen amateur statistician, was able 'to ascertain the weekly expenditure in liquor of all the men – hard working labourers, and skilled artizans, employed by one master'. 'The gross weekly earnings of the 131 men amount to £154.16s., and the aggregate of the weekly sum spent by them in liquor is £34.15s., or 22.4 per cent of their wages'.[122] 'It is the knowledge of the facts like these which renders credible the calculated expenditure in the United Kingdom in intoxicating drink, viz., more *than sixty-five millions of pounds sterling annually! Ten times the usual amount of the English poor rates!*'[123] And the popularity of public drinking as a working-class pastime was confirmed by a survey whose results were presented by a prison chaplain to the 1834 Select Committee on Drunkenness. 'The other fact is, that into 14 of the more prominent gin-shops of the metropolis there entered, in one week only, no less than 142,453 men, 108,593 women, and 18,391 children . . . a grand total of no less than 249,438!' Although there were other reasons for the contemporary increase in crime, the Reverend Ruell was in no doubt that 'the great deterioration in the character and habits of the working classes, either produced or aggravated by drunkenness, more especially by dram-drinking, has been the leading cause, if not the greatest of all.'[124] Estimates of the importance of drink in the aetiology of offending varied: at Pentonville it was estimated that amongst the men in 'the lowest class, full 50 per cent fell from habits of drinking in public houses.'[125] Susan Willis Fletcher put the proportion higher amongst the women at Tothill Fields, Westminster, and blamed, not the women, or the social conditions in which they lived, but the government.

> Nine in ten, and I think a larger proportion, owe their imprisonment solely to drink sold to them by respectable men licensed by government, and so employed to collect the revenue. The government tempts these poor women to drink, pockets a large part of the money they pay for their 'liquid damnation,' and then shuts them up in this dark, cold, and horrible prison to get sober, and then get drunk again.[126]

But contemporary commentators were not content simply to point to drink as an important cause of crime; they were concerned to reduce its abuse by the lower classes. In her book on prison visiting, Maria Shepherd makes a direct appeal to drinkers: 'Oh! working man, pass those doors quickly which stand so invitingly open. Do not stop to listen to the merry song, nor answer the laughing jest of the smiling landlord, as he lounges against the door-post; but hasten to your own fireside – a very poor one it may be, but it will not be a miserable one, if you are a sober man'.[127]

Since her work was specifically directed at 'mothers and mistresses', it is unlikely that her words ever reached any working men, but even if they had, it is unlikely they could have undermined the attractions of 'the beer-house, where they spend their evenings in drinking, gambling, quarrelling, listening to the stirring tales of poachers and thieves, or to one of their number reading one of the detestable pamphlets of the day'.[128] These pamphlets were devoted to lurid subjects – to the life stories of Dick Turpin and Jack Sheppard, and others of their ilk; and young criminals 'although naturally restless in their habits, will sit for six or eight hours together, relating and hearing tales of criminal heroes'. 'Although an advocate for the fullest liberty of the press,' confesses the Newgate Schoolmaster, 'I regret to add that if means could be taken to suppress the low publications, of which there are now so many sold, many boys would be saved from destruction who are now lost entirely by the influence these works have on their vitiated tastes, viz. the fictitious lives of robbers, pirates, and loose women'.[129] Dramatized versions of these tales were also presented to appreciative and uproarious audiences in low theatre houses. The Reverend J. Kingsmill, who had a bad word for most of life's little pleasures, thought that 'The minor theatre *directly* teaches crime and immorality; the superior sort, more speciously, *immodesty and vice, which tend to crime.*'[130]

But this froth of theatrical frivolity concealed a deeper and darker sediment that lay beneath the surface of nineteenth-century crime – a residue of social, physical and economic conditions which most observers, Sir Edmund DuCane amongst them, felt bound to acknowledge: 'A large proportion of the prisoners who form the population of our prisons are of diseased and impaired constitutions, victims of dirt, intemperance, and irregularity, and the sins of the fathers in these respects are visited on the children "to the third and fourth generation".'[131]

Thoughts of this sort raised inescapable issues of free will and moral responsibility. There were those like Michael Davitt, who spent many years locked up with criminals, and who inclined to view the products of adverse social conditions as less than fully responsible for their anti-social acts:

Men whose early years have been vitiated in an atmosphere of crime, whose recollections of childhood are those of neglect, hunger, and theft, and whose after lives have run in an orbit of iniquity, at once fixed and repelled by the operation of that very influence which should have rescued them from thence – the influence of Society – such men can be scarcely any more responsible, from a moral point of view, for the actions they commit than the unreasoning animal which follows the impulse of its passions.[132]

'Speaking proverbially,' quotes Sir Edmund, and less charitably, 'they form a class of fools whom even experience fails to teach.'[133]

Earlier theories did not hold to so determinist a view of human nature; Governor Chesterton asked, for example, ' "Does this vicious subject know right from wrong?" Assuredly, "Yes" would be the universal reply, because, at length, all around conspired to instruct him on the point, in addition to the natural light of reason, which, though obscured, is rarely utterly extinguished.'[134] And Dr Daniel Ritchie, surgeon-captain of a convict transport, rejected the theory outright on purely moral grounds: 'No error can be more erroneous than that which considers all crime a natural sequence of a particular constitution, or mental formation. According to this view there could exist no hopes of reformation.'[135] Determinist thinking was hardly dented by such frail opposition; it remained firmly rooted in a folk tradition that professed to see in the features or physique of the criminal some evidence for the existence of a distinct 'criminal type'. Even the Newgate Schoolmaster, a commentator not normally given to hyperbole, was taken by the appearance of his prisoners. 'They have a peculiar look of the eye, which may be known by any one much accustomed to see them; and the development of their features is strongly marked with the animal propensities.' 'Some of the boys have an approximation to the face of a monkey, so strikingly are they distinguished by this peculiarity.'[136] Here too is Hepworth Dixon: 'A man who has not seen masses of men in a great prison, cannot conceive how hideous the human countenance can become. Looking in the front of these benches, one sees only demons.'[137] 'Such low, misshapen brows; such animal and sensual mouths and jaws; such cunning, reckless, or stupid looks, – hardly seem to belong to anything that can by courtesy be called human.'[138] These impressions were shared by and given savage added effect in the words of Thomas Carlyle following a visit to Pentonville: 'Miserable distorted blockheads, the generality; ape-faces, imp-faces, angry dog-faces, heavy sullen ox-faces; degraded underfoot perverse creatures, sons of in-docility, greedy mutinous darkness, and in one word of STUPIDITY, which is the general mother of such.'[139]

Prisoners also could be carried away with this view of their fellows:

I had noticed, sitting behind this man as I did in chapel, almost directly in the rear of him, that I *could see his eyes*. He had a narrow, straight face, and there was a deep scoop, as it were, taken out of each bone where the forehead joined the cheek, and through this scoop I saw the eye from behind more clearly than when standing in front of the man, for his brows overhung in a most forbidding way.[140]

The popularity of the notion that there was a 'criminal appearance,' in which the marks of Cain were to be readily detected, was lent a 'scientific' respectability by the emerging doctrines of social Darwinism and by the school of 'criminal anthropology' associated with the work of Cesare Lombroso. The more uncritical followers of his teachings were led to make statements of the sort that appeared in an edition of the influential *Nineteenth Century* over the name of Vernon Harris, one-time governor of Dartmoor prison:

As a rule criminals will neither look straight at nor receive the gaze of a person speaking to them.[141]
The hair and eyes of female criminals are usually darker than those of honest women.[142]
General testimony says that prostitutes are very insensible to pain, a fact to be surmised from the readiness with which they allow themselves to be wounded, to be cauterized for certain diseases, and to undergo surgical operations. . . . The voices of prostitutes are very frequently deep and coarse.[143]

These and similar absurdities continued to be repeated as received truths until 1913, when the statistical work of Dr Charles Goring dealt them a more or less fatal blow. In his study of *The English Convict* he looked at the characteristics of 3000 convicted prisoners, *and* at those of selected non-criminal groups. 'From these comparisons,' he concludes, '*no evidence has emerged confirming the existence of a physical criminal type, such as Lombroso and his disciples have described.*'[144] The prison experience of Clifford Rickards predates the publication of Goring's results, but the writing of his memoirs came after it, so it may be that he was being wise in retrospect, but this is his impression of the prison physiognomy:

Here is no Bill Sikes, with the bullet head and cruel beast-like features, such as we meet with in pictures and detective stories, but a quiet, placid, and pleasant-featured youth, such that if you found him in your house at midnight, you would be disposed to think he was the gentleman from next door who had come in by mistake, rather than a burglar intent on robbery.[145]

By strange chance Rickards did once discover just such a gentleman in his study, although at the slightly later hour of '1 o'clock in the morning'.[146] He was armed with a knife and Rickards shot him. 'The gun must have thrown up a bit, as the charge caught him in the forearm.'[147] The intruder (a man called Mollott) was taken to Tavistock Hospital 'where he was seen by four doctors who decided that the arm must be amputated below the elbow'.[148] Rickards attended his trial and pleaded with Judge Vaughan Williams to give him a lenient sentence, which he did in the form of one month's hard labour.[149] Within a few months Mollott was again convicted of burglary and sentenced to 'penal servitude for six years'.[150]

NOTES

1. A. Bidwell, 487.
2. Dawson, 151.
3. Chesterton (1856), II, 140.

4. Joseph, 54–5.
5. Rickards, 99.
6. Sykes, 191.

7. Thomson (1925), 63.
8. A. Bidwell, 488.
9. Ibid., 483.
10. One-who-has-endured-it, 3.
11. No. 7, 9.
12. Martyn, 8.
13. J. Balfour, 6–7.
14. Hepworth Dixon, 349.
15. Horsley (1898), 126.
16. Mayhew, 246.
17. Schoolmaster, 526.
18. Fulford, 143.
19. H. Gordon, 8.
20. Hart-Davis, 270.
21. Bacchus, 269.
22. Llewellin, 13.
23. Bacchus, 269.
24. Carnarvon Committee (1863), 152.
25. Wood, 31.
26. Kingsmill (1854), 100.
27. Fannan, 125.
28. Hart-Davis, 272.
29. Hiener, 3.
30. Shepherd, 71.
31. Wrench, 37.
32. A Governor, 219.
33. W.L. Clay, 291.
34. A Governor, 218.
35. Rossa, 226.
36. Kingsmill (1854), 92.
37. Ibid., 44.
38. Ibid., 49.
39. B. Thomson (1925), 150.
40. Ibid., 152.
41. Fulford, 148.
42. W.L. Clay, 564.
43. Ibid., 567.
44. Leicester Inquiry (1854), 215.
45. Ibid., 236.
46. Ibid., 225.
47. Ibid., 220.
48. Ibid., 223.
49. Holyoake (1893), I, 163.
50. Half-Timer, 78.
51. Bent, 71.
52. Drunkenness Inquiry (1834), 355.
53. Quinton, 16.
54. Joseph, 45–6.
55. Blake, 18.
56. One-who-has-endured-it, 259.
57. W.L. Clay, 522.
58. Henderson, 29.
59. Ibid., 68.
60. Ritchie, 163.
61. Henderson, 66.
62. Wood, 103.
63. Ibid., 104.
64. Ibid., 108.
65. G. Bidwell, 192.
66. Ibid., 195.
67. A. Bidwell, 205.
68. Bowen-Rowlands, 103–5.
69. B. Thomson (1925), 192–3.
70. Jervis, 77.
71. Fannan, 130.
72. WBN, 45.
73. Campbell, 114.
74. Ibid., 113.
75. Woodruff, 458.
76. Davitt (1885), I, 78.
77. Griffiths (1904), 215.
78. Davitt (1885), 80.
79. Ticket-of-leave-man, 121.
80. One-who-has-endured-it, 219.
81. J. Balfour, 72.
82. Foote, 86.
83. A. Bidwell, 487.
84. Ticket-of-leave-man, 108.
85. Hooley, 289.
86. B. Thomson (1925), 169.
87. Ibid., 170.
88. Ibid., 66.
89. B. Thomson (1907), 266.
90. B. Thomson (1925), 123.
91. B. Thomson (1939), 220.
92. B. Thomson (1925), 32–3.
93. Quinton, xi.
94. Ibid., 140.
95. B. Thomson (1925), 33.
96. S. Pankhurst, 235.
97. Ibid., 446.
98. Richardson, 74.
99. Lytton, 120.
100. Ibid., 260.
101. Merrick, 11.
102. Ibid., 25.
103. Ibid., 29.
104. Ibid., 30.
105. M. Gordon, 99.
106. Kingsmill (1854), 63.
107. Horsley (1887), 239.
108. Ibid., 241.
109. Ibid., 242.

110. Ibid., 244.
111. Ibid., 247.
112. Ibid., 251.
113. Hood, I, 64.
114. Horsley (1887), 257.
115. Ibid., 258.
116. W.L. Clay, 461.
117. Parkhurst Report (1839), 9–13.
118. Reynolds, 15.
119. Horsley (1887), 93.
120. Holloway (1887b), 8.
121. Kingsmill (1854), 69.
122. W.L. Clay, 510.
123. Ibid., 511.
124. Drunkenness Inquiry (1834), 307.
125. Kingsmill (1854), 41.
126. Fletcher, 324.
127. Shepherd, 51.
128. Fulford, 145.
129. Old Bailey, 298.
130. Kingsmill (1854), 79.
131. DuCane (1885), 97.
132. Davitt (1886), 33.
133. DuCane (1885), 3.
134. Chesterton (1856), II, 130.
135. Ritchie, 15.
136. Schoolmaster, 522.
137. Hepworth Dixon, 244.
138. Ibid., 245.
139. Carlyle (1850), 70.
140. Roche, 54.
141. Harris (1907), 792.
142. Ibid., 796.
143. Ibid., 797.
144. Goring, 96.
145. Rickards, 66.
146. Ibid., 247.
147. Ibid., 233.
148. Ibid., 234.
149. Ibid., 243.
150. Ibid., 246.

4
THE DAILY ROUND

'The day began early' at Chatham Convict Prison. 'The first bell to rouse out the convicts was at 5.30 a.m.,' says Arthur Griffiths, who began his prison service there as assistant deputy governor in 1870.[1] Between 5 and 6 a.m. establishments at every point on the penal map were stirred into life by the sound of the bell. At Dartmoor it was 5,[2] Parkhurst, 10 past 5;[3] at Millbank,[4] Pentonville,[5] and Cold Bath Fields[6] it was as late as 6 o'clock. Stuart Wood entertained a 'fancy . . . that every prison bell in England was cast by the same hands in the same mould and tuned to the same pitch, for I never heard one which differed in any respect from another. Each and all have that harsh, strident note which seems to embody in its tone all that is brutal, cruel and hopeless.'[7] 'The ugly voice' of the bell marked the moment 'when every man springs from his hammock, and by the time he has given himself a good wash in his bucket, all over if he likes, the warders are on the landings.'[8] This was also the time when 'if a man wants to speak to the warder for anything: to put his name down to see the Doctor, Governor, Chief Warder, or Chaplain . . . he puts out his broom under the door.'[9] At Tothill Fields, Westminster, the doors were unlocked at 6.30, 'when all pass out with their uncovered slop-buckets and water-cans, to empty the former and fill the latter. The water-tank and place for emptying the slops are together; and fifty women of one division are expected to get back to their cells in ten minutes'.[10] In 1840 these were operations that took place in the open air at Liverpool, the inmates being required to 'carry out the nuisance tins – wash them in a large stone trough. . . . Next, we were to undergo ablutions ourselves, in the same stone trough. . . . After breakfast, recourse was had again to the trough, to cleanse our *dishes*'.[11]

At some places, the morning unlocking was one of the two daily occasions when 'prisoners had a brief opportunity, harried by the perpetual shout of "Make haste! Make haste!" to run to the W.C. in the corridor.'[12] Personal ablutions were followed by a cleansing of the cell and such of its contents as could be swept, washed or polished. Stone floors were to be scrubbed. At Dartmoor, 'on his door being opened every man goes down on his knees and scrubs and cleans so much of the slate floor of the landing as is in front of his own cell. Thus the whole landing is done.'[13]

It was also necessary for the tins in the cell to be cleaned regularly. Like other contents of the cell, the items of tinware served a double purpose in the moral economy of the prison. Firstly they were there as utilities – utensils for washing in, or eating off – but, just as important in the eyes of officials, they were objects of a daily discipline that permeated to the minutest detail of the prisoner's life. Austin Bidwell's 'consisted of a jug for water and a bowl for washing in and a pint dish for gruel'. 'Although called tinware, it really was zinc, and was susceptible, through much hard work, of a high polish, but this "polishing tinware" was a fearful curse of the poor prisoner'. 'There were strict and imperative orders, rigidly enforced, that this tinware should be kept polished, the result being that men never washed themselves, and never took water in their jugs, for if they did their tinware would take a stain – "go off," as it was termed – the result being that if the poor devil washed and kept himself clean he would be reported and severely punished for having dirty tinware.'[14] Techniques for producing brilliant results with little effort were developed and shared amongst prisoners:

By well cleaning the dust-pan with whitening, rubbing it up well with the clean rag until it had a nice surface, and then lightly passing a rag saturated with dubbin over it, you could produce a beautiful polish by a few slight touches of the 'finisher.' After this artistic process the dust-pan shone like an oriental mirror, and might have served a belle at her toilette.[15]

The bedding also possessed disciplinary properties. On the first morning, after a first night under prison-issue bed-clothes, the first task 'was to learn how to roll them up again in apple-pie order, a core of white sheets, and a crust of yellow blankets, with a coloured counter-pane outside the lot'.[16] It was a difficult art to master. 'Some convicts', says One-who-has-suffered, 'can roll up bedding in 15 minutes, others 45; but it all depends on strength.'[17] It took O'Donovan Rossa 'an hour to fold these things, and if they were not folded so as to please the officer, he pulled them off the shelf and threw them about the floor, ordering me to go at them again.'[18]

Whilst all this was going on, amidst the 'hurry, noise, dirt and bustle',[19] the first meal of the day would be served. The conditions under which it was consumed were subject to seasonal variations of an unhelpful nature. 'In the winter,' says Mrs Maybrick, 'the prisoners get up in the dark, and breakfast in the dark, to save the expense of gas.'[20] The darkness and the cramped conditions added to the difficulty of doing the housework: 'to get through your cell-cleaning at all is like working a Chinese puzzle, and requires the most adroit management, you have to work ceaselessly (swallowing your cup of cocoa in sweat and dirt) till you go to chapel.'[21]

EXERCISE

At some time in the prison morning, sometimes after breakfast and before chapel, sometimes just after chapel, sometimes after work and before the mid-day meal, all prisoners except those already engaged in heavy work were obliged to take part for half an hour or an hour in an activity universally but not very accurately entitled 'exercise'. When Captain Jebb was drawing the plans for Pentonville he had to find a 'means of affording the prisoners exercise in the open air, without compromising individual separation or entailing a disproportionate number of officers to superintend them'.[22] To him it was just one more of the design problems that followed, as night from day, the initial election for a separate system of prison discipline. For the advocates of silence, it was yet another opportunity to mock the contortions which the theory of separation forced upon their opponents. Few were more skilful at this sport than Sir Peter Laurie, alderman, president of the Royal Hospitals of Bridewell and Bethlem, and author of the anti-separation pamphlet, *Killing No Murder*. He picks on Mr John G. Perry, 'a gentleman who has been recently appointed a Prison Inspector for the Southern and Western Districts, and who seems to be quite prepared to vouch for the perfection of the Separate System, and to palliate and excuse its defects'.[23] He takes three quotations from page 11 of Perry's report, which refers to Shrewsbury Gaol. The first is in favour of exercise. The second is this:

> To those undergoing very short sentences, *no exercise at all should be allowed* unless under peculiar circumstances. Prisoners might be allowed, with advantage, the use of a pair of coarse *horse-hair gloves, wherewith to scrub their bodies well every morning, thereby producing a healthful action of the skin by promoting insensible perspiration.*[24]

The third reverts to support for the saving virtues of 'proper exercise', all of which leads Sir Peter to the observation that Mr Perry, 'from his total disregard of the ordinary mode of consecutive reasoning, cannot fail to become a most useful auxiliary to Messrs. Crawford and Russell'.[25] And it illustrates nicely the ambivalent territory into which thoroughgoing 'separation' led its supporters.

Undeterred by such quibbles, Captain Jebb produced an architectural solution in the shape of 'a large wheel, 100 feet in diameter lying on the ground, it has fifty spokes, and on every spoke there is built a wall ten feet high. Between every two of these walls', says O'Donovan Rossa, 'one of us is confined for an hour each day. The rim of the wheel is an iron grating, around which the Governor walked occasionally, a door enters or opens from every compartment, and within the stock or the hub of the wheel is a room in which the officer keeps a watch upon the convicts.'[26] The wheel succeeded well enough in one of its aims, that of not compromising individual separation, but getting the prisoners to and from their cells, and into and out of what a member of the Carnarvon Committee was pleased to call 'a groove of iron', caused definite problems in terms of the 'number of officers' required to superintend the operation.[27] Governor Gardner explained to the committee how it was managed at Bristol: 'they are removed from the compartments in each yard to the cells in each ward, one at a time. An officer is placed at the cell door, and another at the compartment in the yard. Directly a prisoner is released from the yard . . . they turn a half-minute glass, and when the sand is out they let another go; when the man arrives upstairs he rings a bell to show that he is out of sight, so that they never see each other.'[28]

Difficulties of this sort, allied to the demise of strict separation, led to the demolition of the radial yards and their replacement with congregate, but 'silent' arrangements. It was usual for these to consist of 'three circles, one within another, the arc of each being a flagging about eighteen inches wide. The convicts walk on these flags, and in three different places between each circle there are raised pathways on which the officers walk, and have a view of the whole ring.'[29]

For newly received prisoners, exercise was a first chance to see an assembled body of their fellows, whether men or women or children: Susan Willis Fletcher thought it 'a curious sight to see this regiment of women, from eighty-five years old to twelve, all dressed alike, but looking so different, – a regiment composed almost entirely of drunkards, prostitutes, thieves'.[30] But for Constance Lytton it was a most depressing sight: 'They nearly all of them looked ill. Their faces wore an expression of extreme dejection; the lifeless, listless way they walked, enhanced the look of entire detachment of one from the other; in spite of being so closely herded, each seemed in a world of her own individual sorrow.'[31]

The scene matched that in the yard on the men's side where 'there were boys in their teens, young men, middle aged men and old men tottering round and round – all of them wearing the same, strained, hopeless expression on their faces.' And 'it was no uncommon sight to see boys who were little more than children tramping that Devil's Circle with men of all ages and degrees of vice.'[32] Sometimes, as a sort of gesture in the direction of separatist hygiene, children might be removed as they were at Reading, and 'sent to exercise on small sunless yards, sometimes a stone-yard, sometimes a yard at the back of the mills – rather than that they should see the elder prisoners at exercise'.[33]

The presence of warders in the yard epitomized the great preoccupation of the 'silent' regime: how to control and prevent from talking a gathered mass of criminals whose voluntary co-operation in the enterprise could hardly be counted upon. When One-who-has-tried-them took his exercise, 'some six or seven warders were in superintendence; one placed at each corner, and two or three more skirmishing up and down, ready to pounce upon any man who attempted to open his lips, and keeping a sharp look out that no papers were dropped or picked up.'[34] In a Scottish prison there were 'massive stone pedestals, three on each side – each one with a "Screw" stationed on top, to see doubtless that no prisoner in the exercise yard takes it into his head to diddle off with any Government property.'[35] From these different vantage points the warders kept the rotating prisoners apart: 'Some of us walked fast, others more slowly, consequently we were constantly being held up by the arm of the Law, regulating the distance between us.'[36] The distance between prisoners could also be managed by semi-mechanical means. In the exercise yard at Pentonville, the concentric rings 'consisted of a narrow line of bricken paving let into the soil, and on this lay a long rope knotted at distances of fifteen feet apart: Here the prisoners took up their station, one at every knot.'[37]

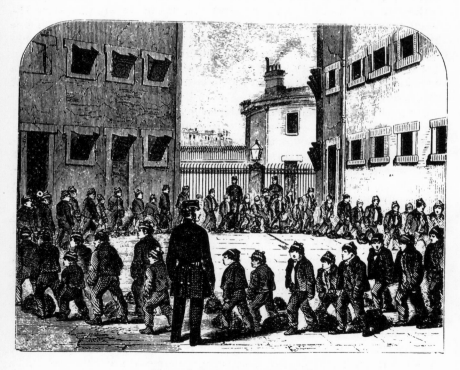

Young boys in an exercise yard

Besides keeping prisoners apart, the officers would, from time to time, vary the whole pace of the proceedings, as they did at Leicester.

There were about 50 men and boys at exercise, and after walking a few times round, 'right about face' was shouted by one of the officers in charge, and soon after the order 'double quick' was given, when 50 human beings had to run five or six hundred yards or so, walking or running like horses at the command of human beings like themselves, and who were possibly not so good as some of the poor prisoners.[38]

But the main aim of the official presence was to prevent talking: 'The average warder watches the lips of prisoners, and the angle at which they hold their heads when at exercise. He doesn't listen so much, he watches.'[39] Quite clearly the officials failed in this ambition: 'absolutely to prevent talking was an impossibility and though hampered considerably, it hummed amongst the files like the breeze in a pine forest.'[40] 'While at exercise,' says Frederick Brocklehurst, 'you frequently hear a voice issuing as it seems from nowhere, and directed upon no object. No movement whatever indicates either speaker or listener.' 'Old prisoners are past-masters in the art of ventriloquism. The words appear to be formed at the back of their throats, and are so low in tone that unless you have a remarkably keen ear they speak to you in vain.'[41] Jabez Balfour 'suddenly detected a voice' behind him, 'hoarsely whispering, "What are you here for, old man, and what have you got?" '[42] ' "Wot's libel?" ' John Dawson was asked. 'I answered the question as well as I could under the circumstances. It was no easy task to say even what I did with lynx-eyed warders watching every movement of the prisoners; and my difficulties were increased too, by having to converse with a man who was behind me. It was comparatively easy to talk to a prisoner who walked in front of you, only it is advisable for the man in front never to turn his head when he is spoken to, otherwise he is likely to betray to the keen gaze of a warder the fact that you are talking, even though you may not so much as move your lips, and your voice may be perfectly inaudible to the officer.'[43]

If speech were not possible; if friends were placed in different files parading round different rings, communication was still feasible since 'the man in the inner ring made more circuits than the man in the ring next to him. So that if we did not strike upon each other when we entered the yard at first, we were sure to pass each other repeatedly during the hour.'[44] As they passed, men would make signals: 'you may at times perceive a prisoner making sly movements with his thumbs and fingers – a fact which leads to the natural observation that the dumb and deaf alphabet is now and then put to uses other than those for which it was originally intended.'[45]

Towards the end of the nineteenth century, the 'sinews of discipline' were loosened to the extent that, on Sunday each week, penal-servitude prisoners in the last stage of their sentences, 'though surrounded by officers and kept in a small circle like people at a fair, could select their companions and even sit down on the ground by the prison side and rest.'[46] They were also permitted to talk, something that provoked fresh fears of criminal contamination. Lord William Nevill, who had himself enjoyed this more relaxed dispensation, found it 'natural that some should like to talk about their past life, and, personally, I often found such narratives full of information and free from anything offensive or harmful.'[47]

Talking at exercise, even as a privilege for men on the point of release, was quite exceptional; the ordinary experience was one of enforced silence. Even when addressed, well-behaved convicts would not reply for fear of disciplinary reprisals. Balfour never answered to the voice that asked 'What are you here for?' Brocklehurst heard the voices of others but said nothing himself; and saw the signs but made none of his own. Exercise remained, as it was intended to be, a profoundly lonely and solitary perambulation of 'between two and three miles', in the company of many others. Helen Gordon, a suffragette, took her exercise in the yard at Strangeways:

> Round she moves – looking up at the windows of one wing of the prison, and counts the windows – one – two – three, etc. It is an old worry of hers – it has bothered her for days – Eleven – twelve – thirteen – no, fourteen – no, she has missed one. Now comes a huge chimney – a high wall behind an open covered passage-way leading from prison to hospital – there is a door in the wall·through which sometimes the under-matron conducts prisoners in their ordinary clothes – they are leaving the prison – three times she has seen this. Once through the open door she sees an ordinary four-wheeler in the court beyond – it is all so fleeting – for as she turns away on her circle it disappears and may have vanished when next the circle is completed. . . . As she turns, her eyes seek the prison windows again – eleven – twelve – thirteen – no, that pipe running up the centre of the wing has put out her calculations – the dull red walls with their regular windows bother her. . . . Now the circle is completed and begins again – the door in the wall – the passage-way – the old bit of the prison – the hospital – the jugs – the high prison chimney – the counting of the windows – the sky over the high wall, and the other great chimney beyond, stretching up to the sky.[48]

Even so, there was visual relief to be found in this arid environment: 'Chiefest among the tiny grains of pleasure which prison life contained' for the author of *Pentonville Prison from Within* 'was the sight of some forget-me-nots – sweet, modest, blue babies, looking up at us with their myriad eyes as we toiled round the prison yard under the stern eye of the armed warders.'[49] Sylvia Pankhurst, poet and painter, took even keener delight in 'a showery day, the sun shining gaily on puddles and raindrops, the white clouds driving briskly across a sky of strong, clear blue, and the wind whisking our bonnets and skirts in playful gusts. The pigeons, dear harbingers of freedom, dwelling in great numbers about that dreary prison, flew low and strutted near us. How gladly my eyes sought the varied hues of their glossy plumage.'[50]

These delights of the senses may have been the privilege of a few; the minds of a more prosaic majority were on lower things. Bill Sykes tells his readers: 'There is one thing wanted very badly at Pentonville in the exercise yard – that is sanitary conveniences for the men; there is no accommodation whatever, of any description for them. And if a man should happen to be in any difficulty, he has to fall out, ring the prison bell, go back to his ward, and lose his exercise for that day. In addition to this, I have, during the time I was at Pentonville, seen men wait for a quarter of an hour and more before the bell was answered, the men suffering most excruciating misery in the interval.'[51] Leonard Hall, a colleague of Frederick Brocklehurst on the Boggart Clough, witnessed similar scenes at Strangeways, which made him 'wonder what is meant by the supporters of the present system when they cant and twaddle to you about the present system being "reformative, no longer punitive." '[52]

It was not however any particular detail of exercise that haunted Lady Constance Lytton, but the whole aspect of the yard, and all that it stood for:

The remarkable feature of the yard, which caused the first feeling of horror that has remained a nightmare in my mind ever since, is the tier upon tier of cell shutters . . . the prison from here looks like a great hive of human creeping things impelled to their joyless labours and unwilling seclusion by some hidden force, the very reverse of natural, and which has in it no element of organic life, cohesion, or self-sufficing reason.[53]

She was never after able to see 'the high central tower, which enables Holloway prison to stand as a landmark for many miles distant . . . without recalling the sensations that gripped my soul and checked my breath when I first set eyes on this inner yard. It seemed the quintessence of prison, the very heart of it.'[54]

NOTES

1. Griffiths (1904), 166.
2. Harris (n.d.), 49.
3. WBN, 123.
4. One-who-has-endured-it, 86.
5. Convict 77, 57.
6. D— S—, 178.
7. Wood, 28.
8. One-who-has-endured-it, 170.
9. Ibid., 172.
10. Fletcher, 325.
11. Wait, 168.
12. S. Pankhurst, 235.
13. One-who-has-endured-it, 171.
14. A. Bidwell, 403.
15. Foote, 125.
16. *Pentonville Prison from Within*, 29.
17. One-who-has-suffered, 15.
18. Rossa, 87.
19. Letter, 497.
20. Maybrick, 179.
21. Letter, 497.
22. Jebb, 12.
23. Laurie, 17.
24. Ibid., 18.
25. Ibid., 17.

26. Rossa, 91.
27. Carnarvon Committee (1863), 328.
28. Ibid., 329.
29. Rossa, 90.
30. Fletcher, 326.
31. Lytton, 133.
32. Wood, 31.
33. Hart-Davis, 272.
34. One-who-has-tried-them, I, 267.
35. Burnside, 8.
36. Biggs, 11.
37. Mayhew, 142.
38. Barrow, 9.
39. Wood, 55.

40. Fannan, 99.
41. Brocklehurst, 98.
42. J. Balfour, 45.
43. Dawson, 106.
44. Rossa, 117.
45. Brocklehurst, 98.
46. Letter, 499.
47. WBN, 241.
48. H. Gordon, 26–8.
49. *Pentonville Prison from Within*, 169.
50. S. Pankhurst, 236.
51. Sykes, 150.
52. L. Hall, 229.
53. Lytton, 188.
54. Ibid., 187.

5
CHAPEL

After ablutions, the prison day proper began in earnest with the call to worship. Half-way through the nineteenth century, the English prison acknowledged only three denominations: Church of England, Roman Catholic and Jewish. It did not recognize at all the right to Dissent, nor that of professing no religion at all. An attempt by Henry Harcourt, in 1864, to register in his own faith ended in failure. 'We have no Mahommedan religion here,' he was told, 'we don't recognise it; you must either go to church or to chapel.' When he remonstrated, the Millbank deputy governor's reply, so Harcourt says, was brutally simple: 'you will have to go to church or chapel, and if you refuse to do so you will be flogged.'[1] Catholics, despite their disproportionate presence amongst the criminal classes, were recent and controversial admissions to the official fold.[2]

But for the great majority of Victorian prisoners, the daily summons was to the rites of the Anglican communion. These, whatever their spiritual pretensions, were experienced by prisoners as unmistakably disciplinary proceedings. 'Each ward is marched off to the chapel in its turn, and on receiving a signal that the way is clear of other prisoners, along the corridors we marched in silence. Such is the rule, although there were many whisperings together among some of the men, which was always checked by the warders.'[3] Women received exactly the same treatment. 'At 8.30 the officers shouted "Chapel". The doors flew open, the prisoners emerged, and were marshalled in single file amid a running fire of rebuke: "Who is that speaking? I heard someone speaking!" "Tie up your cap strings, 27! You look like a cinder picker; you must learn to dress decently here!" "Hold up your head, 30; don't shuffle your feet." "Don't look about you, 12!"[4] At Cold Bath Fields 'the entrance of the prisoners was not conducted on the principle customary in places of worship, but was accompanied by the blowing of whistles and shouts of "Move higher up!", "Come on, there!" "D'you know where you are?", "This ain't a music hall!" and such-like appropriate exclamations. The chief cause of most of this indecent behaviour was one of the head warders, and when this man superintended the chapel parade the scene was disgraceful; and "Take that man's name down!", "I'll send you to your cell, sir!" and bully, bully, bully was the preparation for the service.'[5] A whistle was blown at the House of Detention, Clerkenwell, 'when a prisoner leaves his cell, another when he has entered chapel, and the same when service is over, so that for half an hour several times a day the whistle is sounding through the prisons at intervals of less than a minute.'[6]

'It took nearly half an hour to get the prisoners out of the chapel, and the same time to get them in. They were taken in and out very slowly, with the view of avoiding any disorder', says John Dawson.[7] The time it took to get the celebrants from their cells to the chapel was in fact the first part of a price that prison religion found itself forced to pay to the principles of silence and separation. A second instalment was visible in the elaborate arrangements required to create what amounted to an audience of isolated individuals; a segregated congregation:

> The chapel was arranged in rows of upright coffins (no other word will so well convey an idea of their appearance to the reader), each tier raised some two feet higher than the one in front, like the pit of a theatre, thus allowing the prisoners to see the chaplain, governor and chief warder, who were placed in a sort of gallery facing them, but quite preventing their seeing each other, or indeed looking anywhere but straight to their front.[8]

'This plan', claims Daniel Nihill, 'involves a striking anomaly. On the one hand, we bring Christians together for joint sympathetic worship; for the primary idea, the essential principle, which distinguishes public from private devotion, is sociality – the recognition of brethren – members of the same family – heirs of the same hope – aided by the sight and hearing of each other in a common assembly, where with one heart and one mouth they glorify God. Such is the principle on which the prisoners are brought together in chapel; but on the other hand, whilst so assembled, there is a studious effort to keep them all in a state of separation, and to defeat the idea of their communion.'[9] The general success of these efforts was affirmed by Governor Fulford: 'A more orderly or apparently devout congregation there never was, much of this may be attributed, doubtless, to the fact of a great number never having been at church before, and to their being punished if they misbehave themselves.'[10] In order to ensure that none of those who misbehaved should escape merited punishment, he had 'officers all over the building cross-firing at them, and they cannot communicate'.[11] And in the chapel where One-who-has-tried-them worshipped there was 'a railed platform across the roof from one end to the other' on which 'was placed a warder who was thus enabled to see exactly what any one man was doing, as there were no tops to the coffins below.'[12]

The 'separate system' in Pentonville's chapel

'Chapel', says Stuart Wood, 'was just part of one's punishment. If one looked either to the right or the left or attempted to whisper to another fellow it meant three days' bread and water in close confinement.'[13] Chaplains, or at least some of them, did not hesitate to play an active part in this disciplining of their flocks. Chartist William Lovett saw the Warwick prison chaplain 'from the pulpit point out to the gaoler poor wretches for unavoidably *coughing*, after they had been kept standing in the cold yard for nearly half-an-hour without their hats, in the winter season; and for which trifling offence they would be locked up in the refractory cell for a certain period'.[14] The devotion of one chaplain to discipline is reminiscent of the schoolteacher's daily battle with classes of recalcitrant children. Henry Fielding officiated in the New Bailey Prison at Salford, and this extract from his journal illustrates the problem and his response to it:

Tuesday May 3rd. 1825. Read prayers to the misdemeanants. Perhaps not quite so attentive as the felons, but their behaviour did not justify my pointing out any individual on whom I could inflict such Punishment as might cause him to be a warning example to the rest.[15]

This subversion of the chaplain's role to the demands of discipline, the subjection of the services to petty regulation and the unavoidable confusion of the two in the mind of the average prisoner made up a final, and probably fatal, repayment of the debt that was incurred when mere *prisons* became *penitentiaries*. 'The principal object of these regulations', in the view of A Merchant, 'was to preserve in the convict mind, even in the act of worship, the idea of punishment in a perfectly lively and healthy condition.'[16]

But in the midst of the surveillance, the shouting, the whistles, the punishments, divine service did offer to prisoners one secular consolation above all others: the opportunity to open their lungs after a long night, or more, of involuntary silence.

Imagine between three and four hundred men and some fifty or sixty women shut up day after day, week after week, and forbidden, under the severest pains and penalties, to open their lips, and then twice every seventh day being permitted to shout as loud as they please for five or six minutes; you can then form some conception of the noise that was made and the temptation there was to make it – some conception, and only some, for nobody who has not actually experienced it can form any exact idea of the intense longing, the almost frantic desire that tempts one to shout at the top of one's voice after three or four months' enforced silence.[17]

'The congregation joined in the service with great enthusiasm,' says Arthur Harding, 'and I was amazed at the fervour.'[18] It was an enthusiasm that did not go unnoticed – or unpunished. 'The revival associated with Moody and Sankey made itself known' to David Fannan and his fellow convicts, 'by the introduction of the well-known hymns which we much appreciated. . . . We sang Sankey's hymns with such gusto as to attract the attention of the prison authorities.'[19] 'Considering such joyous song inconsistent with the sombreness of prison life, they forbade the hymns, and sent us back to the psalms and paraphrases with their plain puritanic tunes.'[20] There was another reason for the authorities to be wary of loud singing, which was the perfect cover it provided for illicit conversation.

We will suppose for a moment that the opening hymn is 'Nearer my God to Thee'. An intending conversationalist sings the first word of each line lustily, and then breaks into a lower tone as he asks or answers questions. The following is a sample of the kind of thing one hears in chapel:-

(*Cres.*)	'Nearer'	(*dim*)	'How are you Jack?'
"	"	"	'All right.'
"	'E'en'	"	'When are you going out?'
"	'That'	"	'Monday week, etc., etc.'

The longer the line of the hymn, the greater possibility there is of squeezing a long sentence in the place of the one to be sung.[21]

Another way in which this possibility was exploited was in the singing of 'ribald songs under shelter of the many voices intoning around.'[22]

There were also occasions when these *sotto voce* commentaries broke cover as interjections in the service itself. As part of his sermon, the chaplain at Holloway 'instanced how wrong it would be if, when we were hungry, we yielded to the temptation of stealing bread. At this remark an old woman stood up. She was tall and gaunt, her face seamed with life, her hands gnarled and worn with work. The tears streamed down her furrowed cheeks as she said in a pleading, reverent voice, "Oh, sir, don't be so hard on us." The wardresses immediately came up to her, took her by the shoulders and hustled her out of the ward; we never saw her again. The Chaplain did not answer nor even look at her, and continued his address as if nothing had happened.'[23] A more principled objection was made during a confirmation service at Dartmoor. 'At the conclusion of the Bishop's address a cry was heard from the far end of the big chapel of "*Vive l'anarchie; à bas le [sic] religion*" and an Italian prisoner convicted of the manufacture of bombs was gently seized by the warders and lifted over the heads of the other men and deposited outside without interfering with the Bishop's encouraging words.' 'The Bishop interceded for him and accordingly he was let off very lightly. He gave no further trouble, at any rate when in chapel.'[24] More pointedly, a man 'took off his boot in chapel one morning and threw it' at the Reverend Eustace Jervis. 'It did not touch me', he says, 'but it hit the desk where I was standing, so it was a good shot.' This attack, however, was not a comment on the sermon but retaliation for criticisms the chaplain had previously made of the convict's way of life outside. The man belonged to that 'race of loafers who haunted hotels and theatres and big shops to shut the doors of hansoms, and would not get off the step until they got something. There was no dole in those days and no Poplar Guardians, so even the loafers had to do something for a living.' This particular loafer, 'a hulking brigand', Jervis called him, had 'come into prison for a month for "obstruction" and I had told him what I thought of him. The Act of Parliament states that "the chaplain shall see and admonish all prisoners", and I took care to do it.'[25]

Other 'disgraceful scenes' also occurred in chapel, although One-who-has-endured-it refrains from giving further detail lest the reader 'cast aside the book with horror and disgust'.[26] The author of *Prison Songs* claims that nearly all the fights he saw in prison took place when men were being taken to the chapel,[27] and Captain D— S— says 'we sometimes had a fight to vary the ceremony'.[28] A Manchester Merchant saw an 'affray' amongst the women prisoners at Kirkdale Gaol which caused 'much amusement amongst the male prisoners'.[29]

Equally distracting to the truly pious or repentant was the speed at which the services were conducted; one complained of 'gabbled' litanies[30] and Balfour referred to a 'kind of devotional steeplechase'.[31] The result was 'a religious fiasco',[32] 'a blasphemous farce'.[33] G.W. Foote, himself a 'Prisoner for Blasphemy', makes the same point although for different reasons. He depicts a congregation of which he was a member as 'glancing about aimless as monkeys, or staring listless like melancholy monomaniacs'. 'It was a ghastly mockery, a blasphemous farce, a satire on Christianity infinitely more sardonic and mordant than anything I ever wrote or published'.[34] How little of all this was seen, or understood, by the people responsible for the management of the later Victorian prison system is made clear in one of the conclusions reached by the 1896 Committee of Inquiry into Education and Moral Instruction: 'and though the pleasure which they find in the services may not always be, strictly speaking, devotional, the mere habit of reverence, inculcated by constant attendance, cannot but be a distinct gain'.[35] Felicia Mary Skene visited prisoners out of a deep personal conviction, but her novelist's eye did not fail to register how 'it is the defiant custom of prisoners who . . . have no desire to share in the services, to stand like soldiers on parade, the arms hanging straight by the side, the eyes fixed on the wall, and the lips firmly closed, as if the singing of the hymns and chants were as meaningless to them as the moaning of the wind outside the narrow windows'.[36]

THE PENITENTIARY DESIGN

The disciplinary irritations of the daily service, however distracting in practice, were intended to serve ends that eventually became obscured from those who suffered under them. The ends themselves, and the strange architecture that served them, were enshrined in the theory of the penitentiary. Its arrival on the English prison scene is preserved, like a fault in the geological record, in the proceedings of the 1835 Select Committee on Gaols and Houses of Correction. The Committee had addressed an enquiry to 'the Chaplain of every Prison in England and Wales for the Year ending Michaelmas 1834'. It asked what salary was paid to each chaplain, and also 'the usual Hours of doing Duty in the Prison each Day; the Average Number of Prisoners daily; and whether he has any, and what Ecclesiastical Duty other than Attendance on the Prison and the Emolument derivable therefrom'.[37] Most of the replies were mundane, but on page 579 of the Committee's Report, the contrasting returns made by the chaplain at Millbank, Whitworth Russell, and the Ordinary of Newgate, the Reverend H. Cotton, are printed consecutively:

General Penitentiary, Milbank
My Salary as Chaplain is 400*l.* per Annum.
The Duties actually performed by me are as follows: – From Nine to

Ten o'Clock, every Morning, I receive in my Office such Prisoners as desire to see me; and these are numerous. From Ten to One o'Clock, during Five Days of the Week, I deliver Lectures in Chapel, to different Classes of the Prisoners, on Scriptural and Religious Subjects. During these Three Hours I am engaged, without Interval or Rest, in addressing large Classes of the Prisoners; and the mental and bodily Labour is very considerable. After One o'Clock I visit the Prisoners under Punishment; their Number of course varies; sometimes but little Time is requisite for the Performance of this Duty, at others Two or Three Hours. I then visit the Infirmaries, of which there are Three. The sick vary from Twenty to Fifty or Sixty. I daily read Prayers in each of the Three Infirmaries, besides reading to and praying with such of the sick as require my more immediate Attention.

I read and sign every Prisoner's Letter that either comes into or goes out of the Institution. These amounted in the last Year to at least 3,500. I also keep up a numerous Correspondence: Letters to Prisoners Friends; Letters of Inquiry as to Prisoners Characters and previous Habits; as to Character and Conduct of discharged Prisoners; and Answers to various Inquiries from Prisoners Relations and others. These and their Answers were, last Year, little short of 1,000.

I keep a Journal of daily Occurrences within my Department, for the superintending Committee; also the Prisoners Character Books, in which are entered the various Offences and Punishments of each Prisoner; Remarks from Time to Time upon their Conduct; and I report to the superintending Committee upon each Prisoner who is recommended for Pardon, a Duty of great Responsibility.

I superintend the Prison Schools, which are held for One Hour and a Half every Monday and Thursday Evening.

In addition to my daily Duties, I each Week prepare Two Sermons for the Sunday. Every Sunday I perform Two full Services in Chapel, besides reading Prayers in the Infirmaries; and on Twelve Sundays in the Year I administer the Sacrament to about 100 Communicants.

When these various Duties are performed, which daily occupy at least Eight or Ten Hours, there is no Limit to the Demand upon the Chaplain's Time, Zeal, and Powers. The visiting and instructing Prisoners in their Cells can have no Bounds set to it, and would occupy the whole Time of the most active and able Clergyman.

These Duties are not merely formal and routine, but demand much mental as well as bodily Exertion. My whole Time is devoted to my Calling. I cannot sleep even a single Night out of the Institution without the Permission of the Committee; and I am almost as much a Prisoner as any of the Inmates of the Establishment.

The Average Number of Prisoners daily in the General Penitentiary is as follows:

In 1831 – 543   Male and Female Prisoners.
   1832 – 523   ditto   ditto.
   1833 – 585   ditto   ditto.
   1834 – 643   ditto   ditto.

I have no other Duty than Attendance on the Prison. I am constantly in Residence; and I give my whole and undivided Time and Attention to the Duties of my Office as Chaplain of the General Penitentiary.

   17th March 1835.   WHITWORTH RUSSELL

Gaol of Newgate

The Salary of the Ordinary of Newgate for the Year ending at Michaelmas 1834 was 400*l*.

The usual Hours of doing Duty in the Prison of Newgate each Day was on Sundays at Half past Ten in the Morning and Three o'Clock in the Afternoon; on the Week-days at a Quarter to Ten every Morning.

The Number of Prisoners daily from 150 to 400.

Ecclesiastical Duty, other than Attendance on the Prison, was, every Fifth Week, Morning Prayers at Christchurch, Newgate Street, at Eleven o'Clock. The Emolument derivable therefrom was 8*l*.

   16th March 1835.   H. COTTON

These two reports speak of different worlds; the Reverend Henry Cotton's belongs to a prison in which religion is largely nominal – a recital of the offices and little else; that of Whitworth Russell refers to nothing less than a crusade. The older order was one that saw no need to explain or justify itself; the new was alight with proselytizing zeal. The presence of both on the same page is evidence of the speed with which this spiritual revolution spread, ably assisted by the subsequent appointment of Whitworth Russell to the newly formed Inspectorate of prisons. And yet, following the almost equally dramatic collapse of the penitential ideal, prison religion was to undergo a second transformation; not so sudden as its predecessor, but just as far-reaching in its practical effects. It took the form of a slow and unannounced retreat from the notion that silence and separation could of themselves create the conditions in which wicked individuals would repent and reform. The chapels with their peculiar trappings were the public face of the penitentiary, and they remained as abiding memorials to the spirit that inspired them – except that behind the scenes, the spirit itself had expired. A religious impulse wound tight the mainspring of the penal mechanism during the 1840s. As its great clockwork wound down in the direction of the twentieth century the daily and weekly services continued to mark time, only – like the Julian calendar – it was not quite the right time, and as time went by it was increasingly the wrong time. Eventually theory and practice drifted so far apart that the divorce between them could not be denied, although it never led to the disestablishment of the church from its formal position of pre-eminence in the prison universe.

THE CHAPLAIN'S MISSION

One of the earliest enthusiasts for separation and silence, the Reverend John Clay, thought of his penitentiary work in two ways. In the first place he saw it as a mission to the heathen: 'Whatever may be the claim of the swarthy unconverted natives of an opposite hemisphere', he says, 'it is not a *better* claim than that of our own countrymen'.[38] As to the mechanics of this missionary endeavour, Clay conceived them in the medical terminology then current in reformist circles: 'If it be true . . . that a reformatory prison should be regarded as a moral hospital, what ought to be the treatment of the patients?' He replies to his own query without doubt or hesitation: 'The question may be answered when their symptoms are understood; when it is ascertained that gross ignorance has to be enlightened; that hard hearts have to be softened; that the sparks of humanity and conscience have to be fanned by the breath of kindness; and that the dormant principle of religion has to be called into life by the earnest and judicious use of those means of grace which a merciful Providence places within a prisoner's reach.'[39] There in a sentence is the vocation of the Victorian prison chaplain: to educate the ignorant and to bring the wicked to repentance and salvation by personal appeal and admonition, by precept and example, and by the systematic exposition of the gospels.

Exposition of the gospels was undertaken by various means. Specimens of 'improving' literature were left in cells; there was personal visitation; and there was divine service. The whole organization of the early Victorian prison was shot through with an expectation of repentance and reform. The chapel was the outward manifestation of this expectation, and the service was its engine. At the heart of the service, surrounded by the hymns and collective responses of the prayer book, lay the sermon.

'Preaching to a congregation consisting of the vilest of the vile', was, in the words of Henry Joseph, 'a most arduous undertaking'.[40] Dartmoor chaplain Clifford Rickards also found the delivery of a daily sermon 'rather a trial', although he 'hoped that a few straight words might catch and perhaps be thought over during the long day's monotony of work'. One of the 'trials' he faced was that of addressing what he calls 'a mixed multitude' of 'four or five doctors, some schoolmasters and clerks, journalists, and two clergymen, not both of the established church, and all quite capable of criticising the sermon, besides many murderers, thieves, pickpockets, receivers and professors in crime'.[41]

'Half-Timer' adopted a direct approach in his sermons. 'You have tried all kinds of ways of the world, the flesh and the devil', he told his listeners, 'dishonesty, unclean-ness, gross pleasures, over-indulgence in beer and liquors, and you have tried to the utmost of your power the desires of self and your passions. You have tried the crooked life, you have tried pretty nearly every way but the right way that you could think of, but you have never *tried God*.'[42]

Stuart Wood's summary of a similar sermon is shorter and a lot less tolerant.

The Reverend John Clay

'We were informed how wicked we were and how grateful we ought to be to society for giving us such an excellent opportunity to mend our ways'.[43] It must have been a common refrain in prison preaching, because Oscar Wilde heard a version of it at Reading Gaol; the chaplain 'addressing his shorn and grey-garbed flock, telling them how wicked they all were, and how thankful they should all be that they lived in a Christian country where a paternal Government was as anxious for the welfare of their souls as for the safe-keeping of their miserable bodies; . . . and that the community against which they had previously sinned, was fattening calves to feast them, if they would but undertake to return to the fold and become good citizens'. Wilde later told a sympathetic warder, Thomas Martin, 'I long to rise in my place and cry out, and tell the poor disinherited wretches around me that it is not so; to tell them that they are society's victims, and that society has nothing to offer them but starvation in the streets, or starvation and cruelty in prison'.[44]

Other sermons made different impressions. On the day that Henry Mayhew went to Pentonville, the chaplain related the sad story of a father's grief for his dead daughter, and *her* dead child. 'When the tale was told, there was hardly one dry eye to be noticed among those so-called hardened convicts; some buried their faces in their handkerchiefs, in very grief at the misery they too had heaped upon some parent's head'.[45] Tears in grown men were messengers of hope to the Victorian cleric; signs of that 'softening of the heart' which preceded accep- tance of the message of the gospels.[46] At the beginning of the penitentiary era, when separation was strict and solitary confinement prolonged, tears came easily. 'It is very seldom under other circumstances I find a prisoner melting into tears when I converse with him', says John Clay, 'but with regard to the *solitary* – for him to remain unmoved when "*the things which belong to his peace*" are offered to his acceptance is the very rare exception'.[47] Kingsmill goes even further. 'There is nothing easier', he boasts in his annual report, 'for an affectionate, zealous, Christian minister to accomplish, than to move the feel- ings of prisoners in separation, and to gain control almost over their very wills'.[48] It was an ambition that brought hard words from a brother chaplain in the Irish convict service. 'To be able to gain control over the "very wills" of prisoners, is a power which no Christian minister should desire. He should leave this to religious charlatans, spirit-rappers, and table or brain-turners.'[49]

As the period of solitary grew shorter, and its effects began to wear off, chaplains were reduced to prompting the production of tears by means that strike us now as typically Victorian. 'Undoubtedly', claimed Half-Timer, 'there is magic in the word *mother*, for I have seen young lads whose life has been given up to deeds of ill, rain tears of sorrow or something at the mention of the word'.[50]

More seriously, the place of tears in Christian conversion can be seen in the pathetic life story of Henry Newlake, *The Convict Converted*, in which he tells of his misspent youth, turning aside from the paths of righteousness set out for him by his father, teachers and spiritual mentors:

> I had for years refused to attend the means of grace; but God in his tender mercy and compassion for my soul, brought me into prison, and com- pelled me there to listen to his threats to the wicked and obstinate, and his promises to the penitent sinner. The precise time when God began the renewing of my soul, I do not know; but in a few months, after entering prison, I began to listen with attention to the ministers; more especially to the young minister who preached on the love and mercy of Jesus to poor sinners. Often I would find myself weeping. Satan now began to tempt me to commit suicide, for a long time I was thus. And when I almost despaired of life, he set my feet upon a rock.[51]

The classic mechanics of conversion are present in this account; the sinner's life of progressive evil is checked by a sentence of imprisonment; he hears the Christian message – typically one of threats and promises; there is a period of confusion and doubt, and temptations to self-destruction; and finally the cer- tainty and serenity of his new found identity – that of a saved soul.

DISBELIEF

Also saved was William McCarty, convicted for burglary and sentenced to seven years' transportation: 'As regards my religious character before I came to this place, I used to boast of my *infidelity*. I read nearly all Tom Paine's works, and used to sport at religion.'[52]

Mention of Tom Paine heralds the arrival of a small but worrying cloud on the spiritual horizons of the penitentiary. Christian ministers well knew – and accepted (almost) – that wickedness could be due to ignorance, or contamination, or to the temptations of low-life flash houses and flesh-pots; but a special note of anxiety is reserved in their writing for any hint of reasoned or ideological opposition to the word of God. The new creed of socialism preached a godless doctrine that appalled the devout souls labouring to bring repentance to sinners in prison. Sarah Martin was a simple believer who paid visits to the gaol at Great Yarmouth. Among the rustic delinquents there she found more than one infected with a spirit of scepticism whose possible influence on others she was at some pains to neutralize. 'It seemed my duty', she wrote in her journal, 'having discovered that Edward Johnson and others had heard Robert Owen lecture, and knew much of his system; also, that while he spoke of the wide extent of Socialism, and said he had heard Robert Owen speak, and that the other gentleman could not answer him, it seemed quite time on my part to expose the evils of that system so offensive to God and ruinous to man, and to turn to the Bible as exhibiting the contrast: in its doctrines for our belief, – in its precepts for our practice, – and in the example of Jesus Christ.' Johnson was her first target: 'Today he said in a low voice with his head down, "The rich send poor people to prison; how would they like to be shut up here?" Could I hear such poisonous expressions without a reply? I said, "What made you poor? Was it not drunkenness and wickedness?" '[53] Another 'socialist', called Cullingford, was reported to Miss Martin as having said he would 'join the Socialists because they are for community.' 'It is not surprising that a vile drunkard should wish to be supported in idleness on the property of others,' she replied, 'yet in this respect you would find socialism as false as it is wicked.'[54] The Owenites of Great Yarmouth seem to have been struck dumb by Sarah Martin's attack, but she does not mention whether their socialism was replaced to any extent by more acceptable Christian beliefs.

A more explicit success in this direction crowned the efforts of the chaplain at Exeter. He had to grapple with 'a devoted disciple of the late Mr. Charles Bradlaugh, who when he first came to our prison was quite unimpressionable, and took no interest whatever in the chapel services. In the end, however, his atheism began to give way. At the end of nine months, he said to me that his present view of Christianity was entirely different from what he had been taught by his unbelieving friends. He then wrote on his slate the following address to me – "In every one of your sermons you dispose of some bulwark of atheism. One by one the distorted difficulties conjured up by our lecturers have been disposed of with ease; and in language the humblest can understand; and this is the only cure for atheism." ' 'This testimony from a militant atheist is striking and important', says the Reverend John Pitkin, especially from one who had, in his own words, 'established a strong branch of the National Secular Society', in which 'each member undertook to do all in his power to further the cause of atheism, and thwart the efforts of Christian bodies'.[55]

COMMUNION

For those who *do* profess Christianity, the highest ritual expression of their faith lies in the taking of the sacraments. For the newly converted, holy communion cannot be celebrated until after a proper period of religious instruction and confirmation. Given the missionary aims of the early nineteenth century penal system, it is curious that the first reference to the confirmation of prisoners is made by the Reverend J. Clay as late as 1852: 'in reporting, as I do now with grateful satisfaction, the fact that, in December last, the Lord Bishop of the Diocese conferred, in the chapel of this prison, the rite of confirmation on eighty-eight prisoners, I believe that I place on record the first instance of such a proceeding in the history of prison discipline'.[56] By the time of Clifford Rickards's ministry at Dartmoor confirmation was routine. The Bishop of Exeter visited the prison every two years 'when any prisoners who offered themselves, after careful preparation on my part, extending over some six or eight weeks, were presented . . . and duly confirmed in the presence of all the other prisoners'.[57]

Other prisoners made their own assessments of the motives of communicants, but Rickards rejoiced over one youth he had baptized and prepared for communion who 'was taken ill and died in the infirmary, receiving the Holy Communion at my hands the day before he died, and passing away in the faith and hope of a glorious resurrection'.[58] It was for moments like that that some Victorian chaplains denied themselves the pleasures of an easy living, preached to the 'vilest of the vile', and undertook what a Recorder of London called 'God's work in Hell'.[59]

PERSONAL VISITATION

Preaching in chapel was an instrument of mass persuasion well suited to the size of the populations normally held in penitentiaries. The personal visitation of convicts in their cells promised a potentially even richer harvest of individual conversions. But in view of the numbers involved, who was the chaplain to visit first? A not unexpected set of priorities, enshrined in *Prison Regulation 122*, placed the sick and the wicked at the head of the queue.[60] 'The sick all visited', writes the Reverend J. Kingsmill, 'prisoners in the refractory-ward, and from cell to cell'.[61] Such visiting was often a mainly pastoral affair: 'Found a poor prisoner distressed in mind, and in great agony from sciatica, waiting, half undressed, to put his knife and the implements of his trade out, as the rule is, it being near double-locking time, 8 P.M. I pulled out the basket for him, spoke some words of consolation and hope, and left him free to get into his hammock again.'[62]

Kingsmill, we may be sure, did not neglect the spiritual side of his cell visits, but James Smith, minister to the prisoners at Dumbarton Gaol, logged a more vigorous evangelism in his journal for the period 1842-3. He explained to James Dunn, a poacher, 'the origin and nature of Godly fear, and entreated him to implore God to give it him ere he leave the cell'.[63] With one man he 'conversed on the Death of Infidels – and laboured to show him his natural condition as a child of wrath'.[64] He would pray with prisoners, read passages from the scriptures to them, and set some of them verses or sections of the Catechism to learn before his next visit: 'William repeated today a voluntary exercise – Heb. 1. (accurately repeated).'[65]

One of the great virtues of learning verses by heart was that it could be used to measure religious productivity. 'It astonished' Sarah Martin 'to observe how strictly and constantly the prisoners labour to learn their verses from the Holy Scriptures, every day.' 'T., who, on April 21, could only attempt one, has for some time learned five regularly, and several of Watt's Divine Songs; since yesterday he has learned fourteen, from John XV., perfectly.'[66] The benefits of this type of rote learning could, however, be questionable. Hepworth Dixon came across a convict at Preston who 'was reading of the marriage in Cana with the rapidity of an elocutionist; but being asked what was the meaning of marriage, he stared blankly and replied, "They did no' tell me ony o' th'meanings".'[67]

WOMEN VISITORS

Chaplains were aided and abetted in their visiting of women prisoners by lady volunteers, who drew inspiration from the pioneering work of Elizabeth Fry. Mrs Fry first visited the 'poor female felons' at Newgate on 15 February 1813. She records in her diary that 'before we went away, dear Anna Buxton uttered a few words in supplication, and very unexpectedly to myself, I did also. I heard weeping, and I thought they appeared much tendered; a very solemn quiet was observed; it was a striking scene, the poor people on their knees around, in their deplorable condition.'[68] Although she did not at once realize it, she had discovered her calling – one that was to make her known and admired and consulted throughout Europe, and the heroine of a prolific religious hagiography.

Her work with the women of Newgate began seriously in 1816 with the formation of a school 'for the children of the poor prisoners, as well as the young criminals'.[69] But her passion, and the foundation of her influence both with prisoners and administrators, was her preaching, witnessed on one occasion by Frederic Hill, one of the earliest prison inspectors: 'The address consisted almost entirely of selected portions of the Bible, which she read slowly and in a fine melodious voice, pausing every now and then to give her hearers time for reflection. Her manner was very impressive; I noticed that many of the women were moved to tears.'[70]

Armed with this gift, and the support of a small group of like-minded ladies, Mrs Fry brought industry and order and religion to the women of Newgate. She and her friends formed themselves into 'An Association for the Improvement of the Female Prisoners in Newgate',[71] thereafter referred to as the 'Ladies' Committee'.[72] Like the penitentiary itself was to prove, the 'Ladies' Committees' were instantly popular and copies of the Newgate model sprang up in many places. At Northampton, 'The Visiting Committee consists of eighteen ladies, belonging to various religious denominations: three of these ladies visit the prison weekly during the month; thus each lady is engaged for two months in the year';[73] and it was 'not unknown' for there to be 'from forty to fifty carriages collected at the gate' of a prison during the visitations of the local 'Ladies'.[74]

None of this was achieved without difficulty; women were seen as intruders in the unreformed prison. Mrs Fry distilled her experience of gaining entry and doing good by stealth in such places in her *Observations on the visiting, superintendence, and government for female prisoners*. She concluded a chapter on Deportment with 'the expression of a desire, that the visiters may be at once *wise as serpents, and harmless as doves . . .*'.[75]

Men did not have the benefit of visitors organized along the lines of the Ladies' Committees, but for prisoners of both sexes 'there were Scripture readers, laymen and laywomen, in all convict prisons, to assist the chaplain in his arduous duties'.[76] They did this by officiating at simple services, by visiting men and women in their cells, and by reading passages from the Bible to them. Mr Gibbs, the Scripture Reader at Portland, earned the complete admiration of Ticket-of-leave-man: 'He had himself belonged to the industrial class; he is a conscientious total abstainer; and he was able and willing, as far as opportunity was allowed him to give in a brotherly way sound advice to the prisoners. I know of two or three instances in which he was successful in inducing young and comparatively innocent men to avoid the company and language of the old thieves, and I know of one or two others, who, in consequence of his earnest advocacy, left prison with a determination to make their first call at the offices of a temperance society and sign the pledge. Half-a-dozen such men, with unlimited opportunities of seeing and talking with young prisoners, might have effected an amount of good which cannot be over-estimated.'[77] But eventually, according to Mrs Maybrick, the services of the readers were dispensed with 'on the grounds of expense'.[78]

RELIGIOUS LITERATURE

Not many prisoners refer positively to the private visits of the chaplain, but all of them were exposed to the more passive influences of the religious literature that was made available to them in their cells at all times except when undergoing punishment. In the absence of lighter reading, these items often attracted the attention of otherwise irreligious men and women. For some they proved a literal salvation: a means of preserving their reason at times they most feared to lose it.

When the Bidwells, together with their accomplices, were sentenced to penal servitude for life, they resolved to use the Bible as a means of mutual remembrance during the ordeal that stretched ahead of them. 'As we halted there in the gloom we swore never to give in, however they might starve us, even grind us to powder, as we felt they would certainly try to do. We knew that in their anxiety about our souls they would be sure kindly to furnish each with a Bible, and we promised to read one chapter every day consecutively, and, while reading the same chapter at the same hour to think of the others. For twenty years we kept the promise.'[79]

Stuart Wood never served so long a sentence as the Bidwells but an early committal to prison brought on 'a depression so acute as to become almost a physical pain'. He endeavoured to counteract it 'by reading the Bible . . . and by forcing myself to concentrate on the structure of sentences as well as to try to comprehend the meaning of what I was reading. Since that time I have twice read the Bible from cover to cover in similar circumstances and for similar reasons.'[80] He also mentions a work called *The Narrow Way*, about whose contents he is silent, unlike Brocklehurst who studied 'a bundle of tracts' at Strangeways including some he described as 'octogenarians'. 'One', he says, 'was dated 1815.' Others contained warnings against Owenism and Chartism, both of which were traced 'to a source not generally mentioned to polite ears'. Paine's 'atheism' was refuted, and attention paid to Hume's 'Deism', and other controversies. 'Into this fare imagine a *soupçon* of warning against eternal damnation, and a general exhortation to look upon yourself as the blackest and vilest scum of the earth, and you will have a pretty fair idea of a medium sample of the moral and elevating literature which is ladled out to brighten the lives and cheer the hearts of the unfortunate dwellers in Her Majesty's prisons. Who wants to thrash the dialectical chaff of a hundred years ago?'[81]

Joseph Kingsmill was author of one of these pious works, *The Prisoner's Manual of Prayer*, which comprised 'Morning and evening prayers to be used by prisoners in their cells'. 'Whilst dressing', the devout convict is instructed to 'repeat some suitable Scriptures, as *clli*. Psalm, and some Hymn, as the following:

> "Awake, my soul, and with the sun
> Thy daily stage of duty run;
> Shake off dull sloth, and early rise
> To pay thy morning sacrifice." '[82]

Then the prisoner is urged to bless the Lord 'for my creation, preservation and all the blessings of this life; for my health, food, raiment, and all other comforts afforded to me'.[83] And in the evening, 'Having read such portion of Holy Scripture as time will permit', he is to 'repeat on bended knees the following prayers': 'Take me, O gracious God, under thy protection this night; I am a vile, unworthy sinner; . . . fill me with such fear and love of thy name, that my heart may surely there be fixed, where only true joy is to be found, through Jesus Christ my Saviour. Amen.'[84] Only one of the prayers in the manual makes a direct reference to prison: 'A Prayer, suitable to a Prisoner about to be discharged, for Himself and Others'.[85] Otherwise they appear to accept the ordinary Christian view of man the miserable sinner as perfectly well adapted to the penitentiary framework.

LITERACY

Cell literature held out no hope at all to the illiterate, and little more than that to those who were lettered but yet lacking in knowledge. That there was ignorance amongst prisoners was not in doubt to some who knew them well; the ones brought to the room of the chaplain at Chester Gaol were asked: 'Can you say the Lord's prayer?' and 'In 8 cases out of 20 the reply is "I cannot".'[86] A worse discovery still was made by Maria Shepherd, a member of the Salop Penitentiary Committee: 'I visited two girls from Merthyr Tydvil Ironworks, and it will scarcely be credited, but they had never heard of a Saviour – such was their dense ignorance.'[87] Similarly 'Helen Cook, 22 years of age', seen by the Chaplain of Dumbarton Gaol, 'cannot read, cannot write, cannot cypher' and 'never saw the Bible read or heard a prayer in her Father's House'.[88] John Clay examined twenty-five randomly chosen members of his flock as to the extent of their religious and secular knowledge. None of them knew in which month of the year Christmas fell, and sixteen had no idea what year it then was – it was 1843 – 'seventeen were ignorant of Her Majesty's name; four thought it was Prince Albert', and more of them had heard of Dick Turpin and Jack Sheppard than knew the name of the Duke of Wellington.[89]

Against the dismal results of these informal tests must be set the view of a Yorkshire governor that 'the greatest number of those who frequent prisons are not to be called ignorant . . . their educational instruction is as good as that of the generality of the labouring classes of the country, and their worldly knowledge is far more extended'.[90] And, more precisely, 'Of the first 1,000 convicts' on the registry of Pentonville '845 had attended some sort of school as children, for periods averaging about four years'.[91] Out of 702 'first time prisoners' at Cold Bath Fields, 646 could read and write, as could 217 out of 265 recidivists.[92] In 1834, at Salford Gaol, 'of 89 prisoners in the printed calendar for January, two-thirds could read, two-fifths also could write; of those 89, 77 had been at some period or other to Sunday-schools, day-schools or boarding schools'.[93] The chaplains who reported these findings drew equally gloomy conclusions from them: 'It is not the Want of Education', says the Reverend John Ousby, 'but the Absence of Principle, which leads to the Commission of Crime'.[94] The Reverend Bagshaw inferred that 'mere reading and writing will not do unless there be religious instruction with it; the mere reading and writing will not keep them from crime'.[95] And Kingsmill agreed: 'Education, without motive and sound Christian principles, is as the moving power to machinery which has no regulator, or as widespread sails to a ship which has neither chart nor compass to steer by.'[96]

But whatever the actual facts about degrees of literacy, etcetera, amongst prisoners, 'progressive' penal opinion accepted uncritically the link between a lack of education and the commission of crime. Remedial instruction was therefore deemed necessary, although *not* to be supplied as at Preston where, as late as 1825, 'a system of mutual instruction is still practised among the prisoners of all classes. They are supplied with the necessary books; and it is generally found that those who can read are not only willing, but in many cases anxious, to instruct their more ignorant fellow prisoners'.[97] Penitentiary policy made no allowance for the prisoner as teacher and a stop was put to such practices.

THE PRISON SCHOOL

In the 1840s at least one prison – that at Reading – adopted what Sir Edmund DuCane was to dismiss in retrospect as an 'extraordinary crotchet . . . under which prisoners were employed in nothing but education', by which was meant literary education: 'In this prison the inmates learned lessons all day, except when exercising, attending chapel, and cleaning cells, etc. As a privilege they might, "when tired of reading", "pick a little oakum", but this was quite optional, and hard, heavy labour was absolutely forbidden in order that the whole attention might be devoted to literature – the establishment was a criminal university, and acquired the name of the "Read-read-reading Gaol".'[98] Contemporary critics of the scheme were answered by William Merry, one of the Berkshire county magistrates: 'those who imagine that sentences of hard labour are not fulfilled in spirit, because the judicial blunder of the tread-wheel has been remedied, have little idea how much more ingenious as a punishment the spelling-book would deserve to be called, if it did not merit a better title than ingenious'.[99]

The system did not last long at Reading and – as will be gathered from the tone of Sir Edmund's comments – was never a likely candidate for inclusion in the curriculum either of the penal servitude prisons or in the newly national-ized local prisons which came under his control following the Act of 1877.

On a more modest scale, however, chaplains were put in charge of assistant schoolmasters whose job was to test the competence of prisoners and to provide instruction for those who fell below a required standard. The examination undergone by Jabez Balfour 'was not a stiff one'. 'I read half-a-dozen lines from a school history of England, wrote a few sentences from dictation, successfully disposed of two or three sums in arithmetic, and received an educational diploma, which was tersely comprised in three figures, "666". . . . a triple Standard VI man. I need not say that I was very gratified with my success.'[100]

The instruction that followed did not conform to any national scheme: the most usual arrangement was for there to be a 'school hour'.[101] One-who-has-endured-it describes the scene at Dartmoor:

Three assistant schoolmasters were at work, each taking a separate class, and the grey-headed, grey-bearded head master walked about supervising the whole, and taking a ramble along the landings, chatting with those prisoners who needed no schooling. The school orderly attended on them all, seeing to supplies of pens, books, ink etc. One master was teaching writing; another was dictating; and the third, with a blackboard and a piece of chalk, was doing his best to drum some simple rule of arithmetic into the heads of those whose education had been evidently neglected. On

Girls' school at Tothill Fields

school nights the Chaplain also shows himself, and walks round, looking into the cells of those men who welcome his visits, and chats for a few minutes with each.[102]

These assemblies of prisoners were, of course, full of possibilities for the pupils and fraught with difficulties for the staff. 'Disgusting conversations were indulged in, the prisoners keeping their eyes upon their books to avoid detection but under pretence of mumbling their lessons aloud they were engaged in ribald chat with their neighbours, and many were making disgusting and licentious drawings on their slates, and showing them to their pals.'[103] 'Is not the instruction in classes a little inconsistent with the separate system?' the Lord Steward asked Captain Fulford of Stafford Gaol when he appeared before the Carnarvon Committee. 'Precisely so', he replied, 'only that instead of one watcher, as it may be, there are several officers, one to every three or four, perhaps, who is assisting in the teaching.'[104]

The ambiguities surrounding the status of education in the prison, and of the 'teachers' who provided it, found expression in a debate about 'effectiveness'. There were, naturally enough, individual successes to be recorded. A girl in prison wrote to her sweetheart, 'You will, no doubt, notice an improvement in my writing. A little schooling is one of the very few sweets of prison life.'[105] In the case of Mark Jeffrey 'a little schooling' proved also to be a somewhat dangerous thing. He informs his readers that while waiting to be transported from Millbank: 'I learnt to read and write, and the gentleman who taught me said I was one of the most apt of his pupils . . . I made such quick progress under my teacher's guidance that, after a lapse of six months, I wrote a letter to my brother William. Then I became seized with a desire to know something about religion, and I read the commandments over and over again, as well as those portions of the Bible which I could understand. I was particularly struck with the words: "Remember the Sabbath day to keep it holy. Six days shalt thou labour and do all that thou hast to do; but the seventh day is the sabbath of the Lord thy God. In it thou shalt do no manner of work", etc. "It is not right for me to work on Sunday", I said to myself, and communicated my impression to the supervisor. "You must do as the authorities tell you", said he. "No", I replied, "I shall do as God tells me".'[106] We are not told whether God spoke to him, but the Governor did, ordering him to work on the Sabbath. ' "You may hang me to a tree", said I, "but I must and will obey God's commandments." After that reply I was sent back to my cell again, and two clergymen were sent to me, one of whom (Mr. Penny) took the Bible and pointed out where the disciples plucked the ears of corn and ate them on the Sabbath Day. He explained the reply of Jesus, who held them blameless, and he then endeavoured to convince me that there was no harm in pumping water for drinking on the Sabbath day. "Well, then", I said, "What are the commandments of God for, if we are not to obey them?" The chaplain said they were to be obeyed, but my spiritual advisers were better able to discriminate right and wrong actions in accordance with them.'[107] Members of the Carnarvon Committee were keen to establish a more exact balance between these pluses and minuses in the educational equation: ' "Since the system of instruction has been in force in your prison" ', one of them asked Captain Fulford, ' "have you noticed any increase in the general intelligence or educational capacity of the prisoners?" "No, I think not," he said. "The chaplain's return, I think, does not vary much annually with regard to the astounding ignorance of the great bulk of them".'

'Have you observed', the Lord President persevered, 'from what class you get the greatest number of reconvictions; whether from the animal stupid class, or from those who show an anxiety for instruction?'
'With regard to juveniles, of whom we have a great many in Staffordshire, there are a great many who have learned entirely to read and write in the prison, and they are almost certain to come back again.'
'More so than those who have not learned to read and write in prison?'
'Yes, they are the sharpest of the lot.'[108]

With an air of authority that came easily to one whose whole lifetime had equipped him to wield it Sir Edmund DuCane concluded that: 'Experience has shown that literary education has not the reformatory influence on prisoners which was once expected from it, and that moral and industrial instruction are the most potent of the educational influences which can be employed with that object.'[109] And that – for all practical purposes – was that, so far as education in the later Victorian prison was concerned.

THE LIBRARY

But there was another department of the chaplain's literary work which positively flourished – and that was the library. Prison libraries developed in a haphazard fashion up to the end of the nineteenth century, but their contents eventually came to reflect a hesitant approximation to the tastes of the typical prisoner. The original foundation of the stock was what Basil Thomson called 'the goody-goody type of literature, a bequest from the time of our grandfathers, when books were divided into those that the young might not read, and those that they must. The first additions to the prison library were illustrated magazines, and these are still by far the most popular of the books. Next, probably, are the practical hand-books on trades, which the men devour greedily under the impression that when they have read them they become skilled workmen.'[110] 'In the modern prison library there is a very wide range of choice, and if an undue proportion of the books appear to be trashy novels, it is because the men themselves prefer that kind of literature.'[111] In the county prison where One-who-has-tried-them was remanded the library consisted 'of some hundred and twenty volumes, and far the greater number of these were the most awful rubbish'.[112] Rickards' library at Dartmoor comprised 4000 volumes, and when the annual allowance was available for the purchase of new books 'I always gave notice to the men in Chapel . . . and if there were any books they wanted, they could write the names on their slates, and I would see what I could do to procure them'.[113]

An attempt by Lord William Nevill to enrich the library at Parkhurst ended in failure. His friends outside were permitted to send him books on condition they were subsequently donated to the library. All went well until a copy of *Whitaker's Almanac* was barred from the shelves. Appeal was made to the visiting Director, who said 'there was something in the book which was deemed undesirable for prisoners to read'. 'I have since searched Whitaker for 1901 from cover to cover', said Lord William, 'and I think it would be very difficult for the prison officials to point out where the undesirable information is given. Shortly after this all leave for having books from outside was withdrawn and a most hopeful attempt to improve the library was brought abruptly to an end.'[114]

A more personal form of censorship was exercised by one of the schoolmasters at Parkhurst who had 'a positive mania for removing from all books and magazines any drawing or picture containing any human being who was not depicted as fully clothed, male or female'. Lord William 'remonstrated with him for cutting the books about so, and his reply was that it would be highly indecent for people to be seen walking about naked, and he therefore considered it was bad for the men's morals to see pictures of people in the nude'.[115] The most common form of censorship encountered elsewhere in the system was the excision of all references to crime or prisons. Other books and articles were excluded in their entirety, not on moral but ideological grounds: 'not one of the productions of Thomas Carlyle can be found in any prison library. Harriet Martineau and Mr. Froude are excluded, and many other authors who have written with the object of improving and refining the race'.[116] Even so, items not normally thought of as subversive slipped through the net. James Watson, a Chartist prisoner, came across a copy of Mosheim's *Ecclesiastical History* and commented: 'The reading of that book would have made me a free-thinker if I had not been one before.'[117]

The routine of the libraries and the regulations governing the issue of books varied from place to place and from time to time; at Strangeways, Brocklehurst found that he was not eligible for other than approved 'books of moral instruction' until he had served three months; so that since he was committed for only a month he found himself 'suddenly bereft of his closest and dearest friends'.[118] The arrangements did not commend themselves to George Bidwell either:

The plan of distribution of the library books was arranged according to the usual official red-tape stupidity, by which the largest amount of work is consumed to produce the least possible result. In case a man wished to have his book exchanged, on the appointed day he must put it down at his door before he goes out to work. In the course of the day a schoolmaster comes around, followed by a prisoner carrying a tray containing a number of books, one of which the prisoner picks up and drops at the cell door, and puts the one returned in with the others. The book left may be one that the man had a week or a fortnight before, and if he has been there long he is quite sure to have had it at some previous time.[119]

But books in prison were more important than Bidwell's review of the administrative shortcomings of the libraries might indicate. To the author of *Pentonville Prison from Within*, 'books stood alone like bright redeeming angels, between the prisoner and his dreary thoughts and insane impulses'.[120] One-who-has endured-it thought that reading had kept him sane: 'This was my great solace, and without it I fear I should have gone mad, for being so much by myself, my fearful position and fallen estate, and the ruin it had brought on those so dear to me, would rise up before me in condemnation.'[121] For Stuart Wood too, books became a lifeline:

What, after all, are four bare walls to the man who has access to the princely minds of all ages? Of what significance are restrictions of diet and free intercourse with one's fellows when one is able to slam one's door and, in the printed page, watch the pageant of world history and trace the rise and fall of mighty Empires? If anything reconciled me to prison life it was access to standard works on every conceivable subject and the leisure to study them.[122]

RELIGION AND THE PRISONER

Education and library work were never much more than marginal activities for the average Victorian chaplain, and their impact on prisoners was to a large extent secular. More important than either in shaping the prisoner's view of religion appears to have been the character and conduct of the chaplain himself. By this test many of them must be counted as failures. 'It often happens that those who seek office in prisons, asylums, and workhouses have failed to obtain a hearing in the outside world, the assumption being that anything will *do* for prisoners, lunatics and paupers', was the verdict of Dr McCook Weir.[123] 'I suppose these clergymen did their best', a prisoner told Basil Thomson, 'but it was a poor sort of best. They had been at it so many years that the sound of their admonitions must have grown stale even to themselves.'[124]

For some prisoners, the least impressive part of the padre's performance was his failure to visit them personally in their cells. Ticket-of-leave-man for instance: 'I am sorry to say that during my long experience in two convict prisons I never knew a chaplain voluntarily to enter a prisoner's cell and have a little rational talk with him about the good policy of honesty and truth. I am sure that not one of them ever came in this way to me. I never heard of one going to any other prisoner.'[125] David Fannan on the other hand did not wait to be visited, but sought out the chaplain at Wormwood Scrubs for himself. 'I asked for an interview with "Holy Joe", I told him very honestly about my past life, made a clean breast of my crimes, and asked what hope there was of God's forgiveness. Rising up from his seat with hands raised in horror, "Holy Joe" replied – "God will have nothing to do with such a character as you, you're past redemption".' Immediately afterwards Fannan was moved to Millbank where he renewed his study of the Bible. To his surprise, 'Holy Joe' was transferred to the same place, and they met again. ' "Aye", I said "you're the man that tell't me God wad ha'e naething a dae wi' me, but what dae ye mak' o' this text – "Though your sins be as scarlet, they shall be white as snow: though they be red like crimson, they shall be as wool." He fled from the cell without a word.'[126]

Other prisoners took a more general dislike to their spiritual mentors. Of the four chaplains whom Frederic Martyn encountered, he thought that three 'were certainly and palpably out of place in prison', and one of them he described as a 'terrible driveller'.[127] Stuart Wood met one in the Midlands, 'a cynical divine whose chief characteristic was an atrocious Birmingham accent which neither school nor college had eradicated'.[128] The presence of such a man in the ranks of the clergy is a sign of the times when Stuart Wood served many of his sentences, before the First World War. But when M. Moreau-Christophe, Inspector General of French prisons, visited the British Isles in the late 1830s such an appointment would have been unthinkable. 'The anglican minister', he said, 'is a *gentleman*, which is why he has but little influence on the lowest ranks of the social classes. The prisoner feels untouched by the broad statements of dogma he hears preached from the pulpit on high.'[129] Gentleman or no gentleman, Oscar Wilde had no time for any of them:

> The prison chaplains are entirely useless. They are, as a class, well-meaning, but foolish, indeed silly, men. They are of no help to any prisoner. Once every six weeks or so a key turns in the lock of one's door, and the chaplain enters. One stands, of course, at attention. He asks whether one has been reading the Bible. One answers 'Yes' or 'No,' as the case may be. He then quotes a few texts, and goes out and locks the door. Sometimes he leaves a tract.[130]

The weight of prisoner opinion is tilted firmly against the chaplains, but there is also some positive testimony to report. The Ordinary of Newgate earned the respect and affection of One-who-has-endured-it: 'Without being obtrusive, he kindly and lovingly urged his great Master's message. How often have I since recalled to mind the many little acts of kindness, and the encouraging, really sweet words of comfort, "words in season", I have received from him'.[131] These acts of kindness included advice on how to soften oakum, and how best to adapt mentally to a long sentence. 'You must', said he, 'just consider yourself as a slave till your time is out.' But, he added, 'though your body is condemned to slavery, your thoughts, your mind, and heart are free to commune with God, free to pray, free to praise and free to repent. You may in after-life reclaim yourself and actually look back upon this very punishment as a blessing'.[132] And when Stuart Wood, who so disliked the unreconstructed accent of the Birmingham padre, fell seriously ill at Shepton Mallet, he was visited daily by the chaplain: 'A little man, with a tragic, plaintive expression of spiritual pain, he had the heart and soul of a child and a humility that was Christ-like. He told me he thought it his duty to live as plainly and as simply as his prisoners, and I know that he got his bread and porridge from the prison kitchen. He was not in any sense of the word a learned man. He was just a simple, humble man of Galilee to whom the life, teaching, death and resurrection of his Master were the supreme facts of life.'[133] Roman Catholic priests in prison, more often than their Protestant counterparts, seemed to command the respect and affection of their flocks, and even of non-Catholic prisoners. Father M— was 'a true friend' to Lord William Nevill at Parkhurst: 'I think Catholics are more fortunate than their Church of England fellow-prisoners, because of the more frequent visits of the priests.'[134] And George Bidwell (who was no Catholic) says 'all the Catholic priests I have known were without exception faithful and entirely devoted to the duties of their holy calling, speaking fearlessly to the authorities whenever Catholic prisoners were being wrongly treated by the warders.'[135]

'IMPERIUM IN IMPERIO'

The Anglican chaplain was not generally renowned amongst prisoners for speaking fearlessly to the authorities. 'If he attempts . . . to win the hearts of prisoners, he finds the whole system of prison discipline arrayed against him. That discipline breeds and encourages the growth of every evil passion in the heart of man, and he, the chaplain, is part of that system; he lives by it, and he is not allowed to interfere with it, at all events he never did so. When prisoners complained to him of some injustice or some cruelty, they got for reply: "I am here to preach the Gospel, and I can do nothing in the matter." '[136]

An issue which epitomized the tensions between prisoners and chaplains *and* the uneasiness of the relationship between chaplains and governors, was that of letter writing. When One-who-has-endured-it was at Dartmoor, a young prisoner wished to advise his wife – 'she was only nineteen and remarkably good looking' – not to leave the safety, as he saw it, of her mother's house. But he was not due another letter for fourteen weeks. One-who-has-endured-it implored the chaplain to intercede with the governor for permission to write or to write himself to the man's wife, passing on the convict's advice. The chaplain would do neither. 'No, I cannot see it is my duty to transgress the strict rules of the prison. Good evening.' As our author feared, the worst befell the young lady. 'Before I left Dartmoor we heard of her living with a gentleman who was keeping her' . . . and her husband 'began to get careless and was frequently in trouble.'[137] The Reverend Clifford Rickards, who may well have been the guilty party in these proceedings, acknowledges that chaplains are 'to a certain extent handicapped by restrictions and prison rules. This at times makes their task a delicate and difficult one. For instance a man in great trouble appeals to me to write a letter to his wife, as she is in a dangerous and delicate position. If I will send her a word from him it may be the means of saving her from serious danger. It seems hard to refuse, and all I can promise is that if he will get the governor's permission for me to do this I will gladly do so, but not otherwise. It seems rather a hard case and sounds so plausible that many a *locum tenens* officiating during my absence has been enticed to break the rules of the prison out of pity for the man and his wife; but once you do so you are in the man's power, and he will use it by pressing other requests and threaten to expose you for having written to his wife.'[138] Rickards' *apologia* can not have been untypical. So far as Stuart Wood could judge from his knowledge of Anglican chaplains, which was extensive, 'the majority of them saw nothing fundamentally wrong with the system because, after all, it was only the logical application of the Mosaic Code in which most of them had been nurtured'.[139]

'CHAPLAIN'S MEN'

So much then for the esteem or otherwise in which chaplains were held by their involuntary parishioners, but what of the prisoners who made a positive response to the Christian message; those who repented or professed reform, sang in the choir, helped at the altar, or took the Holy Sacraments; what was *their* standing in the eyes of fellow convicts? 'Some of them', according to One-who-has-endured-it, 'were truly pious as far as one could judge in such matters, others were unfit or unworthy partakers, the whole of them were called by the other prisoners "Parson's men", or "Sacrament blokes." It used to pain me to hear them scoffed and mocked at.'[140] They were also referred to as 'Joeys'[141] and 'Pantilers'.[142] John Lee had 'known those who have tried to follow the services devotionally to be openly scoffed at by their companions',[143] and Josh Poole's attempts to spread the word of his own conversion were not universally well received in the kitchens of Wakefield Gaol: 'I began telling the cooks about Jesus – I could not nelp it. Some of them laughed, others jeered, but others came to me by themselves, and opened their heart to me, and I tried to console them as best I could.'[144]

The first opportunity for a display of hypocrisy on the part of the prisoner occurred during the registration of faiths on reception. This as we have seen was limited to a simple choice between Church of England, Roman Catholic, and Jewish. For the truly faithful, the choice was straightforward, but for the less committed a variety of strategic considerations affected the decision. For example: 'If a London thief, professing Protestantism, should have a pal undergoing a term of penal servitude who was a Catholic, he would, to a certainty, class himself as a member of the latter faith after being sentenced, in hopes of falling in with his old chum somewhere and at some period during the lagging.'[145] John Devoy, the Fenian leader, recalls meeting prisoners who 'were always trying to devise means to get sent to one of the "public works" prisons where the food was supposed to be better'. When Portsmouth, which had the reputation of being a 'better prison' in this respect, first appointed a Roman Catholic priest, 'the newly convicted Catholic prisoners were sent [there] for convenience. The word spread among the "old lags" and when sentenced to penal servitude again many of them declared themselves Catholics, in order to get sent to Portsmouth.' When the Prison Commissioners appointed RC chaplains to other prisons, 'the bogus Catholics, finding they could not get to Portsmouth, developed "scruples of conscience", applied for instruction, and at church meetings outside foolish boasts were made about the number of Catholic prisoners who were turning Protestant.' Alas for those who made these claims, 'The "converts" were, of course, all habitual criminals who had no religion at all outside of their stomachs.'[146]

An even more devious motive lay behind the 'conversion' to Catholicism of prisoner 'B' known to Balfour at Parkhurst, and which he thought not unconnected with the fact that the judge in the man's case 'was also a Roman Catholic', and who 'would certainly be consulted about the propriety of remitting any part of B's sentence'.[147] It was, says Captain D— S—, 'a favourite dodge, now pretty well played out . . . to petition for a remission of sentence on the plea of conversion and regeneration.'[148]

Ticket-of-leave-man, a Christian who held aloof from religious observance in prison, is one of the most vocal in his contempt for that 'whole regiment enlisted under the "banner of the cross" ' in the belief that 'one of the ways of fetching an "easy lagging" is to be a canter and a hypocrite'.[149] Amongst the recruits to this army, he says, are to be found 'a large proportion of the vilest and filthiest scoundrels whom I met with, both at Portland and Dartmoor'. They 'were not only members of the church choir, and the loudest in their responses at church, but "regular communicants" of the Lord's Supper'.[150] He cites in evidence the case of 'the present leader of the choir in the Protestant chapel at Dartmoor' who was doing 'his third "lagging". It is well known to the officers of the prison that the display of religion on his part, and that of many others, is a mere sham; that if they get the tip from their neighbours that the chaplain is in their neighbourhood, their Bible will be open on the table, or he will very likely find them on their knees, but as soon as he is gone they will be indulging in obscene conversation through their "chat holes".'[151] They were the men 'acknowledged on all hands to be the meanest rogues in the prison. Every observance that could please a chaplain's heart they conformed to. They joined his preparatory class, were confirmed by the bishop, sang like angels in the choir, partook regularly of communion, and the very men who had received the sacrament of the Lord's Supper in the forenoon, would in the afternoon sneak into the other prisoners' cells to steal their bread.'[152]

The last straw for some of the truly religious was the attitude of the 'chaplain's men' towards the sacraments. A Manchester Merchant overheard one communicant at Kirkdale Prison tell another 'that his only motive . . . was to taste the wine'.[153] Devoy heard another who claimed that 'When ye'r a Protestant yeh gets a bigger piece o' cake w'en yeh goes to Communion'.[154] And at Portland, says Ticket-of-leave-man, 'the chaplains have found it necessary to keep a tight hold upon the goblets while administering the wine. To trust them in the hands of the communicants would be to greatly increase the amount of the prison wine-account.'[155]

The story of religion in the penitentiary, then, is one of a 'glorious revolution'; one that succeeded beyond the imagining of its originators in capturing the minds of prison administrators all over the newly industrializing world. Its immediate appeal rested partly in the moral and intellectual splendour of the proposed edifice; partly in the pretty drawings of the prison buildings that accompanied it – symmetrical representations of order and purpose; and partly in the missionary fervour with which the apostles of separation preached their creed. But most fundamentally these proposals and these plans were of 'machines for the time': the moral equivalents of the engines that drove the wheels of industry and possible means of bringing under control some of the runaway social turbulence that factories and railways and burgeoning towns drew in their train. But if the mechanical analogy was part of the allure that sold the *idea* of the penitential prison, it also suggested the instrument by which its subsequent performance was to be measured. Machines serve no other purpose than ornament if they fail to produce finished goods; as pumps lift water, looms fabricate cloth, and lathes turn out machined parts, so the penitentiary, by the terms of its prospectus, was to re-form the criminal into a morally improved and better behaved citizen. Previous forms of imprisonment had failed to produce the required results. Joseph Kingsmill 'heard the late Chaplain of Clerkenwell say, that out of 100,000 prisoners who had passed under him, he knew only of two cases of true repentance towards God. Subsequently he told me that he found himself disappointed in both. This is a melancholy picture of prisons as they were, even under respectable men such as he was'.[156] Small returns indeed from such a mighty winnowing of souls. The penitentiary promised to do better than that, and for a moment – a very brief moment – it was a promise that seemed to tremble on the brink of fulfilment. Enough of the first few drafts who passed through Pentonville managed to acquire sufficient fluency in the rhetoric of reclamation to convince the chaplains and their supporters that success was almost assured. But it was not to be.

To many prisoners of the later Victorian period, the monstrous chapel buildings, and the empty rituals that filled them, must have appeared like the inexplicable relics of a lost civilization. To their inventors they made sense. The logic of their construction followed impeccably from their basic premises – but the foundations of the great machine had been sunk into the soft sand of an unreal view concerning the human material that was to be fed into it. These men and women and children – a few of them wicked and dangerous by any standard, but most of them convicted of what can reasonably only be thought of as trivial and minimally damaging offences – taught their masters and the moral projectors of the new prison a salutary lesson. It was a lesson that was bought at a dear price, and as usual, it was paid by those least able to afford it, in a despairing currency of broken minds and ill-used bodies.

But the damage the penitentiary did went deeper than broken promises and hurt minds. The void left by its collapse was progressively filled by a disciplinary timetable from which all humanity and all hope were all but extinguished. The original vision foresaw a dark tunnel of suffering, at the end of which there shone – however distantly – the light of redemption and salvation. When the light went out, the darkness closed in around the Victorian prisoner. It was not to be lifted again for a generation.

NOTES

1. Harcourt, *Horrors*, 1.
2. Kingsmill (1854a), 1.
3. One-who-has-endured-it, 87.
4. S. Pankhurst, 234.
5. D— S—, 301.
6. H.P. Fry, 56.
7. Dawson, 120.
8. One-who-has-tried-them, I, 50.
9. Nihill, 66.
10. Fulford, 147.
11. Carnarvon Committee (1863), 157.
12. One-who-has-tried-them, I, 52.
13. Wood, 31.
14. Lovett, 237.
15. Andrew, 24.
16. Henderson, 37.
17. One-who-has-tried-them, I, 218.
18. Samuel, 129.
19. Fannan, 129.
20. Ibid., 130.
21. Brocklehurst, 104.
22. Griffiths (1904), 167.
23. Lytton, 120.
24. Rickards, 128.
25. Jervis, 19.
26. One-who-has-endured-it, 208.
27. R.J. Clarke, 86.
28. D— S—, 98.
29. *Kirkdale*, 100.
30. Barrow, 10.
31. J. Balfour, 333.
32. McCook Weir, 66.
33. One-who-has-tried-them, I, 52.
34. Foote, 96.
35. Prison Education (1896), 12.
36. Scougal, 90.
37. Select Committee on Gaols (1835), 1st report, 563.
38. W.L. Clay, 344.
39. Ibid., 335.
40. Joseph, 112.
41. Rickards, 128.
42. Half-Timer, 31.
43. Wood, 31.
44. Sherard, 353.
45. Mayhew, 167.
46. W.L. Clay, 335.
47. Ibid., 144.
48. Gibson, 98
49. Ibid., 99.
50. Half-Timer, 83.
51. Newlake, 16.
52. Joseph, 61.
53. Wrench, 58.
54. Ibid., 59.
55. Pitkin, 66–8.
56. W.L. Clay, 330.
57. Rickards, 145.
58. Ibid., 145.
59. Jervis, 8.
60. Prison Regulations (1849), 27.
61. Kingsmill (1854), 208.
62. Ibid., 213.
63. R.D. Thomson, 3.
64. Ibid., 10.
65. Ibid., 9.
66. Martin, 112.
67. Hepworth Dixon, 343.
68. E. Fry (1847), I, 201.

69. Ibid., I, 252.
70. Hill (1894), 117.
71. E. Fry (1847), I, 262.
72. Ibid., I, 269.
73. Wrench, 95.
74. Hogan, 131.
75. E. Fry (1827), 25.
76. Maybrick, 171.
77. Ticket-of-leave-man, 195–6.
78. Maybrick, 171.
79. A. Bidwell, 389.
80. Wood, 59.
81. Brocklehurst, 52.
82. Kingsmill (n.d.), 10.
83. Ibid., 12.
84. Ibid., 13.
85. Ibid., 30.
86. Joseph, 2.
87. Shepherd, 107.
88. R.D. Thomson, 8.
89. W.L. Clay, 507.
90. Governor, 218.
91. Kingsmill (1854), 39.
92. Select Committee on Gaols (1835), 1st report, 76.
93. Drunkenness Inquiry (1834), 360.
94. Select Committee on Gaols (1835), 1st report, 76.
95. Select Committee . . . on Drunkenness (1834), 360.
96. Kingsmill (1854), 42.
97. W.L. Clay, 132.
98. DuCane (1885), 79.
99. Merry, 22.
100. J. Balfour, 63–4.
101. One-who-has-endured-it, 197.
102. One-who-has-endured-it, 206.
103. Ticket-of-leave-man, 175.
104. Carnarvon Committee (1863), 151.
105. Harris (1907), 788.
106. Hiener, 53.
107. Ibid., 54.
108. Carnarvon Committee (1863), 151.
109. DuCane (1885), 79.
110. B. Thomson (1925), 115.
111. Ibid., 116.
112. One-who-has-tried-them, I, 47.
113. Rickards, 28.
114. WBN, 65.
115. Ibid., 100.
116. Ticket-of-leave-man, 193.
117. Linton, 20.
118. Brocklehurst, 49.
119. G. Bidwell, 505.
120. *Pentonville Prison from Within*, 41.
121. One-who-has-endured-it, 109.
122. Wood, 71.
123. McCook Weir, 159.
124. B. Thomson (1925), 39.
125. Ticket-of-leave-man, 184.
126. Fannan, 133.
127. Martyn, 70.
128. Wood, 164.
129. Moreau-Christophe, 52.
130. Hart-Davis, 338.
131. One-who-has-endured-it, 20.
132. Ibid., 47.
133. Wood, 133.
134. WBN, 49.
135. G. Bidwell, 225.
136. Henderson, 115.
137. One-who-has-endured-it, 211.
138. Rickards, 118.
139. Wood, 29.
140. One-who-has-endured-it, 116.
141. Mayhew, 169.
142. Ibid., 249.
143. Lee, 98.
144. Poole, 71.
145. Davitt (1885), I, 188.
146. Devoy, 5.
147. J. Balfour, 206.
148. D—S—, 304.
149. Ticket-of-leave-man, 187.
150. Ibid., 185.
151. Ibid., 187.
152. Fannan, 112.
153. *Kirkdale*, 101.
154. Devoy, 5.
155. Ticket-of-leave-man, 185.
156. Pentonville Commissioners, 6th report (1848), 37.

6
HARD LABOUR

OAKUM

Three images dramatize Victorian prison work in the popular imagination; men climbing the endless staircase of the treadwheel; convicts breaking rocks; and the picking of oakum. Oakum was picked by prisoners in cells and workrooms for the greater part of the nineteenth century: 'it may be information to some readers to know that oakum is old tarred ships' ropes, from an inch upwards in thickness. The very worst that can be obtained is used for prison use, and it often, in hardness and firmness, resembles wire pit ropes more than anything of a hempy or flaxy nature'.[1] One-who-has-endured-it was introduced to it the day after receiving his sentence of five years' penal servitude: 'the next morning while I was cleaning my cell, three pieces of junk or old rope . . . were flung into my cell'.[2] For his part, One-who-has-tried-them knew 'that the strands of the rope had to be pulled apart till they were fine as silk'.[3] (The finished product 'was used for caulking wooden walls, and portions went to the fishing ports, but most of it was re-spun into ropes.')[4] 'But though I tugged and dragged', he reports, 'and tried with all my strength to get the stuff abroad, I could make nothing of it.'[5] Oakum was also extremely dirty: 'after working for an hour or so one's fingers would be covered with tar, and stick to everything you touched, necessitating at least a quarter of an hour's scrubbing with soap and water to get them into working trim again.'[6] 'If anyone prides himself on a nice hand and filbert nails,' warns a middle-class prisoner, 'let him steer clear of oakum picking.'[7]

To the dirt and the difficulty was added, under the threat of punishment, the daily 'task', that of picking 'three pounds per diem'.[8] Faced with this target, George Bidwell 'sat there and picked and picked, but the pile did not grow fast'.[9] One-who-has-endured-it 'never' picked his 'quantum'.[10] A Leicester prisoner took 'four days to pick three pounds'.[11] And Stuart Wood claimed that even 'if a visit to the execution shed' had been the penalty for failure 'I should surely have gone there, for at no period of my imprisonment have I ever been able to do it, even by slaving for twelve or fourteen hours a day.'[12] He supposed the authorities to be aware how difficult the task was for many prisoners, and yet 'every day saw several reported just by way of keeping the discipline up to the recognised standard of severity and to stimulate the rest of us to even greater efforts. Imagine if you can,' he says, recalling a sentence served at Shepton Mallet, 'the Hall of a prison on a winter's morning with its four tiers of cells lit with gas. . . . Various cleaners are emptying utensils, filling water cans outside cell doors, and scrubbing the slate gangways which run round each landing, whilst the atmosphere reeks with the stench of slops and excrement. In the centre of the hall, lighted at intervals by gas jets, stands a table containing a pair of scales and a pile of hard junk to be issued to the queue of waiting men, each of whom holds in his hand the oakum he has picked the day before. On all their faces is a mingled expression of fear and hate, for only a very few of them have completed their task. They wait with an animal expression on their faces, because it is in the lap of the gods whether they will get the few rotten potatoes and the eight ounce loaf of brown bread which constitutes their dinner, or not.'[13] Failure to meet the 'task' was an 'offence' under prison discipline, punishable by the imposition, amongst other things, of a restricted or 'bread-and-water' diet; hence the anxiety. Old prison hands had resort to a number of 'shifts and expedients' to make sure of their rations.

One was to 'pick a pound and a half or two pounds which they would damp down with water overnight to bring it up to the required weight by morning'. Another was to use the 'prohibited fiddle'.[14] One-who-has-tried-them received instruction from a convict past-master in this forbidden art.

> He rapidly knotted a couple of strands together, and motioning me to place my foot on the edge of the bedstead, tied them firmly round my thigh; then picking up a loose strand he passed it underneath this cincture, and grasping the two ends, one in each hand, drew it quickly to and fro. The friction soon frayed the strand, the loose, fluffy oakum was drawn off and placed on the floor, and the process repeated until the whole strand was completely frayed out.

The lesson ended with some good advice: 'just try and sneak a nail in with you if you get a chance of picking one up at exercise, and then you can soon manage your oakum with that.'[15] 'It was a regular dodge', he says, 'for any man who had managed to get a nail . . . to slip it between the slits of his ventilator before he leaves the prison, and the first thing an "old hand" does when he is placed in the cell he is to occupy is to open his ventilator and push a strand of oakum through the right hand slit of it, and twist it about until he has ascertained whether the oakum nail is there or not.'[16] Once the secrets of successful picking had been unravelled, with or without the assistance of the illicit nail, there was even a kind of pleasure to be derived from the work: 'When it is the right kind of junk and you give it the right kind of twist and beat it properly on your boot-sole, the fibres come apart like floss silk, and there is something fascinating about seeing the little heap growing in front of you until, by the time you have finished your task of three pounds, it is a veritable mountain.'[17]

But normally, from where the prisoner sat, oakum was a difficult and dirty and distressing occupation, to be avoided whenever possible. From an official point of view, the old rope tied together a bundle of contradictions which were never to be properly straightened out. There were three contending schools of thought on the question of prison work: that it should be *punitive* hard labour; that it should make *economic* sense, helping to defray the cost of the prisoner to the public purse; and that it should be *reformative* in the sense of teaching trades thought useful to ex-convicts in an industrial society. Oakum fell short on all three counts. It had no merit as industrial training, which was why the Gladstone Committee of 1895 recommended it be 'discontinued as much as possible except for penal purposes'; that is as a punishment.[18] It became increasingly less profitable as wood gave way to iron in the construction of ships;[19] one estimate was that picked oakum earned a profit of '$\frac{3}{4}$d per lb', or three pence per day per prisoner.[20] The prisons' only competitors in this uneconomic market were the workhouses, some of which, according to Sir Edmund DuCane, 'actually pay for the privilege of picking junk into oakum'.[21] And, finally, oakum failed because it conformed to nobody's idea of what 'hard labour' ought to be. But it went on being picked, because of its simplicity and its tediousness and because no one could think of any better way of keeping so many unskilled hands from idleness. At Cold Bath Fields there was even an oakum-picking shed, 'built on so vast a plan that it has seats for nearly 500 men'.[22] Its great convenience, though, was as a cell task for men in separate confinement, where it continued to keep afloat the leaky vessel of penal labour policy until into the twentieth century.

SEWING, ETC.

The search for alternative forms of cellwork settled inevitably on sewing. Stuart Wood's 'oakum was taken away and I was put at making coal-sacks. Even so, I couldn't do the task required of me. The canvas was hard and stiff, the palm and needle so cumbersome that try as I might, I failed.'[23] Jabez

Balfour was given the job of 'making the mail-bags that we see at railway stations', and went so slowly that he feared a reprimand, 'but I suppose that through the spyhole the warder had seen that I was doing my best, and far from being reprimanded, I was rather encouraged.'[24] And after a few days' practice he 'succeeded in doing the allotted task, and ultimately a good deal more'.[25]

Lord William Nevill was 'set to knitting stockings' during his nine months' 'separates' and found it was something 'which almost anyone can learn in a few lessons, and which after a while, becomes rather absorbing. There is just enough thought required to keep the mind partly engaged; and, as the knitter can walk or sit, or work in almost any attitude, he gets a certain amount of change.'[26] Bill Sykes did not get on so well, in fact he 'made a terrible mess of the knitting'. 'For the first few days I was continually dropping stitches or else dropping my needles; and when it came to "turning the heels" of the stockings, I nearly went insane'.[27]

One-who-has-endured-it followed Stuart Wood's progression from oakum to sewing, although in his case it was to a more advanced standard than coal-sacks: 'the Irish warder, or "Paddy", as he was called by his flock, came into me, accompanied by a prisoner, bringing materials to set me to work. A bundle of drab coarse cloth was thrown down. . . . After I forget how many days, the jacket was completed, all except the button-holes, which my instructor considerately thought were as yet beyond my abilities. I should be very sorry to say the jacket was turned out in a workmanlike manner, but I assure you I was not a little proud of my work when I held it up complete. In the course of time I became a very fair "botcher", as those who knew nothing of a tailoring before they came to prison were called.'[28]

Another handicraft much used for solitary cellwork was mat-making. Manchester Merchant was 'taught in a few days how to trim fancy mats. The work was clean and not hard, and I was not under any task, as some mats required much more trimming than others.'[29] When a 'task' *was* imposed, it was impossible for many prisoners to achieve; 'I spent about two months at this employment and yet I could never manage to make a mat in less than two days. Now men who were certified fit for first class labour were required to make ten of these same mats in the week.'[30] And lastly there was weaving. John Hay 'had to work at a huge iron hand-loom that requires a great deal of power to move it at all. I was kept at this towel-weaving for fourteen hours a day!'[31]

HARD LABOUR

The Earl of Carnarvon and his 1863 Select Committee were predictably distressed to discover 'the widest possible differences of opinions held as to what constitutes *hard labour*'.[32] During the drafting of the bill that followed their endeavours 'great efforts were made . . . to devise a general definition which should indicate what was intended by the above phrase, and a proposal which was made, though not adopted, that it should be defined as "work which visibly quickens the breath and opens the pores", sufficiently indicates the idea intended.'[33] The report itself concluded that, 'of the various forms which are in force in the several prisons, the treadwheel, crank and shot-drill alone appear to the Committee properly to merit this designation of hard labour.'[34]

The treadwheel, the first of Carnarvon's candidates for 'real' hard labour, appeared to opponents of the purely 'penal' philosophy to be an infernal machine: 'the absence of any human sound – the dull, soughing voice of the wheel, like the agony of drowning men – the dark shadows toiling and treading in a journey which knows no progress – force on the mind involuntary sensations of horror and disgust.'[35]

Its invention was claimed by Mr William Cubitt, a civil engineer from Lowestoft, during a visit to the gaol at Bury St Edmunds. In 1818, 'the inmates', according to the narration Governor Chesterton received from Cubitt's own lips, 'were seen lounging idly about, and the whole aspect indicated a demoralising waste of strength and time.' ' "I wish to God, Mr. Cubitt," said the justice who escorted him, "you could suggest to us some mode of employing these fellows! Could nothing like a wheel become available?" Mr. Cubitt . . . whispered to himself, "the wheel elongated!" ' and thus was conceived the treadwheel.[36] The most obvious use of such a wheel was to pump water, 'as in the old days in some monasteries', says Basil Thomson, which suggests that Cubitt had merely extended an old principle.[37] At Reading, the wheel supplied water to 'various cisterns',[38] and the one at Stafford was 'employed in grinding wheat for the consumption of the prison, and of the two lunatic asylums in the neighbourhood'.[39] A more typical employment was for the wheel to 'grind the wind', a fact which helped to fan the flames of the controversy between those who thought penal labour should be productive and those who thought it should not.[40]

Mr Cubitt had clearly intended his device to be put to some practical use, perhaps in 'a mill or manufactory, near the boundary wall of a prison, through which only a single shaft, or axle, would have to pass to communicate the power and motion'.[41] And Henry Mayhew was assured at Cold Bath Fields 'that advertisements have often been inserted in the journals, offering to lease the tread-mill power, but without any result.'[42] But the 'utility' party in this debate earned for itself the derision of Sir Edmund DuCane, who wrote in the *Nineteenth Century*:

They think the moral disadvantage of mechanical labour, such as the tread-wheel, &c., may be surmounted by connecting it with machinery which does useful work, such as grinding corn for the prisoners' own consumption. It seems to me that this view is founded on an amiable delusion as to the imagination prisoners are likely to indulge in on these subjects, and further in an absolute failure to perceive the mode in which, or the reason why, industrial employment may have a good effect on a prisoner's mind.

Detail from a treadwheel

That Sir Edmund himself harboured few delusions on the subject, and certainly none that could be called amiable, is sufficiently indicated by the title of his article, which was 'The unavoidable uselessness of prison work'.[43]

Once on the wheel, the convict needed to lift 'his body up three feet' at each step,[44] despite which one governor thought it 'merely going upstairs, there is no physical weight upon the foot. The stair drops from under the prisoner.'[45] Prisoners told One-who-has-tried-them, who never personally trod the wheel, that 'it was hard work for the first day or two, until you got into the knack of it, and then it was easy enough.'[46] It was a knack that a sympathetic warder pointed out to a grateful novice: ' "Now look at that old chap over there, look how beautifully he does it." ' 'The chap over there' was an old hand, and he was 'stepping lightly and gently on tiptoe on the wheel, as if he was walking on eggs. He did not try to move the wheel, he let the wheel move him.'[47]

Irrespective of experience, the precise rigour of the wheel depended on several things; the first of them being the height that prisoners were required to climb. At York it was 'equal to walking up Mount Ararat (6,000 feet) every day'.[48] Other prisons followed the advice of the Prison Discipline Society and 'apportioned to each male individual 12,000 feet of ascent per diem', which is more like the Matterhorn.[49] Apologists for the wheel made light of these figures by rearranging them in a different plane: 'Where is the laborer', enquired the Reverend Dent, 'whose *daily task* does not exceed a 'walk of *two miles* even admitting it to be uphill? – *yet this is as great a length of distance* as CAN be performed by the revolution of our Tread-Wheel in SIX HOURS, the average of each man's labor at it per day.'[50] Higher still was the target at Stafford – 16,630 feet, i.e. over half the height of Everest.[51] And overshadowing all of these lesser peaks was the task set in Salford's New Bailey, where the height in feet varied with the hours of daylight, '19,400 in summer, 14,450 in winter'.[52] Exact calculation counted amongst the attractions of a contraption like the wheel, but some administrators were indifferent to them. The governor of Stafford was asked by Earl Cathcart, member of the Carnarvon Committee, 'How many feet of ascent do you require in a day?' Major Fulford – and it was he who thought the whole exercise 'merely going upstairs' – had to admit, 'I scarcely know; I believe it is 57 steps in a minute; the steps are 10 inches wide.'[53]

To the rigours of the ascent, there was added at some establishments a cruel modification of the machine. 'The most serious fault of the treadwheels', according to the Inspector General of French Prisons, M. Moreau-Christophe, 'is that the wooden crosspiece on which the prisoners put their hands, is fixed, and by pressing hard on it, the prisoners reduce to that extent the driving force of their feet and bodies.' The solution, which he saw in action at Petworth and Lewes prisons, was to replace the fixed rail with a 'tread-hand-wheel', which 'moves so easily on its axle that the lightest pressure of the hands is sufficient to turn it, so that the arms necessarily repeat on the upper wheel the action of the feet on the lower'.[54]

The severity of the labour was also determined by age and physical condition. The young and the infirm were supposed to be excused the terrors of the wheel. Dr Quinton, surgeon to the Glasgow Gaol at the turn of the century, thought that 'for novices, or for men who had recently been drinking, it was a very trying, if not a dangerous, form of labour.'[55] Even Major Fulford was obliged to find alternative employment for 'such prisoners . . . as are ordered by the surgeon for a time perhaps to be taken off the wheel, or who are cripples with wooden legs, of whom', he adds, 'I have a large number sometimes.'[56] More than one prisoner however slipped through these precautionary exclusions. William Day was only 14, but after being sentenced to transportation in 1839, he 'was condemned, previous to being sent to the hulks, to the tread mill in Stafford Gaol. There being no corn to grind and no opposing friction to the weight of the steppers on the wheel, if ever mortal boy walked on the wind I did then.'[57]

For the older and the able-bodied, the wheel remained 'in all conscience a dreadful punishment'.[58] Manchester Merchant 'pitied the treadwheel men as they went out to their labour' and 'noticed the sweat running down their faces on their return'.[59] After a spell on it, it was not unknown for 'big, strong fellows' to be 'led away crying'.[60]

A medical opinion was that men forced to this labour 'fall off greatly, as a general rule, both in health and strength, before quitting the prison. They shrink very much in size and look pale.'[61] After 'the first week or fortnight of it', says an observer at Stafford, the prisoner's friends 'would be horrified to see him, and he would scarcely recognise himself if he looked in a mirror'.[62] Also at Stafford, 'one man fell off the wheel from sheer exhaustion. The cry "a man down" was soon raised, and the mill was at once stopped, but not until he had been terribly crushed by it. . . . I think one of his legs was broken'.[63] Worse, according to a report quoted by Frederic Hill, 'a boy was killed when working on a tread-wheel; and an accident which rendered it necessary partially to amputate a foot' was recorded from Norwich.[64] In the face of evidences like these, the Royal Artillery, not otherwise noted for squeamishness in the management of its soldiery, 'abstained from consigning their offending men to Cold Bath Fields, owing to the injurious effects observable, on their return to the regiment, from the mischievous excess of treadwheel occupation'.[65]

Even in the face of these adverse judgements, Governor Chesterton maintained a sturdy defence of the wheel, since without it 'the care, comfort, and solid diet bestowed upon prisoners, tend to strip imprisonment of much of its salutary terrors'.[66] He even put women to work on it, a practice which visitors to Cold Bath Fields, and 'especially ladies and foreigners of eminence', were wont to condemn,[67] although he insists that 'at all seasons the general mass of females, frequenters of the prison, courted that labour in preference to every other.'[68] A leading critic of the practice of placing women on the wheel was John Mason Good, a prison doctor at Cold Bath Fields, who wrote a *Letter to Sir John Cox Hippisley on the Mischiefs Incidental to the Treadwheel*. The least of his objections, that of modesty, was met in one prison by 'raising a linen screen a few feet above the platform, so as to hide the ancles'.[69] But beyond that, 'the first mischief of a serious kind which I apprehended would follow on an extensive employment of the machinery before us, was a premature and excessive periodical influence on females, in consequence of the strain or morbid exertion which it perpetually endangers by its peculiar effects on the muscles and other organs of the loins and abdominal region.'[70] Women were eventually taken off the wheel by order, but male prisoners, who had 'a great dread of it', had to think up 'various devices to escape it'.[71] Not a day passed that Governor Fulford did not get 'a dozen of different sorts of applications for the men to be withdrawn from the wheel'.[72]

Before 1877, the efficacy of the wheel could be studied in just some of the local prisons under the county justices. In 1878, the newly constituted Prison Commissioners asked their medical officer to report on the treadwheel. He did so in such positive terms that 'many new machines were erected in the succeeding years under their auspices,' and continued in use until they were abolished in 1895.[73] In an unusual reversal of the normal order of such things, Scotland had reached this decision much earlier. 'It was . . . with much satisfaction', says Frederic Hill, appointed to be the first Inspector of Scottish Prisons, 'that soon after entering on my official work I saw the last treadmill banished from Scotland.'[74] And when they were on the point of abolition in England, the words of Sir Edmund DuCane, during whose reign they had worked virtually non-stop, were turned to advantage by the Gladstone Committee. 'To men of any intelligence,' he wrote, 'it is irritating, depressing and debasing to the mental facilities; to those already of a low type of intelligence it is too conformable to the state of mind out of which it is most desirable that they should be raised.'[75] More than half a century before, the Reverend Daniel Nihill had already noted and condemned the basic absurdity of Cubitt's invention:

Ancient poets, striving to represent the punishment of more than common atrocity, described Sisyphus as doomed in the infernal regions to roll a stone to the top of a hill, upon reaching which, it constantly fell back to the bottom, leaving him to recommence his laborious but unprofitable task. The poets have omitted to inform us by what self-acting machinery Sisyphus was constrained to this useless and unvaried toil. It was reserved for a modern age to complete this part of their image by the invention of the treadwheel.[76]

Next on Carnarvon's list was the crank; sometimes known as 'Appold's hard labour machine', and which, like the wheel, as often as not 'ground nothing but the air'.[77] It was still in use for the military prisoners at Millbank when Major Arthur Griffiths went there as deputy governor in 1872; it comprised 'a wheel set against cogs that exercised a resisting pressure, and turned by a handle weighted at will to fix the amount of effort required to make the revolution. Apart from the humiliating sensation of labouring hard to achieve no sort of result, the process was to be condemned as inflicting the most unequal toil, for these cranks were of very imperfect construction, continually out of order, so that the precise amount of work could never be exactly calculated.'[78]

Like the wheel, the cranks could also be put to productive use if required. At the Leicester County Gaol they were linked to the production of firewood. 'The "saw" was worked by thirty men, ten changing every quarter of an hour, thus twenty were constantly turning the "crank handles" and ten resting. The "saw" crank was fixed in a long building so that twenty men could stand in one long row, each in a small "stall".'[79] But at Cold Bath Fields, in a fiendish refinement beyond anything William Cubitt had thought of, the cranks had been set up as 'counter-weights at each end of the axle of the tread-wheel . . . so that whilst one group of prisoners is forcing the wheel round with their legs, others are using the strength of their arms to turn the cranks. And as the crank turns in the opposite direction to the wheel it follows that the motion of the one works against that of the other.' 'I know of nothing harder or more degrading than this work,' says M. Moreau-Christophe, 'les détenus que j'y ai vus appliqués m'ont paru le subir avec une véritable humiliation'.[80]

Notwithstanding all its advantages, and the enthusiastic endorsements of the Carnarvon Committee, local prisons did not take up the crank in large numbers. One of the reasons for their reticence may have been a scandal investigated by Royal Commission in 1853. At the Leicester County Gaol, the crank had been the centre-piece of a penal regime that struck even the mid-Victorians as extreme. Men were worked so hard at the machine that they developed symptoms generically described in the surgeon's journal as 'crank oedema'. They were also deprived of their food if they failed to reach the number of revolutions prescribed as their 'task'. The Commission condemned this coupling of the crank to the supply of food, describing it as 'altogether unwarranted by the law of England'.[81] But the practice was common enough for George Bidwell to quote a tariff: 'before the occupant can have his breakfast he must turn the handle 1,875 revolutions. His dinner must be earned with 5,000 and his supper with 4,000 turns.'[82]

Prisoners at Birmingham were subjected to a similar regime. The commission of inquiry there was assured that 'to accomplish such a task, a boy would necessarily exert a force equal to one fourth of the ordinary work of a draught horse; the average estimate of the work of a boy, in ordinary labour out of a prison, being about one tenth of the same.'[83] After the mid-century there were no more public scandals, but the greater and weightier wheel of public opinion turned, leaving the crank and its larger counterpart the treadmill to 'grind the wind' to no good purpose that *anyone* could see. Both disappeared in the reforms that followed the report of the Gladstone Committee in 1895.

The third kind of hard labour favoured by the Carnarvon Committee was shot drill, described by Arthur Griffiths (a former major in the 63rd West Suffolk regiment)[84] as 'the last survival of those barbarous personal punishments by which a century ago military discipline was maintained'.[85] The practice slowly fell into disuse, but One-who-has-tried-them 'once watched the prisoners at Lewes engaged in this cheerful amusement'. 'It consists', he says, 'of stooping down (without bending the knees) and picking up a thirty-two pounder round shot, bringing it slowly up until it is on a level with the chest, then taking two steps to the right and replacing it on the ground again.'[86] Griffiths recalls it as a 24-pound shot, carried six paces, which 'went on for four hours, with only a halt of five minutes every half hour to rest the strained and tortured muscles.'[87] Another version had lines of men stationed between piles of shot, and the exercise then consisted 'in passing the shot, composing the pyramids at one end of the line, down the entire length of the ranks, one after another, until they have all been handed along the file of men, and piled up into similar pyramids at the other end of the line; and when that is done, the operation is reversed and the cannon balls passed back again.'[88] Variations on the theme were limited only by geometry and the capacity of the human frame. Carnarvon recommended it with one proviso; that 'if the shot be slightly raised from the ground, this punishment is free from all possible objection in a physical point of view.'[89] In the event, i.e. with hindsight, his recommendation assumes an almost wistful air, since prisons proved more likely to opt for the crank, and even more the wheel – two true creations of the machine age; and they virtually ignored the military athletics of the shot.

PUBLIC WORKS

Ironically, all of these penal forms of labour so approved of by the Earl of Carnarvon and his committee – the wheel, the crank, the shot – were most often the lot of the prisoner serving a short sentence at one of the local prisons. During their period of solitary confinement, typically but not exclusively at Pentonville or Millbank, the longer-term penal-servitude convicts more often picked oakum or did some form of sewing in their cells. At the end of their nine months they were removed, suitably chastened by solitude and the ministrations of such moral agencies as the penitentiary could muster, to the 'public works' prisons at Chatham, Portland, Portsmouth or Dartmoor. Here, in 'silent association' they were to work out the remainder of their sentences in a limited imitation of the work undertaken by their predecessors in Australia. In the Antipodes, gangs of convicts had laboured upon the construction of roads and harbours and the reclamation of virgin land. So far as topography and a fearful public permitted, these projects were now reproduced on English soil.

The most spectacular of them, after the 'magnificent breakwater and the fortifications at Portland', was the excavation of the 'great basins' on the Medway.[90] A glowing picture of the project at Chatham is painted in Sir Edmund DuCane's *Account of the Manner in which Sentences of Penal Servitude are Carried Out in England*.

the addition to the dockyard covers a space of 430 acres, which is four times the extent of the old dockyard. It occupies the site of St. Mary's Island, the channel which separated the island from the mainland furnishing the position of the three basins. . . . The bottom of the basins is twelve feet below the old river-bed, and thirty two feet below St. Mary's Island. The latter . . . has been raised about eight feet by tipping and spreading on it the earth excavated out of the basins &c. The whole island has been drained and surrounded by a sea-wall and embankment 9,200 feet, or nearly two miles, in length, principally executed by convict labour. In carrying out these works, the prisoners have been employed in excavating, pile-driving and concreting, for the foundations; brick-laying, concreting, stone-dressing and setting, in connection with the construction of the basin walls and entrances; removing the earth from the area of the basin by means of waggons and incline planes, barrow roads, barrow lifts, and tipping waggons; loading and unloading materials; plate-laying; and attending standing and locomotive engines.[91]

Sir Edmund makes no effort to conceal the pride he obviously felt as chief architect of the whole scheme, but his proud basins, it is alleged by a prisoner who worked in them, were places 'where more human blood was spilt and more human lives lost through excessive labour than in any other prison in the country'.[92]

'You were sent here to work, and you will have to do it or I will make you suffer for it,' Austin Bidwell was told on arrival at Chatham by 'a pompous little fellow (an ex-major from the army)'.[93] This was *not* Arthur Griffiths – the

Convicts excavating large basin at Chatham

description fits, but by then he had moved on. It was in fact the governor of the day. Austin's first sight of his fellow convicts was not reassuring either: 'After dinner I saw the men marched out to labor, and was amazed to see their famished, wolfish looks – thin, gaunt and almost disguised out of all human resemblance by their ill-fitting, mud-covered garments and mud-splashed faces and hands.'[94] And when he joined them in the basins it was 'mud, mud everywhere, with groups of weary men with shovel, or shovel and barrow, working in it.'[95] He was put to work with a gang feeding the giant pug-mill with clay: 'the clay was in a high bank; we dug into it from the bottom with our spades, and filled it as fast as possible into our barrows. In front of each man was a "run," formed by a line of planks only eight inches in width, and all converging toward and meeting near the "pug". The distance we were wheeling was from thirty to forty yards, and the incline was really very steep; but that in itself would not have been so bad, but the labor of digging out the clay was severe, and that everlasting "pug" was as hungry as if it were in the habit of taking "Plantation Bitters" to give it an appetite. . . . In an hour's time my poor hands were covered with blood blisters, and my left knee was a lame duck indeed.'[96] Later on he found himself 'loading trucks with mud and clay, and that upon a diet of black bread and potatoes. The cars, or trucks, held four tons, there were three men to a truck, and the task was nineteen trucks a day, and between the urging of the officers, frightened themselves for fear the task might not be done, and the mud and the starvation, it was despairing work.'[97]

When not pushed to this degree of desperation – and Chatham was a special case – many working men would not have found the public works too hard a part of their prison lives. But many of our authors were middle-class gents, quite unused to such exertions. The most strenuous activity in Ticket-of-leave-man's previous existence had been strictly for 'amusement'; e.g. winning 'the silver sculls at Henley'.[98] A man of similar background confessed to Basil Thomson that 'at the end of the first afternoon I thought I should not have strength enough to march back to the prison, nor did I know how I should go through another such day of labour. I thought I would take my ward officer into my confidence'. The officer's advice was: 'if I were you I should stick it for a bit. I have seen quite a lot of men when they first come feeling the same as you do, but they found the work gets easier day by day.'[99] 'How I envied some of my fellow-prisoners,' said another gentleman, 'to whose hard hands and brawny arms the work that was almost killing me seemed like play! I thought then, and I think now, that it is not fair to put a gentleman to the same work as a labourer, their crimes being equal; for the crimes being equal, the punishment should be equal – and that cannot be the case where a man, who has perhaps never carried a heavier weight than a gun all his life, is put at the same labour as a man who is accustomed to it from boyhood.' But, he adds, 'before twelve months had elapsed, I was as good a workman as any navvy.'[100]

Not many prison authors actually broke stone to earn their daily bread. Stuart Wood was one who did – at Shepton Mallet:

In the stone-breaking yard each man sat on a stump of wood or a lump of granite in separate walled recesses and broke iron-stone to mend roads with. . . . The daily task was so many hundred weight – I have forgotton how many – and there we sat winter or summer, pounding away at the hard granite, until one's back ached fit to break and one's hands bled from broken blisters.[101]

Michael Davitt did it too – at Dartmoor, where, he says, it was 'not considered hard labour' even though 'during the past few years the prisoners have had to be supplied with small bags made of the same material as their clothing by which to shield their hands from frost-bite and chilblains.'[102]

Stone-breaking took place inside prisons, but the rock was cut outside, in the quarries of Portland and Dartmoor, from where 'granite for the New Scotland Yard' was supplied.[103] Here the work was both hard *and* dangerous. An accident befell Henry Harcourt in the one at Portland: 'I was kneeling upon the rock which was cut out from the quarry . . . cutting a groove in the large rock to split it again, when a stone fell off the top of the quarry on my loins.' Harcourt appears to have had a gift for bringing out the worst in his captors, or a lively imagination, or both, because 'as I opened my eyes,' he says, 'I saw the prisoner giving me some water, and at the same time this young officer kicking me, and saying, "Now then, get up, get up will you?" '[104] Harcourt's injuries were not that serious, apart from the fact that his 'urine was quite discoloured – a reddish colour'.[105] But the Irish prisoners who worked in a gang near the cell block at Portland had 'an opportunity of occasionally seeing some of those as they were taken to hospital or to the dead-house on stretchers, after being maimed or killed or having committed suicide on the works'.[106] At Dartmoor, it was not unknown for blacksmiths to 'come into hospital with injured eyes, quarrymen with crushed feet, farm labourers with kicks from horses.'[107] And a fatal accident took place in 1897, 'when an old convict, who was already doing his fifth sentence in the quarry, made a miscalculation when a block of granite weighing many tons had been set in motion and, instead of stepping outwards to let it pass, squeezed himself against the cliff-face in the belief that he had room. There he was nipped by the block and slowly squeezed to death.'[108] A part of the granite won from the quarry was used in the construction by convict labour of new prison halls at Dartmoor, and this work too was attended with fatalities. Michael Davitt remarks 'in passing, that three prisoners lost their lives while this building was going on, and in my opinion those accidents were attributable to the ignorance of scaffolding arrangements shown by the warders appointed to superintend them'.[109]

RECLAMATION

Dartmoor also sent out parties to cultivate the moorland. Amongst the convicts who sallied forth each morning during the 1870s was Ticket-of-leave-man. 'The men are organized into gangs or parties of about twenty five each, under the supervision of a warder (or "screw" as he is called by the prisoners). Every morning, weather permitting, the gangs are marched in double file to the scene of their labours, where they "break off" and commence the day's work.'[110] John Boyle O'Reilly remembers it as 'labor too hard for brutes, half-starved men, weakened by long confinement, standing in water from a foot to two feet deep, and spading the heavy peat out of the narrow cutting over their heads.'[111] Ticket-of-leave-man remembers it quite differently:

> We were all marched . . . to the other end of a large field, nearly half a mile off, to fetch a sledge with which to remove some stones from a bog-hole. Returning with the sledge we commenced the removal, and dragged the stones to one corner of the field. An hour thus slipped away, and the principal officer came his rounds. The stones had not been placed where he wished, and we were ordered to transfer them to the gate at the entrance to the field. We did that, and then the afternoon was gone. We were resuming our jackets to return to the prison, when the farm bailiff came along upon his pony. He thought the stones would be in the way where we had last placed them, and directed that tomorrow we should remove them to the next field. The whole twenty five men had not earned one ounce of the brown bread, nor one pint of the cocoa they were returning to make their supper on.[112]

At Portsmouth too, where gangs of men went out to work in the naval dockyard area, 'a great part of the work does not need doing. Blocks of iron and pieces of timber are moved backwards and forwards for the mere purpose of giving something to do.'[113]

PENAL v. PRODUCTIVE

These, and matching experiences of prison work, point up one of the most enduring problems of Victorian penal economics. Alongside the issue of silence v. separation, there was conducted with nearly equal vehemence a debate between those who thought 'hard labour' should be purely penal in character – the more pointless and painful the better; and those who argued, on moral and reformatory as well as financial grounds, that it ought to be productive. As if to exemplify the nature and extent of this rift, two official commissions, reporting within months of each other in 1863, came down on opposite sides of the controversy. The Royal Commission on Transportation held that 'Convicts naturally show much greater industry, and exert themselves more cheerfully, when they feel that their labour is really valuable, than when it appears to them to be wasted or misapplied; and in useful work they acquire a training which is most valuable to them after their discharge.'[114] Lord Carnarvon and his committee men, on the other hand, thought that 'Industrial occupation, though it may vary in amount and character, is so much less penal, irksome, and fatiguing, that it can only be classed under the head of light labour.'[115] They were assisted towards these conclusions by the evidence of, amongst others, Major Fulford. He compared the two modes of labour in more or less tendentious terms.

In the case of the industrial occupation of a man who is not master of his trade, we will say, the less he knows of the business the more he is interested in the occupation, and the more he is interested in the occupation the less he cares for being shut up in the cell; consequently time passes quickly and agreeably, and is no weight to him compared to that which it is to a man who is all day on the wheel.[116]

Elsewhere he says, 'imprisonment cannot be by any means so great a punishment to a man employed at his own trade (still less if he have the interest attaching to being taught) as if he were employed in some strictly penal punishment.'[117]

The Carnarvon view of the matter was enshrined in the legislation that followed the presentation of his report – much to the dismay of those responsible for running prisons such as Wakefield where a commercially successful mat-making business had been built up:

Notwithstanding that industrial labour in some form has made its way into every prison in the kingdom, yet in the eye of the law it is merely a parasite on the penal system – tolerated but not recognised. In the Prisons Act, 1865, the treadwheel, shot drill, crank, &c., are prominent, but the words industrial and remunerative are nowhere to be found.[118]

Sir Edmund DuCane agreed with this interpretation; the Act, he thought, gave 'little or no encouragement to industrial employment'.[119] As events developed towards the government takeover of local prisons in 1877, the management of Wakefield grew increasingly uneasy: 'When the Bill was before Parliament, the West Riding Justices knowing (after consulting counsel) that legal difficulties stood in the way of developing the prison trade, communicated with the Home Secretary, who had charge of the Bill, and requested him to insert clauses "legalising the employment of capital, and the sale of manufactured goods, as well as to designate who might sue and be sued, and the name to be used in criminal prosecutions." The reply of Sir George Grey was, that he "did not think it expedient".'[120] Sir Edmund, whose hand lay as heavy on the 1877 Act as had Carnarvon's on that of 1865, sought to achieve a compromise by incorporating the nostrums of both schools of thought in his planning. On the one hand he wanted there to be 'hard, dull, useless, uninteresting monotonous labour'. But although he thinks it 'necessary to resort to this for its penal effect', there is 'a limit to the time during which a prisoner can be advantageously subjected to it, for it is decidedly brutalizing in its effects'. It must therefore be combined with 'employment which plays its part as a moral reformatory agent on those who unfortunately are subject to prison discipline'.[121] The Act accordingly provided that 'the expense of maintaining prisoners should in part be defrayed by their labour, and that useful trades and manufactures should be taught, so far as consistent with penal discipline and the avoidance of competition with outside industry.'[122]

Outside industry, both before and after the Act, exerted pressure of two sorts against the continued existence of prison enterprise. Captain Armytage, the governor of Wakefield, explained to the Social Science Association that mat-making had its origins in the characteristics of his labour force:

> Prisoners are below the average in intelligence, they are apt to misappropriate tools or materials; they are generally disinclined to work, the labour, therefore, must be of a kind that the quantity performed can easily be tested; their stay in prison is, as a rule, so short, that the handicraft must require little teaching; the raw material must be cheap so that a man by wilfulness or carelessness may not waste more than his work is worth. This desideratum has been met with in every respect in the manufacture of cocoa fibre goods.

But where the prison led out of necessity, others followed for profit. 'For many years,' he went on, 'the trade remained exclusively a prison one; at length, profiting by the experience which the prisons had gained, private manufacturers began to compete with the prisons, and judging from the fact that the private firms are constantly increasing in number, their business transactions have not been altogether unprofitable'.[123]

These private manufacturers readily made common cause with a second source of opposition to the profitable use of prison labour: the trades unions. 'The agitators', as Captain Armytage called them, 'propound a theory, which they wish to lay down as a general principle, that prison labour shall not compete with free labour . . . so that for the sake of avoiding the possibility of somebody, at some time, being injuriously affected in some indefinite manner, they would doom their fellow-men to be kept at a degrading and useless labour, or in enforced idleness.'[124]

Pinned down by this concerted fire from otherwise sworn enemies, Sir Edmund sought safety behind a definition of 'market forces':

> Those who discuss these matters with only theoretical knowledge to guide them think to avoid the charge of unfair competition by laying it down as a condition that prison-made articles must not be sold under the market

price. But what is the 'market price' of anything? It is not a divine decree sent down from heaven, but is the result of what has been called the 'higgling of the market', in which sellers get as high a price as they can and buyers pay as little as they can – in which they are helped by the sellers being ready to undersell each other. The practical effect of the condition so laid down is that outsiders may undersell the prison, but the prison may not undersell the outsiders.[125]

And hand in hand with these mysteries of the market there walked a more political consideration: 'the Government are afraid', the schoolmaster at 'Xshire' told One-who-has-tried-them, 'that if they continue to make more than a certain quantity of things in the prisons the mill owners and mechanics will remember it at the next election.'[126] So between them, 'market forces' and the opposition of Sir Edmund put paid to the spirit of enterprise that had flourished in places like Wakefield. And the right to raise capital, which had been solicited by the West Riding justices – Captain Armytage did not exclude the possibility of 'working collieries, for state purposes, by prison labour' – turned out to be no more than a footnote to a history that might have been.[127]

From then on there is to be detected in official reports and writings a concern to establish some sort of profit-and-loss analysis of the work undertaken by prisoners. Instruction in these simplified economics was given to a tramp at the Devonport Gaol who had been refusing to work, until 'encouraged' with a prospect of bread-and-water:

When being dismissed he was shown the pile of work he had completed, and told both what he had earned and what he had cost, leaving a balance of some shillings towards the expenses of the establishment, or as it was put to him by the *Governor*, 'towards *my* salary'. The lesson, though hard to learn, had its effect. He did not know he could work so well, did not know he could maintain himself, much less earn a surplus for the benefit of others.[128]

Translated to the wider institutional framework however these little sums did not add up. There were many reasons for this, one of them being 'the necessity for giving the warders time for meals and recreation. You cannot have a large body of men in workshops with a depleted staff, because at any moment two or three unruly prisoners may incite the rest to mutiny, and the working day is therefore very short.'[129] The result of these and other restrictions was that 'in practice no man, whether sentenced to simple imprisonment or hard labour, really does a day's work such as he would do if he had to earn his living in free life.'[130] To bolster the argument, one way or the other, laborious comparisons were made between prison and 'free' output; one estimate was that 'two convicts employed in quarrying at Portland, or in making excavations at Chatham, did the work of one free labourer, and this difference, great as it is, does not appear to be more than is accounted for by the previous training of the latter, and the different circumstances under which he works.'[131] One-who-has-endured-it acknowledges that 'they do not really work anything like so hard as a free man,' and suggests why. 'Of course there is no heart in a slave's or a prisoner's labour. Every man does as little as he possibly can. So long as what he does will pass muster, and he gets his marks, it is all a man cares for.'[132] It was a pleasing analogy, developed more fully by another prisoner. '*Imprisonment is slavery*. None of the distinguishing features of slavery are absent. The essence of slavery consists in forcibly depriving human beings of their right to labour as and where it may suit them best, and to receive and enjoy the fruits of that labour.'[133]

RESISTANCE

The first and most obvious tactic that occurs to a slave-labour force, and one typically put into practice by tacit agreement, is to work as slowly as possible. A working party observed by Dr Quinton 'appeared to move with a certain rhythmical precision, in slow time, and in a machine-like manner, as if the regularity of their prison life were stamped on the proceedings, and official routine had entered into their bones and muscles.'[134] 'To see one of these parties playing at work was', he says, 'an object lesson in ergophobia.'[135]

A second form of resistance to forced labour was for prisoners to break the strict rule of silence that supposedly surrounded their physical efforts. They talked on the wheel; in the oakum shed; the tailor's shop; and on the works: 'if it be trenching or brick-making, the men are almost of necessity close together, and they talk quietly, but incessantly, until the moment that the whistle blows to "fall in" again.'[136]

Chicago May had her own method for cheating the system; she had made her own way in the world from the age of fourteen, when she ran away from Ireland to America. A few rules and the attentions of the women warders were not enough to deter her. 'The Lord helps him who helps himself. I wasn't a thief for nothing. I would steal finished work from the other girls, take off their names and numbers, substitute my own, and put it into my own basket. I played fair with the poor girls though,' she reminds us, in case we should think badly of her, 'because I only stole work which had been passed and for which they had got credit.'[137]

Going slow on the job, talking whenever possible, and stealing finished work from fellow prisoners were all covert ways of sabotaging the demands of discipline and productivity, and they avoided head-on confrontation with staff; but some individuals took a quite direct approach to the issue. Mark Jeffrey was a fearsome figure, six feet tall and fifteen stone, and a former fairground bruiser. He was 'put to making coats in the prison, and one day the master tailor came to me and said, "How many coats have you made?" "Never mind," I replied. "I don't intend to give them to you; I want them for a bed to lie on during the day.

Don't worry me too much or I'll 'do' for you." The master tailor did not trouble me much about the work after that, and I did not do much tailoring.'[138]

In matters touching on his future good health, the master tailor was clearly a foresighted person; reluctant prison labourers lacking the persuasive physical presence of a Mark Jeffrey soon found themselves up against an unrelenting system of discipline, as Austin Bidwell saw at Chatham: 'About 10 o'clock the man next to me with an oath threw down his spade and vowed he would do no more work. Putting on his vest and jacket, he walked up to the warder, and quite as a matter of course turned his back to him and put both hands behind him. The warder produced a pair of handcuffs, and without any comment handcuffed his hands in that position, and then told him to stand with his back to the work. No one took the slightest notice and the toil did not slacken for an instant, but one man was out of the game, and we had to make his side good.' At the end of the morning's work, the party picked up its tools and made its way back to the prison for the mid-day meal. 'Our laconic friend was trudging on behind the party, and to my surprise I noticed that several of the other parties had un enfant perdu, hands behind his back, marching in the rear, and as soon as we had reached the prison each poor sheep in the rear fell out quite as a matter of course.'[139] At Liverpool prison too, when Basil Thomson visited the treadwheel shed, there was 'a row of men with their faces to the wall. They numbered from six to about fifteen. These were they who would rather undergo dietary punishment than climb another step up the endless staircase, and they furnished the majority of the "reports." '[140] The delinquents at both places were destined to appear before the governor or his deputy charged with the disciplinary offence known as 'refusing labour'.

But in the end it was not the *number* of men and women who refused to labour that mattered, it was the fact that any of them did so that kept alive in the minds of warders and governors the ambitious nature of their duty, which was nothing less than to quell the spirits of the most disorderly members of the civil community outside the walls. And it kept alive in the minds of the captives that small power they possessed of defeating the system by accepting an even greater degree of physical and mental suffering – a very small power indeed, but one in the face of which the forces at the disposal of the prison authorities were ultimately powerless.

To a different class of prisoner, none of this seemed necessary. Manchester Merchant had difficulty meeting his oakum task, but gave his white bread to the cleaner on his landing, on the understanding that he would 'make matters all right' with the relevant officer, 'which he succeeded in doing, at the cost to me of more than half my food. I knew it to be a matter of impossibility for me to do more than two pounds, however hard I worked, and I told the warder so. He complained every night, but did not report me, my bread worked the oracle.'[141] Captain D— S— had an equally happy arrangement with his warder: 'For a weekly consideration my task was picked daily. Of a morning a bundle was mysteriously thrown into my cell, and a few moments later I proudly descended with "my work," and dropped the unused rope on the stair. . . . The man who actually picked my oakum was the "cleaner", a privileged individual with a roving commission.'[142]

HOUSEWORK

In the absence of an obvious profit motive, and of any clearly articulated policy on either the penal or the reformatory nature of hard labour, one branch of prison work which positively flourished was that of housework; the washing and cleaning and polishing and mending that naturally accompanied the maintenance of establishments holding anywhere between a few dozen to fifteen hundred men and women and children. Of all the tasks that this entailed, the laundry was probably the least pleasant and the nearest that could be contrived to the idea of hard labour. Michael Davitt was moved indoors at Dartmoor following an escape by fellow Fenians from Australia, but not to a more comfortable form of work:

> Another prisoner and myself were told off to the wringing-machine, in which linen, &c., for a thousand men, and washings for officers' mess and rooms, &c., had to be wrung each week, with flannels and sheets for same number once a fortnight and month respectively in addition. My assistant on this machine was changed every week, as men – able bodied men – had been reported for refusing to remain constantly at such heavy labour; but as I was physically unable to wash the linen I was compelled to turn the machine as my principal occupation. . . . In addition to turning the wringer, I had to sort my share of the dirty linen each Monday morning, and singularly enough, the infirmary portion was part of my share, and I had consequently to handle the articles worn by prisoners suffering from all manner of skin diseases and other disgusting afflictions. . . . My weight a week after my liberation was but nine stone four pounds, including my clothes, or some eight stone ten pounds without – not, I think, the proper weight for a man six feet high, and at the age of thirty one.[143]

It may be that Davitt's spell in the laundry was meant, in a roundabout way, to cleanse him of the filth and smell he endured in a previous occupation: 'On the brink of the prison cesspool, in which all the soil of the establishment is accumulated for manure, stands a small building some twenty feet long by about ten broad, known as the "bone shed". . . . All the bones accruing from the meat supply of the prison were pounded into dust in this shed, and during the summer of '72 (excepting five weeks spent in Portsmouth prison) this was my employment. These bones have often lain putrefying for weeks in the broiling heat of the summer sun ere they were brought in to be broken. The stench arising from their decomposition, together with the noxious exhalations from the action of the sun's rays on the cesspool outside, no words could adequately express – it was a veritable charnel house.'[144]

Women too had their share of hard housework to do. Chicago May was made a stoker in the laundry at Aylesbury, 'being strong and husky compared to the others'.[145] Mrs Maybrick spent part of *her* fifteen years at Aylesbury, and part of that time she worked in the kitchen: 'My duties were as follows: To wash ten cans, each holding four quarts; to scrub one table, twenty feet in length; two dressers, twelve feet in length; to wash five hundred dinner-tins; to clean knives; to wash a sack of potatoes; to assist in serving the dinners, and to scrub a piece of floor twenty by ten feet. . . . The work was hard and rough.'[146] Even a subsequent job in the officer's mess 'was very hard and quite beyond my strength'.[147] To an outsider, these tasks did not look quite so arduous. Dr Mary Gordon, the first woman inspector of prisons, was 'surprised to find that hard labour meant an exceedingly moderate day's work in scrubbing, or at the wash tub'.[148]

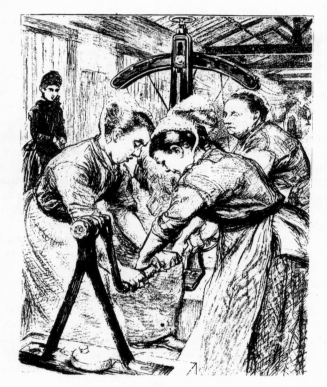

Women's hard labour

BILLETS

Apart from the laundry, which was *real* hard labour, there was great competition amongst prisoners for certain of the 'house-keeping' posts. 'The billet of cleaner', says One-who-has-tried-them, 'is an eagerly-coveted one, as a cleaner gets any amount of food to eat, and is employed out in the corridors all day.'[149] Even more understandably, 'the cookhouse is looked upon by many prisoners as the best position in the prison, on account of the extra amount of food allowed; and it is really surprising to see the altered appearance of men a week or two after their admission as cooks.'[150] Alterations in appearance were not restricted to any weight that might be put on; the cooks were also 'easily distinguished by their hair being greased, no other prisoners having fat enough to waste on such a luxury'.[151] Because of the competition for them, 'these billets were looked on in the light of staff appointments, and were tenable only during good conduct'. They were also 'reserved for those only with a good record for work and conduct, which but few of the petitioners could show'.[152] Old prison hands who knew the routines and had demonstrated their trustworthiness on previous sentences were likely to be reappointed to these semi-official positions if they were reconvicted. David Fannan, a burglar by trade, but not too successful at it, had spent the latter part of his first period of penal servitude working as an orderly in the penal cell-block at Portland. He was released and shortly reconvicted. 'When I turned up at Portland a second time,' he says, 'the warders regarded my reappearance as a matter of course and appointed me to my old tasks as if I had only been absent a week.'[153]

Also prized was any position which took its occupant outside the prison walls. At Dartmoor this privilege fell to the dustbin party, and since 'a handful of men is a microcosm of the great world', it was Basil Thomson's experience that 'the financier who has made a mistake with the trust funds will soon be found expending the same energy in getting into the party that empties the dustbins as, under happier circumstances, he would have expended in getting into Parliament.'[154] Simply to be in the open air was reward enough for many prisoners. Any agricultural work, as distinct from digging the moor, had this added attraction, and was accordingly much sought after. Lord William Nevill did 'hay-making, digging potatoes, and carting manure, and other kinds of farm work' at Parkhurst. 'In the carting as a rule, no horses are employed, but the men draw the cart, harnessed two by two to a long rope. I frankly say this was the part I like best. The open air exercise and the variety were a positive delight after the monotony of crawling along with the hospital party, and as for the supposed degradation of drawing a cart, it made no earthly difference to me, whether I pulled at the rope or sat on the top and drove the horse, as a free farm-labourer does.'[155]

A final and very tiny category of comfortable 'staff billets' was disproportionately occupied by prison authors, on the apparent principle that the great financier might with advantage be put in charge of the library tickets, e.g. Jabez Balfour;[156] or the fraudulent businessman to keep the books in the tailor's shop or the 'engineer's' office, e.g. One-who-has-endured-it.[157]

TRADES

Given the restrictions on free trading that affected all decisions about manufacturing activity in prison, one avenue that remained open was to produce goods for internal consumption, or for use by other organs of government. There is a strangely incestuous aspect to some of this work. Some prisoners were employed at printing the *Criminal Calendar*, for the purposes of catching more people like themselves.[158] And for somewhere to house them, 'a large convict prison arose', under the watchful eye of Arthur Griffiths, 'on the barren brickfields and allotments past the railway station at Acton'. This was Wormwood Scrubs; the bricks were made from clay on the site, and the labour was provided by men who had earned their 'remission' and who 'were so near the day of their release that they gave no trouble'. Griffiths was pleased with their efforts: 'The scene was one of steady, satisfactory industry from morning till dusk; the labour was forced, but was given, I think, ungrudgingly, and my workmen were, for the most part, contented, even happy.'[159] We do not know whether they were equally happy in their work, but 'All the boots for the Metropolitan police were made by the convicts at Dartmoor, as well as for the various convict prisons.'[160] But if productivity is related in any way to morale, then we may infer they were not, since 'there were 190 shoemakers at work, and there were something less than 200 pairs of shoes manufactured in the week, so that making every allowance for the hands employed upon the prison repairs, the work done did not average three shoes to the man in the week. If each man worked in his own cell, he could after three months practice, make a pair of shoes every day with great ease.'[161]

So in a lot of this work, whether it purported to be of an industrial nature or not, there was little that might qualify as 'training'. 'Nobody learns a trade in prison,' complains John Lee after twenty years inside. 'To begin with, the kind of work that is done in prison is utterly unlike anything that is to be found outside.'[162] And even when the work was a valid trade outside, the tempo at which it was conducted inside rendered it useless as any kind of training. 'To a looker-on, obliged by her home-needs to sew with a rapid finger and earnest haste, these work-women seem drawing out the needle at their ease, and putting it in again – *if it so please them*; but no skill or power is ever attained there by the sewing system, and the women on liberation are never found to have acquired there the art of using this species of industry for a living.'[163] In this, as in other areas of controversy, Sir Edmund DuCane affected to spy a basic misunderstanding in the arguments of his opponents.

> It is assumed as a general rule that by teaching a prisoner a trade he will be less likely to fall again into crime, and this is apparently founded on the idea that people fall into crime from want of employment or ignorance of any mode of earning their own livelihood. I believe that it is an entire delusion to suppose that this is true of any considerable number of criminals.[164]

And so it was with every aspect of penal labour policy; pulled this way and then that by conflicting pressures on the policy makers; poorly organized in the prisons – overwhelmed as often as not by numbers and the qualities of a fleeting labour force; undermined by opposition from prisoners and the pecuniation of some officers. It all made most prison work seem more like mere 'make-work' than the 'hard labour' Lord Carnarvon dreamed of. And the machine around which much of the debate had revolved – the tread-wheel – shared an unwitting symbolism with the periods of exercise that decorated the prison mornings. Both were activities in which physical exertion had been separated from sensible outcome – perfect expressions of the effort without profit that was the lot of the industrial serf with nothing but his labour to sell on a buyer's market. And both were journeys without destinations – haunting reminders of the lack of direction that characterized prison management after the collapse of the penitentiary. Hard labour may be seen as one attempt to fill the hole that was left when religion vanished from the centre of the prison stage. It failed. And the prisons themselves came to resemble nothing so much as stranded hulks; their human cargoes neatly stowed below, the staff at their posts and ready to sail – waiting for the orders that never came down from above.

NOTES

1. Payne, 18.
2. One-who-has-endured-it, 47.
3. One-who-has-tried-them, I, 258.
4. Tschiffely, 224.
5. One-who-has-tried-them, I, 258.
6. Ibid., I, 272.
7. One-who-has-endured-it, 44.
8. Wood, 123.
9. G. Bidwell, 405.
10. One-who-has-endured-it, 46.
11. Barrow, 14.
12. Wood, 123.
13. Ibid., 124.
14. Ibid., 123.
15. One-who-has-tried-them, I, 261.
16. Ibid., I, 263.
17. B. Thomson (1925), 38.
18. Gladstone Committee (1895), 23.
19. DuCane (1896), 638.
20. One-who-has-suffered, 9.
21. DuCane (1896), 638.
22. Mayhew, 310.
23. Wood, 35.
24. J. Balfour, 47.
25. Ibid., 48.
26. WBN, 30.
27. Sykes, 140.
28. One-who-has-endured-it, 93.
29. Kirkdale, 60.
30. One-who-has-tried-them, II, 87.
31. Hay, 33.
32. Carnarvon Committee (1863), vii.
33. DuCane (1896), 636.
34. Carnarvon Committee (1863), vii.
35. Hepworth Dixon, 270.
36. Chesterton (1856), I, 225–6.
37. B. Thomson (1925), 28.
38. Field, I., 65.
39. Carnarvon Committee (1863), 142.
40. Quinton, 59.
41. Society for the Improvement of Prison Discipline, Rules proposed, 59.
42. Mayhew, 307.
43. DuCane (1896), 637.

44. Griffiths (1904), 195.
45. Carnarvon Committee (1863), 147.
46. One-who-has-tried-them, II, 256.
47. Nicoll, 6.
48. Twyford, 75.
49. Chesterton (1856), I, 155.
50. Good, 14.
51. Student, 70.
52. Hindle, 11.
53. Carnarvon Committee (1863), 146.
54. Moreau-Christophe, 59.
55. Quinton, 59.
56. Carnarvon Committee (1863), 143.
57. Becke, 27.
58. Hay, 32.
59. *Kirkdale*, 49.
60. Hay, 32.
61. Hill (1853), 200.
62. Payne, 16.
63. Ibid., 33.
64. Hill (1853), 202.
65. Chesterton (1856), I, 156.
66. Ibid., 157.
67. Ibid., 222.
68. Ibid., 223.
69. Good, 8.
70. Ibid., 9.
71. *Kirkdale*, 49.
72. Carnarvon Committee (1863), 143.
73. Griffiths (1904), 196.
74. Hill (1894), 183.
75. Gladstone Committee (1895), 19.
76. Nihill, 13.
77. B. Thomson (1939), 182.
78. Griffiths (1904), 194.
79. Collett, 25.
80. Moreau-Christophe, 61.
81. Leicester Inquiry (1854), v.
82. G. Bidwell, 469.
83. Birmingham Inquiry (1854), vii.
84. Griffiths (1904), 7.
85. Ibid., 194.
86. One-who-has-tried-them, II, 222.
87. Griffiths (1904), 195.
88. Mayhew, 309.
89. Carnarvon Committee (1863), viii.
90. Penal Servitude Commission (1879), lvii.
91. DuCane (1882), 66.
92. No. 7, 104.
93. A. Bidwell, 393.
94. Ibid., 397.
95. Ibid., 398.
96. Ibid., 399.
97. Ibid., 448.
98. Ticket-of-leave-man, 79.
99. B. Thomson (1925), 44.
100. 'Twenty years', 675.
101. Wood, 126.
102. Davitt (1886), 21.
103. DuCane (1896), 635.
104. Penal Servitude Commission (1879), 339.
105. Ibid., 340.
106. Rossa, 135.
107. B. Thomson (1925), 121.
108. Ibid., 141.
109. Davitt (1886), 21.
110. Ticket-of-leave-man, 35.
111. Roche, 56.
112. Ticket-of-leave-man, 57–8.
113. Letter, 498.
114. Transportation and Penal Servitude Commission (1863), 45.
115. Carnarvon Committee (1863), vii.
116. Ibid., 144.
117. Fulford, 147.
118. Turner, 236.
119. DuCane (1896), 636.
120. Turner, 236.
121. DuCane (1882), 57.
122. Quinton, 60.
123. Turner, 238.
124. Ibid., 237.
125. DuCane (1896), 640.
126. One-who-has-tried-them, I, 287.
127. Turner, 241.
128. Row, 6.
129. B. Thomson (1925), 187.
130. Ibid., 89.
131. Transportation and Penal Servitude Commission (1863), 45.
132. One-who-has-endured-it, 348.
133. One-who-has-suffered-it, 589.

134. Quinton, 31.
135. Ibid., 32.
136. Ticket-of-leave-man, 35.
137. Sharpe, 188.
138. Hiener, 73.
139. A. Bidwell, 399.
140. B. Thomson (1925), 29.
141. *Kirkdale*, 97.
142. D— S—, 184.
143. Davitt (1886), 22.
144. Ibid., 19.
145. Sharpe, 180.
146. Maybrick, 98.
147. Ibid., 191.
148. M. Gordon, 33.
149. One-who-has-tried-them, II, 229.

150. *Kirkdale*, 50.
151. Foote, 149.
152. Quinton, 29.
153. Fannan, 92.
154. B. Thomson (1925), 51.
155. WBN, 34.
156. J. Balfour, 339.
157. One-who-has-endured-it, 338.
158. No. 7, 93.
159. Griffiths (1904), 237.
160. One-who-has-endured-it, 178.
161. Ticket-of-leave-man, 50.
162. Lee, 91.
163. Lloyd, 177.
164. DuCane (1896), 641.

7
THE DIETARY

'To all classes of Her Majesty's subjects the mid-day meal is of the highest importance.' Dr McCook Weir [1]

'The meals were given to the ordinary prisoners through a trapdoor. This was about eight inches square. It was locked outside, and when the turnkey opened it he thrust it in and laid the vessel thereon. If the prisoner was not ready to take it off the moment it was laid on, and shut the trap at the same time, he subjected himself to a report.' [2] No other event in the prison day – whether spent in solitary confinement picking oakum, sewing, or winding the crank; or treading the wheel; or labouring on the works or elsewhere – was so keenly anticipated nor so soon after or so often regretted as the arrival of food at the door of the cell. Not that when it did arrive it was ever served with anything like good grace: 'It is wrong to say these articles were handed in to me', says John Dawson, 'because they were thrown on the floor as food might be thrown to a dog, and the door was banged to again.' [3] Dawson was unlucky; the scene that confronted suffragette Annie Kenney when her door was opened was more typical: 'I saw in front of me a wardress and four prisoners. Two of them carried a huge tin can with tea, the others had a large basket with dry, brown, tiny loaves.' [4] The most advanced prison buildings replaced these human carriers with mechanized devices. Visitors to Reading could observe, at one end of the wing, what appeared to be 'two upright bars. By means of a windlass, the provisions for the prisoners, having in the kitchen been placed on trays, are then wound up these bars through a trap door to the corridor; the rations are then removed to larger trays, which run along the rails of the galleries, and are doled out at the doors of successive cells.'[5] The Strangeways version of this machine had 'a curious cage or wire tray which spans from one side of the wing to the other', and which ran 'along on wheels on the top of the rail and over the hall below, three storeys down'.[6]

THE INGREDIENTS

How it was delivered was, however, incidental to the main concern of the prisoner, which was with the quantity and quality of the victuals he or she eventually received. Like nearly every other element of Victorian prison life the menu varied by time and place. Two constants bound together these variations, 'For the first week,' says Frederick Brocklehurst, 'I existed (the verb is carefully chosen) on seven pounds of brown-to-black bread and ten and a half

Lifting apparatus for serving food at Holloway

DIETARIES of County and Borough Gaols 1843.

WEEK	WITHOUT HARD LABOUR.				WITH HARD LABOUR.			
	Class 1. Less than 7 days.	Class 2. More than 7 days, and not more than 21 days.	Class 3. More than 21 days, and not more than 4 months.	Class 4. More than 4 months.	Class 2. More than 7 days, and not more than 21 days.	Class 3. More than 21 days, and not more than 6 weeks.	Class 4. More than 6 weeks, and not more than 4 months.	Class 5. More than 4 months.
	ozs.	*ozs.*	*ozs.*	*ozs.*	*ozs.*	*ozs.*	*ozs.*	*ozs.*
Bread	112	168	140	168	168	140	168	154
Potatoes	–	–	64	32	–	64	32	112
Meat	–	–	6	12	–	6	12	16
TOTAL SOLID FOOD	112	168	210	212	168	210	212	282
	pints.	*pints.*	*pints.*	*pints.*	*pints.*	*pints.*	*pints.*	*pints.*
Soup	–	–	2	3	1	2	3	3
Gruel	14	14	14	14	14	14	14	11
Cocoa	–	–	–	–	–	–	–	3
TOTAL LIQUID FOOD	14	14	16	17	15	16	17	17

pints of "stirabout". Nothing else, *absolutely nothing!*[7] Bread and gruel – variously known as 'stirabout', or 'skilly' from the Irish word 'skillagallee'[8] – were two of 'only six items of food' (the others being potatoes, meat, soup and cocoa) included in 'the dietaries recommended by Sir James Graham in 1843' for use in the local prisons, and used, with adaptations, for the convict prisons as well. 'The dietaries constructed of these few materials were six in number, and provided for the wants of eight classes of prisoners.'[9] The tables divide prisoners first into those with and without 'hard labour', and then sub-divide each of these broad classes into those serving different lengths of sentence. Separate tables were issued for women prisoners, in which some of the staples were reduced – on principles not immediately apparent to casual scrutiny. Together they form the point of departure for all further discussion of prison food for the rest of the century; all subsequent dietaries were consciously either *more* or *less* generous than the 'Graham' suggestions. Sir James, who was Secretary for the Home Department in 1843, warned when the tables were promulgated that 'the diet ought on no account to be made an instrument of punishment.'[10] What precisely he meant by this phrase generated a continuing debate of almost theological intensity. And more critically for prisoners, some of them became the subjects of deliberate experiments designed to test the limits of its meaning in terms of their bodily well-being.

'Number One' diet – the bread and gruel endured by Brocklehurst – was reserved for prisoners without 'hard labour' during their first week. The gruel was described by the 1878 Committee on Dietaries in Prisons, whose members did not have to eat it, as 'a nutritious stirabout, composed of equal parts of oatmeal and Indian meal'.[11] It was described by prisoners who *did* have to eat it every day, sometimes for years, as 'a bad unpalatable oatmeal gruel'.[12] It was unattractive to the cultured palate because 'there was not a morsel of sugar in it.'[13] It was not attractive to any palate when it had 'the consistency of "stickphast" paste',[14] and was 'thick enough to stand a spoon in'.[15] The widespread existence of this revulsion was confirmed by the Gladstone Committee Report. 'The stirabout appears to be so distasteful to a large proportion of prisoners that very much of it is rejected.'[16]

The other 'principal support' of prison diet Number One was the bread, which receives a mixed but mainly critical press from its consumers. At 'a Yorkshire prison' it was pronounced 'Excellent' by A Merchant.[17] 'The bread at times was good', concedes Lord William Nevill, 'but often it was quite the reverse.'[18] Balfour thought it 'well baked' but 'hard of digestion' and because 'a substantial portion of every loaf consists of crust', he says, 'the wise prisoner soaks his loaf in his tea'.[19] But of all the words which prisoners use to convey something of the quality of their bread, 'sawdust' is the most prevalent;[20] 'the bread was quite uneatable. If it had been of sawdust flavoured with road sweepings it could not have tasted worse.'[21]

Potatoes were introduced in Diet Class 3, and retained for Classes 4 and 5. They 'usually consisted of two, or occasionally three, shabby-looking tubers, the dirt still adhering to them, and soft and spongy to the taste'.[22] 'For five weeks together', says Lord William Nevill, 'they gave us rotten potatoes',[23] and Jabez Balfour reckoned that at least 50 per cent of them were inedible.[24] For the fastidious eater 'a careful examination of the potatoes was always necessary, as on tearing them in half, the interior was often found to be a mass of foul, black, spongy disease – a great disappointment to a starving man'.[25]

Perusal of the 1843 tables reveals two further delicacies reserved for Classes 3, 4 and 5 (i.e. prisoners serving more than twenty-one days), namely soup and meat. There were two sorts of soup: vegetable soup, classed as 'delicious' by a Leicester prisoner,[26] but less approved by One-who-has-tried-them – 'it tasted unlike any other pea soup I had ever come across, and when repeated three times a week, week after week and month after month, was simply unbearable.'[27] Then there was 'meat' soup. 'A pint of what was called beef soup' was served up to William Lovett and his fellow Chartists. They felt compelled to include it in a petition of complaint they addressed to Parliament, on the grounds that 'there was no other appearance of meat than some slimy, stringy particles, which, hanging about the wooden spoon, so offended your petitioners' stomachs that they were compelled to forgo eating it.'[28] A later variety was suspected by suffragettes to contain 'lumps of horse-flesh'.[29]

The meat itself, when served on its own rather than in soup, rates little higher in the opinions of our guides to Victorian prison cuisine. It was 'more like *gutta percha* than meat', at Portsmouth.[30] Jabez Balfour 'looked upon tough, stringy and fat meat as part of the punishment',[31] and Henry Harcourt says 'I used to have to hold my nose when I tried to eat it; I could not eat it; it used to make me sick.'[32] Meat was not served every day of the week; one of the 'red letter' days when it *was* happened to be Friday, which created problems of conscience or custom for practising Catholics. O'Donovan Rossa was told by the priest at Pentonville 'that in these prisons they did not alter the prison diet on Friday's for Catholics, but that the church had given them permission to eat meat on those days, and that no fasts need be observed. I did not tell him, nor did I tell you yet, I believe, that I had been a "Friday dog" for the past two weeks. Hunger and reduction in solitary confinement had got the better of my scruples, or rather of my pride, in sticking to this practice of the old faith of my fathers. The first Friday I put out my meat, the second Friday I kept it in my cell and ate it on Saturday. I did not think there was much merit in doing this, and the third Friday I "broke the pledge" quite deliberately by eating the four ounces of mutton and drinking the pint of mutton water with which it was surrounded.'[33]

A final item of the 1843 tables, and one that strikes an oddly luxurious note to the modern ear, is cocoa: 'three quarters of a pint' of it, 'made with three quarters of an ounce of the solid flake, and flavoured with two ounces of pure milk and six drachms of molasses'.[34] 'Cocoa', asserted Dr William Guy, medical superintendent at the Millbank Penitentiary, 'is a very good article of diet, and contains a good deal of that oily element which, if we could manage it, should always exist in food; it is better that there should be some oily element in food, and cocoa supplies that; it contains a good deal of oil in every part of it.'[35] It contained so much oil, indeed, that it tended to float to the surface where it formed an 'oily slick', below which there lurked a 'sediment' that 'equalled the solution in depth'.[36] It was 'positively repellent' to Constance Lytton,[37] but there were others who found it 'excellent'[38] and 'delicious'.[39]

Not on the Graham dietaries, but added after 1864, and intended as a substitute for meat, was 'suet pudding'. This did not go down too well with prisoners either. It was served up as 'blocks of solid' and 'indigestible "duff" ',[40] was 'dry as a bone and tasteless',[41] and 'the suet lay on top in yellow greasy streaks.'[42] A recommended way of coping with the pudding was to allow it to get cold and then eat it, 'in all its clayey substance, like a cold cake, sprinkled with salt'.[43]

Quite independently of what it tasted like, it was difficult to eat some of the food owing to the implements that were issued, or sometimes not issued. Female Debtor, for instance, 'was given a tin of porridge, which I could not eat because there was no spoon, and I was not then accustomed to taking my food in Nature's natural way.'[44] At Pentonville, 'No knives were allowed the prisoners. We ate with a shallow wooden spoon, and must therefore tear our tough meat with our teeth.'[45] And 'the spoon' given to O'Donovan Rossa was 'a timber one, substantial enough by its thickness to fill my mouth, and the plate was timber also.'[46] Washing up could be something of a problem as well. Lady Constance Lytton 'soon learned that if the plate and spoon were greased with food it was very difficult to get them clean again, as they can only be washed in cold water. The pail of water allowed to stand in the cell quickly became greasy itself, and there was no time, when let out to the tap to draw water, to wash up these things at the sink. I therefore used some of the freely supplied brown toilet paper to cover my plate and helped myself with my fingers instead of the spoon as they were much easier to wash.'[47]

MORE OR LESS

Those are the basic ingredients of the nineteenth-century prison diet, which with a few additions and deletions lasted until the First World War. They are simple enough in themselves, but in combination they made up a recipe that satisfied no one. Prisoners complained – constantly – that they were hungry, starving even; a vocal and influential part of public opinion in Parliament and the newspapers complained – loudly – that the diet was too generous by half for the convicted criminal compared with that of the 'honest' poor and the paupers. The pressure they exerted between them on prison administrations and the Home Office is reflected in a seemingly endless series of commissions and committees and inquiries. To make any sort of sense of them, it is necessary to weigh the nominal quantities of food displayed in the diet tables against the actual experience of eating them, not only day by day, but over months and years.

Many of the relevant issues were rehearsed at length in two separate reports that appeared in 1864: the Carnarvon Report on Prison Discipline, and a parallel inquiry into local prison dietaries, commissioned by the Home Secretary Sir George Grey, and conducted by Dr Guy of Millbank, Dr Maitland of the Gosport Military Prison, and Dr Clarke of Dartmoor. Carnarvon began by looking at variations between prisons in the quantities they fed to their prisoners. Dr Guy, in evidence, told them that 'The total of the solid elements of bread, meat and potatoes, taken together varies from a minimum of 100 ounces to a maximum of 340.'[48] That was clearly something that needed attention and correction. But Carnarvon proceeded next, as might be expected, to cross-examine the mid-century dietary with the greatest care, to see if it could be convicted of the slightest generosity towards the prisoner class. Dr Guy was helpful here again; he had made assiduous enquiries during 'a short visit' to Cambridgeshire.

> I went through the houses of the village, and ascertained exactly what the labourers bought in the shape of flour . . . in the shape of meat, in the shape of potatoes, and in the shape of butter, lard and dripping, and I took down the results. . . . the quantity of food per week is about 19 pounds to about 15 pounds. . . . The labouring men and women get about four pounds more than the prisoners in Millbank, or than the prisoners in Class 5 of the county and borough gaols.[49]

Quite apart from what the Cambridge villagers may have thought of Dr Guy's inquisitive visit, the fruits of his labour were not all that helpful to the committee; but another survey, undertaken by Governor Oakely of Taunton Gaol, was more to their taste. He discovered that 'on the average of the 50 county gaols, 267 ounces of solid food, and 17 pints of liquid food, is given per week to the prisoners; and in the 46 union workhouses in Somerset, Devon, Dorset, Wilts, and two in Middlesex, the solid food given to adult paupers is 202 ounces and 16 pints of liquid food'.[50] That 65-ounce difference and the extra pint confirmed a generally held suspicion, voiced in particular by Thomas Carlyle who had visited Pentonville. 'The bread, the cocoa, soup, meat, all the various sorts of food, in their respective cooking-places, we tasted: found them of excellence superlative.'[51] It was an excellence that incensed him when he thought of the diet of the honest poor. 'Here are two sets of people in a densely populated land, always in the balance before the general eye. Is Crime for ever to carry it against Poverty, and to have a manifest advantage? There are the scales before all men. Whirlwinds of dust scattered in mens' eyes – and there is plenty flying about – cannot blind them to the real state of the balance.'[52] The Carnarvon report accepted both Oakely's facts and the spirit of Carlyle's criticisms: 'whilst sufficient in amount and quality to the requirements of the prisoner's health, the diet ought not to be in more favourable contrast to the ordinary food of the free labourers or the inmates of the workhouse, unless sanitary conditions render it necessary.'[53]

The question was: how could the diet be reduced? And could it be done without endangering the health of the prison population? There were three ways in which the effects of diet could be measured: the incidence of physical sickness; rates of mortality; and gains and losses in prisoners' body weights. These were matters investigated with some thoroughness by Drs Guy, Maitland and Clarke. They started by conducting a poll of local prisons on their *opinions* as to the causes of diarrhoea; a 'scientific' method for collecting what amounted to naive beliefs. The diagnoses they received ascribed it to 'imperfect drainage . . . impure water . . . drinking cold water in excess, while perspiring, or to swallowing soup . . . change of diet'. Whilst these returns appear to exonerate the prison diet of direct responsibility for diarrhoea, other prisons mentioned specifically dietary remedies for the disorder: 'substituting cheese', 'substituting cocoa for gruel on alternate days', 'very little diarrhoea since the use of brown bread'.[54] Scurvy was another diet-related disease to which prison authorities were very much alive – an outbreak of it had closed down the penitentiary at Millbank in 1823.[55] Several of the prisons responding to the survey made mention of the condition: e.g. 'From Salford, we learn that in 1847, owing to the potato disease, and substitution of rice, scurvy attacked half the number of prisoners.'[56] The curative powers of the potato in relation to scurvy were well known; the reasons less so. Here is Dr Guy before the Carnarvon Committee:

> The potato contains a vegetable acid, either the acid of lemons or tartaric acid, it is not quite made out which; there is some little difference of opinion as to what the precise acid is, but it is a vegetable acid in combination with potash; whenever that is wholly absent from the food, scurvy will break out, whatever the dietary may be otherwise; and whenever that is supplied, scurvy will be cured.[57]

The uncertainty in Dr Guy's account was due to the as yet undiscovered *vitamin* properties of the potato; also present in the green vegetables so conspicuously absent from the dietary. 'Only once in nineteen years' did John Lee 'taste vegetables'.[58] But an attempt at Portland to introduce onions and lettuces to the diet came to a speedy end when 'some men pitched them with contempt out of their cells into the corridors'.[59] A complete cure had to wait on the introduction of a much fuller and more balanced diet, and even when Sir Norwood East 'joined the Prison Service in 1899 cases of scurvy occasionally occurred about April if indifferent potatoes only were available until the new crops were delivered'.[60]

The relative accuracy with which the weights of large numbers of prisoners could be recorded, and the ease with which their dietary intakes could be manipulated, created ideal conditions under which proper 'scientific' experiments could be conducted. And they were. Two experiments were carried out at Wakefield; in the first 'the greatest loss took place under the best diet'.[61] The second entailed longer-term prisoners passing through all the preceding class diets before entering the one prescribed by the tables as appropriate to the lengths of their sentences. It brought a protest from Dr Wood, the medical officer of the prison:

> On the 18th March 1863, it was my duty to report unfavourably of this diet, and the discipline which accompanied it, in consequence of the failure of the health and strength of the prisoners, the greater loss of weight, and the greater mortality. I attributed them to the altered diet and discipline.[62]

The visiting justices to the gaol, and the medical triumvirate of the inquiry, proved, to their own satisfaction at least, that Dr Wood was mistaken, but the results of the experiment were not a resounding vindication of the dietary.

The three doctors resolved nevertheless to adopt the principle of prisoners in the local gaols passing through all the preceding stages of the dietary prior to arriving at their own, and they also contrived to remove meat as an item in its own right entirely from the diet; henceforth it was to appear only in the soup, or in the unrecognizable guise of suet pudding. Cocoa was also sacrificed to public feeling, although it survived in the convict prisons.

To justify these changes, without real evidence to support them, the committee made appeal first of all to 'experience', from which they drew predictable reassurance, and then to some special pleading. Sir George Grey, they say, 'recognises the fact that a diet which shall not be more than sufficient to maintain them in health, must of necessity "be penal, as it respects the class constituting the vast majority of prisoners who, when at large, possess the means, and are in the habit of indulging in articles of food and drink which are not necessary to health." '[63] The doctors felt able, later in their report, to elaborate a little on this point. 'Again, all prisoners who, when free, lead a life of reckless self-indulgence, eating highly nutritious food, and drinking stimulant liquors, naturally accumulate fat, which they may lose with advantage; so that in the case of this entire class, an improvement of condition would be accompanied with a loss of weight: such loss of weight, be it remembered, does generally attend that improvement in health and vigour which follows upon training for athletic combats and sports, on pedestrian tours, and in sportsmen during the season.'[64] The debt to 'modern' science in this reasoning is clearly less than to a healthy, old-fashioned kind of moralizing, and one, moreover, that harmonizes nicely with Carnarvon's own conclusion that 'The low animal natures of too many of the criminal class, and the admitted efficiency of reductions in food in cases of prison offences, render plain the value of diet as one form of penal correction.'[65] So in the end 'science' had very little to do with these decisions, but the dabblings at Wakefield and other places had left a mark on the debate that was to be visible for a long time to prisoners on the look-out for someone to blame for the state of their diet: 'Doctors, skilled in such matters, consult and experimentalise; and experience has taught them on how little a man can live in good health, and perform a full amount of labour – that amount, and no more, they gave us.'[66]

A measure of meat was restored to the local dietary by the Committee of 1878; but it was a small measure: 'now what is the good of three-quarters of an ounce of bacon; let anyone weigh that quantity out and see how much it represents'.[67] To round out these infinitesimal quantities and to make a more satisfying meal, the bacon was served with beans. 'Searching for the bacon among the beans is like looking for a needle in a bundle of hay. And when it is found, it is not a tempting morsel. It is very fat bacon, suitable for greasing engine wheels.'[68] The whole dish was 'a gruesome and nauseating mixture – apt to cause sickness.'[69]

Between them, the 'Graham' tables and the 1864 recommendations had fixed what was to be the basic prison diet for the better part of the nineteenth century. Their worst defect lay in the fact that although the 'classes' recognized the sex of prisoners; the durations of their sentences; and whether they were sentenced to 'hard labour' or not, they did not take account of differences in the sizes and appetites of the individuals who composed them. One-who-has-tried-them 'always had a very small appetite, and therefore', he says 'if I could not get on there must have been something radically wrong with the diet'.[70] It was a phenomenon that caught the attention of Dr Quinton: 'The conditions of prison life, with the necessity it entails of issuing carefully measured diets to men in separate cells, tend to bring out prominently the marked differences of appetite in men of apparently similar physique, and to lend probability to the doctrine that appetite is to a great extent a matter of training and habit.'[71] And it moved Henry Harcourt to assert that the diet 'was wholly insufficient for a big man, say a man six feet'.[72] Mark Jeffrey was a 'big man' and he complained forcefully to a warder about the size of his dinner: ' "There is many a man in London who does not get as much as that," he said. "London!" I exclaimed. "They are all dwarfs there, but I am a man six feet one inch in height and fifteen stone in weight, and it requires more than what I get to support me." '[73]

On this diet, calculated if not with precision then at least with deliberation to fall as far this side as possible of anything that might be called 'luxurious living',[74] and only just beyond the minimum limit at which it might begin to cause 'loss of health and strength',[75] many prisoners felt 'eternally hungry'.[76] 'A man goes to bed hungry and gets up hungry, in fact he is always hungry; and this lasts for not weeks, not months, but for years.'[77]

More palpably Balfour suffered from 'a severe and constant form of indigestion'.[78] Dr McCook Weir found out 'what it was to have a pile'. He also became uncomfortably aware of the 'extreme flatulency' of a fellow prisoner. This colleague attributed his condition – and in McCook Weir's opinion 'rightly too – to the unvaried regimen of his prolonged incarceration'. In a tone that concedes nothing to any possible vulgarity the doctor warms to his medical theme: 'Nor is his flatulency merely an inconvenience. A prisoner can soon poison the limited column of air in his cell, and if not attentive to the ventilation such as it is, he will soon find himself in a mephitic atmosphere.'[79] Lord William Nevill noted 'the enormous number of prisoners who were admitted to the infirmary where he worked 'suffering from indigestion in various forms – spots, boils, and rashes and other skin diseases'.[80]

And a compendium of ill-effects – all of them ascribed to the prison diet – is supplied by One-who-has-suffered-it. 'When, by-and-by, he can eat the unpalatable mess provided, he acquires chronic indigestion, dimness of eye-sight, tinnitus aurum, roarings in the head, gastric spasms, shortness of breath, sickly giddiness, and absence of "staying" power generally. In addition', as if the rest were not enough, 'he may contract heart disease.'[81] Missing from this catalogue is the most obvious symptom of a reduced diet, which is loss of weight: Brocklehurst 'rapidly lost flesh';[82] Balfour 'lost two stones in weight';[83] Ticket-of-leave-man 'went down from twelve stone to nine';[84] the Tichborne Claimant 'lost 7 st. in weight in seven months'.[85] 'It is commonly asserted by prison surgeons and officials', says One-who-has-tried-them, 'that prisoners usually gain weight while in prison.' His privileged position in the prison office gave him access to records from which he was able to check the accuracy of the official view. 'When the Criminal Registry came into my hands I carefully examined into this matter, and found that more than ninety per cent of the prisoners *lost* weight.'[86]

He also translated some of the official arguments about diet into terms he could convey to some of his fellow prisoners:

> It is frequently urged by members of Parliament and others that the class of men who ordinarily find their way into prison never have been accustomed to good food, and this is perfectly true in many cases; and I have used this argument myself to several prisoners, but the reply I invariably got, if vulgar, was unanswerable. 'Quite true, sir, our food is rough, but we get a bellyful of it; here it's very rough, and we don't get as much in a day as we should eat at one meal when we are out of prison.'[87]

The diet also had consequences that went beyond mere weight loss. Austin Bidwell witnessed the effects on Chatham convicts 'of hunger and torment of mind. The first part visibly affected was the neck. The flesh shrinks, disappears and leaves what look like two artificial props to support the head.'[88] A man that Brocklehurst saw 'was sunburnt and healthy' when he came into prison, but 'at the end of a few days this splendid specimen of humanity was crawling round the exercise-yard, with head bent, and with feet scarcely lifting from the ground'.[89]

Prisoners countered what many of them clearly saw as a threat to their physical integrity – their earthly survival even – with a number of defensive strategies. The first of them was an acute sensitivity to the weight of the food they were given, and especially of the bread. The author of *Revelations of Prison Life* insists that although 'the loaf of bread is reputed to be of six, eight and ten ounces in weight, according to class', it 'is *always* short weight'.[90] Old lags were reputedly able to gauge the weight of their loaves to the nearest ounce simply by weighing them in their hands. Prison cooks took precautions against accusations of deficiencies by affixing to short-weight loaves small cubes or 'jockeys' of bread to make up the full amount;[91] and it was the practice to have handy a pair of scales so that bread and other items could be weighed on the spot and supplemented if short. 'For some months', Jabez Balfour 'had charge of the scales which are kept for weighing the rations when a convict desires it, and when I speak of men always hungry I speak of what I know.'[92] The quantities of the published dietary were also subject to alteration during the baking: 'The bread as a rule was half baked at Portland in order to keep it wet and damp, so as to take less bread to keep it up to weight; at Portland the bread was what you call soaked, you could squeeze it up like a lump of putty.'[93]

Cooking was one of the keys to a second sensitivity developed by prisoners, which was to the quality of the rations served up to them. At its worst the food earned simple abuse: 'I should imagine that every swine's trough around the metropolis must have been plundered to provision Holloway Gaol.'[94] A more balanced perspective was that 'the materials are good, but the cooking bad'.[95] Part of this problem lay with cooks whose 'knowledge of cookery was of the very slenderest description',[96] and part, prisoners suspected, in arrangements of the kind where 'the cook did all the private baking for the governor's family for nothing, and, in addition, assisted the chief warder to make a very comfortable thing out of the stores'.[97] Suspicions sometimes alighted on the suppliers as well: 'I only wish the contractors could be made to suffer as we suffered from bad and indifferent food.'[98] Such suspicions may have had at least some foundation in reality. An 1899 committee of inquiry into the prison dietary affirmed that the 'wheat supplied shall be good, sweet, dry, clean wheat, of best quality', but also reports that it 'received samples of whole-meal flour from every prison in England and Wales; we examined them, and the result of our examination could not be called satisfactory. Many of the samples contained an excess of coarse bran, and other defects were recognisable.'[99]

Provision was made in the prison rules for prisoners to make known any complaints they had about food. Prison Rule 9 states: 'If any prisoner has any complaint to make regarding the diet, it must be made immediately after a meal is served, and before any portion of it is eaten.' The rule struck One-who-has-tried-them as 'particularly foolish; how on earth is a man to know whether the food is bad before he tastes it?'[100] An unfortunate prisoner at Lancaster made his complaint too late. In a suicide note he 'referred disparagingly to the food given', but fortunately for the good name of the prison kitchen, 'he was assuredly insane, as the Coroner declared at the inquest.'[101]

There was a point however beyond which the reactions of prisoners to their food could not be brushed aside; a point where collective trouble brewed in the empty bellies of individuals. 'One Sunday – which was known as pork-soup day, because the dinner consisted then only of one pint of pork-soup and eight ounces of bread for full labour men – the pork that the soup was made of was absolutely putrid. . . . There was a tremendous noise in our hall during the whole dinner-time which on Sunday is from twelve to two, the men banging their doors and making all the disturbance they could.'[102] Mindful of such possibilities, the authorities at Pentonville took no chances with one consignment of meat: 'when some of the mutton was rather yellow, and suspected of not being what it should be, a prisoner who was by trade a butcher was brought down to examine it. He pronounced it of excellent quality throughout. This incident shows the care used.'[103] 'On one occasion,' says the governor of Oxford, 'nearly the whole of the bread brought into the Prison on a Saturday was sour. I applied to the contractor to change it; he declined – I sent it back and bought fresh, the contractor came to the Magistrates and complained against me, he had every opportunity afforded him to state his case most fully and completely, and I am happy to say, one Magistrate said emphatically, "I think the Governor did his duty", and left the room.'[104]

Hunger also sharpened perceptions in other directions; those who had the serving of the food were watched like hawks by those who were about to eat it. When penal servitude was at its strictest in Pentonville, the rule was simple: 'No prisoner can give out bread or measure drink; everything must be distributed impartially by an impartial officer',[105] since 'if a prisoner had the distribution of these loaves it would be his fortune while in office. He would be the prince of the ward.'[106] The 'impartial officer' did not always escape the jealous attentions of hungry men either: 'a prisoner at Coldbath Fields, on the mere supposition that the bread served to him at dinner was smaller than that of his neighbour, was so angered, that, breaking open one of the warder's boxes, he obtained possession of a knife, and two days after the imaginary wrong had been committed, stabbed the officer whom he taxed as the author of it.'[107] Local prisons with more relaxed regimes permitted prisoners to serve food, but 'The warders always give their cleaners plenty to eat, so as to prevent their taking the food belonging to the other prisoners while they are engaged in arranging the mess tins on the trays ready for distribution.'[108] Despite these precautions the cleaners would 'often hand a six ounce instead of an eight ounce loaf to prisoners whom they have a spite against, and give them gruel instead of porridge; whilst to their own "chums" who are on the smaller scale of diet, they give the large loaf and the porridge.'[109]

WORMS

Acute hunger cut two ways for prisoners; at the same time as it sharpened up their perceptions of quantity, and quality, and equity in distribution, it also served to dull their ordinary sensibilities about what it was proper to eat. 'To find black beetles in soup, "skilly", bread, and tea, was quite a common occurrence', according to Michael Davitt, 'and some idea can be formed of how hunger will reconcile a man to look without disgust upon the most filthy objects in nature, when I state as a fact that I have often discovered beetles in my food, and have eaten it after throwing them aside, without experiencing much revulsion of feeling at the sight of such loathsome animals in my victuals'.[110] O'Donovan Rossa went one better than his compatriot: 'if when eating my eight ounces of bread I found a beetle or a ciarogue cracking between my teeth, instead of spitting out in

Carrying food trays

disgust what I was chewing, I would chew away with the instinctive knowledge that nature had provided for the carrying away of anything that was foul and the retaining of what was nutritious from what I swallowed'.[111]

Beetles, bad as they sound, were to be found only a short way into that strange territory where hungry convicts went in search of food. 'In our hunger', says Austin Bidwell 'there was no vile refuse we would not devour greedily if the opportunity occurred.'[112] Convicts in this state were known to 'eat all sorts of green weeds, and if they can secretly get hold of a carrot or onion, they ram it into their mouth, tops, dirt and all'.[113] They ate 'railway grease',[114] or 'brown paper mingled with ravellings from a hole in the dirty sheet',[115] and even the paper 'issued weekly from the stores for sanitary purposes'.[116] Men were seen 'to eat a soft sort of earth at Dartmoor',[117] and at Chatham, 'with serious results to the un-natural feeders.'[118] They would eat candles; 'notwithstanding that a highly offensive smell is purposely given to prison candles to prevent their being eaten instead of burned'. Michael Davitt even saw 'bits of candles pulled out of the prison cesspool and eaten, after the human soil was wiped off them!'[119] A 'man of the name of Harrison' – a convict at Dartmoor, was observed to eat 'grass, candles, and dubbing, which they used to allow to rub your boots with'.[120] And at Portland, 'it was considered by a certain class of prisoners quite a privilege to be attached to the "cart party", on account of the refuse, food and poultices which could be fished out of the infirmary ashes'.[121] Not to be outdone, Harrison was also seen 'to eat a poultice'.[122] At Portland, Ticket-of-leave-man came across 'half a dozen men who fed themselves daily upon snails, slugs, and frogs, and they did this not only without any interference on the part of the officer in charge, but to his evident amusement'.[123] Another Dartmoor convict – not the semi-legendary Harrison this time, but certainly one worthy of licking his boots, 'had a handful of earth worms and was in the act of putting salt on them to eat them, when the officer took them away from him.'[124]

The Penal Servitude Commission of 1879, which heard about these practices from former prisoners, appeared keen to allay any anxieties their report might create in its readers.

> It has been stated in evidence that some prisoners eat candles, but we believe this to arise from a desire to eat more fat than the dietary affords, and not from any deficiency in the quantity or quality of the diet. . . . A few convicts were also mentioned as having eaten refuse of various kinds and of disgusting quality whenever they had the opportunity. Similar cases of depraved voracity are sometimes met with among persons other than prisoners, and notably among persons of weak mind.[125]

So it was just a question of greed on the one hand, and of simple minds on the other. Perceptive readers, then as now, would find it easier to interpret this sort of behaviour as that of men made desperate by hunger.

REDISTRIBUTION

Whenever it proved possible, hungry prisoners made efforts to redistribute their irrationally allocated rations on a more equitable basis. 'In the Surrey prison,' says A Merchant, 'the practice of exchanging and trafficking in food amongst the prisoners counteracted the evils that would otherwise have resulted from the regulations being strictly adhered to.'[126] The suppliers in this life-saving market were those with smaller appetites, men and women who could not consume all the food they were given – sometimes because they were too ill, or because they were cleaners or cooks with access to institutional supplies of bread and other foodstuffs. It was also a market that was partly based on altruism. 'The allowance was not enough to support a big man in life,' says David Fannan who worked as orderly in the punishment block at Portland, 'and I could not help pitying them, and smuggling odd bits of bread into their cells.'[127] 'Sometimes,' says Chicago May, 'another prisoner, not so voracious as I was, would slip me a hunk of bread.' 'When I would get this extra food, I would soak it in water until it became twice its usual size. Then, when I ate it, I tried to kid myself that it was quite filling and satisfying.'[128] The same trick could be done internally with salt; some men 'were in the habit of eating a spoonful or two after each meal, in order to make themselves exceedingly thirsty, as they were then enabled to fill their stomachs out with a large quantity of water.'[129] If bread was not offered, it was often asked for, and just as often willingly given. A youth gave the author of *Pentonville Prison from Within* 'his brown roll when I told him I was hungry, and never failed to whisper as he passed me the magic words, "Cheer up!" '[130]

Venally minded prisoners on the other hand, needed no bidding to cash in on the hunger of their companions; Captain D— S— 'found that prisoners would do anything for food' and for the rest of his sentence 'bartered it in exchange for soap &c.'[131] Manchester Merchant 'managed to obtain a constant supply of tobacco' in payment for his surplus bread.[132] A more sinister form of barter was attempted with the young Stuart Wood. 'Each day,' he says, 'I found one or more loaves in my cell and, my hunger satisfied, I began to feel that God was in His heaven and all was right with the world.' One night his hitherto anonymous benefactor, the wing cleaner, came to capitalize on his 'investment'. 'In one hand he held a long knitting needle with which he had dexterously picked the lock, and in the other he had some dubbin. . . . "You're going to be nice to Papa, ain't you?" he said. Even then', says Wood, 'I was too utterly green to take his meaning.' 'There can be no manner of doubt,' he thought, 'that this particular cleaner, and others like him, having in their hands the powerful bribe that extra food actually was to hungry boys, succeeded in seducing many of them in those bad old days.'[133]

If charity and trade both failed, thieves resorted to theft to secure their extra supplies of food. 'Habitual thieves frequently prey on each other even in prison if they get a chance, and act apparently on the "fair game" theory amongst themselves.'[134] 'Pinching food is a favourite trick.' Manchester Merchant caught one in his cell: 'one of the loaves dropped from underneath his jacket, then he implored me to forgive him, and declared that he was starving. I felt sorry for him, and allowed him to eat the bread, but warned him to never enter my cell again. This kind of thieving is of daily occurrence, and creates no small amount of disturbance.'[135]

JAM

Remarkably, some 'luxurious' items slipped through the fine nets that were repeatedly trawled through the Victorian prison diet with the express intention of fishing them out. These were the little treats that could be bought out of the gratuities credited to long-term prisoners like John Lee against the day of their release. He was allowed to spend one and threepence. 'Amongst the things you can buy are the following "comforts", of which I also give the prison prices':-

Oranges	¾d. each.
Figs	4d. per lb.
Dates	4d. per lb.
Apples	4d. per lb.
English Tomatoes	7d. per lb.
Nuts	5d. per lb.
Bananas	1d. each.
Plum Jam	4d. per pot.

But even when the regime allowed these 'comforts' the prisoner was required to exercise a continuing vigilance. 'I soon discovered that sometimes you would get forty dates, another time you would only get twenty for the same money. I went to the governor and asked him if we could have the things put down in a list with the prices, and he made out the list I have already given. Perhaps you smile as you think of the idea of counting up dates. But I can assure you that after years of prison fare, most of which is not fit to eat, dates are a rare luxury, to be counted carefully and husbanded as long as they can possibly last.'[136]

Another rare luxury, only experienced from the end of the nineteenth century onwards, was the marking of royal occasions with some extra food. When the Prince of Wales visited Portland, he asked the governor to give the men 'some special treat by way of commemoration', and they had 'half-a-pound of suet pudding and two ounces of golden syrup for dinner'.[137] Likewise, the 'Coronation of His Majesty the King' was marked with a menu 'the same as that of Christmas Day – even tho' it might be mid-summer, as it was when our present gracious Sovereign was crowned. The fare included a lusty helping of beef and vegetables, and secondly, excellent plum-pudding.'[138] The women at Aylesbury were similarly treated: 'one Christmas, after George ascended the throne, we got roast beef and plum-pudding. The heavy meal nearly killed many of the convicts, they appreciated it so much.'[139]

THE MEDICAL OFFICER

Food in the Victorian prison was weighed on scales as delicate as those of Justice herself. A little too much on *this* side and the likes of Carlyle would hurry to dip their pens in vitriol; a little too little on *that* and prisoners would fall ill or die – 'a punishment not contemplated by law' according to Sir James Graham, 'and which it is unjust and cruel to inflict.'[140] Equally powerful sections of opinion supported the latter view: 'I presume that your medical officer will inform you', Mr Justice Byles told the Grand Jury of Maidstone in December 1862, 'that, with the infliction of the separate system, a diet more or less generous, is, to the bulk of the labouring classes, *absolutely indispensable*. If you deviate from it, it may be that you deprive the labouring man of his only wealth – his constitution – and in comparison to such a sentence as that, to sentence him to be hanged would be comparative mercy.'[141]

Prison officials sought unceasingly to strike a balance between the two sides; tending to agree with those who cried 'luxury', whilst taking what precautions they could to prevent too much damage being done to the prisoners in their charge. The 1878 committee on prison dietaries conceived 'that we should ill-discharge our functions if we were to lose sight of the fact that prisoners are, to some extent, maintained at the expense of those whom they have injured'.[142] They visited a number of prisons, and 'conversed with many prisoners; we have watched them at all hours of the day; and we cannot avoid the conclusion that, in a large number of classes, imprisonment, as now generally conducted, is a condition more or less akin to that of "physiological rest". The struggle for survival is suspended; and the prisoner appears to feel that the prayer for daily bread is rendered unnecessary by the solicitude of his custodians. Tranquillity of mind and freedom from anxiety are leading characteristics of his life.'[143] Under the influence of this idyllic delusion the committee decided that to give short-term prisoners 'a diet necessary for the maintenance of health during the longer terms would, in our opinion, be to forgo an opportunity for the infliction of salutary punishment'.[144] 'In other words', says Lord William Nevill, 'they deliberately urged that starvation should be added to imprisonment and labour as a punishment in English gaols.'[145]

Lord William was right, but he omitted one thing. When the previous committee on diets of 1864 made their recommendations for reducing the existing dietary scales they did so subject to a number of conditions, and 'unless these conditions are observed', they warned, 'we do not hold ourselves responsible for any injury to the health of prisoners which may result from their adoption'. The first of them was: 'That it shall be the duty of the medical officer of the prisons in which these dietaries are in force, to see every prisoner on admission, and to certify his fitness or otherwise to be placed upon the several dietaries in succession; and that if the prisoner be found unfit, it shall be incumbent upon the medical officer to indicate the dietary upon which he shall be first placed.'[146] Two things flowed from this proviso. It allowed the tables and scales to be retained intact, whilst allowing a degree of flexibility in individual cases, at the discretion of the medical officer. But the discretion thus placed in the doctor's hands raised tantalizing visions of food before the eyes of hungry prisoners. It was a discretion that helped swell the ranks of those who went 'sick' each day, and helped as well to turn the practice of medicine in prisons into a battleground between desperate and cunning convicts and suspicious and resentful surgeons.

NOTES

1. McCook Weir, 90.
2. Rossa, 103.
3. Dawson, 80.
4. Kenney, 93.
5. Field, I., 68.
6. H. Gordon, 12.
7. Brocklehurst, 119.
8. Kerr, 123.
9. Dietaries (1864), 26.
10. Sir J.R.G. Graham, *PP* (1843)
11. Dietaries (1878), 11.
12. Cooper, 238.
13. Dawson, 81.
14. Brocklehurst, 119.
15. Gladstone Committee (1895), 286.
16. Ibid., 35.
17. Henderson, 36.
18. WBN, 111.
19. J. Balfour, 47.
20. McCook Weir, 86.
21. Mitchell, 148.
22. McCook Weir, 93.
23. WBN, 110.

24. J. Balfour, 265.
25. *Pentonville Prison from Within*, 37.
26. Barrow, 9.
27. One-who-has-tried-them, I, 154.
28. Lovett, 223.
29. Allen, 17.
30. Howard Association, 96.
31. J. Balfour, 264.
32. Penal Servitude Commission (1879), 352.
33. Rossa, 103.
34. Mayhew, 130.
35. Carnarvon Committee (1863), 360.
36. McCook Weir, 89.
37. Lytton, 70.
38. J. Balfour, 259.
39. Female Debtor, 13.
40. J. Balfour, 264.
41. McCook Weir, 93.
42. Foote, 130.
43. *Pentonville Prison from Within*, 36.
44. Female Debtor, 6.
45. *Pentonville Prison from Within*, 37.
46. Rossa, 87.
47. Lytton, 183.
48. Carnarvon Committee (1863), 361.
49. Ibid., 364.
50. Ibid., 311.
51. Carlyle (1850), 252.
52. Carlyle (1850a), 99.
53. Carnarvon Committee (1863), ix.
54. Dietaries (1864), 51.
55. Griffiths (1875), I, 84.
56. Dietaries (1864), 51.
57. Carnarvon Committee (1863), 359.
58. Lee, 76.
59. Fannan, 103.
60. East, 68.
61. Dietaries (1864), 54.
62. Ibid., 65.
63. Ibid., 22.
64. Ibid., 54.
65. Carnarvon Committee, IX.
66. 'Twenty years', 677.
67. One-who-has-tried-them, I, 154.
68. Nicoll, 5.
69. *Pentonville Prison from Within*, 134.
70. One-who-has-tried-them, I, 155.
71. Quinton, 209.
72. Penal Servitude Commission (1879), 352.
73. Hiener, 72.
74. Dietaries (1864), 27.
75. Ibid., 22.
76. Wood, 64.
77. Howard Association, 92.
78. J. Balfour, 265.
79. McCook Weir, 85.
80. WBN, 114.
81. One-who-has-suffered-it, 588.
82. Brocklehurst, 122.
83. J. Balfour, 75.
84. Ticket-of-leave-man, 80.
85. Orton, 29.
86. One-who-has-tried-them, II, 240.
87. Ibid., I, 156.
88. A. Bidwell, 456.
89. Brocklehurst, 122.
90. One-who-has-suffered, 14.
91. One-who-has-tried-them, II, 283.
92. J. Balfour, 265.
93. Penal Servitude Commission (1879), 352.
94. Foote, 130.
95. Letter, 495.
96. One-who-has-tried-them, II, 29.
97. Ibid., II, 29.
98. Lee, 74.
99. Dietaries (1899), 20.
100. One-who-has-tried-them, I, 173.
101. Llewellin, 15.
102. WBN, 106.
103. Letter, 496.
104. Kebbel, 24.
105. Rossa, 131.
106. Ibid., 130.
107. Mayhew, 350.
108. One-who-has-tried-them, II, 231.
109. *Kirkdale*, 31.
110. Davitt (1886), 17.
111. Rossa, 95.
112. A. Bidwell, 451.
113. WBN, 115.
114. Griffiths (1904), 176.

115. One-who-has-suffered, 18.
116. No. 7, 71.
117. Penal Servitude Commission (1879), 355.
118. Griffiths (1904), 176.
119. Davitt (1886), 18.
120. Penal Servitude Commission (1879), 355.
121. Ticket-of-leave-man, 226.
122. Penal Servitude Commission (1879), 527.
123. Ticket-of-leave-man, 225.
124. Penal Servitude Commission (1879), 355.
125. Ibid., xxxviii.
126. Henderson, 187.
127. Fannan, 98.
128. Sharpe, 187.
129. One-who-has-tried-them, II, 237.
130. *Pentonville Prison from Within*, 72.
131. D— S—, 210.
132. *Kirkdale*, 15.
133. Wood, 65.
134. Quinton, 79.
135. *Kirkdale*, 67.
136. Lee, 74.
137. Ibid., 77.
138. Llewellin, 20.
139. Sharpe, 188.
140. Dietaries (1864), 22.
141. Gibson, 54.
142. Dietaries (1878), 19.
143. Ibid., 5.
144. Ibid., 7.
145. WBN, 103.
146. Dietaries (1864), 76.

8
SICK . . .

Daily medical care was available to the mid-Victorian prisoner on demand. But to prevent its being seen as in any sense a disinterested service to the sick or afflicted, its provision was hedged about with procedural obstacles, and an air of deterrent unpleasantness. The routine at Parkhurst was for the prisoner to hand in 'a small wooden ticket or token', when his door was first opened in the morning.[1] At Leicester County Gaol the doctor would pass along the landings each day: 'the doors used to be opened, and they used to say, "Surgeon, surgeon", but you scarce had a sight of the surgeon; he went like a puff of wind by your door'.[2] Either by handing in a tally, or catching the eye of the surgeon as he wafted past the door, or by some other means, prisoners signalled their desire for medical attention and were duly assembled for the 'sick parade'. In one prison at least, this took place *alfresco*, since the doctor 'paid a daily visit to the exercise yard, which saved him the trouble of going the round of the prisoners' cells. Feelings of delicacy are totally ignored in prison. It was not perhaps pleasant to have to state the particulars of one's ailment in the hearing of other prisoners, but one had to do so, or deny oneself the luxury of being physicked.'[3]

Procedures elsewhere were rarely quite so barbarous. The Parkhurst tallies, for example, were taken to the hospital, and the names of the applicants entered into a ledger. 'Every morning, immediately after the "cease labour" bell at

11.10, the "casual sick" are collected from their parties as they return to the prison, and are escorted to the office or consulting room, where they are received by one of the assistant medical officers.'[4]

Large numbers of men joined this 'parade'; 'Seventy or eighty would not be an unknown number.'[5] The daily sick list at Portsmouth, where Dr Quinton began his career in the prison medical service, 'amounted to almost 10 percent of the population, although the men were all supposed to be able-bodied and fit for a Public Works Prison'.[6] Similarly, 'out of about 1,000 men at Dartmoor,' as Ticket-of-leave-man recalls it, '150 applied to see the doctor every day. Not all of them of course were ill. I speak entirely of my own knowledge and from information gained from the men themselves, when I say that certainly 100 out of the 150, had nothing on earth the matter with them, and had they been free men, would no more have thought of going to the doctor, than they would of going to church.'[7] Quinton's estimate was lower still: 'out of a hundred of these daily applicants, not more than a dozen really needed medical treatment of any kind'.[8]

The queues were swollen by the powers of the surgeon, almost miraculous in the circumstances, to transform the daily life of the convict. He could pass men fit for hard labour or not – he could remove them from this working party or that, and have them placed elsewhere; from outdoors to indoors, or vice versa; he could order the issue of additional and temptingly different items of diet; he could admit men to the restful and nourishing confines of the prison hospital; he could pronounce them fit or unfit to withstand the imposition of dietary or corporal punishment; and in extreme cases he could recommend the immediate release of prisoners on medical grounds. And in none of this could he be gainsaid by the discipline staff; not by the governor or the chief or any of his officers. 'The position of the medical staff in convict prisons is very remarkable', according to Lord William Nevill. 'In some respects they are more powerful than the Governor or even than the Directors, for though they have no authority over the general discipline of the prison, they have entire control of the men in hospital, and they also have absolute discretion in all cases of punishment.'[9]

The manner in which surgeons accomplished their different duties clearly reflected the state of Victorian medicine at large. In the absence of any really effective treatment for many nineteenth-century ailments, it was normal to prescribe rest, nutritious diet, and in some cases a change of air. Prison doctors, within obvious limits, also prescribed these remedies, and therein lay the overwhelming attraction of the sick parade. Rest from hard labour, on the crank or the wheel or the back-breaking public works, and the possibility of extra food from the well-stocked medical larder appealed equally to the sick *and* the well; the exhausted *and* the indolent; to the hungry *and* the greedy.

Extra food could mean anything from a dose of 'castor oil',[10] or 'cod liver oil',[11] to the bounteous fare supposedly dispensed in the infirmary at Pentonville: 'Flesh, fish and fowl, port wine, brandy, stout, and bottled ales, custards, puddings and other un-prison-like luxuries, are all at the disposal of the medical staff.'[12] But such luxuries were beyond the hopes of the average convict who reported sick to improve his diet. One-who-has-tried-them for instance, received 'extra milk'.[13] Oscar Wilde was 'allowed by the Doctor to have white bread to eat instead of the coarse black or brown bread of ordinary prison fare'.[14] And the Tichborne Claimant was 'ordered a little boiled mutton every day'.[15] Thomas Cooper made an impassioned protest against being 'starved' on 'skilly and bad potatoes', and 'the surgeon prescribed some extra food . . . two boiled eggs, with coffee and bread and butter'.[16] All of these were far from rare events. 'While engaged balancing the provision books', One-who-has-tried-them 'carefully went over the list of men for whom the surgeon had ordered extra food, and found that there was not a single man who had been in the prison more than twelve months, that was not in receipt of extra food of some kind or the other'.[17]

So every day the hopefuls queued to see the doctor; some in search of food, others 'anxious to be taken off the tread-wheel or hard labour',[18] others for 'an opportunity of conversing with their "chums" '[19] and some who would 'do anything, take anything, or go anywhere for variety'.[20] In order to weed out some of these undeserving cases, *all* the applicants were subjected to long delays and other 'ordeals'. 'I will not detail', says Jabez Balfour, 'the various wearisome formalities which the "casual sick" go through before they obtain access to the doctor – the marchings and counter-marchings, the calling-out of names, the falling into position, and the weary waiting involved.' He found objectionable the exposure of supposedly ill individuals to 'the fatigue which this process inflicts, and what is still more . . . the severities of English weather.'[21]

'NO. 1 AND NO. 2'

These preliminaries made little impression on the numbers presenting themselves, which created an immediate problem for Dr Quinton and his colleagues. 'As about a hundred had to be seen in the space of three-quarters of an hour it was essential to be quick in diagnosis and ready with treatment, which was accordingly administered on the spot from the compounder's tray.'[22] As an added deterrent, but also partly to satisfy the craving for something different to taste, these instant 'treatments' would consist of three or four not very pleasant palliatives; one or two substances to be taken internally, and some kind of embrocation to be applied externally. The administration of the assorted potions is described by One-who-has-endured-it.

The Doctor, the apothecary, and a hospital orderly carrying a tray with a few bottles of medicines, and a hospital warder come round, attended by the principal of the prison on duty. The cell door is opened; the prisoner stands at the door and salutes the medico, who does not trouble to ask what is the matter: the man tells or shows what it is.

'I've sprained my wrist, sir,' or my leg, whatever it may be.

Doctor looks at it.

'Give him some liniment.'

'Hold your hand,' shouts apothecary.

The man holds it out, and it is filled with some stuff – hartshorn and oil, or opodeldoc. The door is slammed to, and there stands the man, his dinner half finished, and his hand full of some filthy smelling stuff, to make the best use of he can. Perhaps instead of a sprain it is a sore.

'Give him some ointment.'

'Hold something to put in in', shouts the apothecary. The man turns round to find something; apothecary cannot wait; so with the spatula he puts a dab of ointment onto the side of his plate where his dinner is. This actually happened to me; I never used my plate for dinner after that, but always ate it out of the tin it came in.[23]

The non-medical nature of this activity is underlined by the names attached to the various substances on the apothecary's tray. ' "Number one," cried the surgeon. "Put your tongue out," echoed the nurse, and with a spatula he would lay on a great slice of some pasty substance, which was swallowed without protest, not seldom with manifest relish. "Number two" would be some species of uninviting black draught.'[24]

DISORDERS

Amongst the malingerers and the sensation-seekers who crowded out the sick parade there were of course genuine sufferers from different diseases and disorders. Some of these they had brought into prison with them, and some were brought on by the conditions of imprisonment itself. Of the latter, the most prevalent were disorders of the digestion caused by the diet. Diarrhoea and constipation made a dialectical commentary on the bread and skilly and potatoes. William Lovett would not eat gruel after he 'took up a black-beetle in about the first spoonful', and tried to satisfy his appetite 'for a few days with a little bread soaked in cold water for breakfast, and a morsel of bread and cheese for dinner. But this diet in a short time brought on a horrible diarrhoea.'[25] The surgeon to whom he appealed for help was not sympathetic. 'Even when I was so weakened by the diarrhoea as not to be able to sit upright, he certified that I was suffering from a mere attack of the bowels common at that season of the year.'[26] Diarrhoea was not to be unequivocally linked to diet for a long time. The Royal Commission which investigated Leicester Gaol in 1853 was of the opinion that 'it is not improbably connected with an impure state of the air within the prison, since the area surrounded by the high boundary-wall is much too limited for the number of buildings and of the prisoners it includes, and the ventilation of the cells is far from being perfect'.[27]

There were no corresponding theories about the origins of constipation. After he 'had been six weeks without a motion', Henry Harcourt begged the doctor: 'give me some opening medicine'. The doctor said ' "What a stink there will be when you do have one," and he laughed at me, and brought the prison assistants and officers, all laughing at me.'[28] A 'dose of cascara . . . repeated every morning'[29] was given to another prisoner as a matter of routine, and it was systematically applied to Steinie Morrison, although probably for different reasons:

> From the very moment of my admission to the hospital they began to ply me with opening medicine three or four times a day, besides bromide and sleeping draughts. Such food, therefore, as was given to me, ran right through my system before it had time to do any good, and every day they kept repeating to the doctor that my bowels were closed, and every day he kept on ordering some more opening medicine.[30]

Morrison was a notoriously troublesome and violent man, and the laxatives were probably designed to incapacitate rather than keep him regular.

Haemorrhoids prospered under these conditions. A companion of O'Donovan Rossa, William F. Roantree 'put his hand in his boot one day, and when he drew it out it was full of blood; not spotted with it, but as he slanted the palm of his hand the blood streamed off.' 'He was in this state for three months before he was allowed to rest in the hospital.'[31] No doubt as a consequence of his chronic constipation, Henry Harcourt had haemorrhoids as well, which 'were very large round the orifice'. 'I could neither sit nor stand', he told the 1879 Penal Servitude Commission, 'I used to have to lie in this position (*describing the same*) and raise my leg.'[32]

Prisoners also suffered bodily from the cold and damp that prevailed in many places, even in the modern penitentiaries equipped with 'luxurious' heating and ventilation systems. George Bidwell 'had for some years been troubled with dyspepsia, lumbago and a throat complaint. The nature of the prison food aggravated the first, and the damp atmosphere of the English climate the others.'[33] Fellow American Mrs Maybrick suffered almost as much from the English climate, and along with 'the majority of inmates in the winter time, seldom had dry feet, if there was much rain or snow, the natural result being catarrh, influenza, bronchitis, and rheumatism, from all of which I suffered in turn'.[34]

An affliction practically unique to cellular prisons was suffered by Oscar Wilde. The time he spent 'in a white-washed cell with a flaring gas-jet at night', caused him to become 'conscious of great weakness and pain in the nerves of the eyes, and objects even at a short distance become blurred'.[35] The same condition was remarked by Inspector John Perry at Bedford Jail: 'viz. opthalmia in various stages aggravated, he thinks, by the constant view of the prisoner of whitened walls, particularly when the gas is lighted. Mr. Perry therefore recommended that the convicts be furnished with shades to their gas jets, and that the walls of each cell be tinted with drab instead of white as at present.'[36]

'FAKING'

In the ranks of the daily queues to see the doctor there were many who had no genuine affliction but who were not at all deterred by the waiting, or the prospect of a dollop of 'Number Two'. They were men in whose eyes the prizes at the doctor's disposal were worth pursuing at virtually any cost. Perfectly well men therefore simulated the symptoms of disease as various as 'paralysis, epilepsy, and insanity, spitting of blood, and vomiting of food',[37] and inflicted terrible, sometimes fatal, injuries on themselves. Doctors for their part were determined not to be taken in by these impostors. As a result, prison medicine became a battleground in which the surgeon had 'to measure his shrewdness and judgment against the deceit and the cunning of the most villainously artful and deceitful body of men in the world'.[38] The first and most serious casualties of this struggle were almost certainly the genuinely sick.

The simplest symptoms to 'fake', those of a disordered digestion, could be brought on by swallowing 'soap or soda'.[39] 'Soap would be "pinched", and rolled into pills, in order to found the plaint of diarrhoea.' 'Inordinate saline potations would be swallowed expressly to derange the stomach.' 'Lime-white was applied to the tongue, and any available rubbish would be bolted to force on a momentary sickness.'[40] In more extreme cases men would 'swallow ground glass' or 'eat poisonous insects.'[41] Soap eaten in quantity could also produce temporary disturbances of the heart rate and 'another favourite dodge was to press strongly on the ground with the big toe as the doctor was applying his stethoscope, and then suddenly relax the pressure, so that he felt their heart working violently and then gently in the most perplexing and alarming fashion.'[42]

The first defence of the doctor against these minor impositions was the threat of report and disciplinary action. Michael Davitt went to the doctor at Dartmoor with a bad throat. 'He examined my throat and told me to put out my tongue, he said that there was a little inflammation, but nothing serious, and he ordered me to be reported for falling out without sufficient reason.'[43] John Lee had a bad chest and 'saw the doctor, but he refused to give me anything. He even wanted to report me.'[44] It was the innocent who suffered most from this method for discouraging bogus applications and it was not, in any case, sufficient to deter men who were willing to raise the stakes of the game to the point where they wagered their own permanent health, and even their lives, against the chance of some temporary benefit. It was 'by no means an uncommon practice for men to make a wound on one of their limbs, and scratch it to keep it open until a really bad sore comes, or else to tie a string tightly round a limb so as to produce inflammation',[45] or to 'poison their flesh by inserting in it copper wire or worsted'.[46] One of Dr John Campbell's patients, 'invalided for disease of the leg, had a sinus extending to a great depth between the bones; and on probing it one day I discovered something loose, which on extraction was found to be a large darning-needle bound round with thread.'[47]

Alone amongst our prison authors, Stuart Wood performed such an operation on himself: 'with teeth gritted and sweat pouring down my face, I forced that needle through the fleshy parts of my knee, leg and foot and through my left hand, taking up large pinches of flesh, so that at least an inch or more of solid flesh was pierced and then drew the thread through the wounds, cutting it off so that it remained in them. I still bear the scars of that painful operation, but it was wholly futile.'[48] Other men were more inventive still. A young prisoner at Portland 'in his desperate desire to escape work severed the sinews at the back of the leg with a piece of glass'.[49] Also at Portland, one convict was asked by another 'to strike his hand with a hammer and smash it'; but he 'would not do it'. Another man did it for him 'so as to get his limb amputated and to get him into the hospital.'[50] There was a man who 'cut off his finger with the large blunt scissors used in mat-making.'[51] And a 'violent prisoner, who feigned stiffness of his index finger to avoid oakum picking, was so irate when the finger was forcibly bent that, on returning to his cell, he promptly placed the offending finger in the hinges of his table which was attached to the cell wall, and violently raised the leaf, with the result that the finger was absolutely shattered and had to be removed.'[52]

Sometimes these efforts escalated into more drastic projects involving the larger limbs. At Chatham, says Arthur Griffiths, 'there was a lamentable frequency of self-caused injuries amongst the convicts on the works. For some time the practice might be styled endemic; the motive has been variously attributed to abject despair, the reckless desire to end a life of misery, and to deliberate craft, aimed at a long and recuperative detention in the comparative ease of the hospital.' A favourite device for inflicting these 'self-mutilations' was provided by the waggons in which the clay from the excavations at Chatham was moved about the site. 'One day a convict would rush from his party, and, before he could be caught, deliberately lay his legs on the rails, immediately in front of a line of running trucks.'[53] One man known to Lord Nevill, 'a very good worker, and well behaved when I knew him, had only one arm. The other arm he had lost at Portland by deliberately placing it to be crushed between two trucks in a stone quarry, in order that he might be sent to Parkhurst.'[54] The practice of placing arms and legs under railway trucks on the works was so prevalent at one convict prison, says Dr Quinton, 'that no less than twenty-five major amputations were performed in one year.'[55] There were enough of these incidents to cause the 1879 Penal Servitude Commission to look into the matter; but not enough to make them take it seriously. 'In 1872 the number of such mutilations amounted to sixteen; in 1874 there were none. We do not think that these acts on the part of a certain number of prisoners justify the conclusion that the severity of the punishment is excessive.'[56]

Convicts who shied away from subjecting themselves to physical pain sometimes feigned 'fits', or paralysis, or insanity. They soon discovered that the tests
applied by doctors to distinguish true mental disorder from false could be just as
painful. Manchester Merchant recounts 'on one occasion, when waiting for the
doctor, seeing a man fall down and lie full length on the floor. . . . Mr. S—, the
doctor's assistant, stood by, and told him to get up, but the fellow remained
motionless. Mr. S— then went into a cell and procured a quantity of salt, which
he thrust into the man's mouth. The patient now struggled violently, and it was
manifest that the salt was not to his palate; however Mr. S— persisted for some
time in making him swallow it, and then the man sprang to his feet, and took
his place among the other prisoners.'[57] Dr Campbell favoured a slightly more
severe test in a case where he suspected that a fit was being feigned: 'we had at
once recourse to the cold *douche*, which made him jump to his feet. Before
leaving, he begged me not to report him.'[58] More severe again was the treatment meted out to a 'faker' at Cold Bath Fields during Governor Chesterton's
time; 'His head was shaved, and a blister was applied from the crown – and
thence right down the back to the termination of the spine, while other suitable
applications followed.'[59] And most drastic of all was a case known to One-who-
has-tried-them: 'On Thursday they applied a large blister to the nape of his
neck, Friday a huge mustard plaister about the size of a small bed pillow was
placed on the pit of his stomach, Saturday and Sunday they left him to enjoy the

George Bidwell (before prison)

delights of these practical jokes, and on Monday, I believe, started at him with the stomach pump.'[60] In this battle between the medical staff and the malingerer, accurate information about the symptoms of imitable conditions became assets of great value. 'To prevent this malingering, every care is taken to hide any genuine fit from the eyes of other prisoners, lest they should be able to imitate what they have seen.'[61]

PARALYSIS

To prisoners in search of a disabling condition which could be simulated without great pain or cost to themselves, paralysis of the legs must have seemed a most attractive option. No previous knowledge or experience required, just a determination not to move a muscle when the doctors or hospital staff could see. But they were wrong; a developing medical technology lay in wait for them.

George Bidwell, who up till then had been a rebellious prisoner, mentally tormented, minded to suicide, and with an eye constantly on the possibility of escape, collapsed in despair during a period of punishment. He lost consciousness, and with it, he claims, the use of his legs. As consciousness returned, 'gradually I recovered my powers of observation, and found that they were giving me a shock of electricity from a powerful battery, which had no effect on my legs, but as they applied it to other parts of the body it caused the most excruciating pain, and shook me as though it would tear every bone out of my body'.[62] The battery, a combined treatment and diagnostic tool, much favoured by prison doctors of the period, was used 'to good effect' in a case dealt with by Dr Campbell at Woking Hospital Prison. A young man was brought in, seemingly helpless.

When examined he showed a great dislike to being touched, whining and crying, and at the same time using filthy and threatening language. As the cradle appeared unnecessary, and might enable him to move his legs without being observed, I ordered it to be removed. Upon this the night officer reported that he used his legs in turning in bed. Though various remedies had been administered without effect, but galvanism had not been used, this was tried in the usual way, and as the muscles acted freely, was continued daily in spite of his insolent and violent behaviour. On the sixth day I found him standing by his bedside, but he still refused to walk. A pair of crutches were then provided for him, and in three days he was walking in the corridor. Next day, on going into the ward with the assistant medical officer to apply the battery, he was gone; and the warder informed me that he had walked down to the exercise yard with the other patients.[63]

In ordinary dealings between doctors and patients such a use of the battery would not be admissible, but prison medicine was an extraordinary branch of what was then a most inexact kind of science. Besides, we have Dr Campbell's word for it, 'that as a general rule galvanism was not brought into play till after other remedies had failed. Patients suffering from the real disease gladly submit to this or any other remedy likely to benefit them; but malingerers show a great repugnance to it.'[64] George Bidwell does not say anywhere in the 560 pages of his autobiography whether he was or was not faking his symptoms (Ticket-of-leave-man encountered him at Dartmoor and asserted that 'from the first he has steadily refused to use his legs')[65] but he certainly disliked the battery. 'So powerful a current is used that the handles once grasped, cannot be relinquished, for the muscles become cramped around them as rigid as iron, doubling up the arms, twisting and wrenching at the nerves and tendons, cords and muscles, and throwing the victim into an agony of pain which continues for as long as the doctor directs. . . . It was applied to me two or three hundred times, and when, each day I heard them coming with the battery, I began to tremble despite myself, then set my teeth to bear it, while the agony caused the perspiration to start from every pore of the body.'[66] The battery was also used on Bidwell, so he says, as a punishment for refusing to answer questions put to him by prison officials. One of the warders 'suggested to the assistant doctor that the battery would make me talk or scream . . . it caused most indescribable torture, especially when applied to the nerve centers, the eyes, mouth and ears'.[67]

Henry Harcourt, another ill-behaved prisoner, claimed to have received similar treatment with a battery, as well as being burnt 'in 11 places with a red hot instrument'.[68] George Bidwell was also plunged into a boiling bath, 'in the hope that if I were shamming inability to walk, the sudden scald would make me jump out. I felt as if every inch of skin was coming off, and made out to raise myself into a sitting posture, and there I sat in the hottest spot I had ever known'.[69]

Batteries, hot baths, and much other ill-treatment besides – their continuing application evidence of the doctors' disbelief in the reality of the symptoms – failed to shake Bidwell's insistent paralysis, so that by the time Dr Quinton 'saw him at Dartmoor at the end of eight or nine years of his sentence, long disuse of his legs had rendered him almost a cripple. The muscles were extremely wasted, and both hip and knee joints were contracted in a state of semi-flexion, so that he lay doubled up in a bundle.'[70] Shortly afterwards, he was moved permanently to Woking, the invalid prison for convicts, where Dr Campbell examined him and found the sinews of his legs 'so contracted that they were very crooked, and there was not much but skin and bone left, being quite atrophied.'[71] If his behaviour had been a pretence at the beginning, by the end, what he pretended had become real, and the photograph of Bidwell after his release from prison shows a man with bowed and deformed legs, standing with the support of a stick.[72] If it was a pretence, it had been maintained with an obduracy of purpose that was truly remarkable; but it was certainly not unique in the annals of prison medicine. A man with identical

George Bidwell (after prison)

symptoms had been 'shipwrecked on his way back from Bermuda' where he had first feigned paralysis. 'It will be acknowledged', writes A Merchant, who met him in hospital, 'that he played his part well, when even during the shipwreck he had never made the slightest attempt to move.'[73]

'PUTTING ON THE BARMY STICK'

Michael Davitt made a close study of 'fakers' in prison. ' "Fetching the farm" [obtaining infirmary treatment] is the one thing in the lagging which the worst type of these men will strain every nerve and resort to every possible device that may be calculated to impose upon the doctor and other officials to get.'

One form of it, known as 'putting on the barmy stick' or 'simulating madness', was 'often resorted to in hopes of securing removal to some other prison'.[74] It was a proceeding not without its own dangers since too effective a performance could lead to certification as a criminal lunatic, and removal to Broadmoor, from where release might prove extremely difficult. It was also a difficult impersonation to carry out successfully. To Governor Chesterton's practised eye, it was 'inconceivable how difficult is the task effectually to copy the gestures and incoherency of the really insane. There is something so touchingly sad in the disordered demeanour, and senseless discourses of that afflicted class, that factitious cheats utterly fail to produce any other impression than that of contempt and disgust.'[75]

Someone who did achieve the deception was Mark Jeffrey. 'I felt an inward prompting to feign madness. Mechanically I yielded to this strange inspiration, and, stripping every particle of clothing off my body, I tore it into shreds. Then I devoted similar attention to the writing-table and my bedding, meanwhile using my powerful voice to the best advantage and ramping and roaring around my cell like a newly caged beast.'[76] He kept up this performance for several days and was treated by the doctor as genuinely insane. Eventually he grew 'heartily tired of maintaining the deception'. On the doctor's next visit, Jeffrey 'greeted him most cordially, and laughingly referred to all that had transpired. But the doctor was a passionate man, and he did not accept my revelation with good grace, as he had been befooled and belittled before all the officers of the gaol. "I presume, doctor, you have not had much experience in mental diseases?" I queried sarcastically, as the strait jacket was being removed from me.'[77]

The real cost of this sort of 'heartless imposture' was paid by 'the poor wretches who really do become insane in prison, as it prolongs the period during which the prisoner exhibiting such symptoms must be kept under close observation.'[78] As with paralysis, these lunatic tricks for 'taking in the croaker' had 'begot detection dodges on the doctor's parts also'.[79] One of the 'dodges' was explained to Michael Davitt 'by an educated man who had "done a lagging" in C— convict prison.' Upon any convict showing symptoms of insanity, real or imaginary, he was at once placed under close observation. He was then given 'a powerful aperient disguised in some article of food', and 'an ordinary empty dinner tin would be slipped inside the door. . . . When the medicine began to operate, the patient would utilise the dinner-tin as the only utensil or convenient article to be found in his cell. The tin, is . . . after a while, handed in again as if containing the rations of the prisoner. He is again closely watched. *If he eats the contents, he is believed to be insane. If he does not, he is reported to the director for a flogging for simulating madness.*'[80]

'Fakers' who were adept in sustaining their symptoms in front of officials would sometimes take a rest from them when in the company of other prisoners. A man of this description worked alongside David Fannan: 'His gift of facial contortion was marvellous, and from the relaxed features of good sense which he wore in conversation with me, he could at once change to a look of utter imbecility and wonderment when any warder came near us.'[81] Fannan later worked as an orderly in the penal wards at Portland, where it was a part of his duties to enter the cells of refractory prisoners. One of them was a violent 'lunatic' who attacked warders but not, apparently, other prisoners working as orderlies: 'I went in and out without the slightest apprehension. We had many a pleasant chat, and a more completely sane and self-possessed man it would have been difficult to find.'[82]

The temptation to sham insanity was strong in the Victorian prison. Following the events at Pentonville in the 1840s there was a great sensitivity on the part of prison officials to any accusation that their regimes produced mental derangement in those who endured them. Prisoners, alert to the slightest weakness in their masters, soon fastened on insanity as an area that could be exploited to their own advantage. Its signs and symptoms were to be seen everywhere around them and a real fear of it was never very far from conscious apprehension in many minds. Prisoners could be heard going mad: Constance Lytton heard another woman prisoner. 'The wolf-like barking sounds of her voice turned into a human yell as she screamed out, "Nurse! Nurse! Let me out." '[83] 'The distressful cries went on intermittently for several days, after which they lapsed into groans like those of the dying.'[84] And prisoners could be *seen* going mad. A soldier called Prince was observed at exercise in Reading Gaol by Oscar Wilde: 'The hideous and deliberate grace of his gestures made him like an antic. He was a living grotesque. The other prisoners all watched him, and not one of them smiled. Everybody knew what had happened to him, and that he was being driven insane – was insane already.'[85]

SUICIDE

The most eye-catching feature of the later Victorian prison hall was the wire netting suspended between the galleries that ran round the upper stories of the building. To Lady Constance Lytton, it was what gave 'the building an abnormal appearance; newcomers question "Why is it there?" The explanation fills the mind with horror and revolt.'[86] The origins of the wire, claims Basil Thomson, lay in an incident he witnessed at Liverpool prison:

> There were four tiers and the top landing was thirty-three feet from the stone floor of the wing. Suddenly there was a crash, which I took for the slamming of a heavy door. The warders began to run towards the end of the wing, where a battered heap was lying on the stones. A young Irishman, who had had repeated convictions for drunkenness, had taken a header from the top landing, and his head and shoulder took the impact of the blow. He was still breathing when he was removed to the hospital, and the medical officer found a fracture at the base of the skull that according to all medical rules should have cut short his career, but he got better and at the end of three weeks, his discharge being over-due, he demanded his release. His eye was still dilated from the fracture, but he would listen to no advice and out he went. The result of this occurrence was that in all the sixty prisons in England and Wales, wire netting was stretched from landing to landing.[87]

No greater reproach could be laid at the door of prison discipline than that some of its subjects should decide to do away with themselves and great efforts were devoted therefore to preventing its occurrence. Hence the universal provision of netting.

The inference to be drawn from Thomson's story is that the young Irishman leaped over the balustrade in a fit of *delirium tremens*, or at least with his judgement still impaired by alcohol. Others appear to have been brought to the fatal act by the bullying of officers, instances of which can be multiplied from the writings of ex-prisoners. Ticket-of-leave-man knew of 'a very young man named Wills, of former respectability, and of some education and intelligence', who occupied a cell on the top landing: 'He had been suffering for several weeks from diarrhoea, and had been on more than one occasion subjected to punishment for committing an act which it was quite impossible for him to avoid. . . . On this Sunday morning he repeated the so-called offence under necessity, and his warder notified him that on Monday morning he should report him to the governor.' Wills was due for release the following week and a report meant the possible loss of a week's remission. 'The threat was too horrible to the poor boy; he was in exceedingly delicate health – consumption had wasted his frame. . . . He made one spring over the balustrade and his body lay upon the flags below; the leap was as from the top of a four-story house, and it was fatal. He was carried to the infirmary, and, when the prison bell tolled for vespers, he had gone to his everlasting rest.'[88]

Other suicides were caused not so much by the malevolence of individual warders as by the intractability of the system as a whole.

HILLOA! there's a great commotion on our landing this morning: what's up? A man opposite has hung himself by means of his braces. . . . And he only had a letter from his little daughter yesterday, enclosing a lock of her hair. She was on her death-bed, but the authorities would not let him have the little tress: 'tis against the Christian rules and regulations of English prisons.[89]

Several prison authors were either tempted to commit suicide, or made actual attempts on their own lives. Dr McCook Weir was deeply affected by his remand in prison on a charge of wounding his wife. After four weeks his feelings finally overcame him during the Christmas Day service in chapel, and he 'wept like a child in company of many others'.[90] That night, in his cell, having had 'the inexpressible happiness to lose consciousness for an hour or thereabouts' during the dinner period,[91] the voice of temptation came to him, 'Have you not at your hand the means of ending your miserable existence?'[92] 'See here is the cord which binds up your miserable bed, and there the handle of your gong, or better still, your stout gas bracket; and whilst you get ready, I will just shift the little wooden table out of your way, and adjust the noose. Abandoned and hopeless wretch, put forth thy hand and slay thyself.' The doctor wrestled with 'Beelzebub' who spake to him thus 'on that accursed night' and prayed,[93] and survived till 'dawn ushered in another day, and Christmas, eighteen hundred and seventy-nine was a thing of history'.[94]

Having the means to hand – a ligature of some sort, a handkerchief, boot-laces, braces, the hammock-straps – and somewhere to tether them – the window bars, the hammock-hook, or a protruding gas-pipe, was in itself no guarantee of success for the would-be suicide. The gas-pipe in particular was situated not very high up the wall, so to succeed in the last of life's tasks, another quality was required as well. It was obviously possessed by the man who 'was found stone dead, having no other means for accomplishing his purpose than the pocket-handkerchief with which he suspended himself from the gas-pipe, and the extraordinary determination which enabled him to keep his knees bent until he expired. If he had risen to his feet even for a moment, he could not have died.'[95] An even more determined man, in a cell with no gas bracket, 'succeeded in strangling himself by means of a bandage round his neck tied to a looped sheet, in the bight of which he placed his feet, and by extending them tightened the ligature. The act was unexampled for cunning and deter-mination,' says Vernon Harris, one-time governor of Dartmoor.[96] It was also 'unexampled', it might be thought, for the human unhappiness that lay behind it.

A more direct method, not so popular as hanging, was to cut one's own throat. A prisoner told the Reverend H.S. Joseph: 'I was quite tired of my life and attempted to commit suicide in the dock, at the Town Hall, during my trial: It was with a razor, which I picked up in the City Gaol, and which I believe belonged to one of the prisoners.'[97] George Bidwell took 'the tin strip used for a knife, and after sharpening it against the stone wall,' he says, 'I tried to cut my throat, but discovered that it was tough – so tough that I sawed away with all my force for some minutes, when, by the rate at which it bled, I thought it was enough to put an end to my troubles. I lost consciousness, and when I came to myself the doctor was pushing a needle through to sew up the gash, the cicatrice of which is still visible.'[98]

A novel method that occurred to George Jacob Holyoake involved the use of the furniture in his cell: 'There was just width enough in my cell to admit of the heavy iron bed-frame being raised on one end. By marking a circle round one of the legs, which I did with a fragment of stone, I determined the place on which the leg would fall when the frame was pulled down. My head once placed on that spot, the great weight of the frame would have sent the narrow leg through the brain, and death must have been instantaneous.'[99] But, then again, it might not have been – at any rate Holyoake never put his theory to the test.

Perhaps the most obvious way to certain death was simply to refuse food. In later years the 'hunger strike' became a political weapon in the hands of the suffrage campaigners, but it had a long history as a merely secular occurrence. In the first cases of self-starvation encountered by Governor Chesterton, the consumption of food was spontaneously resumed after intervals of only a few days. 'With these two examples to guide me', he says, 'I became indifferent to an occasional exhibition of this nature.'[100] His nonchalant attitude is in marked contrast to the practice which became standard later in the century. 'Obstinate refusal of food, and an attempt to die by starvation were of common occurrence,' in Arthur Griffiths's experience, 'always to be overcome by forcible feeding'.[101] At Parkhurst during Lord William Nevill's time 'there was a black man undergoing a life sentence for murder who made up his mind to starve himself to death'. After several days 'the doctors attempted to feed him by artificial means. As they could not force the feeding-tube between his teeth they made shift to feed him through his nose. About an hour afterwards he was found dead from a sort of convulsion or paroxysm of rage at the doctors having succeeded in feeding him against his will.'[102] David Fannan worked as orderly in the hospital at Portland where such cases were dealt with. 'As regards the suicides', he says, 'it was astonishing the length of time they continued to live so long as they got water to drink. When this was stopped they collapsed at once.'[103]

A popular method of suicide in outside society, then as now, was poisoning – but more difficult to achieve in prison because of the rarity of suitable materials. When Stuart Wood decided to kill himself, he looked around for a way of accomplishing the act.

I had noticed that the twine for sewing coal sacks had an acrid smell as if it had been steeped in some acid or other; I noticed too that if it got into a cut it would quickly fester. Surely it was poisonous! and if it were steeped in water it could poison the water. . . . So I took a large skein of it and soaked it in water for twenty-four hours and drank it! It was vile! But it didn't work. I was sick and ill, but not ill enough; the doctor merely glanced at me and ordered a dose of white mixture.[104]

The doctor then did something else which was symptomatic of the official response to prisoners who tried but failed to kill themselves. 'A report was made charging me with malingering', says Wood. 'I got three days bread and water and the usual solitary confinement.'[105] A man who survived a fall from the landings 'was brought before the visiting justices, and in consideration of his youth only got seven days in the punishment cells'.[106] A prisoner at Pentonville 'was cut down in a very sad condition, and conveyed as soon as possible across the road to the police court, where he was charged with attempting to commit suicide.' They 'let him off with a caution.' But whilst the magistrate was lenient, the prison authorities passed a different judgement on him. He was, on his return, 'conveyed to a padded cell in the hospital, and there, dressed in a strait-waistcoat, was fain to lie prone on the ground of the cell at meal-times, and lick up, as a cat might the crumbs of bread which were sprinkled about for him, it being impossible for him to use his arms.'[107] These apparently unfeeling reactions grew out of deeply rooted attitudes towards both the 'sin' and the 'criminal offence' of suicide and attempted suicide. Some of them are clearly revealed in the sequel to a suicide that took place in Cold Bath Fields Prison at the beginning of Chesterton's governorship. Captain H—, a respectable gentleman, had resorted to counterfeiting bank-notes to pay his bills, and after his arrest and remand in custody made a determined and successful bid to hang himself. In a letter he left to his wife, 'he spoke of his unfortunate children with equanimity, and counselled their mother as to their education and destination, and, in short, displayed so clear and discriminating a judgment, even in that solemn extremity, that the jury, on the inquest, unanimously pronounced a verdict of *Felo de se*. . . . His dishonoured remains were consigned to the earth at four cross roads in the parish of Clerkenwell, not very far from the scene of his degraded exit.'[108]

THE HOSPITAL

For prisoners on the 'sick parade' admission to the hospital came second only to medical release in the desirability of the benefits at the disposal of the surgeon. The hospital was correspondingly high on the list of positions which doctors took good care to fortify against entry by all but the most obviously ill, or the most determined of impostures. So when admission was granted to Austin Bidwell, without his having sought it, it was for him a piece of 'happy fortune'.

A smallpox scare was existing outside, and all hands in the prison were ordered to be vaccinated. When the doctor came round a few days afterwards to examine the effects of the operation, he found my arm so swollen that he directed me to be taken to the hospital. . . . With nothing to do but read my Shakespeare, the cravings of hunger for the first time since my imprisonment satisfied, I was tempted to believe – that the world had few positions pleasanter than mine.[109]

And nor did it – in prison anyway; it was 'a haven of rest'[110] and a promised land of abundant food.

Dr McCook Weir's 'change of diet to a mutton chop daily, a good supply of well-stewed rice pudding and new milk; tea, instead of the filthy cocoa, which was also retained, and an extra pint of milk, at eleven o'clock daily, soon cut short my illness.'[111] There was so much food in the hospital that behind the warder's back, Captain D— S— saw 'bread, potatoes, and lumps of meat flying about with a rapidity, precision of aim, and a profound silence, only disturbed by the "flop, flop" as they reached the various hands, that would have done credit to the most expert Oriental-Whitechapel juggler.'[112] And David Fannan, recovering slowly from an attack of rheumatic fever, was amused at 'the tricks of my convict attendants, though I had no reason to complain of their conduct – they were kind and attentive to me in my illness. In my utter weakness I could only partake of liquid food, but they informed the doctor that I had managed to swallow a bit of egg; and when he gladly ordered for me light solids, such as egg and chicken, the rascals gobbled them all up themselves.'[113]

Discipline too was necessarily relaxed; at Kirkdale the hospital began to resemble the old days in Newgate:

> The hospital warder always closed our door at six o'clock in the evening, and we then had no fear of again being disturbed until six o'clock the next morning. After we had finished our tea, the tea leaves were collected and put upon the hob to dry. We then made cigarettes and smoked them instead of tobacco. Disgusting and obscene language was predominant, tales of crime were unblushingly told, and acquaintances were formed which would soon add considerably to future records of crime.[114]

DOCTORS AND HOSPITAL WARDERS

The actual quality of prison medicine was to a great extent dependent on the knowledge, character and temperament of the men and women who practised it, whether that was in the yard, the cell, or the hospital ward. The medical officer was specially instructed by the Regulations for Prisons that:

> Whenever he shall have reason to believe that either the mind or body of a prisoner is likely to be injuriously affected by the discipline or treatment, he shall report the case in writing to the governor, together with such directions as he may think proper; and he shall call the attention of the chaplain to any prisoner whose state of mind appears to require his special care.[115]

It was a responsibility that Dr Quinton, for one, did not take lightly. 'He is the recognised and responsible protector of the prisoner from any undue harshness of treatment that may tend to his physical or mental detriment, and he is very often the confidential repository of the prisoner's grievances, or complaints of unfair dealing on the part of the staff.'[116]

On a personal level, says Dr Campbell, 'it was my invariable practice, in prescribing for the patients, to treat them with as much consideration as if they had been delicate ladies – at the same time enjoining a kindly treatment on the part of the attendants.'[117] One of the patients on the receiving end of this 'consideration', during Campbell's reign at Woking hospital prison, was George Bidwell: 'the doctor wound up the interview with the clincher, in his high squeaking tones: "Well, my man, you know you were sent here to die, so you must not make any trouble, for there is nothing I can do for you." This was his stereotyped reply, no matter what the case or the nature of the disease, which had usually been aggravated or brought on by hard work with insufficient food.'[118] His summary of the doctor's long career is in similar vein. 'Dr. Campbell', he writes, 'resigned from the service and retired to private life with a pension and the inexpressible hatred and contempt of all prisoners who ever had the misfortune to come under his treatment.'[119]

An altogether more serious allegation, that of professional incompetence, is frequently made by prisoners about both their own treatment and that of others known to them. After John Hay had been treading the wheel for a week he 'petitioned the Governor', complaining that he was 'suffering from sciatica'. 'The doctor ordered me to strip, and, having made me get on the scales, said that I was four pounds heavier than when I entered the prison. I don't know how this showed I was not suffering from sciatica.'[120] When David Fannan reported sick to the doctor because of 'a slight spitting of blood that I feared was a symptom of lung weakness . . . he immediately ordered me off to plank bed and bread and water for imposition, but as my cough and blood spitting did not improve under this treatment, he was compelled to put me on the sick list and send me to hospital.'[121] At Shepton Mallet, Stuart Wood's symptoms were ignored until 'great sores had broken out all over my scalp, and large fissured ulcers in the anus made stool an intolerable agony'.[122] Prior to that he says, 'My appeals to the doctor, a part-time official with a practice outside, were received with scepticism, and daily doses of salts, which made me vomit and weakened me more and more.'[123] Oscar Wilde's indignation over the handling of the lunatic soldier called Prince turned mere dislike into a more fundamental attack on the competence and ethical standards of prison medicine.

Prison doctors have no knowledge of mental disease of any kind. They are as a class ignorant men. The pathology of the mind is unknown to them. When a man grows insane, they treat him as shamming. They have him punished again and again. Naturally the man becomes worse. When ordinary punishments are exhausted, the doctor reports the case to the justices. The result is a flogging. Of course the flogging is not done with a cat-of-nine-tails. It is what is called birching. The instrument is a rod; but the result on the wretched half-witted man may be imagined. . . . This man A.2.11 will, I have no doubt, be able to tell his name, the nature of his offence, the day of the month, the date of the beginning and expiration, of his sentence, and answer any ordinary simple question; but that his mind is diseased admits of no doubt. At present it is a horrible duel between himself and the doctor. The doctor is fighting for a theory. The man is fighting for his life. I am anxious that the man should win.[124]

Doctors were officially charged with making daily visits to their prisons and to their patients, but the continuing care of the hospitalized sick was entrusted, in the first place, to warders and wardresses drawn from the discipline staff of the institution, and secondly to inmate 'orderlies'. Warders and orderlies were criticized because they ignored the sufferings of sick prisoners. 'Sympathy is not part of their official duty', said the normally mild-mannered Mrs Maybrick of the wardresses in Aylesbury prison hospital, 'and be the warder never so tender in her own domestic circle, tenderness must not be shown toward a prisoner.'[125] And when a man at Gloucester would sometimes 'fall out of bed in an epileptic fit, and lie groaning on the stone floor for an hour or more together', it was in vain that George Jacob Holyoake and his colleagues shouted to the turnkeys. 'They who can hear a man *think* of escaping, cannot hear when he breaks his neck.'[126]
But alongside the criticisms of the prison medical service, there were also compliments to be paid. George Bidwell, who so disliked Dr Campbell, 'with one exception . . . never saw among prison authorities a nobler-hearted Christian gentleman than Dr. P. Power, the medical officer in charge of Dartmoor prison at the time of my arrival there.'[127] At Pentonville, 'The doctor and his assistant were unremitting in their attentions' to Balfour;[128] and Convict Number 7 reports 'I had every consideration and care shown me by the medical staff, and particularly by the doctor.'[129] One-who-has-tried-them was treated 'very skilfully' by one doctor.[130] Dr Pocklington was 'kind' to Jeremiah O'Donovan Rossa.[131] At Dartmoor, Ticket-of-leave-man found himself 'under the penetrating eye of the assistant-surgeon, Dr. Bernard', who was later 'dis missed the service on account of his supposed neglect of a prisoner who died'. 'I watched Dr. Bernard very closely', he says, 'for the simple reason that I used to hear all the schemers and habitual thieves abuse him, and whilst I admit that he was sharp and severe with tricksters, his treatment of men who were really ill was skilful and kind.'[132] And Stuart Wood was at last admitted to the hospital with his misdiagnosed illness: 'Now that I lay stretched helpless on my back everyone was gruffly kind to me, so kind indeed, that in my weakness I often cried softly into my pillow with gratitude.'[133]

DYING

Stuart Wood survived, and revived from his illness, but says 'I have known many men to die because their complaints, whatever they were, were allowed to develop beyond the point at which a cure was possible before the doctor believed there was anything really the matter with them.'[134] There was no shortage of men in prison who when they heard of any sudden death in the hospital were 'ready to swear "his light has been put out by the doctor," '[135] and some of the men who died, did so 'screaming aloud that they were poisoned'.[136] Accusations of the same nature were frequently made by recently released prisoners, including some normally sober observers of prison life:

> James McDermot, had been complaining daily, for months, of yellow jaundice. . . . The doctor told him there was nothing the matter with him, and that if he troubled him again he would send him to the punishment cells. At length, when he was no longer able to walk, he did trouble him again, and was admitted to the infirmary; but it was too late, for after three weeks infirmary treatment he was buried.
>
> Ticket-of-leave-man [137]

> I noticed that this man fell out several times to see the doctor, and he was never admitted to the infirmary to my knowledge. One morning I observed him drop dead on the parade, and I believe it was from heart disease, or from bursting a blood-vessel or something of that sort. I think that when he was examined by the doctors, if they had had sufficient knowledge to have detected his disease, they would have admitted him to the infirmary.
>
> Michael Davitt [138]

> Another time a healthy looking old man, with chest disease, complained to the doctor of pain in that region. He was dosed repeatedly with salts and senna – the medicine for schemers – and in less than a fortnight he was buried.
>
> A Merchant [139]

One-who-has-tried-them narrates the story of the man who

> complained that he was subject to heart complaint; but the doctor and Old Bob [the hospital warder] had got it into their heads that he was shamming and the former certified him fit for first class labour. It was very hot summer weather; the man was placed upon the wheel, and used to puff and blow and exhibit signs of intense distress while at work; but this was looked upon as a dodge, and no notice was taken of it, and the man continued at wheel work. A few nights later the warder, going round to lock up

cell-doors at bedtime, heard a strange gurgling noise in this man's cell, and looking in, saw him stretched upon his bed gasping for breath. . . . There was the usual inquest on the body, and the doctor stated the man had died from heart complaint, and the verdict was of course 'Death from natural causes'.[140]

Inquests were necessary, but not all that welcome to the prison authorities, for reasons that Dr Quinton explains. 'One manifestation of the popular interest which was taken in prison affairs after the transfer (i.e. to Government control in 1877) and which was commonly seen at the inquests held in accordance with law on the death of every prisoner, was frequently embarrassing, if not annoying, to the prison witnesses, especially medical officers. A fixed idea seemed to possess the minds of jurymen that prisoners were either starved, or done to death under the new management.'[141] 'So captious and unreasonable were some juries that an intelligent onlooker remarked that "medical officers were practically tried for manslaughter at every prison inquest." '[142] Inquest proceedings were looked on no less unfavourably by prisoners. There was a 'general belief' among Dartmoor men 'that it is one jury which is always summoned, and this jury is composed of men who are dependent upon the prison'. 'Discharged warders and others, who supply vegetables, or are employed about the prison'.[143]

MEDICAL RELEASE

One way of avoiding these proceedings, and any possible public criticism, was to release sick convicts on purely medical grounds before the expiry of their normal terms. 'This was a regular dodge; as soon as a man's case was hopeless they got an order form from the Home Secretary and sent him home, so that his family might have the expense of burying him.'[144] Captain D— S— was subjected to 'a minute medical examination' and his lung was found to be affected. 'Later on, a further examination proved that the malady was slowly progressing. To remain in prison was certain death, so my case was submitted to the Home Secretary, who, with the humanity that has characterised his term of office, ordered my immediate discharge.'[145] The captain at least lived long enough after his release to write a book about it all; a man whom Balfour 'knew very well' was not so fortunate. He 'had to be removed in an ambulance, was with difficulty conveyed to his home in the North of England, and died within three weeks of his release'. The decision to release him was, he thought, 'prompted not by humanity but by a desire to keep down the prison death rate, and avoid the inconvenience of an inquest.'[146] It was only possible to release a prisoner on medical grounds if he had somewhere to go. In some terminal cases, Dr Campbell noticed 'the constant craving for liberty of those who are destitute of friends able or willing to receive them'.[147]

REQUIEM

Men like these were destined to be numbered amongst those who died in prison. 'Many died like the brutes, and a very few departed in peace, with a prayer on their lips. The great majority died as they had lived, and were forgotten by the spectators almost before their bodies had been laid in the grave.'[148] The very thought of it was appalling to One-who-has-endured-it: 'to die a convict, to be buried in an unknown, uncared-for grave, thrust into a prison coffin filled up with dirty sawdust, as I have seen them done at Dartmoor, so that the ragged old shirt given out to do duty for a shroud may be saved for other purposes, is but a sorry end for a man who has once lived respected and beloved'.[149] But as they died, some of these men and women elicited unexpected qualities in those they were about to leave behind them. 'There is one estimable trait in the character of prisoners, observable even among the roughest criminals' – this is Dr Campbell – 'I mean the great attention and kindness they bestow upon the sick.'[150] This was partly, in some hospitals at any rate, *faute de mieux*. 'The prisoner must attend to her own wants, and if too weak to do so, she must depend on some other patient less ill than herself to assist her.'[151] Mrs Maybrick performed this office for a woman prisoner and 'when she was in the agony of death she called to me: "I don't know anything about your God, but if he has made you tender and loving to a bad lot like me, I know he will not be hard on a poor soul who never had a chance. Give me a kiss, dear lass, before I go. No one has kissed me since my mother died." '[152] Dr Campbell also witnessed what passed between a dying convict, who had been refusing the last rites, and his prison friend:

> This man was extremely rough in manner, and apparently completely hardened; but when brought to the bedside of his dying friend he was quite overcome, and on being told that he refused to see the chaplain, he implored him to change his mind and not to die like a dog, the tears all the time rolling down his cheeks.[153]

These touching and sentimental scenes from institutional life do nothing to rescue the practice of Victorian prison medicine from the consequences of its appointment to fundamentally disciplinary tasks. The doctors patrolled the narrow straits that separate hunger from starvation and punishment from outright cruelty, hauling aboard the life raft of their dispensations this drowning soul or that, and repelling, with brute force if necessary, the efforts of the others to climb to safety. In so doing, they lent to the work of preserving their employers' reputations whatever dignity and authority their emerging profession possessed – and lost it. What these scenes *do* do is to reveal the suppressed humanity of the prisoners in acts that shine forth – like the unexpected forget-me-nots on the yards at Pentonville – as small beacons of affection and hope in a dark and hopeless world.

NOTES

1. J. Balfour, 349.
2. Leicester Inquiry (1854), 218.
3. Dawson, 110.
4. J. Balfour, 350.
5. Ibid., 351.
6. Quinton, 19.
7. Ticket-of-leave-man, 81.
8. Quinton, 19.
9. WBN, 83.
10. Griffiths (1904), 176.
11. Ticket-of-leave-man, 82.
12. Convict 77, 60.
13. One-who-has-tried-them, I, 241.
14. Hart-Davis, 212.
15. Orton, 29.
16. Cooper, 241.
17. One-who-has-tried-them, II, 236.
18. *Kirkdale*, 36.
19. Ibid., 37.
20. Ticket-of-leave-man, 81.
21. J. Balfour, 350.
22. Quinton, 19.
23. One-who-has-endured-it, 196.
24. Griffiths (1904), 176.
25. Lovett, 229.
26. Ibid., 231.
27. Leicester Inquiry (1853), xii.
28. Penal Servitude Commission (1879), 348.
29. Martyn, 71.
30. Timewell, 15.
31. Rossa, 144.
32. Penal Servitude Commission (1879), 337.
33. G. Bidwell, 413.
34. Maybrick, 124.
35. Hart-Davis, 145.
36. East, 82.
37. Campbell, 65.
38. Ticket-of-leave-man, 167.
39. Ibid., 169.
40. Chesterton (1856), II, 93.
41. Ticket-of-leave-man, 169.
42. Fannan, 116.
43. Penal Servitude Commission (1879), 538.
44. Lee, 69.
45. WBN, 91.
46. Ticket-of-leave-man, 169.
47. Campbell, 71.
48. Wood, 36.
49. Fannan, 115.
50. Gladstone Committee (1896), 326.
51. Bacchus, 268.
52. Quinton, 14.
53. Griffiths (1904), 177.
54. WBN, 91.
55. Quinton, 13.
56. Penal Servitude Commission (1879), li.
57. *Kirkdale*, 37.
58. Campbell, 69.
59. Chesterton (1856), II, 95.
60. One-who-has-tried-them, II, 127.
61. Rickards, 112.
62. G. Bidwell, 444.
63. Campbell, 66.
64. Ibid., 67.
65. Ticket-of-leave-man, 107.
66. G. Bidwell, 498.
67. Ibid., 478.
68. Penal Servitude Commission (1879), 338.
69. G. Bidwell, 445.
70. Quinton, 17.
71. G. Bidwell, 485.
72. Ibid., 16.
73. Henderson, 57.
74. Davitt (1885), I, 142.
75. Chesterton (1856), II, 91.
76. Hiener, 71.
77. Ibid., 72.
78. Davitt (1885), I, 145.
79. Ibid., 143.
80. Ibid., 144.
81. Fannan, 120.
82. Ibid., 122.
83. Lytton, 140.
84. Ibid., 142.
85. Hart-Davis, 274.
86. Lytton, 178.
87. B. Thomson (1925), 28.
88. Ticket-of-leave-man, 144.
89. Sykes, 170.
90. McCook Weir, 119.

91. Ibid., 122.
92. Ibid., 124.
93. Ibid., 126.
94. Ibid., 127.
95. Scougal, 172.
96. Harris (n.d.), 59.
97. Joseph, 36.
98. G. Bidwell, 470.
99. Holyoake (1850), 91.
100. Chesterton (1856), II, 103.
101. Griffiths (1904), 223.
102. WBN, 146.
103. Fannan, 115.
104. Wood, 36.
105. Ibid., 36.
106. D—S—, 207.
107. *Pentonville Prison from Within*, 69.
108. Chesterton (1856), II, 88.
109. A. Bidwell, 455.
110. *Pentonville Prison from Within*, 47.
111. McCook Weir, 142.
112. D—S—, 232.
113. Fannan, 118.
114. *Kirkdale*, 95.
115. Regulations for Prison (1849), 32.
116. Quinton, vi.
117. Campbell, 58.
118. G. Bidwell, 485.
119. Ibid., 511.
120. Hay, 32.
121. Fannan, 117.
122. Wood, 130.
123. Ibid., 129.
124. Hart-Davis, 275.
125. Maybrick, 87.
126. Holyoake (1850), 98.
127. G. Bidwell, 456.
128. J. Balfour, 115.
129. No. 7, 92.
130. One-who-has-tried-them, I, 80.
131. Rossa, 248.
132. Ticket-of-leave-man, 89.
133. Wood, 130.
134. Ibid., 130.
135. Henderson, 61.
136. Ibid., 64.
137. Ticket-of-leave-man, 86.
138. Penal Servitude Commission (1879), 536.
139. Henderson, 61.
140. One-who-has-tried-them, II, 63.
141. Quinton, 188.
142. Ibid., 189.
143. Penal Servitude Commission (1879), 540.
144. One-who-has-tried-them, II, 113.
145. D—S—, 351.
146. J. Balfour, 209.
147. Campbell, 62.
148. Henderson, 64.
149. One-who-has-endured-it, 118.
150. Campbell, 59.
151. Maybrick, 126.
152. Ibid., 193.
153. Campbell, 115.

9
DISCIPLINE

Even after forty years, Dr R.F. Quinton could clearly recall the shock of reporting for duty at Portsmouth convict prison:

> The armed sentries, gates and bars, fetters and triangles, with other paraphernalia of the establishment, were sufficiently stern and gruesome features to me as a novice entering the service to relieve suffering, but they counted as nothing when compared with an actual acquaintance with the human beings for whose control and safe-keeping they were required. I felt I had been suddenly transplanted into a veritable community of pirates capable of any, and every, crime under the sun. Although penalties for misconduct were very severe at the time, they had apparently but little deterrent effect.[1]

Out of the character of that 'community of pirates' came the sternest practical test of everything that continued to be represented in the idea of a 'reformatory' prison. Convenience and necessity, as well as considerations of economy, had dictated the historical development of the prison as a place where large numbers of wrong-doers were assembled and held together. Before the reforms of the later eighteenth and early nineteenth centuries, prisons had acted largely as ante-chambers to the administration of justice. The assize courts were charged with 'delivering' the gaols – rather than with filling them;

and they delivered the 'innocent' into freedom, and the 'guilty' to death or mutilation or banishment. The problem of order in these waiting rooms was secondary to their purpose and was more or less maintained by making fast the outer wall, and virtually delivering over the wards and yards to whatever form of society the prisoners chose to devise for themselves, often in collaboration with profit-minded keepers and their families. Cases of persistent disruption met with physical restraint; with irons and chains. But in the new prisons, with their punitive and reformatory ambitions, the congregation of law-breakers in large groups over long periods of time created two main problems for the officials in charge.

The first was that of physically controlling numbers of difficult and some-times dangerous individuals; the second was how to prevent moral contamination. Separate cellular confinement had promised a theoretically short answer to both; its failure in practice resurrected both questions in especially acute forms. But it left behind, in a legacy of specialized buildings and spaces, a useful, if partial means of imposing order; namely the division of potentially surly masses into smaller more manageable units, often consisting of single individuals. Two other applications of the principle were also employed to control prisoners. One – widely used in the early reform prison – was to divide them into classes: men, women, children, those awaiting trial, those convicted of criminal offences, first offenders, second offenders – and so on, minor offenders, serious offenders, etc., etc. The urge to classify followed the success of the naturalist in bringing order to the chaos of an unnamed world, and pro-vided besides an intrinsic intellectual satisfaction of its own. But by themselves these static categories lacked laws of motion; which were supplied by the division of time. Time in prison was treated in two distinct ways; first, the day was dissected by a minutely detailed timetable that spoke for every second of the prisoner's existence. Secondly, time in the longer term was ordered by the division of sentences into discrete sequences or 'stages'.

The 'stage' system was first developed for dealing with convicts sentenced to transportation, but its main features were taken over practically intact for use in penal servitude, the sentence that replaced it in 1853. 'A sentence of penal servitude', Sir Edmund DuCane tells us, 'is divided into three principal stages. During the first stage, which endures for nine months in all cases, the prisoner passes his whole time – excepting the period allotted to prayers and exercise – in his cell, apart from all other prisoners, working at some employment of an industrial or remunerative character. During the second he sleeps and has his meals in a separate cell, but works in close association under a close and strict supervision, at employment suited to him. The third period is that during which he is conditionally released from prison, but kept under the supervision of the police, and liable, for any infraction of the conditions of his release, to be returned to prison, there to fulfil the portion of his sentence which remained unexpired at the time of his release.'[2]

To these three stages were normally added four 'classes': a 'probation' of twelve months – nine of them in separation and three on the works; 'third' and 'second' classes of twelve months each; and a 'first' class which lasted for the remainder of a sentence, except for those few prisoners who were promoted into a 'special' class. 'Promotion into each of these classes is followed by certain privileges, and each class wears its own distinctive badge. These privileges are necessarily very limited but still they offer inducements which are much sought after.' They consisted of greater frequencies of permitted letters and visits, 'more freedom for exercise on Sundays', and 'the earning of a higher gratuity of money to be paid on the prisoner's discharge'.[3]

In the early days of penal servitude, prisoners were able to earn gratuities for 'good conduct' and for 'industry' amounting to 15 pence per week.[4] Over a period of years these tiny payments could accumulate into substantial sums, and they were therefore reduced so that by the time One-who-has-endured-it came to be released it represented 'a small sum of money', which was enough to keep a man 'for a few days, or perhaps a week or so after leaving'.[5]

The most important inducement of all held out to the prisoner was that of slightly diminishing the duration of his sentence by obtaining 'Conditional Release'. Promotion from each class to the next was to be 'gained by industry alone, and not by "good conduct" ', says Sir Edmund, 'which, in a prison, can be little more than passive, or abstaining from acts of indiscipline or irregularity. The time has long gone by, if ever it existed, when he could profit by any lip professions of piety or reformation.'[6]

All of this meticulous systematization of sentences was translated into a 'form easily intelligible' to the prisoner; i.e. as 'the duty of earning a number of marks proportioned to the length of his sentence'.[7] Each day's marks had to be earned by hard work, 'recorded from day to day by the same officer, the signs used for the purpose being V.G. (very good), G. (good), and O. (Ordinary)'.[8] The threat of their removal was one of the most important pieces in the disciplinary armoury of governors in their efforts to secure good behaviour. The prisoner was given a card on which his marks were recorded, the whole system clearly giving the greatest satisfaction to Sir Edmund. 'In this manner, day by day, week by week, and year by year, he can count and record the progress he is making towards an advance in class, in accumulation of money, and towards conditional release; and he is made perfectly to see and feel that his fate is in his own hands, and that he has something more to work and to hope for than the mere avoidance of punishment.'[9]

From this summary of the stage system it will be clear that it laid prime emphasis on the prison behaviour of the individual and tended to neglect characteristics related to the offence and other behaviour prior to imprisonment, which had been the basis of earlier schemes of classification. These had, to a great extent, been pushed aside in the rush to separation – prisoners in solitary confinement constituted so many unique classes of their own – but it was partly reintroduced in 1879, with the designation of a 'star' class of first offenders.

A version of the penal servitude stages and classes was installed in the 'local' prisons after the transfer of power to government in 1877 – one of its refinements for shorter-term prisoners being that they were allowed no mattress at all during the first stage, which in some cases meant the whole of their sentences, and the 'right' to a mattress on every night of the week was one that had to be earned gradually by good behaviour.

Dr Quinton looked back on the introduction of marks and stages as 'a truly beneficent change which at a stroke enabled the prisoner to lighten his punishment, and at the same time help to work out his own reformation if he felt so inclined.'[10] Part of the appeal of these arrangements, as with the penitentiary in its hey-day, lay in their self-regulating and machine-like nature. The Reverend C. Gibson, chaplain to Spike Island Prison in Ireland, saw clearly the same idea at work in both, although he admired neither. 'According to the rule which prevails in England, any day on which a prisoner obtains the letters V.G. for good conduct and industry, *he has gained a certain number of hours towards obtaining an earlier liberty*, so that the motive and reward of good conduct are always in operation, like the hands of a clock.'[11]

In the last two decades of the nineteenth century, this regime was brought by those responsible for it, chief amongst them Sir Edmund DuCane, to a state approaching mechanical perfection. Each part of the mechanism had been drawn up in theory then tested and polished in endless practice. All of its parts were catalogued, and their interconnections set out clearly in written manuals of rules and regulations that catered for nearly every eventuality. Then the whole 'vast machinery' had been set on rails where it ran along the tracks of an iron routine – for the day, the week, the month, the year, an entire sentence; picking up and setting down its unwilling passengers at predetermined points. The motive force for the complete works was supplied by 'discipline', a word with more than one meaning in the dictionary of late-Victorian corrections. In its most basic sense, 'discipline' was a finite, almost palpable presence that permeated the tiniest facet of the prisoner's daily life. It was a printed code of rules. It was a set of procedures and methods for securing compliance with the rules. And at its most abstract, 'discipline' was an almost metaphysical spirit that drew together and gave coherence to the concrete activities that bore its name.

PRISON OFFENCES

In each prisoner's cell hung a copy of the 'rules' (see pp. 289–90). One-who-has-suffered read them and remembered that 'each clause begins "No prisoner shall," and ends with "Shall be severely punished." '[12] His memory was not accurate but he conveys well enough the intent with which the rules had been framed. An anonymous convict, giving evidence to the 1879 Inquiry into Penal Servitude, expressed a view that commands wide support amongst men and women who described their prison lives. 'The present rules are so drawn up that I do not consider it possible that they can be fairly administered to the prisoners by the officers; I do not consider it possible that those rules can be carried out.'[13] His view is supported by another convict – also anonymous – writing in the *Hibbert Journal*: 'Nineteen-twentieths of the breaches thus castigated could not claim, and would not receive, as between man and man, a moment's regard outside prison walls. They are the creations of an abnormal condition wherein human feelings are legally suppressed by certain printed paragraphs.'[14] The minute nature of these breaches of the disciplinary code can be seen in the following catalogue of offences presented in the Fourth Report of the Prison Inspectors by the governor of Northallerton House of Correction: 'R.G. Shoving and making signs to another prisoner, and constantly looking about.' 'W.M. Taking his wrong place in the rank.' 'J.W. Blowing his nose out in an improper place.' 'M.P. Stopping too long in the privy.' 'C.P. Making water against the wall in the tread-room.'[15] 'A misdemeanour', in other words, 'is very easily made out against a prisoner – an ugly look, a quick reply, an impatient manner, even silence itself is construed into an offence; there is really no way of guarding against being reported.'[16] And no wonder Warder Martin was convinced that 'some of the rules are made with no other object than to be broken, so that an excuse may be found for inflicting additional punishment.'[17]

'SILENCE!'

The most unnatural of all the prison rules, the most difficult to supervise and enforce successfully, and the most productive by far of offences, reports and minor punishments, was the silence rule. Its importance was signalled in Newgate by the visual equivalent of a shout – 'a blackboard with "silence" marked in large letters' that stood in the middle of the hall.[18] Strictly speaking the rule was not about 'silence' at all, but about communicating, and no noise was necessary for a breach of the rule to occur, as Balfour soon learned at Portland: 'Once a prisoner in passing me smiled. It was not a smile of recognition, for he had probably never seen me before. It was not a secret communication. It was nothing but a casual and kindly smile. But the warder saw and was swift to shout, "Now then, Balfour, smiling is not allowed here".'[19] He was not actually placed on report for this, but on Sunday, 1 January 1899 he 'committed the heinous offence of wishing a prisoner a "Happy New Year" ' and was placed on report for that.[20] 'The penalising of speech begets seventy or eighty per cent of prison offences', says Michael Davitt, 'but produces absolutely nothing of a counterbalancing reformatory or moral effect which could not be better obtained by more humane and rational regulations.'[21] 'Nay,' he continues, 'it can be truly said that this infliction of the dumb torture must inevitably keep alive all the propensities to trickery, deception, and subterfuge which are the most prominent features of criminal character. These cunning faculties are kept in hourly exercise throughout long and short sentences by the very rule which was instituted with the object of keeping them in check!'[22]

198 VICTORIAN PRISON LIVES

Daniel Nihill was an early supporter of separation; he described prisoners held under the congregate system as 'steeped to the lips in society, and at the same time *Tantalised* by a rule which prohibits the slightest intercourse.'[23] 'The officers of the prison', he says, 'whose duty it is to maintain the observance of the rules, find themselves baffled in ten thousand instances, in which the prisoners, availing themselves of the construction of the building, and the various movements belonging to the system, contrive the most extensive intercourse.'[24]

The same restrictions, and the same evasions, applied not just to 'intercourse' between people in the prison, but between them and the outside world as well. It was intrinsic to the nature of reformed imprisonment that contacts between those held inside and their friends and relatives at liberty were kept to a minimum. The only communication officially allowed to convicts undergoing penal servitude was via visits and letters. Both channels were subject to conditions which greatly reduced their usefulness to anyone genuinely seeking to keep alive an emotional attachment to someone outside. For a start they were severely rationed:

> During the first two years letters are allowed to pass between prisoners and their families, and also visits to take place every six months, the second year every four months, and after that every three months, provided always that a prisoner did not forfeit his privilege by misconduct, and that he earned his proper quota of marks.[25]

This last proviso meant that 'the meanest official in a convict prison can, by systematically reporting a man for the most trifling and trumpery infringement of the prison rules, prevent him during the whole, say, twenty years of his imprisonment from ever seeing, hearing from, or writing to, friend, wife or children.'[26]

Visits, when they did fall due, were very rarely joyful reunions; most often they were miserable occasions. 'Under the present system the prisoner is either locked up in a large iron cage or in a large wooden box, with a small aperture covered with wire netting, through which he is allowed to peer. His friends are placed in a similar cage, some three or four feet distant, and two warders stand between, to listen to, and, if they wish, stop or interrupt the conversation such as it may be.'[27] In some prisons, a more public version of these cages or boxes was provided. Bill Sykes took part in a mass leave-taking by convicts en route for Portland, Chatham and Dartmoor at which there were 'about twenty or thirty men at one time bidding farewell to their wives and relations, separated from them by two rows of iron railings, about three feet apart, covered with wire gauze. The decent man, the habitual criminal on one side, and the virtuous wife and the foulest prostitute, all mixed up together on the other side, taking their farewell of each other. And thus it was, amidst the prayers of some, and the vilest oaths and blasphemy of others, that I said good-bye to my wife.'[28]

It need occasion no surprise that 'many prisoners, rather than support such an ordeal, refuse to see their friends at all.'[29]

The public nature of the proceedings, the presence of prying officials, the general babel – all were added to and made worse by the transformed appearance of the convict, sympathetically noted by the Reverend Clifford Rickards.

> Anything more disfiguring and disgusting than the dress and tonsure of the man in prison it is impossible to imagine, and some of them feel it acutely, especially when a friend or relative is allowed to visit them, and they see how shocked their visitor is when faced with the grotesque Guy Fawkes opposite and realises that that is the man he has known outside in decent garments.[30]

The right of writing a letter too, to a friend or relative, even when it had been earned, turned out to be so circumscribed as to rob it of any spontaneous pleasure. All letters were, for instance, read before they left the prison and 'if a prisoner . . . makes any complaint of the prison system, that portion of his letter is cut out with a pair of scissors', or the offender is 'brought up before the governor and told to write another letter'.[31]

Just as off-putting as the censorship to the sensitive correspondent, when Jabez Balfour first went to Portland, prisoners' letters were not even put in envelopes, but were 'fastened up in the old fashion in which notes were folded before envelopes came into general use. The consequence was that they could be identified as coming from prisoners, and their contents could even be scanned by gossiping post mistresses and inquisitive postmen.'[32]

The rules that regulated letter-writing further threatened that 'Any which are of an objectionable tendency, either to or from prisoners, or containing slang or improper expressions, will be suppressed.'[33] The only way therefore that strong or unfettered feelings could be expressed was by sending letters illicitly out of prison, care of a corrupt warder. Shortly after receiving his life sentence from Mr Justice Archibald, Austin Bidwell received a letter from his wife, accusing him of deceiving her (which he had); insisting on a divorce (which she got); and bidding him adieu (they never met again and the child she bore him the month after his conviction died within days). He replied, presumably *not* through the official channel, as follows:

> Mrs. A. B. Bidwell.
> Thou worse than Babylonian whore, thou strumpet, false heart and traitor. That night, when lone and diseased, forsaken and starving, you walk to London or Waterloo Bridge, think of the heart great as Caesar's you were false to, and what you left to consume itself to ashes, that heart that loved you and on which you had often lain and sighed out your love. Oh thou worse than whore, thou traitor heart, may water turn to blood when you drink, scorpions be your pillow. May the grass wither from thy

Friends visiting: on the left is the visitors' compartment and on the right the prisoner's

feet, may the woods deny thee a shelter, earth a home, dust a grace, the sun her light, and thy mother as she will welcome thee with a curse and a beating. Then think of me thou false heart one – that never spek to you but to bless you and whose prosperity you revelled in, but deserted in the first breath of adversity. 'Finis' is not written after my name and I will live (a fortune is mine) to make you pray and pray in vain for death. Thou worse than whore, be a whore with the curses of your

Husband
Austin B. Bidwell[34]

Materials for writing unauthorized letters were carefully concealed by prisoners, and strenuously sought after by the authorities. The pencil might have been nothing more than 'a small piece of common plumber's lead',[35] or it might be one of prison manufacture: 'The pencils were thus made: a little of the pewter was scraped off the pint, and this being run with a hot iron, (which the prisoner gets to carry on his tailoring), was easily attached to a bit of wood or quill.'[36] Or it might have been a ready-made one imported from outside, or stolen from a prison official, and then concealed: 'I hid my lead pencil in a hole in the wall, which I found very conveniently ready-made for me by some other prisoner.'[37] Paper was the next prerequisite; Ticket-of-leave-man was in the habit of learning poetry by writing it down on the 'brown wrapping paper . . . served out for necessary purposes.'[38] The author of *Pentonville Prison from Within* was committed to prison for refusing to agree not to 'molest' a woman – the 'actress in the background' from the subtitle of his book. He used his illicit pencil and supply of paper to write a letter to her. 'This letter I handed to my young prisoner-friend, and he smuggled it out, and either delivered it or posted it to the actress. . . . I got into great trouble for sending this document out.'[39]

TOBACCO

Possibly the principal prize in officialdom's war against possessions was tobacco; and no effort was spared in the search for it. Under the older county administrations it had been a simple matter to import contraband items, including tobacco, into the gaol. The cleaner at Warwick was quick to offer Thomas Cooper and the other Chartists 'Some bacca, if you like. . . . We can get 'owt you like, throo th'debtors. There's a chink i'th'wall where we get things through.'[40] Under the stricter discipline of a later period the 'chink' through which most of the tobacco arrived in prison was located in the pockets of turnkeys, which had to be lined with money before they would release their precious cargoes. But the warder's official duty was to find and confiscate tobacco and to report for punishment those found in possession of it.

Like other Irish political prisoners, Jeremiah O'Donovan Rossa did not have a high opinion of his fellow convicts at Portland. 'They were hard characters most of them, thieves, garotters, and every class of criminal that grows in English society.' Unaware of these sentiments, one of them offered him a chew of tobacco, for which he asked neither 'fee or reward'. On his way back into the prison, Rossa was taken to the bath-house. 'I stripped with an officer looking at me, and as he had his head to one side, I let the bit of tobacco fall on the floor. When I was in the bath he took hold of my clothes and searched them; his eye fell on the black thing on the floor, and he picked up my bit of tobacco.'[41]

The prison-wise way to dispose of tobacco was *not* to drop it on the floor. A convict of A Merchant's acquaintance 'just about due for his liberation had half-an-inch of tobacco given him by another prisoner. . . . He was "chaffed" a good deal by his "pals" for neglecting to swallow the quid when he saw the officer coming to him.'[42] But warders were themselves wise to this manoeuvre on the part of the convict, and 'if they think that he has tobacco in his mouth, will rush at him and seize him by the throat, one before and one behind, or, as they say in prison slang, will "choke" him, to prevent his swallowing the tobacco'.[43]

THE ENFORCEMENT OF DISCIPLINE

To the prohibitive prose of the rule card, and to their own generally intimidating presence, prison staff added a set of disciplinary procedures with which to enforce order; to maintain silence and separation so far as that might prove possible; and to suppress the possession of any item not sanctioned and issued by the prison administration itself.

The most straightforward of these methods was the daily inspection of the cell. 'About ten o'clock every morning one or other of the chief warders, sometimes two together, would come round. On their entering the corridor either the warder or his assistant would run on before them and unbolt every door, flinging it wide open. Slowly did the officials pass along, carefully scrutinising every cell, and if any man's bedding or other things were out of order, he speedily heard of it unpleasantly.'[44] Only occasionally did these inspections lead to disciplinary action, but the threat of it served to impart a little fear to the beginning of the prisoner's day.

But there was another version of these cellular visits that was more forceful. 'I remember well the first time my chamber was "turned over" as it is called', says One-who-has-endured-it. 'One day, on going in after exercise, I was surprised, on passing the doors of several cells, to see everything in confusion, and on reaching my own I found some one had been there kicking up "Meg's diversion" – books were thrown in one corner, bedding unrolled and cast about in every direction, not an article but had been misplaced and thoroughly examined; even the little bag with the bath brick and rags was turned inside out and its contents strewed all over the place.'[45]

When warders on a similar errand had finished with Stuart Wood's cell, it 'looked as though a bomb had been dropped on it'.[46] And Balfour says that 'the bed-clothes would often be foul with the searcher's footprints, and besmeared and blackened by all the dirty and dusty accretions of the grimy stone floors.'[47] If that was not enough, warders would also sometimes contrive to sprinkle salt on the cell tinware, so as 'to give the convict extra cleaning work, as the salt readily eats into the zinc, causing black holes very difficult to remove. This weekly cell searching causes many hours' labour to the convict to clean his cell.'[48]

Like the cell inspection, the body-search was part of the rhythm of everyday life in prison. At Cold Bath Fields, in its simplest form it was 'a thrice-fold daily periodical search', in which 'the sub-warders passed their well-pressed hands down from the arm-pits to below the hips of each individual.'[49] A more rigorous 'rub-down' was imposed on the penal-servitude convicts, the warder passing 'his hands down the body and legs of the prisoner, right down to his very heels,

much after the fashion of a dexterous shampooer at a Turkish bath'.[50] Given its
frequency, and relative innocuousness, the 'rub-down' was little resented by
prisoners, but its advanced form, the strip-search, already encountered in the
reception room, was not so readily accepted. Jabez Balfour took more exception to it than most. 'Once a month every working party is searched by the
process known as the "dry bath". . . . The commands given will best indicate
the disgusting business that then went on.' The first set of instructions related to
the removal of clothing:

> The wretched prisoner was now stark-naked. 'Open your legs
> wide – stretch out your arms above your head – don't mind me, it has to
> be done. Open your mouth wide, so that I can see inside it. Turn about,
> stoop down, and touch your feet with your fingers. Keep like that until I
> tell you to move.' If the reader will only pause as he reads each order, so as
> to realise what it meant, and what is involved – of degradation to the
> unhappy prisoner and outraged delicacy to the reluctant warder – he
> will need no words of mine to stimulate his indignation and his horror.[51]

To Mrs Maybrick, too, 'it was a bitter indignity. I was never allowed to forget
that, being a prisoner, even my body was not my own. It was horrible to be
touched by unfriendly hands, yet I was compelled to submit – to be undressed
and searched. During the term of my imprisonment I was searched about ten
thousand times.'[52]

PROCEEDINGS

Any particular breach of the many general rules of the prison led, if detected by
a warder, to a 'report' for disciplinary action. The more minor of these, that is
the majority, were heard by the governor or his deputy; the more serious had to
be referred to the visiting magistrates in the local prisons, or to one of the
directors of the convict prisons. 'The governor or deputy "sits" at twelve
o'clock, and first hears the reports. The prisoner is brought from the cell to the
governor's room on the ground floor. This is an ordinary office, with a door at
each side. The prisoner on entering is divided from the governor and his clerk
by strong iron railings, reaching from the floor to the ceiling.'[53]

In places where there were no railings (as at Pentonville), the governor was
'surrounded with a mighty staff of warders, who formed a complete phalanx of
well-stuffed uniforms about him'.[54] The warders were there to protect him, but
were not always successful. At Portland, the convicts 'would throw various
missiles which they had cunningly concealed, at the poor governor's head; it
might be a sharp stone flung with terrific force from a pocket-handkerchief, or
a long nail, rusty iron or pieces of granite. With these relics Mr. Clifton
adorned the walls of his room.'[55] The warders' efforts at restraint also sometimes
went astray, as Arthur Griffiths observed during an inspectorial visit.

Governor hearing disciplinary charges: with prisoner in punishment dress

One day a prisoner who had misconducted himself, when invited to speak in his defence, stooped down quickly, and taking off his shoe, launched it at the Governor's head. Whereupon the warder on one side of the culprit drew his staff and knocked the other warder down. The tableau has never been forgotten by me: I can see them still, the Governor indignant and much perturbed, the warders rescuing their prostrate comrade, the prisoner, and, I am ashamed to say, myself convulsed with laughter.[56]

Proceedings themselves were brief. The warder made his statement, and the prisoner was invited to reply in his own defence. Prisoners believed this to be a waste of breath. 'Whatever lie a warder may proffer is accepted as truth. Whatever truth a prisoner may proffer is held a lie.'[57] And 'Any report, however garbled, is necessarily believed; and if corroboration is necessary, a dozen turnkeys, from every part of the prison, will come forward, and emphatically endorse their comrade's charge.'[58] The general principle was endorsed by the governor of Chatham convict prison, that 'when a man becomes a convict he is necessarily placed in such a position that under no conceivable circumstances is his word to be believed as compared with a free man.'[59]

In these circumstances, cases were heard with despatch. At Liverpool 'reports were heard at ten o'clock. Man after man was marched into the room, followed by his warder-accuser. The common offences were idleness, refusing labour, and "back-chat". Mr Walker, the governor, wore his hat while dealing with them because he regarded the whole prison as the open air. . . . "Can't pick oakum. Blind men pick oakum! Two days' bread and water." '[60]

The author of *Pentonville Prison from Within*, charged with sending out the illicit letter to his actress, received a common combination of punishments: 'three days' bread-and-water, close confinement to cell, and earn 56 marks in the first stage – Right about turn.'[61] He was not particularly perturbed – 'whenever I got three days' bread-and-water, and all the rest of it, I found it a welcome break in the awful monotony of the barren, brutal months'.[62] 'To the rough-bred London criminal', on the other hand, 'a bread and water diet was a punishment particularly trying. Their god was their belly, of which they never tired speaking. They were continually grumbling about their food'; and to David Fannan, as a Scot, their favourite reproach was 'You Scotchmen don't eat beef.'[63] In short doses the bread and water did no more harm to the constitution than the already impoverished diet, but ill-behaved inmates could be condemned to successive three-day periods of it, broken only by one day's ordinary food. Jeremiah O'Donovan Rossa once had to endure a four-month spell of punishment diet, and towards the end of that time he found his 'body covered with small pustules, like little boils. Not an inch of me was free of them, and they looked very ugly with their white heads.'[64] To Dr Quinton, dietary punishment, 'though it has always seemed to me a more or less barbarous and senseless proceeding to apply to human beings, was nevertheless very necessary with unruly prisoners. I know of nothing approaching a scientific excuse for its use, except the principle on which a horse has his oats reduced in order to tame his spirit.'[65]

'Close confinement' took place in one's own cell, a familiar enough if none too palatial environment, but the governor could also order offending inmates off to the penal or punishment cells. These were descended in a direct line from the dungeon. At Brechin Gaol Frederic Hill 'found a wretched vault below ground, called by the prisoners the "black hole", still in use, although it had been pronounced by the sheriff to be "unfit for a dog." '[66] The refractory cell at Warwick Gaol in 1839 was no better. William Lovett 'knew a boy of the name of Griffiths, of the age of 17, locked up in it for three days and nights in the month of February . . . and when he came out he was so swollen as hardly to be known; he had several holes in his feet, and *two of his toes festered off.*'[67] In the course of penal 'progress' the dungeon was raised to ground level and made more sanitary, but although it was no longer replete with the rats of the story books, it was still designed to create 'darkness as intense as imagination can conceive',[68] a darkness 'like that experienced in Egypt, such as might almost be felt'.[69] And to be absolutely certain, 'The punishment cells at Folkingham House of Correction were not only completely dark, but were also blackened inside.'[70] The Reverend John Pitkin worked at Wandsworth, where the 'Black

Hole was in existence and often used. The prisoner was literally encased in this cell, and two substantial doors, three feet apart, isolated him from the rest of the prison. He could neither see, nor hear, anything that was going on. When I opened the doors, I found the prisoner in a half-dazed condition, and being out of touch with the progress of the day, he generally asked me the time. It was a terrible form of punishment, and its abolition, under the Act of 1878, was a happy event for the inmates of prisons.'[71] Following the ban on 'dark cells', those undergoing punishment were placed in cells containing 'nothing in the way of furniture except a raised platform of hard wood on one side large enough for the occupant to the down on, with a piece of wood fastened at one end for a pillow'.[72]

All of these formal procedures for the maintenance of discipline were normally accompanied by a barrage of admonition and abuse from the subordinate ranks of the prison staff. Its effects on prisoners could be extreme. Lady Constance Lytton, reprimanded by a woman warder, 'felt mentally stunned, physically cowed, morally indignant, a blend of sensations which I think must be common to many prisoners'.[73] 'As with so many other prisoner sensations', she thought, 'it is akin to child life, engendered from complete helplessness, subjection to others, ignorance and uninformedness as to what is happening outside the cramped horizon of the life to which one is subject.'[74] And Irish political prisoner John Daly often went back to his cell and lay down 'on the hard floor, prostrate mentally as well as physically. The nagging, the ordering about, the mental kicking and hammering, so to speak, crush you to a pulp. I really cannot describe it all; I loathe to think of it.'[75]

REDRESS

As if to forestall any attempt at retaliation on the part of the prisoner, the authorities provided an elaborate series of checks and balances against the unbridled exercise of their own power. It comprised a three-part complaints procedure. In the first instance prisoners could complain to the governor of an establishment about any aspect of their treatment. Secondly they could go to the magistrates who ran the local gaols until 1877, and who were kept on after that date to perform a number of vestigial functions – the hearing of complaints being one of them. Alternatively, appeal could be made to the centrally appointed inspectors, who visited the prisons in their regions on a regular basis; or to the directors of the convict prisons who did likewise at Chatham, Dartmoor, Portsmouth and Portland. Failing satisfaction from any or all of those quarters, prisoners could make their complaints directly to the Home Secretary via a written petition.

In one sense these procedures were over-used. There was for instance 'a class of prisoners at Aylesbury known as the "wishers". That is to say, they are continually expressing a wish to see the governor without' – as a visitor to the prison put it – 'any adequate reason or cause'. [76] At the same time, the way that serious complaints were treated created scepticism about their value. 'If you speak about anything while you are a prisoner', according to Henry Harcourt, 'about the weight of your bread, for instance, you give what they call unnecessary trouble; no matter what you speak about, it is all construed into unnecessary trouble.' [77]

One-who-has-tried-them once complained about an 'issue of salt beef' that was 'musty and bad'. After carefully studying the government dietary he came to the conclusion that the governor had no power to serve out salted beef since 'the substitutes permitted in the list are, Colonial beef preserved by heat, and American or other beef, preserved by cold'. [78] Despite warnings from friendly officers, One-who-has-tried-them persisted with his complaint, and won the day in the sense that the regulation meat was issued instead. But he emerged from the encounter a loser since he was simultaneously removed from the cosy staff billet he had obtained in the prison office.

Complaining about the behaviour of officers was also an activity that had its hazards. John Lee thought that he was being unfairly allocated to the wringing machine in the laundry at Portsmouth, and intimated to the officer in charge that he 'would see the governor about it. According to the prison rules that is a threat. He reported me, and I lost sixty marks and two months probation.' [79]

Next port of call for the determined complainer was the visiting inspector, although he was not necessarily a figure who inspired respect amongst the prisoners it was his job to protect. 'On one occasion a lavender kid-gloved gent, with cane, and shining patent shoes, and horned imperial, came from London to test the ventilation of the cells' where Manchester Merchant was serving his sentence. 'Not one did he enter, but being surrounded by a troop of officers, he had all the doors opened, and standing about ten feet from the entrance of each, he sniffed the air, like a fondled poodle at a rat-hole. The result was a report of them being in excellent condition.' [80] One-who-has-tried-them tells what happened to a man who actually lodged a complaint with one of these officials that he had been assaulted by an officer. The inspector reprimanded the culprit, and quit the scene:

He had been gone about five minutes when I heard the warder come stamping across the corridor, dash open one of the cell doors, and shout out in a furious voice, 'You ungrateful young scoundrel, I'll teach you to tell the inspector;' then there was the thud, thud, of heavy blows or kicks, interrupted by a scream of agony, and followed by a succession of short, spasmodic screams, evidently produced by intense pain. [81]

Last resort, in most ordinary circumstances, for airing a grievance was a petition to the Home Secretary himself; a literary device that defeated many prisoners, and which as often as not drew the blank response: 'No grounds'. [82] To someone like Stuart Wood on the other hand, articulate, literate, intelligent, the whole complaints system was one to be manipulated to his own advantage. 'The truth of the axiom that "knowledge is power" is nowhere more experienced to greater advantage than it is in a prison. Confront any prison official with a rule which is legally binding on him as it is upon you, and, if he is breaking that rule, you have got him by the short hair. Some governors, of course, bully and threaten all sorts of things, but a courteous request for a petition will generally turn the trick, especially if a fellow knows how to draft one in terms likely to command attention.'[83]

BREAKING-OUT

The ability to work the system in the way recommended by Stuart Wood was not widespread in the prison population; a more common protest took the form of violent assaults on the inanimate objects that constituted confinement: 'few days passed but some desperate wretch, maddened by silence and solitude, smashed up everything breakable in his cell . . . in a vain rebellion against a System stronger and more merciless than death.'[84] For reasons not difficult to guess, women were more prone to vent suppressed emotion on their immediate surroundings than on the personal representatives of authority – although that was not entirely unknown either. A girl of 12 was confined in the 'penal' cells at Wandsworth when Henry Mayhew made a tour of inspection. She 'had been singing in her cell against the prison rules. . . . She was drumming in passionate mood at the door of her cell. On our looking in through the eyelet opening, we saw her sitting crouching in a corner of the cell with only one garment wrapt around her, and her blue prison clothes torn into a heap of rags by her side.'[85]

'It might seem at first sight as if this system of periodical "breakings out" which is largely adopted by the lower class of female prisoners, were a mere unreasoning indulgence in temper; but it is not so', explains Felicia Mary Skene, 'it has a distinct *rationale* of its own, illogical enough, no doubt, but a well-considered method in the apparent madness. The object of it is simply one of deliberate revenge for the pains and penalties to which their imprisonment subjects them. The women are perfectly aware that by these paroxysms of violence they give a great deal of trouble and annoyance to the officers, whose duty is to carry out all the unpleasant conditions of the sentences they have brought on themselves by their offences against the law.'[86] Susanna Meredith, another prison visitor, talked to a woman after one such outburst 'and began reasoning with her on the foolishness of her conduct, at first with no effect, but finally she burst into violent fits of weeping, frequently repeating, "They have treated me like a beast and I have become one." I argued and talked and got her to finally tell me why she acted as she did, and she said, "Well, I did it for *variety*. Oh, the monotony of a prison life! I had to smash the glass of the cell and glass everywhere I could or I should have gone mad." '[87]

Prison staff were not slow to interpret a 'breaking out', or 'smash-up' as it was also known, as a public affront to their authority, nor to deal with the

Female convict in canvas dress
(under punishment for tearing her clothes)

offending prisoner accordingly. 'When the warders thought the paroxysm had exhausted itelf they would go to his cell, drag him out, hustle him into the punishment cells, fasten his hands and feet into shackles and leave him till morning. If he flared up and resisted in any way at all he was "disciplined" by the warders, and the whole prison was disturbed by his screams for mercy.'[88] Steinie Morrison was a practised exponent of this art, and the recipient of much staff violence. 'I smashed up the furniture, and was set upon and beaten (always on the head) and then put in an empty cell. I tore up my clothing, and was beaten again and then handcuffed.'[89] The handcuffs to which he refers were not ordinary ones:

Around my waist they put a leather belt a quarter of an inch thick, and three inches wide. The belt they pulled as tight around my waist as they possibly could, locking it behind with a hanging lock. At each side of the belt was a handcuff in which my wrists were firmly locked in. . . . In a few days my wrists swelled up so big that the biggest handcuffs they could find in the prison were not sufficiently big to fit with ease. . . . Finally the skin broke. The matter all coming out caused the handcuffs to rust; the rust got into the open wounds and my arms and wrists were poisoned.[90]

Handcuffs had a history of use that paid no heed to age or sex. Visitors to the chain room at Millbank were shown 'little baby handcuffs, as small in compass as a girl's bracelet, and about twenty times as heavy' – objects which impressed Henry Mayhew with a notion, that 'in the days of torture either the juvenile offenders must have been very strong or the jailers very weak otherwise, where the necessity for manacling infants?'[91] The advent of an ostensibly more enlightened nineteenth century did not mean that children were always excused manacles and chains, and even in the twentieth century, so Mrs Pankhurst claims, 'Delicate women were sentenced, not only to solitary confinement, but to handcuffs for twenty-four hours at a stretch.'[92]

There was, also, a special mode of restraint reserved to women, called 'hobbling', which consisted 'in binding the wrists and ankles of the prisoner then strapping them together behind her back'.[93] The 'hobbles' themselves were 'strong leather straps and wood appliances which fasten the leg and foot back behind the knee to the thigh, the arms being fastened down so that the hands could not be raised to the mouth, and the unhappy individual in the hobbles had only her knees to rest upon, and with her back to the wall had to be fed like a baby'.[94] Mrs Maybrick condemned them as 'barbarous'.[95] But beyond the handcuffs and the hobbles, the last destination of the recalcitrant was the straitjacket. Susanna Meredith went to the cell of a prisoner who had been 'smashing up', 'and saw a woman lying on a plank bed whose only garment seemed to be a long green baize straitjacket which reached from her neck to her feet, and was so narrow that it prevented her bending her knees or moving in any way. She was spitting violently all around the cell, so that no one could approach within any distance of her without risk'.[96]

BIRMINGHAM

The use of all these methods of restraint was a source of some anxiety to the central prison authorities, and of careful scrutiny for concerned outsiders. Mrs Fry was 'always fearful of any punishment beyond what the law *publicly authorises*, being *privately inflicted* by any keeper or officer of a prison'.[97] In 1853 a scandal occurred which fulfilled the worst of her fears, and of those who thought like her. The conduct of discipline at Birmingham Borough Gaol became the subject of local concern following revelations at the inquest of Edward Andrews, a boy of fifteen who had hanged himself in the prison on 27 April. A public meeting was held at which allegations of severity and cruelty were made by two recently dismissed members of the prison staff. A delegation

of Birmingham citizens proceeded to memorialize the Home Secretary, Lord
Palmerston, in person. 'If a criminal must suffer death', they urged on him, 'it
should be by the doom of the law, and the sentence should be carried out in a
legal manner, but it should not form part of any system that a man or any set of
men should have the power to inflict such a prison discipline as will daily lessen
the prisoner's love of life, until finally goaded to madness, and no longer able to
endure that discipline, he consummates his life of crime by the great crime itself
of self-destruction.'[98] The proceedings of the Royal Commission that followed
were focused on the activities of the Governor, Lieutenant Austin, RN. He had
worked as deputy to, and then succeeded as Governor, the renowned penal
administrator and reformer Captain Maconochie. Maconochie had first
formulated and then operated, in Van Diemen's Land, the mark system, which
was to become the cornerstone of English prison discipline. The Commissioners
questioned present and previous staff and prisoners of the gaol and uncovered a
legacy of severity and illegal punishment which led back to Captain Maconochie
himself. He, they say, had 'punished for prison offences by depriving prisoners
of their bed and of their gas, by keeping them from exercise, by preventing
them (even in the case of untried prisoners) from seeing their friends, by com-
pelling them to stand with their faces to the wall for all the working hours
during the day, and in some instances for several successive days – all of them
unquestionably illegal punishments.'[99] Prisoner Richard Scott was asked by
one of the Commissioners:

> Were you ever placed in the hall by the old governor? – Yes.
> How were you placed? – Standing by the wall.
> Without moving? – Yes.
> (Dr Baly) What prevented you moving? – I durst not; the governor
> stationed me not to stir.[100]

Encouraged by these precedents, and aided by a new chief officer lately
arrived from the county gaol at Leicester, Lieutenant Austin had waxed
inventive in his search for yet more stringent forms of constraint and punishment. He had had made some leather collars or stocks, which were produced to
the Commissioners. 'They were of various sizes, but those which appeared to
have been most commonly used, were about 3½ inches deep at the deepest part
in front, somewhat more than thirteen inches long, and rather less than a
quarter of an inch thick, made of leather perfectly rigid.' The mode of use of the
collar consisted in 'the prisoner being first muffled in the strait jacket, having his
arms tied together on his breast, the leather stock fastened tightly round his neck,
and being, moreover (where the punishment was inflicted by day), in almost
every case strapped to the wall of his cell, in a standing position, by means of
strong leather straps passed round the upper parts of the arms, and fastened to
staples or hooks in the wall, so tightly as to draw back the arms into and keep
them in a constrained and necessarily painful position, at the same time compressing them.' It was obvious 'that such a mode of restraint must necessarily, if

continued for several hours, be productive of great pain, – in truth it must be an engine of positive torture. So strapped to the wall, prisoners – chiefly boys – were kept for periods of four, five and six hours, and in some instances for a whole day, by way of punishment for the nonperformance of the crank labour, and for other prison offences, frequently of a very trivial character.'[101]

As the Commissioners observed, these methods were not only used for trivial offences, but like the handcuffs at Millbank were used without discrimination of age. One of the victims 'Lloyd Thomas (the little boy of ten years old), declared that he was kept in the jacket and collar, but not strapped to the wall, for the whole of three consecutive days.'[102] The evidence of another boy, William Barnes, illustrates the experience of others besides himself.

WILLIAM BARNES sworn
How old are you? – Going of 12.
When is your birthday? – I do not know.
Do you remember being put into the strait jacket? – Yes.
What was that for? – Why for ringing the bell on a Sunday.
What did you ring if for? – I did not know it; I could not tell; I just went to touch the handle and the little door fell open.
Did this strait jacket hurt you much? – Yes; about my arms and my body.
Did you cry out? – Yes.
What did you cry? – I cried out as loud as ever I could; I had as lief be dead as alive then.[103]

To add to the discomfort of the jacket, Isaac Shaw – aged 16 – was drenched in water as well. 'The governor came, and by his order the crank-warder threw over the prisoner a bucket-full of cold water as he lay on the floor; the governor himself threw over him two buckets-full more.'[104]

This treatment was also applied to Edward Andrew, whose condition prompted a memorandum from John Wood, the prison schoolmaster. Andrew, he said 'had the strait jacket last Sunday morning, two hours. It made shrivelled marks on his arm and body. A bucket of water stood by him in case of exhaustion. He stood with cold, red, bare feet, on a sock soaked in water. The ground was covered with water. He looked very deathly and reeled with weakness when liberated and previous to liberation. . . . Too weak and jaded to be taught; could only be talked to; always appeared wild. His crime, talking and using obscene language; was also threatened with trial before the magistrates.'[105]

The Commission's ultimate findings were unequivocal: 'With respect then, to the case of Edward Andrews, we are of the opinion that, by the order and with the knowledge of the governor, he was punished illegally and cruelly, and was driven thereby to the commission of suicide.'[106] Captain Austin was ordered dismissed the service; Dr Blount, the surgeon, came in for criticism over his attempt to give the drenching of a prisoner with buckets of cold water some sort of medical gloss, 'but he was, with some difficulty, brought to admit that in his judgment the man had no disease whatever, and that the water was in truth thrown over him solely by way of punishment for his supposed obstinacy and his filthiness.'[107] He saved the Commission the duty of giving him the sack by resigning.

VIOLENCE

Violence by prisoners was not restricted to the damage they could do to the physical contents of their cells. On occasions they would lash out at fellow prisoners. In a fight that Dr Quinton saw, a large man had picked on one smaller than himself, but 'the small man gave him unexpected sport, and a regular hammering – the officer in charge, I inferred, not intervening prematurely when he saw how things were going'.[108]

But higher in the scale of seriousness by which prison offences and their punishments were measured, were attacks on warders, governors or other officials. One day Mark Jeffrey, 'when more than usually hungry and exasperated . . . seized an additional piece of bread from the turnkey as he was serving out the allowance. "You have one piece," said he. This was provocation enough for me in the condition I then was, and I immediately retaliated by knocking him down.'[109] Violent as he was, there was a quality of impulsiveness about Mark Jeffrey, and an engaging frankness about his recollections, which rob them of innate nastiness. The same could not be said of some other prisoners, one of whom, 'with the mind of a devil and a heart of stone unless it had cankered away with hate, imagined a grievance with an officer, and in order to be revenged planned a terrible and dastardly act. He fashioned the handle of a spoon to a point, and removing the glass from the spy-hole of his cell, pierced the eye of the warder when making an observation in the course of his duty.'[110] Another man with an 'imaginary' grievance, 'cut a warder down with a heavy blow on the head, and then attempted to kill him as he lay on the ground. The reasons he gave were of the most trivial kind – the warder (he said) had reported him once, had refused him a pair of dry stockings at another time when his feet were wet, and denied him a drink of water just before the assault occurred. Even these accusations were proved to be false.'[111]

During David Fannan's stay at Portland no less than two warders were murdered, and 'it is a sad commentary on the desperate elements to be found in our penitentiaries', he says, 'that they were the most amiable warders on the staff. One of them, Trevitt – an admirable man – was struck dead by a blow from a pick; and the other, called Blyth – a man full of cheery, good nature, had his legs mangled by blows from a spade, and died shortly after.'[112]

That women were by no means immune from these outbreaks soon became apparent to George Chesterton when 'various metropolitan workhouses caused their refractory paupers to be committed to Cold Bath Fields, up to September,

1850, and we witnessed in the demeanour of the young girls, from fifteen years of age and upwards, such revolting specimens of workhouse education, that the exhibition was at once frightful and disgusting. The inconceivable wickedness of those girls was absolutely appalling. Their language, their violence, and their indecency shocked every beholder.'[113] Whether such behaviour was due to moral degeneracy or to corruption as Chesterton thought, Arthur Griffiths, who encountered women prisoners for the first time at Millbank, insisted that 'it has been officially recognised nowadays that the most effective government is that exercised by a doctor; so many questions of hyper-emotional tempera- ment, of hysteria, of peculiar physical conditions arise, that the chief official in every large prison today is invariably a medical man.' Griffiths had written a book on the earlier history of Millbank and recalls that 'the first batch of women received were found to be suffering from fits. The affliction promptly disappeared when the Governor stated that the best treatment was to shave and blister the heads of all who were attacked.'[114]

So far as the workhouse women were concerned, Chesterton complained that 'the punishment provided by law, for their offences in prison, was restricted to solitary confinement, on bread and water, at which they positively mocked.'[115] He attributed their unruliness, in part, to the fact that he could not order them flogged. Whilst agreeing that 'the exhibition of a woman, stripped to the waist, and flogged, with the cat-o'-nine-tails, by a man, gave evidence of a barbarous age and people,' he still thought that 'manual correction by a woman, in the presence of women only, would infuse salutary intimidation.'[116]

FLOGGING

Chesterton was no stranger to these questions. A favourite sentence of the Victorian courts was for a whipping to accompany a period of imprisonment. Prison governors were charged with seeing that both were properly imple- mented. In Chesterton's early days, judicial floggings had been public events. 'The culprit was conducted to the spot by my officers and made fast to the cart's-tail, while I also repaired to the place selected, where I found crowds of assembled spectators. On the production of the warrant, and the necessary intimation, the cart moved slowly on, and as it travelled onwards, the cat fell heavily, at intervals, on the prisoner's bare back, and at the conclusion, the condition of the skin amply proved the severity of the castigation. My first reflection, after this exhibition, was that I and the police had been degraded, and the public outraged by so savage a spectacle, and I heartily rejoiced when the custom fell into desuetude, or became prohibited; I know not which.'[117]

Only the publicity attending the event 'fell into desuetude', the sentences continued to be imposed, but behind prison walls. Henry Holloway underwent the ordeal in Manchester:

I shall never forget the morning I was brought out to be flogged, which happened about a week after I went in. When I got into the great yard I saw the governor, the surgeon, the chaplain, and about forty prisoners, the latter with their faces towards the wall. When the triangle was brought out I began to shake from head to foot. It appeared that several had to be flogged; and to make matters more unpleasant, so far as I was concerned, a number had to undergo the punishment before me. When the first was strapped he began to shout and roar like a child, but the lash was nevertheless, administered with great force. Such crying and groaning I never heard before or since, and I hope I may never hear again. Amongst the rest were the following ejaculations: 'Do have pity!' 'Lord, save me!' 'Mercy! Mercy! you'll kill me!' My name was called at last, and I in turn began to cry for mercy and pardon; but it was only like the prophets of Baal calling unto their god – no help came. On the contrary, the more I cried for mercy the more severely was the lash felt. At length I was released from the triangle, and marched slowly to my cell. On arriving there I fell down from exhaustion, and was scarcely able to lie in bed for pain.[118]

For a time, the floggings in the prison yard had formed part of a moral pageantry, to which assembled bodies of the imprisoned were exposed; so as to edify them, by one view, or to terrorize them, by another. 'I had never seen corporal punishment administered', recalls a man sentenced to twenty years' penal servitude, 'and I felt a sort of horror at being forced to witness it. I applied to the governor to be allowed to be absent, but he would not hear of it. . . . A dead silence reigned through the place. The warders, at regular intervals, stood in front of the prisoners with their staves in their hands; and a party of the prison-guard stood near the triangle with bayonets fixed.'[119]

These semi-public displays in prison did not long survive the disappearance of floggings and hangings outside the gates for the instruction of the mob. The reasoning in both instances may have been similar: an official feeling perhaps that displays of brutality were no longer in keeping with the 'modern' style of punishment and reformation. And there was the constant danger of fresh disorder excited by the spectacle. But although it could no longer be seen, flogging continued to be an audible presence in prisons . At Pentonville it took place at the end of the day. 'When the door banging is *done*, night is not silent. They choose this time when all the prisoners have gone to bed, for administering the cat-o'-nine-tails to men who have been sentenced to that punishment. You are awakened by the voice of the doctor calling to a warder, as he stumbles along the dark halls towards the room where the dread chastisment is administered. Then there are the frantic and furious cries of the unhappy victim, and his hellish, dismal howls continue to resound through the otherwise silent watches of the night, long after the operation is finished.'[120] During these performances, in Jabez Balfour's experience, 'a kind of awe-stricken silence and stupor pervaded the whole company'. He affirmed 'that at such times a feeling of nausea overpowers all others, with the result that many a dinner that day would be left untasted'.[121]

Men varied widely in their capacities to withstand the pain, or even to tolerate the prospect of an imminent flogging. The Reverend Clifford Rickards once 'blundered' onto the scene when a man was 'tied to the triangle, waiting

Whipping-post, Wandsworth

for the first stroke of the cat. As long as I live', he recalls, 'I shall never forget that man's face or its expression. I had often heard the saying "In a blue funk," but had never before seen an example of it.'[122] Some men 'roared awfully' under the lash.[123] Manchester Merchant had never heard such 'roaring, screaming and appealing for mercy'.[124] But one young man 'never made a murmur. I had occasion to go into his cell soon afterwards, and he stripped his back bare so as to show me the impression left upon him. He was in a dreadful state; in fact his back presented the appearance of raw meat. I asked him if he had suffered much while undergoing the punishment, and he replied "Rather; I thought they would have cut me in two, but I had fully made up my mind to die before I would roar out and be laughed at".'[125]

Henry Harcourt made the same resolve when he was flogged – for hurling a chamber pot which missed a prisoner and struck an officer instead. It was an experience he found difficult to put into words: 'a number of lights of different colors seemed to pass and repass before me, and I thought a quantity of hot dust had been thrown over me.' 'The chief officer, who was calling the strokes, gave extra instructions to the flogger, saying, "Lower down, more to the left," and so on, knowing that the first few lashes are much more acute than those that follow, for they know that those who can bear a dozen without flinching can bear the whole number without uttering a sound. It was a great disappointment to the doctor, and his friend, the governor not to hear me bellow.' [126]

Such men were not numerous. 'An odd case may arise', says O'Donovan Rossa, 'where a prisoner would utter no cry, and this person would be a hardened wretch in the estimation of the jailers, while his fellow-prisoners would look upon him as a hero.' [127] One such, the only man to be flogged during Arthur Griffiths's tenure of the governor's office at Wormwood Scrubs, 'endured it all without a sign or a groan', and when he was taken down from the triangle, turned to the assembled officials 'and said coolly, "Now, I'll fight the best man among you." '[128]

As for the effects on men's minds, as opposed to their backs, George Bidwell, who narrowly escaped the cat, said afterwards that 'had they flogged me, there is no doubt that I should have been put into a state of mind that would have led to murder.'[129] George was merely surmising, but Henry Holloway actually was flogged, and the effect on *him* was definitely not the one intended:

> The day after I was flogged the warder came into my cell, and said, 'They have been warming your back, have they?' So hardened was I that I asked him what it had to do with him. As I got better the thought of the lash grew weaker, and I began to care very little about anything else. When I got out of prison I became worse than ever, and in less than four months I was put upon my trial again for felony, but was not convicted.[130]

Floggings were relatively rare occurrences in English prisons; Chesterton boasted that during the last year of his authority at Cold Bath Fields, 'out of 10,000 inmates, in the course of the whole year, *four* only were visited with corporal chastisement.'[131] So why do nineteenth-century prison authors spend what appears to be a disproportionate fraction of their literary effort on it? It is partly due, no doubt, to the brutal and dramatic spectacle it presented, and partly to its powerful illustration of 'man's inhumanity to man'. But were there, beyond these fairly obvious explanations, any other reasons for the obsessive interest in all the details of the instruments and procedures of judicial flogging? Here are two physical descriptions; the first, by the Reverend Henry Ryder, is of a young Irishman about to be flogged for his part in a robbery. 'Though not above middle size he was wonderfully good-looking; a brilliant complexion, large violet eyes, and dark hair with just a glint of fire in it.'[132] In the second, a 'Warden' refers to 'A man we will call "X". He had a fine athletic figure, and was very goodlooking in rather a boyish manner. A few days after his reception he was examined one morning by the doctor and told to come along to the punishment cells. There he was stripped. He had a perfect frame, this young Irish giant – he would have served as a model of masculine perfection.'[133] An overheard conversation between two boys in the unreformed Newgate suggested to one observer one of the reasons for this sort of interest. 'Two of them very circumstantially described the effects of witnessing an execution at the Old Bailey. . . . The same effects transpire under the punishment of flogging – *that is, priapism*; the fact is in itself curious.'[134]

TRANSIT

Compton Mackenzie, whose memories of childhood were vivid, remembers seeing 'a chained gang of convicts who were working in Portsmouth harbour' in the summer of 1886. 'At the far end of the gang was a tall gaunt man who seemed to lift his fettered leg with difficulty as he walked and whose expression was one of utter agony. Were I able to draw I could draw his features with complete accuracy. It was finely cut profile and his eyes seemed to be staring at despair.'[135] Lines of manacled convicts like these were common enough spectacles in the vicinity of Portsmouth, Chatham and Dartmoor, and they were not unknown elsewhere as prisoners were moved from place to place in an unending penitential progress. They were most regularly to be seen at railway stations, and their appearance in public rarely failed to create a sensation. 'No sooner' did One-who-has-endured-it and his party 'draw up at the Great Western Railway than immediately a crowd collected to see us alight. I cautiously cast my eyes around dreading to catch sight of any known face, and I tried to keep as much behind other men as possible. I noticed that many gazed for a moment at us, and turned away with a look of contemptuous pity and disgust, which strange to say, rather amused me than otherwise.'[136]

For many convicts, the experience of being 'chained together like beasts, stared at',[137] 'stared at, like so many wild beasts',[138] was unforgettably unpleasant. 'Men looked at us', says David Fannan, 'as if unable to realize our humanity.'[139] On the other hand, it is all too easy to realize the inhumanity of the crowd that gathered round the solitary figure of Oscar Wilde:

> From two o'clock till half-past two on that day I had to stand on the centre platform of Clapham Junction in convict dress and handcuffed, for the world to look at. I had been taken out of the Hospital Ward without a moment's notice being given to me. Of all possible objects I was the most grotesque. When people saw me they laughed. Each train as it came up swelled the audience. Nothing could exceed their amusement. That was of course before they knew who I was. As soon as they had been informed, they laughed still more. For half an hour I stood there in the grey November rain surrounded by a jeering mob. For a year after that was done to me I wept every day at the same hour and for the same space

of time. That is not such a tragic thing as possibly it sounds to you. To those who are in prison, tears are a part of every day's experience. A day in prison on which one does not weep is a day on which one's heart is hard, not a day on which one's heart is happy. [140]

For outsiders, the sight of prisoners between prisons opened a rare window into a closed world; for the prisoners themselves the journeys provided an equally rare glimpse of the outside. And although they were tightly manacled there was a perceptible relaxation of the less tangible aspects of discipline. 'You left the separate system behind you in passing out of Pentonville, and the officers who accompany you treat you as men passed into a comparative state of freedom.' [141] 'The moment we stepped outside the prison door a tacit licence seemed to be given to the men to chatter and talk as they liked and most of them availed themselves of it at once.' [142] When they reached the railway station, the bolder spirits of the party made practical use of this licence. 'A large third-class saloon carriage was set specially apart for us in the night mail train for Plymouth, and so soon as we were all in and our warders, the men began begging tobacco from the people thronging the platform. . . . "I say you, Sir, in the white choker, give a poor devil a bit of bacca," cried one, thrusting his head from the window, and holding forth his free hand. . . . "We ain't any of us proud, so if you haven't all got sheeroots, throw us baccy," seeing one man about to take some out of his pouch; "don't be stingy, do it well while you are about it. Pitch the lot here and I'll return you the case the next time I see you." A hearty laugh from all around greeted this, and the man did actually throw the pouch, which one of the warders in vain tried to obtain possession of. In an incredibly short time the pouch was emptied, and the prisoner who first caught it threw it back to the man in the crowd. . . . Several people threw tobacco in at the windows of our carriage, which the officers in vain tried to prevent, both by appealing to the people on the platform to desist, and by endeavouring to get it from the men. . . . the engine's last shriek was heard, and we moved out of the station. The warders soon desisted from their scuffling with the men about the tobacco. I do not believe one of them got a scrap of it, nor do I think they either cared or wished to. What they did was but for show, and to keep up the appearance of doing their duty.' [143]

Journeys like these were also opportunities for escape-minded prisoners. Chain-gangs were virtually escape-proof, but when Jeremiah O'Donovan Rossa was being moved by himself from Portland to London, en route to Chatham, he thought that there might be a chance of getting away from his guards where the train made one of its scheduled stops. At the station where he had resolved to make his bid, one of the warders brought him some food from one of the vendors who plied the platforms with refreshments.

He gave the money to the little girl and gave me the cakes. As I took them into my manacled hands, whatever blood was in my body seemed to rush into my face. I felt it, I felt the thrill through my whole frame. I know there was some impulse toward throwing them into his face, or throwing them out of the window, but another impulse counteracted that, in the thought that the man was acting against his orders; that there was some kindness in the act, and the last thing I could do would be to hurt the feelings of a man who did not mean to hurt mine. I suppose if my blood was ever hot, it was somewhat cooled down at this time. I ate the cakes, and never spoke a word till I reached London, meditating on that escape of mine.[144]

It may seem a tender-hearted response from a man who advocated the violent ejection of the British from Ireland, and who later organized a dynamiting offensive against targets in London, but the fact is, he says he did not care to attack a man who had just done him a small favour.

ESCAPE

There was nothing that so animated both the spirit and the mechanism of discipline, nor so quickened the public interest in prison, as an escape, or the threat of it. Prisons were built like fortresses and castles, in part to symbolize their impregnability to attack from without, but also so as to emphasize their immunity to escape from within. The legal authority that accompanied the convict from court was a warrant to hold the person for as long as the judge or magistrate had seen fit to specify in the sentence; so many days, weeks or years. To lose a prisoner was to fail in that fundamental duty and prisons went to great lengths not to do so. And yet, for reasons that are not entirely clear, many prisoners not only made no attempt to escape, they did not appear even to contemplate it. In the case of short-sentence men and women that may be understandable, but for those condemned to spend many years behind bars, under conditions of great hardship and deprivation, it is less easy to see why escapes were not more often attempted. There are a number of possible reasons for this reluctance; the greater likelihood of identification through the pages of the criminal registry or the marvels of M. Berthillon's multi-form measurements or the patent processes of finger-printing; the growing numbers and effectiveness of the various police forces; the increasingly intimate grip of civil authority on the towns and cities; a populace progressively schooled to its place in the official scheme of things; an acceptance of court proceedings as legitimate and just; a sense of awe engendered by the presence of personal representatives of an impersonal power. . . .

Neither of the Bidwell brothers was apt to stand in awe of any man, let alone the lower functionaries of the English prison system. Nor were they inclined to wait and see whether their sentences were fair or not. They determined instead to escape from Newgate before they came to trial. Like their assault on the Bank of England, the plan of escape was simple and audacious – and that was simply to walk out of the prison through doors unlocked for them by bribed warders. 'They proposed to let us out at night when on night duty, or even in the daytime should a favorable opportunity present itself. They also proposed to go with us, vacating a responsible position of trust, thus incurring the penalty of penal servitude should they ever be caught. And all this for what consideration? £100 – about $500!' After his release, more than fourteen years later, George Bidwell professed doubts about the plan. 'It was too cheap!' His comrades perceived that he 'was cold on the project', but he did not feel 'authorised in attempting to put a veto on the matter, for the others would always feel that I had caused them to throw away a chance of escape'. 'Neither of us knew at the time that every cell door was double-locked at ten P.M., so that only with the master key, which was kept by the governor, could a cell be unlocked.'[145] The plot was, in any event, discovered when one of the bought warders could not resist displaying his new-found wealth, and talking about his imminent emigration to a new life abroad. Bidwell later 'heard that Norris was sentenced to eighteen months imprisonment, and that the other two were dismissed the service. Of course this looks, on the bare facts, as though they got off very lightly for such a breach of duty.'[146]

Few prisoners possessed the resources, either organizational or financial, necessary for an escape attempt of that nature. For them, the barriers were physical ones – getting out of a locked cell, getting over a high wall, getting away from the neighbourhood of the prison. To be successful in breaking out from a cell, the would-be escaper needed first of all some sort of tool, quite a bit of persistence, and not a little luck. Sometimes the tool was at hand. A prisoner sentenced to fifteen years' transportation waited until the night warder had passed by. 'After he had been round I got a piece of iron from the loom in my cell. I then prized the door open with it, which took me at least two hours before I had accomplished it.'[147] There was also a claim that 'a thick iron bar was cut through with a saw made of a watch-spring.'[148] Possession of the tools did not in itself solve the escaper's difficulties. He also had to deal with the noise it was necessary to make in dislodging masonry or metal windows. A cunning solution to the problem was hit upon by a prisoner who 'had concealed the head of a sledge-hammer in his clothing when he came in from work. It was a Sunday evening, and as the warders slammed door after door in serving the suppers he beat out the cast-iron framework of his window with blows timed to coincide with the slamming of the doors.'[149]

By far the most promising starting-point for any would-be escaper was from one of the working parties which went out each day to dig the dock basin, or reclaim the moor. After he had left Dartmoor, Ticket-of-leave-man received a letter sent illegally to him by a friend still there. In it he describes how a group of men at work on the moor had decided to make the dash for freedom. Ticket-of-leave-man's correspondent urged caution upon them; but 'the vision of convicts, artful and cunning as the majority of them are, seems to be obfuscated when the very possibility of regaining liberty is dancing before their eyes. . . . I suggested to them that Captain Harris, the Governor, and Captain

Johnson, the Deputy-Governor, had swift horses, and were probably dead-shots with the rifle.' His colleagues were not to be deterred and waited for an opportune moment to flee.

> We had stacked our rakes and forks, so that we were entirely unarmed, and three officers armed with loaded rifles were in charge of us. We were unwisely allowed to go alone to the hedge, which was at a considerable distance, to fetch our clothes. 'Now is our chance!' said Morgan, and over the hedge went the conspirators. As I was one who remained behind I could take stock of the officers in charge. They were supposed to be 'on guard'. I must say I never saw men so completely taken 'off their guard.' They looked very like the historical 'stuck' animal, the brothers and sisters of which they are far better qualified to take charge of than convicts.[150]

The members of this particular party may have surprised the officers, but they did not get very far. There was at Dartmoor 'a standing reward of £3 to anyone arresting an escaped convict, so that the whole country round about are always on the lookout for anyone that has a prison crop.'[151] On this occasion, 'thirty or forty Devonshire labourers had heard the alarm-whistle and the signal gun. They were soon joined by others, and in strong parties started in pursuit.' The men were recaptured and 'a score or more of poor Devonians . . . anticipated Michaelmas and became the joyful possessors of a whole golden sovereign; perhaps some poor slipshod daughter will get a new pair of boots'.[152] These ancillaries aided the strenuous efforts of the prison staff; Basil Thomson, for example, mounted his horse and rode after one man. He found him 'shivering, and irresolute, anxious only to be recaptured. In fact, when he saw me, instead of running away he approached me and scrambled over the wall to my side. I have never seen so miserable an object.'[153]

Other escapers at Dartmoor were pursued by members of the civil guard, 'armed with carbines, loaded and to be fired in case of a man trying to escape.' They were 'instructed to fire low and as far as possible avoid killing the man.'[154] But even when the instructions were followed, to the extent that circumstances permitted, they could still have fatal consequences. 'The men were called upon to halt. One obeyed, the other scaled a stone wall, and in the failing light, while he was actually stooping for the jump down, the civil guard fired at his legs, but the charge of buckshot struck him in the back. He died almost immediately.'[155] The Reverend C. Rickards 'met the bearers bringing him into the prison, and, removing the handkerchief from his face, saw that he was dead'.[156] Some time later, in his capacity as censor, Rickards came across the following phrase in a prisoner's letter, 'The one they killed is the best off. If I could make sure of being shot dead, as he was, I too would make a bolt for liberty.'[157]

In the breast of the general public, escaped prisoners did not evoke simple emotion. On the one hand, 'he grows suddenly in popular fancy into being half-giant, half-ogre, a terrible creature who may come round the corner at any moment and devour babies'.[158] But there is another perception of him, an unexpected quirk in the character of public opinion, and an indication perhaps that the legitimacy of the legal and penal systems was, for some Victorians at least, a lightly worn garment. The unmanned 'lock-up' in the county town of Huntingdon backed onto the river. A prisoner locked up in it – probably for drunkenness – began to demolish the outer wall of the cell and 'although several persons, by either hearing or seeing something unusual, stopped to see what was happening, no inkling of the proceedings was carried to anyone in authority. By the time the hole in the wall was large enough for the prisoner to squeeze himself through, there was a numerous group of interested and amused onlookers. . . . the man quietly waded to the bank, nodded a friendly recognition to those who had been witnesses of his exploit, and he was again a free man. The work of making the hole in the wall had gone on for some time, and the wonder was that no one in authority got wind of what was going forward when so many of the townspeople not only heard of it, but assembled to witness the gaol-breaking.'[159]

Similar populist sentiment surfaced in unexpected places. Mary Gordon was a doctor and the first woman to be appointed to the inspectorate of prisons:

> Once I was in a town where a man who had been committed for trial escaped on the morning when he should have been tried. In the afternoon I met the judge who was seeing over the prison. He said: 'Well – that fellow has got clean away.' I said (really without thinking of what I was saying): 'I'm so glad.' 'What!' said the Judge, severely, 'His Majesty's Inspector *glad* when a prisoner escapes from justice?' 'Yes', I said, stoutly, 'I am'. The judge looked cautiously round about him. 'Don't tell anybody', he whispered, 'but *so am I.*'[160]

No caution at all marked the reception of an escaped Dartmoor man when he was recaptured in a Devon town some way from the prison. 'He was placed in a wagonette and driven smartly through the crowded street, greeted with the cheers of the onlookers, a very improper but very natural recognition of his pluck and cleverness,' says Clifford Rickards.[161] And at South Tawton, when two escapees were taken, 'the inhabitants sided with them, and attempted their rescue. They also supplied them with tobacco and beer to such an extent that one of the prisoners was quite drunk when finally secured.'[162]

Even in Princetown, where most of the population consisted of warders and their families, there was an unseemly enthusiasm for some escapes: 'round the corner at the bottom of the street came warders and convicts, apparently without any order, but all in a crowd. They were soon surrounded and followed by a mass of spectators, school children, visitors, and villagers all marching confusedly together. There was laughing and joking, and apparently none seemed to be enjoying the joke so much as the prisoners, who appeared to be having the time of their lives, and were evidently the heroes in the play.'[163] What happened next to the returned absconder was often less of a laughing matter. At Dartmoor 'it was the age-long tradition of the place that he should be taken down to a separate cell and be beaten indiscriminately' by the warders.[164]

CONTROL

At the very heart of Victorian prison discipline lies a mystery; a puzzle that first presents itself as a disproportion of numbers. One thing that struck Captain D— S— at Clerkenwell 'was the small number of warders in comparison to the prisoners. Seven or eight, from the Governor to the lowest turnkey, comprised the entire staff, and were responsible for the safety of some two hundred prisoners.'[165] It was a phenomenon that fascinated many observers, including William Hepworth Dixon.

> Standing in the centre of a large room, in which 140 are employed in tailoring and picking oakum, it is thrilling to think what a mass of disorderly passion, of brute ignorance, of criminal desires, is held down and prostrated before and within a few yards of you by the presence of a few unarmed officers. In former times – not many years ago, indeed – these men would all have been chained to the walls, and manacled with irons, hand and foot. Now they are perfectly free. There is no more restraint upon them than is exercised over the work-men in a well-ordered manufactory. Silence and attention to work are alone enforced. This however, is enough. The order is perfect. The silence is profound. The march of industry is steady and regular. There is a unity of action, a promptness in obeying orders, which would do no discredit to a well-drilled regiment on parade.

The perfection of Hepworth Dixon's picture is illusory – prisoners were never that well behaved. But there is a reality in the fact of so few officers controlling so many potentially rebellious men. 'The stranger cannot divest himself of the feeling', says our intrepid author, 'that he is standing on a volcano which may, for anything he can safely assume to the contrary, explode at any moment, and make sad havoc by its violence – the more fatal for being only temporary. He feels himself in the position of Van Amburgh in the cage of lions.'[166]

The image of the volcano recurs at several points in the writings of senior officials. 'The Governor of a convict prison never forgets that he is sitting upon the crust of a volcano – a crust which may wear thin at any moment,' said Basil Thomson.[167] Chaplain Clifford Rickards likened it to 'living in a powder magazine, that a spark might blow up at any time'.[168] The strain of living on the edge of this volcano sometimes proved too much for those who bore the responsibility. At Dartmoor, when Basil Thomson first went there as deputy, the then governor was in such a state that whenever staff approached him about any matter to do with the prison 'they were to begin chanting a refrain of "It's all right, sir," as soon as they came within earshot'.[169]

Practical Hand recalls the proposal; 'I don't know who first spoke of it – that convicts should exercise in gangs, in which they should not be permitted to speak or make signs to each other. I remember how frightened we all were

when the plan first came out. We thought the profession would be an excessively dangerous one, because the convicts would be continually rising and
murdering their officers. When it was tried, however, by degrees, this did not
happen.' Practical Hand was puzzled by this docility; 'No doubt, if you take a
hundred free-born Britons, innocent of any offence, and put them into a field
with a circular path round it, and tell them to walk round, keeping six feet
apart, and this at the bidding of some three, or at most four, taskmasters quite
unarmed, the free-born Britons would fall in and secure their guards at all risks
of consequences.'[170]

A prisoner who had considered the problem from the other side came to a
different conclusion. 'This phenomenon, like many others peculiar to prison-
life, exemplifies and illustrates one of the strange mysteries in the criminal
character. Much of course is done by sheer force or terror to subdue the prisoner
to the exigencies of his lot; but much, too, is accompanied by the facilities – the
amiable facilities they might be called – of the criminal nature. . . . This part
of his nature includes a signal exemption from irritability or angry excitement,
and a bland courtesy of obedience that has a strange similarity to a high tone of
Christian resignation.'[171]

The obedience may have assumed the outward appearance of Christian
resignation, but its achievement was a product of deliberate planning and
effort on the part of the authorities. An Old Warder quotes approvingly a
passage from the Third Report of the Prison Inspectors in which they say that
'the prisoner, on entering his cell, ought to see at once that all his efforts to
struggle with that discipline will be utterly unavailing. Every thing around him
should present the appearance of a barrier, against which the utmost exertion
of his strength, seconded by his most skilful ingenuity and the most untiring
perseverance, must contend in vain.'[172] A part of this impression was created by
architectural means; what Daniel Nihill called 'passive and inanimate obstacles which cannot be made the subjects of hostility' – although as we have seen,
they often were. 'If prisoners are not to look out of windows,' he goes on, 'let the
windows be out of reach – if they are not to converse with those in adjoining
calls, let the partition walls be made too thick.' The aim of this policy, in
Nihill's opinion, was to deflect hostility from the persons of the officers
'towards whom on moral accounts, a friendly and grateful feeling should be
cherished'.[173]

The officers however, personified an impersonal regime in which 'Things
which in another situation would be ridiculous to notice, are here of necessity
inflated into unnatural importance, and made matters of grave discussion, of
formal investigation and trial – and for this plain reason, that when a multitude of bad characters are collected under the control of a few officers, they
form a very combustible mass. Little matters might easily be blown up into a
mighty flame, and it is therefore necessary to notice every slight tendency to
disorder, and promptly to check it by punishment.'[174] Against these 'little
matters' then, the threat of extreme force was brought to bear. 'Do you not see',
Governor Cope of Newgate enquired of Mark Jeffrey when he was refusing to

work on Sunday, 'that by this persistent refusal to obey orders, you incite the other prisoners to rebellion? We must keep order and discipline in the prison.' And after one of his violent outbursts, the governor approached him and said, 'Jeffrey, don't you know that all this resistance to authority is useless, and only makes your punishment more severe? We can call the soldiers, and you will certainly be injured if you persist in such mad behaviour.'[175]

Success for the staff in instances like this was important for the atmosphere of intimidation and fear it created amongst other prisoners, an atmosphere captured by Stuart Wood in a purple passage:

> I have not actually seen men flogged or hanged, but I have seen them *after* being flogged and noted their cowed look and twitching limbs. I have seen men streaming with blood from blows with truncheons and seen them thrown from the top of the steel staircases to the bottom. I have seen men sustain broken limbs in resisting transfer to the punishment cells. I have heard them shrieking under the lash of the cat-o'-nine-tails and have seen them trussed like beasts in strait-jackets lying helpless on the floors of padded cells. I have seen and worked with men in chains with hideous sores on their ankles.[176]

'If I have myself escaped personal violence in prison,' he said, 'it is solely due to the fact that I early realised the utter futility of resistance.'[177]

There was, in these circumstances, only one kind of safety available to dissenting prisoners, and that lay in numbers. An example of successful mass action is documented at Stafford – not during Governor Fulford's time, but later. When the tickets outside cell doors were first inscribed with details of their occupants' crimes, suspicion fell upon the chaplain as the author of the scheme. Direct protests by individuals would have done no good, but 'there was nothing in prison discipline that could prevent them from coughing whilst at service in the chapel on Sundays. So as if by instinct, on the first Sunday after this innovation was made, several of them began to cough vigorously and the others catching up the meaning of it, almost every prisoner was suddenly seized with a fit of coughing which created a noise almost as bad as that which greets the ear on a visit to a dog show. The warders were powerless. They looked wild. They grinned savagely until they shook with passion, but they could not do anything.'[178] Staff were equally powerless in the presence of numbers of determined suffrage prisoners. When Sir Thomas Beecham went to Holloway to see his friend, fellow-conductor, and composer of the Women's March, Dr Ethel Smyth he 'arrived in the main courtyard of the prison to find the noble company of martyrs marching round it and singing lustily their war-chant while the composer, beaming approbation from an overlooking upper window, beat time in almost Bacchic frenzy with a toothbrush.'[179]

Numbers were not, however, a perfect protection for those prisoners who did not have the moral support of outsiders enjoyed by their political comrades. A set of events at Portland prison makes the point painfully. 'It had been a custom for many years', Ticket-of-leave-man says, 'for the prisoners to sing songs in their cells on Christmas-night. So long as this custom was kept within bounds it was to a certain extent tolerated; but at Portland the evil grew more obnoxious and unbearable every year. . . . On the Christmas of 1876 all sorts of vulgar, indecent, and beastly songs were sung aloud, and the prison reverberated with obscene and disgusting language, shouts of defiance to the authorities, and the free use of damnatory epithets. On the following day a good many men were reported and subjected to bread-and-water punishment, loss of marks, &c. This had no effect whatever. On the Christmas night of 1877 the same game was not only repeated, but in the prison called F north, in which the Roman Catholic prisoners are located, the blasphemous and obscene language and the filthy and disgusting songs were beyond all description horrible and hellish. Mr Clifton was called up after midnight, and was himself a witness of what was going on. He carefully and very properly satisfied himself of the identity of a score of the worst offenders, and at the next visit of the director, and on the recommendation of the governor, these men got "two dozen". On the Christmas-night of 1878 perfect order and quiet reigned throughout the prison.'[180]

As on that Christmas night, so for gaolers the aim was to reproduce every night 'perfect order and quiet' – and during the daytime too. And for almost all of the time they succeeded. Just occasionally, the half-articulated fear that haunted warders and governors, and their government overseers and pay-masters, almost edged into physical expression.

On July 22nd, 1901, a convict had thrown up his work, and as he was marching back to the prison in the rear of the other parties, he began to shout to his fellows to come and rescue him. It is a favourite trick of disorderly convicts when no one is touching them to emit piercing cries for help as if they were being murdered, in the hope of exciting the other men to violence. The ranks were broken and there was very nearly a mutiny.[181]

Very nearly, but not quite, since such appeals rarely, if ever, evoked a positive response from other convicts. 'Incitements to mutiny imply the existence of a good deal of mutual confidence and co-operation between the inciters and the incited, but just as it has been said that there never was an Irish conspiracy of three without one of the conspirators being a traitor, so I am sure that, except under very special circumstances, no three "old lags" would dare to trust one another in so serious and hopeless an enterprise.'[182]

So rare were disturbances involving more than one or two convicts during the whole of the nineteenth century that there are no readily accessible personal records of them. Susan Meredith, the prison visitor one day 'saw from a corridor window the whole yard full of riotous women, throwing their wooden clogs up into the air, the warders not daring to approach them. A friend with me volunteered to go with me and quiet them and afterwards mediate between them and the prison authorities. First taking the precaution of holding our chairs over our heads we worked our way into the middle of the yard, the women's surprise being so great that they stopped while we stood on the chairs and began expostulating with them on their conduct.'[183] It is a measure of the spontaneity, and ineffectiveness, of these *émeutes* that two lady visitors were so easily able to quell one by their unafraid presence in the yard. Unafraid, that is, so far as we know, since Miss Meredith reveals nothing of her feelings at the time. It could be that her activities as a visitor had conferred on her a non-combatant status which the prisoners respected. Lieutenant Colonel Rich enjoyed no such immunity at Maidstone where he was the governor. A group of convicts engaged on building work 'refused pointblank to fall in' at the end of one day's work. They were quickly surrounded by armed officers and a company of soldiers was summoned from the local barracks. 'It was at this stage of the affair', admits the Colonel (who had served with distinction in the Boer War), 'that I, trembling in every limb with blue funk, sailed into the middle of a seething and blasphemous mass of convicts armed with sticks and stones, all only waiting for one of their number to throw a brick or strike a blow, when the fat would immediately have been in the fire'. He addressed them in soldierly terms and ordered them to their cells.[184] To his surprise they obeyed, although, as he later reflected, 'how hopeless a mess we should have been in had the convicts only included one man game enough to throw the first brick'.[185]

There is an irony, perhaps an inevitability, in the fact that one of the very few major disturbances to take place in a nineteenth-century prison broke out at Chatham. Many of the men, and some of the officers there, had been transferred to the convict station from the hulks where discipline had been much more relaxed. On 6 February 1861 'a gross irregularity in serving out the men's dinners' was noticed by the chief officer and abruptly terminated. 'Two days after this occurrence one ruffian, more desperate than the rest, mounted on one of the tables in the mess-house, made an inflammatory speech upon the alleged bad quality of the soup, and finished by hurling his dinner into the centre of the room.' On this occasion 'acts of serious insubordination were confined to about a dozen', and 'nothing further of moment took place till the men were assembling on parade for labour on the afternoon of the 11th, when one man refused to join his party, raised a shout, and then threw up his cap. The spark of insubordination thus thrown upon the inflammable minds of the convicts spread like wild-fire, and, in a few minutes, all hope of restoring order, except by force, was at an end.'[186] Troops had to be employed to restore order; the ringleaders were flogged; many other prisoners forfeited remission and gratuities, and the prison reassumed its reputation as the epitome of repressive penal discipline. 'In all these matters the Chatham organisation was perfect', says Arthur Griffiths. 'Everything worked with clock-like precision; the worst that could be said was that it was too mechanical, the inmates were treated too much *en masse*, with no attempt at distinguishing between them. They were as one in the eyes of the authority, a single entity, ground under the hard and fast rules of the prison system. The wheels went on and on, round and round, with ceaseless, methodic movement, and everyone must conform, and either fall out or be crushed; the happiest were those who allowed themselves to be carried along without protest or hesitation, adapting themselves automatically to the monotonous movement.'[187]

Austin Bidwell who passed most of his prison years there agreed with much of Arthur Griffith's eulogy, but added to it a bitterness that could only come from experience of the juggernaut *beneath* its wheels.

An English prison is a vast machine in which a man counts for just nothing at all. He is to the establishment what a bale of merchandise is to a merchant's warehouse. The prison does not look on him as a man at all. He is merely an object which must move in a certain rut and occupy a certain niche provided for it. There is no room for the smallest sentiment. The vast machine of which he is an item keeps undisturbed on its course. Move with it and all is well. Resist, and you will be crushed as inevitably as the man who plants himself on the railroad track when the express is coming. Without passion, without prejudice, but also without pity and without remorse, the machine crushes and passes on. The dead man is carried to his grave and in ten minutes is as much forgotten as though he never existed.[188]

NOTES

1. Quinton, 13.
2. DuCane (1885), 156.
3. Ibid., 163.
4. Transportation and Penal Servitude Commission (1863), 14.
5. One-who-has-endured-it, 356.
6. DuCane (1885), 164.
7. Ibid., 168.
8. Transportation and Penal Servitude Commission (1863), 14.
9. DuCane (1885), 169.
10. Quinton, 50.
11. Gibson, 274.
12. One-who-has-suffered, 5.
13. Transportation and Penal Servitude Commission (1879), 440.
14. One-who-has-suffered-it, 593.
15. Fourth Inspectors' Report (1839), II, 112–14.
16. 'Twenty years', 677.
17. Sherard, 354.
18. Cecil, 219.
19. J. Balfour, 69.
20. Ibid., 153.
21. Davitt (1894), 878.
22. Ibid., 879.
23. Nihill, 23.
24. Ibid., 43.
25. One-who-has-endured-it, 84.
26. Sykes, 157.
27. Hart-Davis, 337.
28. Sykes, 111.
29. Hart-Davis, 337.
30. Rickards, 198.
31. Hart-Davis, 337.
32. J. Balfour, 256.
33. Maybrick, 137.
34. Huxley, 175.
35. Ticket-of-leave-man, 146.
36. Nihill, 51.
37. *Pentonville Prison from Within*, 210.
38. Ticket-of-leave-man, 145.
39. *Pentonville Prison from Within*, 200.
40. Cooper, 243.

41. Rossa, 186.
42. Henderson, 195.
43. Penal Servitude Commission (1879), 520.
44. One-who-has-endured-it, 94.
45. Ibid., 118.
46. Wood, 28.
47. J. Balfour, 89.
48. One-who-has-suffered, 17.
49. Chesterton (1856), II, 298.
50. J. Balfour, 87.
51. Ibid., 92–4.
52. Maybrick, 111.
53. One-who-has-endured-it, 329.
54. *Pentonville Prison from Within*, 200.
55. Dent, 33.
56. Griffiths (1904), 202.
57. One-who-has-suffered-it, 598.
58. D— S—, 205.
59. Penal Servitude Commission (1879), lii.
60. B. Thomson (1925), 29.
61. *Pentonville Prison from Within*, 201.
62. Ibid., 34.
63. Fannan, 113.
64. Rossa, 248.
65. Quinton, 27.
66. Hill (1894), 124.
67. Lovett, 238.
68. Field, I, 63.
69. Pitkin, 15.
70. East, 105.
71. Pitkin, 14.
72. G. Bidwell, 467.
73. Lytton, 97.
74. Ibid., 103.
75. Daly, 4.
76. Adam, 117.
77. Penal Servitude Commission (1879), 343.
78. One-who-has-tried-them, II, 164.
79. Lee, 68.
80. Collett, 49.
81. One-who-has-tried-them, II, 172.
82. Lee, 68.
83. Wood, 127.
84. Ibid., 126.
85. Mayhew, 528.

86. Scougal, 35.
87. Lloyd, 184.
88. Wood, 127.
89. Timewell, 13.
90. Ibid., 14.
91. Mayhew, 246.
92. E. Pankhurst, 154.
93. Maybrick, 117.
94. Lloyd, 186.
95. Maybrick, 117.
96. Lloyd, 183.
97. E. Fry (1847), II, 386.
98. Allday, 8.
99. Birmingham Inquiry (1853), xxviii.
100. Ibid., 185.
101. Ibid., viii.
102. Ibid., xxv.
103. Ibid., 355.
104. Ibid., xviii.
105. Ibid., x.
106. Ibid., xi.
107. Ibid., xvii.
108. Quinton, 37.
109. Hiener, 48.
110. Half-Timer, 67.
111. Paterson, 22.
112. Fannan, 105.
113. Chesterton, (1856) II, 134.
114. Griffiths, (1904), 205.
115. Chesterton, (1856) II, 132.
116. Chesterton, (1856) II, 134.
117. Ibid. (1856), II, 135.
118. Holloway (1877a), 8.
119. 'Twenty years', 676.
120. *Pentonville Prison from Within*, 167.
121. J. Balfour, 301.
122. Rickards, 201.
123. *Kirkdale*, 81.
124. Ibid., 61.
125. Ibid., 81.
126. Harcourt, *Twelve Years* 7.
127. Rossa, 291.
128. Griffiths (1904), 239.
129. G. Bidwell, 442.
130. Holloway (1877), 10.
131. Chesterton (1856), II, 131.
132. Bacchus, 262.
133. Warden, 128–30.
134. *Old Bailey*, 311.
135. Mackenzie, 120.

136. One-who-has-endured-it, 138.
137. Wood, 19.
138. Fannan, 94.
139. Ibid., 94.
140. Hart-Davis, 219.
141. Letter, 497.
142. One-who-has-endured-it, 137.
143. Ibid., 141.
144. Rossa, 208.
145. G. Bidwell, 388.
146. Ibid., 393.
147. Joseph, 72.
148. 'Twenty years', 676.
149. B. Thomson (1925), 130.
150. Ticket-of-leave-man, 136.
151. One-who-has endured-it, 152.
152. Ticket-of-leave-man, 137.
153. B. Thomson (1925), 128.
154. Rickards, 55.
155. B. Thomson (1925), 34.
156. Rickards, 57.
157. Ibid., 108.
158. B. Thomson (1925), 127.
159. Bird, 42.
160. M. Gordon, 75.
161. Rickards, 171.
162. Harris (n.d.), 59.

163. Rickards, 181.
164. Ruck, 11.
165. D— S—, 93.
166. Hepworth Dixon, 140.
167. B. Thomson (1925), 53.
168. Rickards, 151.
169. B. Thomson (1925), 53.
170. Practical Hand, 25.
171. *Reminiscences*, 22.
172. Old Warder, 9.
173. Nihill, 61.
174. Ibid., 57.
175. Hiener, 66.
176. Wood, 190.
177. Ibid., 127.
178. Payne, 36.
179. Beecham, 85.
180. Ticket-of-leave-man, 229.
181. B. Thomson (1925), 133.
182. J. Balfour, 292.
183. Lloyd, 185.
184. Rich, 40.
185. Ibid., 43.
186. Convict Prisons Report (1862), 251-2.
187. Griffiths (1904), 166.
188. A. Bidwell, 460.

10
THE SCAFFOLD

William Makepeace Thackeray retired early one Sunday evening in 1840. 'As I was to rise at three in the morning', he says, 'I went to bed at ten, thinking that five hours' sleep would be amply sufficient to brace me against the fatigues of the coming day. But, as might have been expected, the event of the morrow was perpetually before my eyes through the night, and kept them wide open.' The event in question was the public execution of François Courvoisier, a Swiss-born butler. He had been tried and condemned to death for murdering his master, Lord William Russell, by cutting his throat. After a sleepless night, Thackeray got up, met his friends and set off for Newgate. 'How cool and clean the streets look, as the carriage startles the echoes that have been asleep in the corners all night.' 'As we enter Holborn the town grows more animated . . . it is twenty minutes past four as we pass St. Sepulchre's: by this time many hundred people are in the street, and many more coming up Snow Hill.'

Arrived at the prison, what first arrested the eye of the spectator was the gallows. 'There it stands black and ready, jutting out from a little door in the prison. As you see it, you feel a kind of dumb electric shock, which causes one to start a little, and give a sort of gasp for breath.' The throng that gathered beneath and beyond its shadow was, according to Thackeray, 'extraordinarily gentle and good humoured'. 'A ragamuffin in the crowd (a powdery baker in a white sheep's-wool cap) uses some indecent expression to a woman near; there is an instant cry of shame, which silences the man, and a dozen people are ready to give the woman protection.'[1]

George Jacob Holyoake attended a couple of public executions, and his recollection of the crowds was quite different. One of them took place in Glasgow in 1853:

> At every angle perspiring mobs of dirty men and tattered women rushed past like an avalanche of ordure. Hans Smith Macfarlane and Helen Blackwood were out in Jail-square, and the operation of strangling them was about commencing. The Salt-market was wedged full of raw depravity. You could take the dimension of villany by the square inch. The cubic measure of Scotch scoundrelism in the city of Glasgow could be ascertained that morning.[2]

He also saw Franz Muller hanged at Newgate, for the murder of a Mr Briggs in a North London Railway carriage. 'The sympathetic and serious were there, within the precincts of the public pollution, but overwhelmed and out-numbered by mobs of horsey, doggy, thick-necked, bull-headed, turbulent felons in embryo.'[3]

Both the novelist and the rationalist agitator were concerned to turn their accounts of the hanging crowd to polemical ends. On that day in Glasgow, relates Holyoake, 'A fog hung over the city, and you could only discern the edge of the mob on Glasgow green like a deadly exhalation. Its thick murmur resounded like the coming of the cholera cloud, said to be heard by its first victims.'[4] Outside Newgate, when Courvoisier was about to be hanged, the clock began to strike the hour, and 'a great murmur arose, more awful, *bizarre*, and indescribable than any sound' that Thackeray had ever heard before. 'Women and children began to shriek horribly.' The condemned man appeared on the scaffold 'dressed in a new black suit, as it seemed . . . he turned his head here and there, and looked about him for an instant with a wild, imploring look. His mouth was contracted into a sort of pitiful smile.' The executioner pulled the cap over Courvoisier's face. At this point, confesses Thackeray, 'I am not ashamed to say, that I could look no more, but shut my eyes, as the last dreadful act was going on, which sent this wretched, guilty soul into the presence of God.'[5]

The novelist was of the party that wished the whole bloody business abol-ished. But before that item came to the top of the reformist agenda, the terms of the argument were rehearsed in a prolonged debate about whether hanging should continue to take place in public, or should be made more decently 'private' inside the prison. A Select Committee of the House of Lords reported in 1856 on the 'present Mode of carrying into effect Capital Punishments'. The evidence they heard was almost all in one direction. They heard from the Venerable Archdeacon Bickersteth how, for the execution of Josiah Misters in 1841, the town of Shrewsbury 'was converted for the day into a fair. The country people flocked in in their holiday dresses, and the whole town was a scene of drunkenness and debauchery of every kind.' He also quoted to the committee parts of a letter written to him by the chaplain of Aylesbury Gaol, who observed 'that the breathless silence which had prevailed during the short time intervening between the culprit's appearing on the scaffold and the moment of his death was immediately afterwards followed, as it had also been preceded, by the most incongruous sounds of low jesting and indecent ribaldry. The brief silence,' he thought, had originated 'in the morbid curiosity of the crowd to catch the expected words of the hero of the moment.'[6]

One of the effects that was looked for from public execution was the deterrence of further crime amongst the onlookers. On this point there was no shortage of evidence to the contrary. A prisoner 'of great mental powers and superior education, who was acquitted of a charge of forgery', assured Edward Gibbon Wakefield, author of *Facts Relating to the Punishment of Death in the Metropolis*, 'that the first idea of committing a forgery occurred to him at the moment when he was accidentally witnessing the execution of Fauntleroy'.[7]

George Jacob Holyoake used the occasion of Muller's execution to deliver himself of a broadside concerning the supposedly moral effects of the state's publicly doing to death some of its citizens. 'Yesterday morning', he wrote to the editor of the *Morning Star*, 'was devoted by the Government to public instruction by the Hangman.' The government, he believed, had discovered a secret that was hidden from other moral educators. 'Exchange the black board for the black cap of the judge – exchange the desk of the professor or the pulpit of the preacher for the gallows and the noose, and the scholars rush up in crowds – every student is eager – you cannot count their numbers – you require formidable and far-extended barriers to restrain their impatience for instruction.' The reasons for this enthusiasm, he thought, were not far to seek. 'The mob was tired of melodrama. Bombast, blue lights, and penny tragedies had palled on its whisky-blistered stomach. Rows and minor bloodshed had kept up its criminal spirits for a time. It now wanted a *real* murder – as safe as cowardice could make it, as public as ferocity could wish it; and it was all prepared by "lawful authority".'[8]

CONDEMNED PRISONERS: THE NEWGATE ERA

The campaign against public execution rested in part on evidence about the brutalizing effects of the spectacle on the spectators. Having seen a hanging, it was argued, seemed to encourage rather than deter the commission of further crimes. Ironically the same effect was to be seen at work inside prisons themselves where prisoners were not permitted to witness actual executions. This was a curious omission in view of their compulsory attendance at floggings, but the prolonged presence amongst them of numbers of men and women under sentence of death could hardly fail to create very special situations.

Edward Gibbon Wakefield chronicled some aspects of their existence at Newgate during his imprisonment there between 1826 and 1829. He was a gentleman by birth, a cousin of Elizabeth Fry – convicted together with his mother of abducting a young lady. After his release, he became an influential theorist of colonial development in Australia and New Zealand, as well as a brilliant witness for the case against capital punishment. Whilst he was imprisoned 'a batch of convicts' was 'sentenced to death every six weeks in London'. The members of these 'batches' who had been sentenced to die for crimes other than murder, 'of whom the average may be stated at twenty',[9] found themselves trapped in an historic delay between the 'progressive' movement of public opinion and the eventual abolition of the death sentence for property offences. Between 1825 and 1831, for example, out of 85,257 convictions for criminal offences in England and Wales, no less than 9316 attracted sentences of death; but of those no more than 410 were actually executed.[10] These sentences had to be confirmed – or commuted – by the monarch, and 'the average period of detention in the cells – that is, between sentence at the Old Bailey and the decision of the King in Council – is about six weeks'.[11] 'In former days', says Sir Edmund DuCane in a brief history he wrote of capital punishment, 'the signature of the king in council on the death-warrant was . . . necessary to justify the sheriff in carrying it into execution, but on the Queen's accession it was thought proper to relieve her by Act of Parliament, from a duty so painful to any woman, and to a young girl, as Her Majesty then was, so impossible.'[12]

Until the law 'relieved' them too, condemned property offenders had no choice but to sit and wait for the decisions on which their very lives hung. Wakefield described them as 'engaged in a lottery, of which the blanks are death, and that an attempt to foretell the result in any case would be mere guesswork'.[13] Meanwhile the condemned men and women, and occasionally children, were objects of great interest and earnest attention from their fellows, to whom they were most visible in the chapel:

Some tremble, and sigh or weep – some swagger to their places, tossing their heads, smiling, nodding to their friends, and pretending to glory in the distinction of their danger; others appear stupified, creeping into the pew, looking around them vacantly as if unconscious of their state; and some again really behave with the most perfect, I mean with real composure, appearing, as they really are at the time, proud of the distinction of being amongst the condemned, but without any admixture of fear, – since these last are either boys whose youth they know protects them, or men convicted of offences, such as returning from transportation, which are never punished with death – or criminals so hardened by constant contemplation of death by the hangman, that they can look forward to it as their own fate with comparative indifference.[14]

Others were materially affected by the strain of waiting for their decisions: Wakefield saw 'several instances' in which 'brown hair turned gray, and gray white, by a month of suspense such as most London capital convicts undergo. In the same short period the smooth face of a man of twenty-five becomes often marked with decided wrinkles on the forehead, and about the eyes and mouth.'[15] At length the decisions came down. 'One sees twenty-five fellow creatures, who yesterday were all under sentence of death – twenty of them are saved, and five are utterly condemned.' Wakefield's own strongly felt sentiment on these occasions was one of 'anger – of that sort of anger, which is commonly produced by witnessing gross injustice'.[16]

The decisions also acted as a signal for the onset of activities that provoked him to even greater wrath. 'As soon as a man is ordered for execution, the great increase of his danger produces extraordinary exertions on the part of those who administer the offices of religion to the inmates of Newgate. . . . The Ordinary and his assistants visit the press-yard frequently every day, and indeed almost live with the condemned men, exhorting them to repentance, prayer and faith.'[17] The condemned men and women became in fact the focus of protracted religious ceremonies which celebrated death and some of its many meanings for the faithful and the infidel, both in and out of prison. There was no shortage of willing would-be helpers in this missionary work: 'When a batch of capitally condemned prisoners are confined in the cells of Newgate . . . the prison is beset with applications for admittance, by persons who wish to be allowed to administer consolation to the unhappy malefactors: these applications are generally made by dissenting ministers.'[18] 'In London too, as in the country', says the author of *The Schoolmaster's Experience in Newgate*, 'many ladies, who are connected with those who have the power . . . to secure admittance into the prisons, engage in the work of preparing men for death.'[19]

The religious interests of all these divines, and of the ladies drawn from a genteel laity, cannot be reduced to any sort of simple list. There was no doubt an element of that 'morbid interest' that must attach to human beings with certain advance knowledge of the hour and the manner of their own dying. There was besides, an evident desire to vindicate both the course of justice in general *and* the justice of particular capital sentences, by securing from the accused or the condemned, confessions of their guilt. Confessions also provided saleable copy for the best-selling broadsheets with which some pre-reform prison clerics had been wont to amplify their official stipends. Beyond these quite earthly concerns, preparing the soul for death was a clear Christian duty, and one that might yield, in the case of a condemned person, a series of lessons, both bitter and sweet, for the edification and inspiration of a large religious reading public beyond the prison walls. Traces of all these purposes are to be discerned in the descriptions that survive of nineteenth-century death-cell missions.

The fullest account that still exists of such a mission was written in 1832 by Mrs Elizabeth Lachlan, otherwise an author of improving 'tales', typically dedicated to female members of the royal family. It concerns James Cook, a Leicester bookbinder, who in May that year bludgeoned to death Mr Paas, a brass-ornament manufacturer, for the purpose of acquiring the very large sums of cash he carried with him. What made the offence especially notorious was the fact that Cook tried to destroy the evidence of his murderous deed by burning the body of Mr Paas in his bindery fireplace; and what made it even more ghastly was that 'after despatching his victim, and before committing the body to the flames, the cold-blooded murderer divided it into four parts, by cutting and sawing it across the abdomen, and above the knee-joints. The head and legs appear to have been burned first.'[20]

Two local county ladies who read a printed 'confession' of this crime, thought they detected in it 'one expression . . . which appeared to indicate some desire for spiritual advice. The ladies consulted together as to what they could do; as to what their duty to their gracious and merciful God would require of them to do in this deplorable and awful case. One said to the other, – suppose we write to him? The other immediately agreed to this proposal; and thus began the mighty work of this grievous sinner's conversion.'[21] They wrote an earnest letter to the murderer and sent it off together with some 'religious tracts and handbills' which included 'a little book of verses called Sunbeams'.[22] To their surprise, they were rewarded with a reply from Cook inviting them to meet him. They wrestled with their repugnance at the idea of meeting face to face so horrid a murderer; appealed in prayer for guidance as to their religious duty; and duly attended Leicester County Gaol to interview James Cook. 'There, behind the door, sat a youth of most interesting, handsome countenance, heavily ironed, leaning over a table, on which was placed a writing desk, and on this lay the little book, called "Sunbeams." '[23] It was a scene that might have been drawn straight from the pages of one of Mrs Lachlan's own pious romances:

> The keepers, stood on one side; Mr. William Owston (the Governor) also was near them; and there as transfixed in the deepest emotion of horror, pity and concern stood these two elegant and accomplished ladies, both formed to adorn the most exalted stations of society, even according to human doctrines of delicacy and refinement, but then, according to THE WORLD, degrading themselves by this sweet and touching effort made in prayer.[24]

By the time of their second visit, there was a startling change to report: 'And now, what will you say, when I tell you, that no sooner did we enter the cell, than we beheld a new creature! O what a change was there! His countenance shone with a sweet expression, and he really seemed as much changed in body as in mind. He held out his hands to us with a look beaming with heavenly gratitude, and wept the bitterest tears I ever saw drop from human eyes.'[25]

Cook went to trial a repentant sinner pleading guilty. The proceedings were brief: 'the prisoner betrayed no outward signs of emotion; and at the conclusion he turned away from the bar, and, gently inclining his head and moving his hand to some person on the bench, descended calmly into the room below.'[26]

Something of Mrs Lachlan's motives in dashing off a 300-page book in less than three months can be gathered from the tone of her opening chapter. Who, she demands, can deny the right of a murderer, even one as wicked as Cook, to seek forgiveness and redemption? She singles out in turn specimen sinners of the age: the *blasphemer*; the *adulteress*; and then the *fornicator*:

And now, come forth, thou pestilence that walks the earth, and nips the blossom, and the bud, and the early fruit, and then leaves it to the blight and the mildew. Thou serpent, often clothed in the exterior of an elegant accomplished gentleman, as often, in the enticing one of the pleasing and quietly attractive man, turning your eye keen for your prey on this side and on that; – now sending forth a smile, then a glance, then a soft word, then an ardent one, heated in the unholy fire of unlawful love; say, you, that lurk in the ball-room and the cellar, the village and the town, you that lavish your fiendlike smiles, and spread your greedy and sensual nets for any prey, the innocent virgin, the wedded wife, the bereaved widow; and then having caught your prey, and unplumed it of all its loveliness and all its worth, then with a smile of scorn cast it far behind, and loathing, from you. I ask YOU, murderer of innocence, and honour, and virtue, and secret assassin of the dark, whence do you ground your expectation of mercy, while you deny the same privilege to the wretched murderer of man? [27]

THE EFFECTS

As to the effects of all this activity on the condemned, there are conflicting views; 'in nineteen cases out of twenty', according to the author of *The Schoolmaster's Experience in Newgate*, 'there is no true repentance; most of them die apparently careless about their former course of life, or of the world to come.' [28] The estimate of Edward Gibbon Wakefield is that 'in about half such cases, the exertions of religious teachers are most successful'; [29] 'there can be no doubt that a considerable number of those who are executed, die with a firm expectation of happiness in another world.' [30]

Whatever the exact proportions, the immunity of some other prisoners to the consolations of religion as their deaths approached could have been due to any of a number of factors. The Newgate Schoolmaster met with scepticism when he tried to convince one sentenced man of 'another state of existence'. ' "What," he exclaimed, "you too can gammon as well as the parson: that's what they do; they take your life away, and then think to make you amends by telling you of another and a better world; for my part, I am very well satisfied with this, if they would let me stay in it." ' [31] Another source of indifference to the spiritual possibilities of an execution was disclosed to Frederic Hill. He had asked Mrs Fry 'what she found to be the chief thought of a prisoner under sentence of death shortly before her execution.' 'I grieve to say,' she replied, 'that commonly the chief thought relates to her appearance on the scaffold, the dress in which she shall be hanged.' [32]

A different kind of demeanour in the face of death – not bravado exactly but something simpler and more admirable – was illuminated by the Newgate Schoolmaster with a literary quotation: 'Fazakerly says, with great truth, "Sir, there is something in the nature of man that disdains to be terrified; and therefore severe punishments have never been found effectual for preventing crime." '[33]

Wakefield reckoned that the different responses to religion were reflected in the physical states of the condemned; in 'nearly all such cases of religious fervour, the bodily health of the enthusiast is excellent, his sleep sound, his appetite good, his pulse steady, and his skin moist; whilst, speaking generally, he who goes to the scaffold scoffing at religion is full of bodily disease, of which the main symptoms are want of appetite and sleep, a rattling or fainting pulse, and a skin hot and dry as if he were in a burning fever.'[34] A woman to whom Mrs Fry ministered in the death cell, far from being 'hot and dry', had cold hands and was 'covered with something like the perspiration preceding death, and in an universal tremor'.[35]

These differences dogged the condemned prisoner right up to the last few steps onto the scaffold. Some of them were besides themselves with fear: 'The next morning, when brought out of his cell to be pinioned, you behold a man already half dead, – his countenance has fallen, his eyes are fixed, his lips are deadly pale and quivering, whilst his whole aspect, in anticipation of the reality, gives you the personification of death's counterpart.'[36] Some were resentful: 'on almost every execution day, on which several are hanged, the chaplain is subjected to the most outrageous insults from one or more of the doomed men.'[37] And some, like the young man whom the Reverend C.B. Tayler accompanied to the gallows, were composed and anxious to put to good use their last moments in this life: 'It was a deeply affecting sight, to see him, prepared as he was for immediate execution, stop successively, before the iron palisades of the several yards where the various inmates of the gaol were assembled: but I was astonished to hear the short and admirable warnings which he addressed to them as he passed along.'[38]

The party reached the scaffold, and the hangman did his work:

The kind-hearted governor had partly descended from the platform, and stood weeping like a child on the ladder; the drop had fallen; but I was standing aloft and alone, with my eyes steadily fixed on the dying man. I saw his head drop on one side, and an inward flutter rise upon his open chest. I caught a glimpse of the executioner below, skilfully hasteningt his horrid work. The death-struggle was but for a moment, and all was over.[39]

Even after death, tradition dictated that the corpses of the executed could continue to serve instructive purposes. Disembowelling and decapitation and the cutting of the cadavers into four quarters were the most common items in these *post-mortem* festivities; the last to disappear was the hanging of the body in chains; and the last instance of it in English legal history proved to be that of James Cook at Leicester. 'The body was dressed in the same clothes that he was hung in – black coat, black waistcoat, white duck trousers, and a pair of white

Berlin gloves. His face was covered with a pitch plaster, and over it placed the cap he suffered in.'[40]

There was 'an immense concourse of spectators' attended by 'several ranting preachers', and the authorities, either out of a sense of distaste or a fear of disorder, ordered an end to the spectacle.[41] The move was of a piece with the contemporary drift of penal policy, and coincided with other changes described by Sir Edmund DuCane. 'By a law passed in the reign of Henry VIII, some bodies of murderers were given over for anatomical purposes, and in 1829 this course, which had also been very usual, was prescribed for all. Instances occurred of this proceeding being followed by the resuscitation of the body. In 1832 these laws were superseded by one directing that the bodies should be buried within the precincts of the gaol.'[42] If certain of the corpses had revived under the attentions of the student anatomists, the conclusion is inescapable that others of them, not so delivered over in the interests of medical education, must have been laid to rest in beds of quicklime and literally buried alive.

PRIVATE EXECUTION: A NEW ERA?

The possibility of being hanged for offences other than murder was progressively excluded by a series of parliamentary measures that spanned the 1820s and 1830s. The movement to abolish the death penalty altogether made much slower progress, and had become, in the middle years of the nineteenth century, a debate about whether hanging should take place in public or not. The 1856 Select Committee on Capital Punishments had examined many 'expert' witnesses from inside and outside the prison services about the advisability of continuing to hang convicted murderers in full public view. 'On reviewing the whole of the evidence,' the Select Committee recommended 'that executions should in future be carried into effect within the precincts of the prison, or in some place securing similar comparative privacy'.[43] Ten years elapsed without any legislation being brought forward to enact this recommendation, and a Royal Commission was set up in 1866 to examine precisely the same question.

The Commission endorsed the findings of its predecessor, and the Capital Punishment Act of 1868 finally put an end to public executions outside the prisons of England and Wales. 'It was decided', says Sir Edmund DuCane, 'after full consideration that the scenes at a public execution were so demoralising that they could no longer be tolerated; they collected all the scum of the neighbourhood, and were little less disgusting than the former practice of the procession to the distant place of execution, while the deterrent effects were certainly no greater.'[44]

The last *public* execution in England was that of Michael Barrett. He was a Fenian, and the only one of four defendants to be convicted of causing the explosion which breached the wall of Clerkenwell Prison in December 1867; a vain attempt to rescue Colonel Ricard Burke – O'Donovan Rossa's companion at Chatham – and Joseph Casey.[45] Barrett's execution took place outside Newgate on 26 May 1868, just three days before the Royal Assent was given to the Act that finally abolished hanging in public. It marked the end of an era of popular participation in the implementation of justice. Thereafter, only the trial was open to popular view; from the moment of sentence the offender became virtually invisible – executions and floggings took place behind closed doors; all the impositions of imprisonment were suffered in private.

Overtly then, everything was different; in practice there were many continuities between the old and the new arrangements. The same agonies were suffered, only in the isolation of the condemned cell rather than semi-publicly as formerly at Newgate; the same religious efforts were made to prepare the condemned for death; and the same gruesome drama was enacted on the scaffold unseen by all but a handful of official spectators. There are also first-hand accounts of these experiences, from Florence Maybrick and John Lee. Mrs Maybrick underwent her ordeal at Strangeways in 1889: 'For nearly three terrible weeks I was confined in this cell of the condemned, to taste the bitterness of death under its most appalling and shameful aspect. I was carefully guarded by two female warders, who would gladly have been spared the task. They might not read nor sleep; at my meals, through my prayers, during every moment of agony, they still watched on and rarely spoke.'[46] John Lee was less affected as he waited in the death cell at Exeter prison. Lee, from Babbacombe in Devon, was convicted in 1885 of murdering the lady who employed him as a servant. He swore his innocence of the crime, a claim he was never to relinquish, but for an 'innocent' man he remained remarkably composed as death drew near. 'If anything I felt relieved. All the suspense was over. I knew now what to expect, and I made up my mind to face it as cheerfully as I could.'[47] Mrs Maybrick was incapable of such composure: 'I was too overwhelmed for either analytic or collective thought. Conscious of my innocence, I had no fear of physical death, for the love of my Heavenly Father was so enveloping that death seemed to me a blessed escape from a world in which such an unspeakable travesty of justice could take place.'[48]

Mrs Maybrick fell quite naturally into a religious state of mind; John Lee was more impressed by the fact he was on 'hospital diet'. 'I could have practically what I wanted.'[49] It was not unknown for this indulgence to cover otherwise banned items. 'A frequent request is for tobacco,' says Arthur Griffiths, whose duties as a prison inspector included the arrangements for executions, 'the weed so strictly tabooed within our prison walls, and it would be cruelty to withold the comfort of a smoke from the man who is on the brink of the grave. The concession rests with the medical officer of the prison, and he is generally indulgent, although I have known him refuse on the grounds that there was no medical reason, a perfectly sound objection, but rather cruel and far fetched. If it was left to me to advise, I invariably recommended the issue of the tobacco. Stimulants might be and were given, even on the very morning of the dread ceremony, in cases where the strain was too severe upon the wretched sufferer.'[50]

To certain of the staff, however, and certainly to a section of the public beyond the walls, the prolonged ordeal of the condemned remained of spiritual rather than corporeal importance. A vast and pious correspondence converged on the cell where John Lee awaited execution at the hands of hangman James Berry. 'I used to receive letters from all parts of the country. There was one from some Brotherhood. I forget what it was about but somebody in the prison had scribbled on the letter: "Confess, dear brother, confess!" '[51] 'Books, large bundles of tracts, and letters, which would take three months to read, if two or three hours daily were devoted to the task, have been sent to poor men awaiting execution, who had perhaps only eight or ten days to live', says the Reverend John Pitkin who ministered to Lee's spiritual health. And as if to emphasize the nature of the events as a kind of wake for the living, there were delivered to Lee's cell 'many gifts of flowers'.[52]

REPRIEVE

As the period of waiting lengthened, the tension increased for those men and women who still hoped for a stay of execution from the Home Secretary. 'The date of my execution', says Mrs Maybrick, 'was not told me at Walton Jail, but I heard afterwards that it was to have taken place on the 26th of August. On the 22d, while I was taking my daily exercise in the yard attached to the condemned cell, the governor, Captain Anderson, accompanied by the chief matron, entered. He called me to him, and, with a voice which – all honor to him – trembled with emotion, said: "Maybrick, no commutation of sentence has come down today, and I consider it my duty to tell you to prepare for death." "Thank you, governor," I replied; "my conscience is clear. God's will be done." He then walked away and I returned to my cell. The female warder was weeping silently, but I was calm and spent the early part of the night in my usual prayers. About midnight exhausted nature could bear no more, and I fainted. I had barely regained consciousness when I heard the shuffle of feet outside, the click of the key in the lock – that warning catch in the slow machinery of my doom. I sprang up, and with one supreme effort of will braced myself for what I believed was the last act of my life. They read my expectation in my face, and the governor, hastening forward, exclaimed in an agitated voice: "It is well; it is good news!" When I opened my eyes once more I was lying in bed in the hospital.'[53]

Relief was the normal feeling felt by the newly reprieved, but it was not always so. Basil Thomson conveyed the good news to a convicted murderer at Liverpool, and, saw him shortly afterwards in an ordinary convict cell. 'Never have I seen such a change', he said. 'A few minutes before he had been in a class by himself; now he was just one among a thousand. They had clipped his hair to a pattern, and with his own clothing he seemed to have cast off every link which bound him to the past. He was the most dejected man in the prison.'[54]

THE HANGMAN

The central actor in all these proceedings was the hangman. In England and Wales he was an employee not of the prison but of the local county sheriffs. When James Berry, who had been a Bradford policeman for eight years, 'made application to the Sheriffs of London and Middlesex in September, 1883 . . . there were some 1400 applicants for the post'.[55] He was, on that occasion, passed over by the sheriffs, mainly, he thought, because 'members of my own family petitioned the Home Secretary to dismiss the application on the ground that if the appointment was given to me, a hitherto respectable family would be disgraced.'[56] He did not, however, have to wait long before being given a chance to demonstrate his abilities – as yet untested. In March 1884, he was invited by the magistrates of Edinburgh to hang two poachers, Vickers and Innes, on the 31st of the month. The deputy city clerk wrote to Berry to say that the magistrates 'agree to your terms of ten guineas for each person executed and 20s. for each person executed to your Assistant, with second-class railway fares for both of you, you finding all necessary requisites for the Executions.'[57]

William Calcraft, the most notorious of the Victorian hangmen who preceded Berry, was employed on a different basis. He 'was paid by the Corporation of London £1:1s. per week a retaining-fee, and an extra guinea for each execution. He had 2s. 6d. for each flogging he carried out, and an allowance for "cats" and birch rods.'[58] Calcraft, the executioner of Courvoisier and of Franz Muller, and of countless others besides, in a career that lasted from 1829 to 1874, left no proper literary remains of his own, but his reputation was of some roughness and incompetence in the basic skills of his calling. At one of his executions in 1879 'signs of life were visible for a longer time after the bolt was drawn' than could be remembered by a reporter who witnessed it.[59] Another eye-witness to his handiwork thought he would never forget 'that ghoul of a Calcraft, with his disreputable grey hair, his disreputable undertaker's suit of black, and a million dirty pinpricks which marked every pore of the skin of his face. . . . Where everything was strange and dreamlike, the oddest thing of all was to see Calcraft take the pinioned fin-like hand of the prisoner, and shake it, when he had drawn the white cap over the face and arranged the rope.' The same observer noted the fine detail of what happened at the fatal instant: 'The white cap fitted close to his face, and the thin white linen took a momentary stain, as if a bag of blackberries had been bruised, and had suddenly exuded the juice of the fruit. It sagged a way a moment later, and assumed its natural hue.'[60]

Despite all this fascination with the minutiae of judicial killing, the vast numbers who had flocked to witness executions, and the smaller but still extraordinary numbers who always applied for any vacancy in the ranks of the executioners, the hangman was a far from popular figure. It was Calcraft's habit 'to leave his home either very early or else after dark so that he would not attract attention';[61] and when some men in his 'local' made remarks about his occupation one day he left the pub and never returned to it.[62] Edward Barlow, an earlier executioner at Lancaster Castle, known – but not at all affectionately – as 'Old Ned', received rougher handling than Calcraft: 'there were very few houses into which he was permitted to enter; he was ever the butt of scorn for all persons; many times he was seriously abused; often pelted with missiles of the foulest description; and not infrequently was he rolled in the mud, and as often much worse treated in nameless manner.'[63] Later in his career, James Berry also received attentions he did not much care for, especially in Ireland, and he always carried a revolver for self-defence. In a reflection of this general view, the first time that the Reverend C.B. Tayler set eyes on one of these public servants, he 'felt a kind of instinctive horror'. 'That man, Sir', the governor of the prison told him, 'is the hangman; and he is so inveterate a drunkard, that we shall have to shut him up in close confinement all night, to keep him sober and ready for the execution tomorrow morning.'[64]

It was normal practice for the hangman to be lodged in the gaol, not only to ensure his sobriety, but also his safety from the curious and the malevolent. James Berry reported to Calton Gaol in Edinburgh on Thursday, 27 March 1884, in readiness for his first execution the following Monday. He went to his room and 'knelt down and asked the Almighty to help me in my most painful task, which I had undertaken to carry out. . . . After, I filled my time walking about the prison grounds, and thinking of the poor men who were nearing their end, full of life, and knowing the fatal hour, which made me quite ill to think about. My meals did not seem to do me good, my appetite began to fall off, nothing felt good to me, everything that I put into my mouth felt like sand, and I felt as I wished I had never undertaken such an awful calling. I regretted for a while, and then I thought the public would only think I had not the pluck, and I would not allow my feeling to overthrow me, so I never gave way to such thoughts again.[65] . . . Saturday night I was very restless, and I did not feel so much refreshed for my night's sleep, as I was thinking of the poor creatures who was slumbering their hours away, in the prison cell, just beyond where I was laid, thinking of the dreadful fate that awaited them in such a short space of time. Two men, in full bloom, and had to come to such an untimely end, leaving wives and large families. . . . My dinner did not arrive until 4–0 o'clock, which is called late dinner, consisting of rice pudding, black currants, chicken, vegetables, potatoes, bread and the usual teetotal beverages. I tried to make the best of it, but all that I could do was to look at it, as my appetite was gone; but I managed to eat a little before going to roost for the last night.[66] . . . I retired at 10.0 on Sunday, but only had cat naps all night, one eye shut and the other open, thinking and fancying things that never will be, and which is impossible. I was dressed and up at 5.0 a.m.; and felt more dead than alive as I had such a responsible part to play in the programme for the day. I fancied the ropes breaking; I fancied I was trembling, and could not do it; I fancied I fell sick at the last push. I was nearly frantic in my mind, but I never let them know.'[67] His first efforts were in fact successful, but Berry sought continuously to improve the technical aspects of his art, so as to spare the condemned from

James Berry

anything other than the most instant form of death. The key to this technique turned out to be the relationship between body-weight and the length of drop that was allowed. At first he relied on some calculations given him by Marwood his predecessor, but these failed to produce the required results on one occasion at Norwich in 1885.

> The whole of the arrangements were carried out in the usual manner, and when I pulled the lever the drop fell properly, and the prisoner dropped out of sight. We were horrified, however, to see that the rope jerked upwards, and for an instant I thought that the noose had slipped from the culprit's head, or that the rope had broken. But it was worse than that, for the jerk had severed the head entirely from the body, and both had fallen together to the bottom of the pit. Of course death was instantaneous, so that the poor fellow had not suffered in any way; but it was terrible to think that such a revolting thing should have occurred.

'The inquest', he says, 'was a trying ordeal for all concerned.'[68] In the opinion of Felicia Mary Skene, 'the manner' in which Berry 'treated the matter at the inquest was not calculated to allay the universal indignation aroused by the event: he spoke of it with careless unconcern, as a little accident which was quite likely to happen often on these occasions, and which simply could not be helped.'[69]

JOHN LEE

1885 was not a good year for Berry. Earlier in the year he had been called to Exeter to hang John Lee, whom we have already met in the condemned cell: 'John Lee, born at Abbots Kerswell, Devon, went early as a page-boy into the service of a lady named Keyse, who lived in a lonely house on the beach in Babbacombe Bay. She had been connected with the Court of Queen Victoria, as a maid-of-honour, and, retiring from the activities of Court-life, she settled down in her mother's house, called the Glen.' After an interval, when he served in the navy, Lee returned to Devon and 'continued in his kind mistress' service for some months, until, in fact, November 15th, 1884, the day on which the cruel murder was committed'.[70] Miss Keyse was beaten and stabbed to death and attempts were made to set fire to the body, using oil from the pantry where Lee slept. The other servants gave evidence that substantially incriminated him, and after a trial lasting three days, the jury took thirty minutes to return a finding of Guilty. On 4 February 1885 Mr Justice Manisty sentenced him to death. He awaited his execution on 23 February with what the Reverend John Pitkin called a 'nerveless demeanour'.[71]

'On the morning of the 20th ult.', wrote Berry in his report to the Under Sheriff for Devon, 'I travelled from Bristol to Exeter, and on the morning of Saturday, the 21st, from Bristol to Exeter, arriving at Exeter at 11.50 a.m., when I walked direct to the County Gaol, signed my name in your Gaol Register Book at 12 o'clock exactly.' He went out to get some dinner and 'returned at 1.50 p.m. Shortly afterwards I made an inspection of the place of Execution.' We may assume that such an inspection was routine, mandatory even, before any execution; an unremarkable event. What *was* remarkable was the fact that Berry recorded it at all; and he did *that* because of the singular events that followed.

> The execution was to take place in a Coach House in which the Prison Van was usually kept. Two Warders accompanied me on the inspection. . . . Two Trap-doors were placed in the floor of the Coach-house, which is flagged with stone, and these doors cover a pit about 2 yards by 1½ yards across, and about 11 feet deep. On inspecting these doors I found they were only about an inch thick, but to have been constructed properly should have been three or four inches thick. The ironwork of the doors was of a frail kind, and much too weak for the purpose.

Executioner Berry was not impressed with the trap, and made recommendations to the governor of Exeter that thicker doors be supplied in future, and also 'that a spring should be fixed in the wall to hold the doors back when they fell, so that no rebounding occurred'. The inspection continued: 'There was a lever to these doors, and it was placed near the top of them. I pulled the lever, and the doors dropped, the catches acting all right. I had the doors raised, and tried

PRICE SIXPENCE

THE MAN THEY COULD NOT HANG

THE LIFE STORY OF JOHN LEE

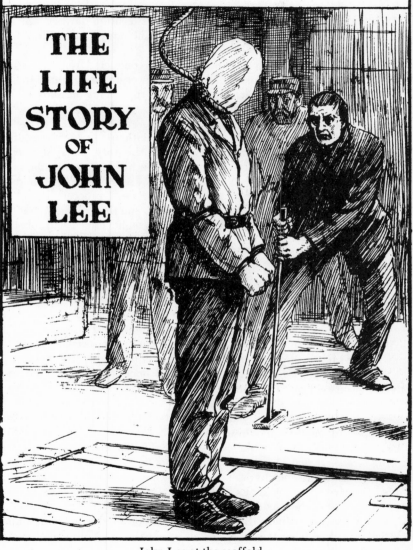

John Lee at the scaffold

the lever a second time, when the catch again acted all right.'[72] Having assured himself that all was well, Berry spent 'all the Sunday' in the room allotted to him, and did not go outside the Gaol. 'I retired to bed about 9.45 that night.'[73]

The Reverend John Pitkin visited Lee 'late in the evening of February 22nd for spiritual preparation'.[74] Lee then went to bed for his last night on earth, and whether it signifies an innocent mind, or an uncaring one, he fell sound asleep: 'And whilst I slept I had a dream. I thought I was on the scaffold. I heard the bolts drawn, but the scaffold would not work. Three times the bolt was drawn, and three times it failed to act.' The day of his execution dawned. 'As I was putting on my socks', he says, 'I told the warders about my dream. They did not say a word, but gave me some tea and toast.'[75]

Meanwhile James Berry 'arose at 6.30, and was conducted from the Bedroom by a Warder, at 7.30, to the place of execution. Everything appeared to be as I had left it on the Saturday afternoon. I fixed the rope in my ordinary manner, and placed everything in readiness. I did not try the Trap-doors as they appeared to be just as I had left them.'[76] The Reverend Pitkin came to Lee's cell 'early in the morning of the 23rd, and remained with him until the executioner arrived to pinion him'.[77] In John Lee's version of the story, 'Berry stepped forward to shake hands with me, but the governor pushed him to one side, saying: "I will shake hands with Lee first." '[78] Berry simply says that he 'was conducted to the condemned Cell and introduced to John Lee. I proceeded at once to pinion him which was done in the usual manner, and then gave a signal to the Governor that I was ready.'[79] At two minutes to eight, after I had robed, the solemn procession started for the place of execution', says Pitkin, 'the chief warder leading the way.'[80]

'What was I thinking about?' asks Lee, rhetorically, or more likely in reply to the journalist who took down his story. 'Certainly about none of the awful things that are said to haunt the last moments of men who perish on the scaffold. Mr. Pitkin', he thought, 'seemed to be much affected. His voice trembled as he read.' 'As he jerked the rope into position, Berry asked me if I had anything to say.'[81] In Pitkin's account the executioner received 'a negative reply'.[82] Lee's recollection, twenty-two years after the event, is of saying ' "No, ... Drop away." I held my breath and clenched my teeth. I heard the chaplain's voice. I heard the clang of the bell.'[83]

Berry: 'I pinioned his legs, pulled down the white cap, adjusted the Rope, stepped on one side, and drew the lever –'
Pitkin: '. . . he passed to the lever whilst I was concluding the service with the Grace. It was expected that, in a moment, the prisoner would have been hurled into eternity.'
Lee: 'I heard a wrench as of a bolt drawn, and –'
Berry: '. . . but the trap door did not fall.'
Lee: 'My heart beat! Was this death? Or was it only a dream? A nightmare?'
Pitkin: 'I asked if all was over, when an emphatic "No!" came from the schoolmaster.'

Lee: 'What was this stamping going on?'

Pitkin: 'The executioner moved the lever to and fro with great force, but the drop refused to fall.'

Lee: 'Good Heavens! I was still on the trap! It would not move! "This is terrible" I heard someone say.'

Pitkin: 'The criminal stood erect upon the drop, and no word of any sort escaped from his lips.'

Berry: 'I unloosed the strap from his legs, took the rope from his neck, removed the White Cap, and took Lee away into an adjoining room until I made an examination of the doors.'

In Lee's temporary absence, Berry tried the doors, and they worked – twice. Lee was sent for again.

Lee: 'When I got back to the shed the officials were waiting for me. Some of them turned away as if they could not bear to witness a second time a scene similar to that which had taken place. Mr. Pitkin, the chaplain, was so distressed that he looked as if he would collapse. The warders were as white as ghosts.'

Berry: 'Lee was then brought from the adjoining room, placed in position, the cap and the rope adjusted, but when I again pulled the lever it did not act, and in trying to force it the lever was slightly strained.'

Lee: 'I sank two inches just as before, and there I remained. The horrible stampings and hammering were repeated, but all to no purpose.'

At this point, in Berry's report to the Under Sheriff, the execution was abandoned. Both Lee and Pitkin insist that a third attempt was made. 'Whilst awaiting this third attempt', says Lee, 'the rope was left round my neck, the cap over my head, I was stifling, choking for breath.'

Pitkin: 'Without the prisoner the machinery worked well, but when he was upon it the drop remained stationary as before. There we all stood, mentally paralysed by the hopelessness of the task we were all by law expected to perform.'

Lee: 'What was passing in my mind all this time I cannot say. I had prayed to be delivered from these men's hands, and something told me that my prayer was being answered.'

Pitkin: 'In this dilemma the Surgeon of the prison came to me and urged me not to allow any more attempts, and I acted upon his suggestion, and told the Under Sheriff that as he had failed three times to carry out the execution, I should stay no longer. An execution cannot be carried out without the presence of the chaplain, who is required to sign the official record of death. The Under Sheriff then ordered the prisoner to be taken back to his cell.'

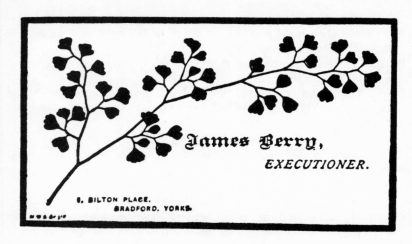

James Berry's visiting card

Lee: 'All that day I lived in uncertainty. I did not know what my fate was going to be. Still uncertain I went to bed. But at ten o'clock the cell door opened, and the governor came in. "Lee," he said, "I am to inform you that you are respited." I don't think I said anything. I was too tired. I just went to sleep.'

So ended the only failed attempt, in modern times, to hang a convicted murderer. The Reverend John Pitkin checked on the story of the dream which Lee had told him: 'The warders, to whom he told the dream, did not see him again that day, but while I was in the cell, after the event, they went to the Governor and told the dream.' Pitkin omits to tell us how these events affected him, but his colleague, Clifford Rickards, chaplain at Dartmoor, says (in what is almost certainly a reference to him) that he told him 'that it was always the most upsetting experience of his life, and one that was never got over by its frequency. He said that the only cure for its awful nerve-racking was a change of scene, and that whenever possible, he always made a point of getting away after the horror of the execution to some fresh scene abroad, going straight away from the prison to the railway, and taking passage to Calais or to some foreign port; but even with the change it took him a week or ten days to rally and become his normal self. I was glad', says Rickards, 'to escape this ordeal during my long term of prison experience.'[84]

NOTES

1. Thackeray, 150–3.
2. Holyoake (1864), 3.
3. Ibid., 4.
4. Ibid., 3.
5. Thackeray, 156.
6. Capital Punishment Report (1856), 11.
7. Wakefield, 177.
8. Holyoake (1864), 2–4.
9. Wakefield, 91.
10. *Old Bailey*, 432.
11. Wakefield, 84.
12. DuCane (1885), 26.
13. Wakefield, 95.
14. Ibid., 146.
15. Ibid., 148.
16. Ibid., 149.
17. Ibid., 155–6.
18. *Old Bailey*, 162.
19. Ibid., 167.
20. Lachlan, 41.
21. Ibid., 99.
22. Ibid., 113.
23. Ibid., 130.
24. Ibid., 130–1.
25. Ibid., 168.
26. Ibid., 236.
27. Ibid., 5.
28. *Old Bailey*, 160.
29. Wakefield, 156.
30. Ibid., 153.
31. *Old Bailey*, 161.
32. Hill (1894), 117.
33. *Old Bailey*, 158.
34. Wakefield, 154.
35. E. Fry (1847), I, 259.
36. *Old Bailey*, 177.
37. Wakefield, 157.
38. Tayler, 199.
39. Ibid., 206.
40. Lachlan, 249.
41. Ibid., 250.
42. DuCane (1885), 26
43. Capital Punishment Report (1856), v.
44. DuCane (1885), 24.
45. Anderson, 19.
46. Maybrick, 58.
47. Lee, 43.
48. Maybrick, 58.
49. Lee, 42.
50. Griffiths (1904), 330.
51. Lee, 43.
52. Pitkin, 232.
53. Maybrick, 59–60.
54. B. Thomson (1925), 25.
55. Berry, 17.
56. Ibid., 18.
57. Ibid., 20.
58. DuCane (1885), 23.
59. Bleackly, 225.
60. *St James Gazette*, 31 August 1892.
61. Bleackly, 225.
62. *Daily Telegraph*, 17 December 1879.
63. J. Hall, 56.
64. Tayler, 170.
65. Berry, 24.
66. Ibid., 26.
67. Ibid., 27.
68. Ibid., 64.
69. Scougal, 151.
70. Pitkin, 190–4.
71. Ibid., 204.
72. Berry, 61.
73. Ibid., 62.
74. Pitkin, 205.
75. Lee, 46–7.
76. Berry, 62.
77. Pitkin, 205.
78. Lee, 47.
79. Berry, 62.
80. Pitkin, 205.
81. Lee, 48–50.
82. Pitkin, 207
83. Lee, 50.
84. Rickards, 200.

11
WARDERS AND GOVERNORS

OFFICERS *AND* GENTLEMEN

Alexander Bethune was a self-educated working-class writer and poet who lived at Newburgh on the North Fife coast. In 1840 he had some correspondence with Martha Hill, the wife of Frederic Hill. She knew him only through his literary and epistolary efforts – and those of his brother – and had clearly formed a good impression of him. She also clearly wished to lend him a helping hand – one that might help her husband at the same time. 'I do not know whether chance has ever brought before you', she enquires, 'any account of the exertions that my husband, as Inspector of Prisons for Scotland, has made for the reformation of "our criminal brethren". Although his wife, I have no hesitation in saying, that during the five years he has been Inspector, the good that has been effected in the prisons of Scotland, with limited means, has been surprising.' She dilates on the 'highly talented as well as benevolent men' who are taking posts as governors, and how 'excellent instructors' are able to 'teach new habits of industry, self-employment, and honourable feelings to the poor individual whose ignorance and recklessness, or wretched early training, have made him the inmate of a prison.'[1] 'Would you like to aid in this good work?' she asks him, 'do you feel, that to help to snatch the unfortunate from guilt and misery, is a great and noble employment?'[2]

Mrs Hill may have anticipated some objections from Bethune because she tries to deal with some of them in advance. 'Perhaps you are not aware, that the order and arrangement of a well-conducted prison, is wholly different from all our old ideas of a prison. In the separate system, no swearing, quarrelling, or displeasing conversation assails the ears.' 'Perhaps you may think', she goes on, 'that your habits of life having been so contrary to the habitual control, zeal, and watchfulness necessary in an officer of a prison, you might not be able to adapt yourself to so new a position.' This, however, need present no difficulty, for there was a 'regular training in the Glasgow Bridewell' which he might attend.[3] In her letters, Mrs Hill identifies some of the fundamental changes taking place at that time in the nature and purposes of imprisonment, and implies some of the qualities thought necessary in a new breed of officials being brought in to replace the turnkeys of the discredited old regimes.

The same emphasis is made by the Rev. Daniel Nihill when he compares the qualities required of officers recruited to work the *separate* as opposed to the *silent* system of prison discipline. Under the latter type of regime, he says, 'regard to the safe custody of the prisoner, and to the danger of personal collision, has made it necessary to choose men distinguished for great bodily power, for animal courage, for austere and commanding temper – men who will make themselves feared.'[4] By way of contrast: 'The Separate System, by taking away the danger of collision, and presenting abundant opportunities for the exercise of kindness and the quiet inculcation of truth, so far from giving occasion to religious persons in humble life to shrink from the duty, offers them powerful inducements to undertake it. It is calculated to raise up a new class of prison officers, both men and women, whose chief qualifications will be rather of a moral than of a physical order – integrity, intelligence, amiability, and christian zeal.'[5]

Christian zeal was enjoined on officers, above all, by prison chaplains. 'Far from a whining, canting class of men, they should be manly and upright persons, who feel it their highest pretension that they are religious; their greatest praise that they are sedate; and their pride (if any) that they are rational characters, who have undertaken an office with the intention of honestly discharging its duties.'[6] The author of this glowing encomium, the Reverend George Heaton, chaplain at Gloucester County Gaol, rather spoils the effect when he adds: 'These men should be religious; but and if not, still they should seem to be. Their example is of the greatest importance.'[7] He advises, in other words, that they should simulate a religiosity they do not feel in order to further the ends of the reformatory prison.

The Convict Prison Standing Orders do not mention religion, but they define the primary duty of the prison officer in high moral tones:

The great object of reclaiming the criminal should always be kept in view by all officers, and they should strive to acquire a moral influence over the prisoners by performing their duties conscientiously but without harshness. They should especially try to raise the minds of prisoners to a proper feeling of moral obligation by the example of their own uniform regard to truth and integrity, even in the smallest matters; such conduct will, in most cases, secure the respect and confidence of prisoners, and will make the duties of the officers more satisfactory to themselves and more useful to the public.[8]

It was to a vision of prison discipline, and to a practice of prison work of this sort, that Mrs Hill sought to win Alexander Bethune. She knew from his letters that he was in straitened circumstances and offered to 'undertake the necessary expenses of your residing at Glasgow, while daily attending the Bridewell, as well as your travelling expenses'.[9] Bethune politely declined her kind offer, but stayed only a few days in his trainee position at the prison. He admitted to a friend the reason for his abrupt departure: 'I could not help disliking the society of the other turnkeys, some of whom, notwithstanding the very great praise which had been bestowed on them, I soon came to regard as the very pink of puppyism and self-conceit.'[10] Bethune's judgement may seem harsh, but it sprang from a trap in which the 'new' prison officers found themselves inescapably caught by a moralistic definition of their work. Measured against that kind of standard, few human beings would emerge with credit.

These far from flattering opinions of officers, by one who declined to work alongside them, are repeated, but less politely, by some of those who suffered under them. 'They were all a set of brutes', says the Tichborne Claimant, speaking of Dartmoor warders, 'most of whom are Cornish miners, being about the roughest type of men a man can meet with.'[11] Captain D— S— described the ones he met at Cold Bath Fields as 'a set of ignorant, cringing, underpaid warders and turnkeys – in many cases ill-conditioned by nature, and brutal, eye-serving, and untrustworthy by habit'.[12] The majority, in Thomas Barrow's opinion, 'are surly men and utterly unfit for the offices they hold'.[13] At Millbank, the 'subordinate officers' were said to be 'especially fond of affecting a military demeanour, and making an ostentatious display of their staves'.[14] And according to Stuart Wood, 'the conditions of the service attracted only the lowest moral types of men and women – those who carried out orders blindly and without question.'[15]

These observations point to one of the main sources of many, if not most, of the men who filled the ranks of the ordinary prison warders. 'A very large proportion of them', says Ticket-of-leave-man, 'are discharged soldiers and sailors.'[16] In his view, military men were not at all suitable people for the job. He was 'quite conscious that army reform has greatly raised the moral status of soldiers during the last fifteen years, but is it not a fact that twenty or twenty five years ago, the army was recruited chiefly from the dregs of the population, largely indeed from the very thief-class?'[17] Amongst these soldiers and sailors, it is former marines, men with a foot in both camps and a motto to match – *per mare, per terram* – who were singled out for special censure by One-who-has-tried-them. 'Out of the seven or eight warders I came across who had served in that corps', he says, 'I only found one decent man among the lot.' 'The others were all the same foul-mouthed, bullying, completely uneducated men, and totally unfit for any position of trust, and, least of all, fitted for prison employment.'[18]

Higher officials in the prisons where use was made of these men's services naturally disagreed. 'Military men seem, at first sight, qualified above others for offices of watch and ward', says the Reverend G. Heaton. 'I think a mixture works very well – it has been, apparently, tried with signal success in the prison with which the writer is most conversant – a mixture of civilians with men that have spent their primes in military scenes, and are now sobered down into the better complexion of domestic life.'[19]

A member of the governor class who did find soldiers unsuited to prison duties was Charles Pannell Measor, a former deputy at Chatham. Some idea of the qualifications of old soldiers 'for the office of moral reformers', he says, 'may be formed from the fact that out of the lowest classes of officers at Chatham Prison, numbering not more than a hundred men, there have been dismissed for neglect of duty and insubordination since the opening of the prison, a period of four years, no less than 54, besides compulsory resignations, of which 16 were dismissed for drunkenness on duty.'[20] Nor was drunkenness their only fault. Foul-mouthed warders were also of common occurrence. George Bidwell 'heard many of them telling or exchanging obscene stories with prisoners, and using the vilest language and bandying thieves' slang, in which they become proficient. I am bold to say that at least one-half of all I have known are in morals on a level with the average convict, or as I have heard more than one assistant warder say, "too much of a coward to steal, ashamed to beg, and too lazy to work" – therefore became a soldier, then a prison warder.'[21]

WARDERS AND PRISONERS

Before the rise of reformatory prison regimes, relations between prisoners and turnkeys had been relaxed – and corrupt. Part of the new disciplinary codes for officers therefore regulated the way in which they were permitted to relate to their prisoners. Under the county managements there were sometimes explicit rules against the holding of any kind of ordinary conversation. One example was spelled out to the Carnarvon Inquiry by Governor Gardner of Bristol:

Is the turnkey at liberty to talk to a prisoner at all?
No, except to direct him as regards his work, and then the prisoner whispers only; and the officer is compelled to speak out loud, and to stand at a distance of six feet.
Is that rule strictly adhered to?
It is. There is no officer on the premises that would dare let me see him nearer a prisoner than six feet.[22]

Since they were 'strongly discouraged from holding ordinary intercourse with prisoners',[23] or from talking with them 'familiarly or unnecessarily',[24] warders and wardresses developed a peculiar manner for addressing those in their charge. Lady Constance Lytton first encountered it when she complained to a wardress about the size of the shoes she had been given. 'She seemed not to have heard what I said, did not look my way, but shouted past me into the air, speaking in a loud voice . . . and without any variety of intonation in a way that sounded strange and unnatural, as if she were proclaiming an edict written by another person: "It's-no-good-complaining-about-those".'[25]

PROVOCATION

Verbal style apart, the officers covered the widest range of possibilities in their behaviour towards prisoners. At one end of this spectrum were officers described by John Lee as 'eternally wishing to report men on the slightest pretext. Such men are quickly marked by the prisoners. They become unpopular.'[26] Ticket-of-leave-man saw these officers as pursuing a reputation for vigilance at the expense of certain prisoners. 'The men selected to be reported are invariably green hands, and the most innocent in the gang. . . . I have known many prisoners do twenty-one days out of a month upon bread-and-water, and in every case the victim was a man unaccustomed to prison discipline, who had been made a mark by some prison-warder anxious for promotion, and who had goaded the poor fellow into using violent or threatening language.'[27]

Either way, the outcome could be counted satisfactory to bloody-minded officers, but if their tactics failed to elicit any kind of reaction from the prisoner, more physical methods could be tried. Lady Constance Lytton was a genteel person who observed the strange world of prison with a fresh, and ironic, and normally tolerant eye, but the use of physical restraints drew from her a reproach.

> Some wardresses allowed us sometimes to come and go freely . . . others, or the same wardresses on different days, would allow only one of us out of the ward at a time. This and all the other rules of the kind would hardly ever be told to us in so many words, but suddenly the wardress would step out and block the way, laying her hand upon us without a word as if we were animals. This being handled when there is no occasion for it seems very insulting.[28]

A more understated form of provocation was practised by 'a huge warder' at Pentonville, 'the worst bully of the flight', who 'placed himself so that we had to brush against his coat each time we passed him at the corner'.[29] Another officer used to 'go behind old men and pull their ears in a very brutal manner'.[30] Jabez Balfour on one occasion 'found it difficult to keep in step' with the man in front of him whilst executing a 'lock' step. 'The warder seized me by the shoulder, shook me violently and told me he would report me if it occurred again. . . . I had never in my life been treated in this way, and I found it very difficult to control my temper. . . . Had I given way to anything like anger I should certainly have been "run in" and punished, as many a poor fellow provoked by such treatment has bitterly experienced.'[31] But when prisoners did respond to this kind of treatment, their efforts were not always ineffectual. Henry Holloway threatened his landing officer following what he considered to be a provocation: 'I ran up to him in a great rage, and said, "Do you know what Seven has got? Seven has got seven years, and if you don't let me alone I'll make it hot for you." I then passed on, expecting to be brought before the governor, but I was not. I had frightened the man.'[32]

Mark Jeffrey, never a man to mince his words, or make empty gestures, instilled fear into nearly all the warders who ever had to do with him. 'Treat me well', he said to one, 'and you will be safe; but use me harshly, and I'll wait for a time and then attack you treacherously, and you may as well tell the mates that will relieve you the same thing.'[33]

Warders, in fact, went in fear, not just of violent individuals but of whole assemblies of prisoners from whom they somehow sensed a threat. The activities of a warder called Long-nosed Smith, for instance, aroused great antagonism towards him at Dartmoor.

> The men one and all took such a hatred to him, and so unmistakably expressed it, not only in words but in most significant looks, that he was afraid to go out with any of the bog gangs, for fear he should have been set upon. When appointed to the quarry gang he was suddenly ill and went off duty. That is the most dangerous gang for an unpopular officer to go with. A chance may arise for a man, *quite by accident on purpose*, to loosen a large block of stone over the head of anyone beneath him.[34]

In other cases, the needling of the officers provoked prisoners into direct physical attacks. The author of *Pentonville Prison from Within* witnessed such an incident in the exercise yard:

> There was a *broad*, short, dwarfish man amongst us, who was subject to terrible fits; and whose temper at times was very dangerous. I once saw him (when threatened by a warder who was new to the yard and did not quite understand the discretion that is used when dealing with epileptic prisoners) – I saw this little man wrench the warder's truncheon from him and strike that young official several times very heartily on the temples and head with it, rather than allow himself to be reported for talking. To my own mind, this was the only time I ever saw a truncheon *properly* used. I think it gave a lesson to a very young warder who carried himself with all the insolence of a Napoleon, though he had not a single qualification to recommend him to any man. . . . I stood by and watched this assault; nor do I blame myself now for not interfering with it.[35]

Given the nature of the two groups of men, the violence that occurred between warders and prisoners was inevitably a two-way affair. A man called Farrier, at Chatham with Austin Bidwell, 'pulled out from his waistband a piece of rag, and unrolling it, produced two of his front teeth with the information that a certain warder had struck him with his fist in the mouth and knocked them out.'[36] Another officer 'of the name of Pearce', was seen by Henry Harcourt to 'use his truncheon to a man while he had the handcuffs on. I should say that he was about 6 feet 4, or 6 feet 3, a big robust man. I have seen him take up his truncheon and knock them down as you would knock a bullock down.'[37]

More often the violence was not visible and could only be inferred from the noises that came from other cells. Thomas Barrow 'heard a poor fellow shout "Oh, Oh, Oh, Oh!" most piteously, and then a heavy door banged too, and I heard the same again a morning or two afterwards, the last Sunday but one before I came out, a man was undergoing more or less punishment all the day long; it seemed as if some one was sitting on his stomach and occasionally jerking on him. Let me tell all cruel men', he says indignantly, 'that God sees them and all their wicked actions and will assuredly punish them.'[38] According to Michael Davitt, 'It frequently happened in Dartmoor that prisoners were felled by warders, and in punishment cells, where I was detained for several months in 1875 and 1876, prisoners have been frequently beaten underneath me in punishment cells in the night time by visiting warders. That happened often.'[39]

By one view of prison warders, these acts of cruelty were the work of cruel and vindictive individuals, but the author of an article in the *Hibbert Journal* held to another theory of human nature. 'Men who in all other relations of life are kind, considerate, patient, lovable, become, in this particular relation, unkind, inconsiderate, impatient, odious. Man in these circumstances is an intolerable tyrant.'[40] 'In truth, there is no office which a human being is less qualified to fill than that of jailer. Here he is not descended from the ape, but from the wolf. Once give a man unconditional power over his fellow, and the brutalisation of the one becomes complete as the brutalisation of the other.'[41]

DISCIPLINE

'Warders were cruel and inhuman,' says Stuart Wood, 'because the system demanded cruelty and inhumanity in its officers. They were themselves subject to a code of rules every bit as strict as those they had to enforce. They were not only forbidden to talk to prisoners, they were not even permitted to hold conversations with one another whilst on duty.'[42] The 'code of rules' that applied to officers was as minutely detailed and every bit as draconian as Wood implies:

Swearing and improper language, incurring debts which he is unable to pay, the habit of frequenting public-houses or keeping bad company, and gambling or card-playing will be considered a sufficient reason for the dismissal of an officer.

Order No. 616 of the Standing Orders for the Government of Convict Prisons (1902) illustrates the extent of the control which the authorities claimed over the conduct of their employees, not merely within the prison walls, but outside as well. Standing Orders even pursued officers into their quarters where they forbade 'the covering of wood block floors with kamptulicon, linoleum, oil-cloth, or any other waterproof substance', since they caused 'the decay of such floors'.[43] And when they returned home at night, the rules went with them into their bedrooms:

> No person of the male sex above the age of ten years is to use or occupy a sleeping apartment used or occupied by persons of the female sex, except in the case of husband or wife.[44]

The rules could not of course cover absolutely every possibility for misbehaviour beyond the walls. But some prison chaplains professed a pastoral responsibility for warders and their families, and a concern for the moral welfare of the official prison community as a whole. 'Cases have been known', said one, 'where Governors and Chaplains have found it next door to impossible to keep their female servants decent and respectable, on account of the dead-set made upon their virtue by the Officers of the Prison.'[45]

Some of the blame for the poor state of affairs amongst officers at Dartmoor was ascribed by Basil Thomson to 'the lack of recreation for the staff. There was no railway to take them to Plymouth; no theatre, or place for dances or concerts; no library or billiard table. They were driven for relaxation to the public-house, and for the rest of their time to quarrelling among themselves. The quarrels extended even to the superior officers, who seem to have been morbidly sensitive about their dignity.'[46] The chaplain who was so worried about the corruption of servant girls thought that one answer could be to build officers' quarters close to the prison, where 'the Chaplain might consider all who lived in them as part of his parish, and under his spiritual care, through wives and children he would learn in a week more of the husbands and fathers than he would know of them in a year at their duties in the Gaol. The Governor might drop in when he felt disposed, when one of his staff was sick, or on any other occasion; the possibility of these visits either from Governor or Chaplain would tend to keep the Officers' homes tidy and comfortable, and more, they would prevent a very common occurrence in the case of feigned sickness, thus: the remaining at home just for the doctor's visit, the time of which is generally pretty accurately known, and the going out to the public-house or elsewhere, either before or after it takes place.'[47]

Like the plan for the penitentiary reform of the convict, this positive vision of moral supervision for officers and their families was never much more than a pipe-dream, and discipline for staff, like that of prisoners, remained wedded to mainly negative sanctions. The seamless nature of the disciplinary code that bound warders and prisoners alike in the Victorian prison was epitomized for Henry Mayhew in the governor's reports he witnessed at Cold Bath Fields. 'After the prisoners, two sub-warders were brought in, accused by their superior officers with breaking the prison rules by sleeping in church during the sermon. Both were fined.'[48]

Older hands amongst the officers would never have been caught napping like that; a number of them known to George Bidwell 'would sleep hours in an upright position, and one at Dartmoor Prison – an old soldier of the Indian mutiny – named Varney, who while on night duty on my ward used to sleep, snoring so loudly as to awaken me. Suddenly he would break off in the middle of a snore and shout, "All right, sir" to the governor, chief, or orderly officer, as either made the customary rounds.'[49] These tours of inspection by principal warders were designed to keep the subordinate staff on their toes, as Lord William Nevill observed:

> Their one idea, seemed to me to be not so much to maintain discipline as to catch the officers tripping, and get them into trouble. I have known them give an officer a 'half-sheet' – in other words, report him to the higher prison authorities, with the risk of being fined or otherwise punished – for the most absurd things, and sometimes without any justification at all. The effect of this excessive sharpness and severity is to make young officers sometimes nervous and flurried, and it has a tendency to make them unnecessarily hard on the prisoners.[50] . . . For the first few years it is neither more nor less than a dog's life owing to the insane delight some of the principal warders take in harassing newly-joined officers.[51]

Officers in search of a quiet life for themselves turned not infrequently to the prisoners for assistance. 'Reconvicted men knew more of the rules; they could instruct an officer when he was, perhaps, rather ignorant of his duties, and so save the officers trouble. As a rule the officers do not care about trouble; they take no interest in their occupation, and as soon as they can get the work done, and get the time passed away, that is all they look to, in order to get to the guard room.'[52] 'There is a tacit understanding between all "second-timers" and old thieves, and the officers who have charge of them. If the officer is caught in any dereliction of duty he is liable to a fine; these old thieves act as his spies, and take care that he is *not* caught. In return he allows the thieves to fetch what they call an easy lagging, to do as little work as they please, and to talk as much as they please.'[53]

Balfour noted the same conspiracy at Parkhurst, and how it worked in relation to official visits. 'Nearly every gang or party has a man who is recognized as the warder's "crow", who is stationed as near as possible to the spot where the visitor makes his appearance.' 'Prison life thus becomes one long trial of skill between prisoners and subordinate officers on the one hand, and the principals and superior officers on the other.'[54] But this conspiracy of convenience should not be mistaken for friendship: 'the old gaol-birds are content to act as spies for the warder, but, exercising the cunning which is one of the essentials of their vocation, they take pains to post themselves up in all his little weaknesses and derelictions of duty, and would not hesitate to betray him at some opportune moment, should he dare report them'.[55]

CORRUPTION

Between the mutual convenience of the warder's 'crow' at one extreme and the reciprocal threats and acts of violence at the other there nestled a third species of relationship between officers and prisoners – a relationship of corruption. Ticket-of-leave-man discovered its benefits early on in his sentence. He wished to write unsupervised letters to a friend (a practice not officially allowed). He 'very soon discovered that it was possible to communicate with him and yet elude the scrutiny of the Governor's office over my letters. . . . As a result of my first letter by this "underground railway", my friend called at the house of the corrupt, but, to me, useful warder. The next morning I had the daily papers with my breakfast; the same evening I had my Pall Mall with my supper; and they *were* breakfasts and suppers, for I was supplied with dainties and luxuries which had no place in the "bill of fare" of her Majesty's prison. . . . This continued during the whole of the nine months of my stay at Pentonville. On my removal to Brixton, where I only stayed seven weeks, I could have made equally favourable arrangements. . . . this Mr. Warder had, to my knowledge, half-a-dozen other clients upon his landing, so that he was able to double his salary at the very least. . . . I whiled away a large portion of my time in the store-closet, in conversation with other "paying prisoners", the warder himself keeping watch at the staircase to give the 'office' in case of the approach of visitors.'[56]

It was not unknown for warders of this nature to tout for custom among men they thought able to pay for it. One prisoner was asked if he wished to write to his friends 'for money', and was then told by the warder that 'he would bring me in a pie or any little thing which I wanted. . . . paper and pencil were put under my cell door more than once.'[57] Nor were these thought to be exceptional cases; it was widely believed that 'perhaps with the exception of one or two, any of the officers will do it.'[58] The reasons for this venality were not, according to some observers, all that difficult to elucidate. 'Where', asks one author, 'can you get intelligent men to work *ninety-two hours every week for a wage of twenty-three and tenpence per week upon the average*?'[59] John Dawson conversed with an Irish warder at Clerkenwell who received this wage: 'He had a small pension. He had a wife and four young children to provide for as well as himself. He lived in —— Road, Kentish Town, and to avoid spending any money in 'bus fare he walked to the prison every morning, and back home again in the evening. Though he was a teetotaler, he said he often experienced

The Chief Warder at Pentonville
and the Principal Matron at the female convict prison, Brixton

great difficulty in making both ends meet.' In Dawson's opinion, this low rate
of pay 'has a very great deal to do with much of the laxity of prison discipline,
tempting the warder, as it does to accept bribes from prisoners'.[60]

According to the report of the 1879 Penal Servitude Committee,

The offence most frequently committed by warders is trafficking with the
prisoners, especially in tobacco. A return which we have obtained shows
that there were 240 cases in which convicts were reported and punished

for trafficking with tobacco during the year 1877 and in 1878 up to December 4, the date of the return. . . . in the majority of cases we think it must be assumed that it was introduced by warders. It is needless to point out how prejudicial such practices are to discipline by weakening the authority of the officers, and tempting prisoners to disregard the rules of the prison.[61]

The prices placed on these illicit imports into the penal economy varied enormously; from 'a six ounce loaf for a quantity of tobacco about as thick as your pencil', to ten shillings,[62] or up to thirty shillings per pound,[63] and even as much as 'a sovereign for every ounce so delivered will they sometimes pay, and as it only costs the warder two or three pence, his profit is pretty good.'[64] These subterranean dealings in the tobacco trade were concealed for the most part from official view, but sometimes announced their presence in an indirect way. 'At Dartmoor it used to be an understood thing that when there was an epidemic of fights it was a sign that some warder had been trafficking in tobacco.'[65] Despite all the efforts of the authorities, this traffic could not be eradicated, and its continuing existence – on any scale – undermined the whole edifice of prison discipline.

Not all warders, of course, were corruptible, and some of them earned the ungrudging respect of their captives, both for that, and for their other qualities. The Fenian prisoners at Chatham met with failure when they tried to recruit one disaffected officer as a postman. 'This Jones was a very honest fellow, honest towards us and towards his employers. He was a Welshman and a military pensioner. He got into a difficulty, on account of which he lost his position. A prisoner and an officer had some altercation on the works; they came to blows; the prisoner got the better of the officer. Jones, who was in charge of a gang of men near by, ran to the officer's rescue . . . but as he did not use his sword on the captive and cut him down instead of tying him up, he was given to understand that he was not fit for his situation, and had better resign, which he did. . . . Thinking that he was in a disaffected or disgusted state of mind at his being thus treated, I suggested the advisability of testing him to see if he would take out a letter from me if I wrote one. Mike Moore approached him on the question, and he proved faithful to his employers. . . . We respected his scruples and did not press him.'[66]

Austin Bidwell and his work party 'had a very good officer by the name of James. He wanted the work done, and used his tongue pretty freely; still he was a man who would speak the truth and treated his men as well as he dared under the brutal regime ruling in Chatham.'[67] And during 'nearly four years experience' of prison life, Lord William Nevill 'saw scores of men being taken into the punishment cells. . . . I must say that, though they constantly bit, kicked, and did everything they could to injure the officers, I never once saw the latter use undue force. . . . many a time when I myself would have given a man a pretty sharp crack with a kosh, I have seen the officers keep their temper in a most extraordinary way.'[68]

The same point was frequently made; not, it must be said, by prisoners in constant conflict with the authorities, but by those who gave no trouble, or who worked closely with warders in the role of orderly, as David Fannan did: 'The warders, about whose petty tyrannies complaints are ordinarily made, I found, without an exception, reasonable and kindly; and was rather surprised at the amount of self-restraint and forbearance they were able to maintain in the management of such tricky and rotten humanity.'[69] More than that, he knew 'a warder in Perth called Wallace. He used to come into my cell during my "solitary" time, and chat with me as I was teasing the oakum, and in his presence all that was best in me seemed to rise to its feet, and I seemed strong enough to break the bonds of an evil past.'[70] Fannan's feelings of admiration were not unique. Alongside the catalogue of brutalities that mark what passed for normal relations between some warders and their prisoners, there must be registered a smaller number of kindly acts that illuminate the common origins of the two groups of men. One warder 'found an apple in his pocket' and 'kindly' gave it to George Jacob Holyoake.[71] Another 'came and kindly said "Good night", the first kind word' that the author of *Startling Disclosures* received in prison.[72] A one-time warder at Lancaster Castle, Isaac Smith, who found his work so uncongenial that he evaded the duty of flogging prisoners as far as he was able and left the service to become a sanitary inspector, tells how he took pity on an old Irish labourer from Preston. 'He was too clumsy for prison life – awkward at shot-drill, not able to do his task at oakum-picking – and being very untidy in his cell he was continually in trouble, – reported nearly every day, and every time reported he was put upon bread and water for the usual number of hours. I felt really sorry for the old man, and when an opportunity occurred for re-arranging prisoners, I contrived to have him removed into a cell under my charge, so that I could help him a little.'[73]

Between Oscar Wilde and Warder Thomas Martin of Reading Gaol there developed an even deeper relationship of mutual regard. Wilde relates an incident when a prisoner with diarrhoea had requested permission to empty his pot before being locked up for the night. The principal officer on duty refused. 'Martin, however, rather than see this wretched man in such a loathsome predicament, said he would empty the man's slops himself and did so. A warder emptying a prisoner's slops is, of course, against the rules, but Martin did this act of kindness to the man out of the simple humanity of his nature, and the man was naturally most grateful.'[74]

Martin himself remembered 'a certain bleak, raw morning in early March', when he found Wilde still in bed, complaining of 'pains in my inside'. The warder advised him to see the doctor, but Wilde refused, 'saying he would be all right when he had had something warm to drink'. Knowing that this would not be for some time, the warder made up some hot beef tea in a bottle, put it under his jacket, and set off for Wilde's cell. The bottle slipped between his shirt and his skin just at the moment when the chief officer chose to interrogate him about the previous night's muster report. 'I was in frightful agony. The hot bottle burned against my breast like molten lead. I have said "there are supreme moments in the lives of men". Those were supreme moments to me. I could have cried out in my agony, but dared not. The cold, damp beads of perspiration gathered on my brow; I writhed and twisted in all manner of ways to ease myself of the dreadful thing, but in vain. . . . I bounded up the iron stairs, and entered the Poet's cell, and pulling out the burning bottle, I related, amid gasps and imprecations, my awful experience. The Poet smiled while the tale was being told, then laughed – actually laughed.'[75] The week after Wilde's release from Reading, and his flight to France, Thomas Martin was forced to pay a high price for his inadmissible good nature. On 27 May 1897, the playwright wrote from Dieppe to the editor of the *Daily Chronicle*:

> Sir, I learn with great regret, through the columns of your paper, that the warder Martin, of Reading Prison, has been dismissed by the Prison Commissioners for having given some sweet biscuits to a little hungry child. I saw the three children myself on the Monday preceding my release. They were quite small children, the youngest – the one to whom the warder gave the biscuits – being a tiny little chap, for whom they had evidently been unable to find clothes small enough to fit.[76]

Martin was never to meet Wilde again, but following the death of the poet in 1900, the warder contributed an emotional tribute to Robert Sherard's biography of him – a tribute that ends like this:

> Farewell! I have kept my promise. I have remembered you during all the years that have intervened since that memorable day we shook hands and parted in your cold and cheerless cell. You asked me to think of you sometimes. I have thought of you always; scarcely one single day has passed since then that I have not thought of you – you who were at once my prisoner and my friend.[77]

FEMALE WARDERS

Like their male counterparts women warders were a mixed group, but they receive a rather better press from their charges. 'Considering the sort of persons who would naturally seek for such an employment,' said Susan Willis Fletcher, 'the warders are better than one would expect. There are, however, in all prisons, I fear, officers quite the reverse, – ignorant, low-bred, drunken, and innately, constitutionally cruel.'[78] At Walton Gaol, Liverpool, where she was received under the pseudonym of 'Jane Warton, spinster', Lady Constance Lytton found that 'the manner of nearly all the officers was severe; one or two were friends but most of them treated me like dirt.'[79] Female Debtor, on the other hand, thought the ones she met 'with scarcely an exception, to be models of everything desirable in woman – brave with the courage of heroines, patient, gentle, kind and self-disciplined.'[80] And Mrs Maybrick was impressed with 'the patience, civility and self-control which the officers exhibit under the most trying circumstances'; qualities which, 'as a rule, mark them as men and women possessing a high sense of duty, not only as civil servants, but as Christians'.[81] 'Add to this,' says Female Debtor, 'that many of them are still quite young and very pleasing in face and form; my own special officer having the daintiest little figure, large, true eyes, a big, affectionate mouth, and a most agreeable appearance generally.'[82] Constance Lytton was also taken with the appearance of the wardresses at Holloway. 'They were fine-looking women, young and vigorous, most of them had good figures and all of them had beautifully-kept hair which gave me a deal of pleasure to look at. . . . They held themselves very upright, and their general bearing brought to my mind certain types of the chaperon's bench at Court balls.'[83]

A part of this interest in appearance, so Governor Harris surmises, may have been related to a curious feature of female prison discipline: 'Female prisoners often like to be under the care of a good-looking officer, and will obey her and conduct themselves properly with her, though she may be a very indifferent disciplinarian. It has been said, and often confirmed, that a plain-featured officer of unsympathetic address finds it difficult to discipline her charges.'[84]

Relations between wardresses and women prisoners, like those on the men's side, were regulated by the rule book, but some women, and particularly the suffragettes, appeared able to pierce the official mask and get to the real person beneath. During a prolonged hunger strike, a principal wardress entered Sylvia Pankhurst's cell after she had cried out in her anguish. 'She took my hands, chafing them, and drawing me to her. "Darling, darling," I heard her say. She helped me to bed.'[85] A hospital wardress came to see Constance Lytton when she was crying. 'She was kind, she inquired tenderly why I was crying, sat down on my bed and held my hands, told me that my sister would not remember my reproaches but would be unhappy if she knew of my present distress. . . . She stayed talking to me in whispers for a considerable time, though looking continually towards the door as if in fear of being detected in a kindness. . . . I longed to return her kindness and ventured to propose that I should rub her chest to ease her hacking cough. A first she would not hear of it, but at last, after I had fetched some ointment from the bed-head of one of the patients who had a cough, she consented and allowed me to open her dress. She seemed much afraid and told me she would probably be dismissed if we were seen.'[86] These exceptions to the severity prescribed by regulations were not entirely restricted to the suffragettes. Susan Willis Fletcher was convicted of fraud and served her sentence at Tothill Fields in the 1870s. 'Let me', she entreats her readers, 'give a portion of a letter I received soon after my release, from a woman-warder who cared for me:

MY DEAR DARLING BABY, – If I may still call you so, – and I think you will let me, for indeed you are very dear to me, – you don't know how miserable and unhappy I feel, now you are gone. It is not like the same place. It was very bad, but now it is much worse. As I am passing that old cell, I look in. It is empty – no one there. Then I don't know what to do with myself. Oh, *do* forgive me. I ought not to remind you of this dreadful place, but I do miss you so much! I hope you will keep well. Let me beg of you to take care of yourself. I was so pleased to see your dear, dear boy; and I love him so much! He has your dear old face, bless him! . . . With fondest love, yours ever.

'It is needless to add', she needlessly adds, 'that a warder like this did not remain long in the service.'[87]

In Annie Kenney's case, the feelings ran in the other direction. 'One class of people who have my sympathy in prison are the wardresses. Their work is monotonous, and their lives are spent with the undeveloped and disharmonized souls on life's ocean. They are on their feet all day, and their pay when I was in prison was poor. . . . Some of them were far too good to be wasted there, and yet such kind, gentle natures could be greatly utilized if the women prisoners could be divided up in groups, each group representing the different stages of personality or development or education, and these groups organized and utilized according to their capacity.'[88] And another suffragette, Mary Richardson, struck a blow for women when she was ushered into the presence of the governor (male) and the visiting magistrates (male) and the matron. 'The sight of the matron standing behind his chair like a lackey while he and his portly brethren sat back in comfortable armchairs inflamed me. "It is a disgrace that the matron should have to stand while you all sit round in your comfortable chairs", I said, "A disgrace!" '[89]

GOVERNORS AND GENTLEMEN

In the army and navy of the nineteenth century, class and caste continued to draw a near impermeable line between 'officers and gentlemen' on one side, and 'other ranks' on the other. In a prison service that was largely manned by former members of the armed forces, the same strict division was made, not once but twice. It was drawn first and most strongly between prisoners – who now constituted a new and more lowly 'other ranks' – and warders, newly promoted to the more elevated status of 'officer'. Secondly, and in order to preserve the pre-existing military distinctions, the qualities of a 'gentleman' were detached from those of the 'officer', and reinvested in the positions of governor and deputy-governor. These were posts that were increasingly, and ultimately almost exclusively, filled by people like *Captain* Harris, *Major* Fulford and *Colonel* Rich.

Before the fusion of local and government prisons in 1877, senior appointments to the county gaols had been in the gift of the magistracy. George Laval

Chesterton, 'formerly of the Field Train Department of the Royal Artillery, subsequently a Captain in the Army of Columbia',[90] found himself in 1829 'returned to England with impaired health and impoverished means'.[91] He had, he says, 'at length, under advice, determined to seek holy orders . . . and for that purpose . . . had been reading with Mr. Ousby'.[92] Mr Ousby happened to be chaplain to be Middlesex House of Correction, and it was he who first urged Chesterton to apply for the vacant post of governor at Cold Bath Fields. Once decided on this course, he applied himself vigorously to the task.

> Traversing the length and breadth of the county, I visited every locality in which a magistrate resided, and, with one solitary exception, experienced the utmost courtesy. . . . My canvass progressed favourably, but I failed to extort a single promise. . . . On the 23rd July, 1829, I was nominated to the post by a vast majority of votes and the crowd assembled in the court and purlieus of Clerkenwell Green exceeded anything I have ever since seen, so much was public interest excited by the contest.[93]

After the nationalization of local prisons in 1877, all staff appointments were made in the office of the Prison Commission. There were no more magistrates to be canvassed, and certainly no meetings attended by 'public interest' in the proceedings. But the element of patronage remained strong in the system. In 1901, Major Wallace Blake returned home on sick leave from colonial service in British East Africa; 'when I arrived in England', he says, 'my people did everything in their power to prevent my returning to that insalubrious region'.[94] One day, he and his father were lunching with Captain Price, then governor of Wormwood Scrubs, when the idea of the younger Blake's applying for a job in prisons was broached. ' "In your case I should call and see Clayton at the Home Office. He runs the show", said Captain Price.'[95] 'Now it so happened that my father knew Major Clayton well; as a matter of fact they were in the habit of forgathering at the Naval and Military. "A good chap, Clayton," said he . . . "We'll go and look him up." So after lunch my father and I took a hansom to the Home Office, where we asked for Major Clayton and were at once shown into the office of the Secretary of the Prison Commissioners. However, it turned out that Colonel Garcia, one of the Commissioners, was also a friend of my father's, and we went to his office and tackled him.'[96] And so Major Blake became a prison governor.

Personal acquaintance played a similar role in the progress of Basil Thomson to a post in the prison service.

> My name had been put down for a Deputy Governorship with many others some years before. In 1896 Sir Evelyn Ruggles-Brise, to whom all the great reforms of the past thirty years were due, had been appointed to the chairmanship of the Prison Commission, and it fell to him to make recommendations for a number of new appointments. He knew something of me from old Eton days [Basil had been 'President-elect of "POP" ' and

had 'every prospect of becoming Captain of the Boats']⁹⁷ and he sent up
my name. It chanced that the Home Secretary's private secretary, who
had stayed with me when I was acting as Prime Minister of Tonga, saw
my name among the others and telegraphed to me asking whether I would
accept the appointment.⁹⁸

The men appointed by these means formed a striking contrast to some of
their predecessors in the unreformed era. 'The governors then', said Maria
Shepherd, 'were mere gaolers – men raised from the office of turnkey, often as
ignorant and immoral as their very prisoners. . . . Now look at the present class
of gentlemen holding these appointments. Men of standing in society – men of
education and ability – chiefly chosen from amongst naval and military officers.'⁹⁹ (In a footnote, though, she has to acknowledge: 'It is true, sadly true,
that the hardheartedness, cruelty, and severity of Lieutenant Austin, as shown
in the late disclosures of Birmingham prison, has deeply stained the purity of
the naval flag.')

Prisoners too, and especially those with pretensions to gentility themselves,
could tell a gentleman at a glance: 'He was an exceedingly tall fine-looking man

The governor's house and planked courtyard at Tothill Fields

with a handsome, kindly face, and a thoroughbred look about him that stamped him at once as a gentleman.'[100]

But the stamp of the real gentleman went deeper than mere appearances. George Jacob Holyoake, never an easy man to please, admired without reservation the governor at Gloucester: 'Captain Mason . . . was a study – a type of the gentleman, official and conventional, whose qualities were instructive. Bland, imperturbable, civil, and firm, he was never weak and never rude. . . . I watched his manners with pleasure – he governed the gaol like a drawing room, excepting that the *desserts* were not quite the same. I saw rude men baffled, they could not make out how.'[101] Even so, good manners, no more than velvet gloves, could not conceal an inner iron in the Captain's character. 'As blandly and courteously as he wished me good morning, he would have conducted me to the gallows, had instruction to that effect reached him. He would have apologised for the inconvenience, but he would have hung me while I was saying "pray don't mention it".'[102]

Besides manners, gentle birth brought with it other attributes and attitudes. Some of these are somewhat muted in the writings of former officials; some of them are quite explicit. Lieutenant-Colonel Rich earned his first full governorship at Northampton County Gaol before the First World War: 'Northamptonshire was in those days a real piece of Old England, full of fine historical and sporting estates belonging to splendid old families who for centuries had been looked up to and loved by a happy and loyal tenantry.'[103] His admiration for these yeoman virtues was matched by a nostalgia for a past age – 'when men used to work and there were jobs for them, and when the trade unions and Socialists had not yet ruined the country by their endeavours to get more money out of industries than there was in them.'[104] 'Let some strong man be appointed to bring England to its senses' is his appeal on the last page of his memoirs.[105] The key to curing the national malaise lay, he was convinced, in the restoration of discipline both outside and inside prison, and he had no doubts about who was best equipped to impose it. 'Now I am fully aware that nowadays it is almost an offence to make use of the expression "gentleman", but nevertheless I am going to risk it and say what is, after all, obvious: prisoners are more easily controlled by a gentleman.'[106]

All governors, however, did not match up to the high standards set by Captain Mason or Colonel Rich, either in their behaviour or in their social origins. 'The Government theory', according to One-who-has-tried-them, 'is to give these appointments to gentlemen only, but like various other Government theories it is continually broken in practice in order that those in whose hands prison patronage rests may satisfy the claims of personal hangers-on.'[107] Prisoners who were themselves gentlemen, or who aspired to the status, reserved a special contempt for such men. At one of the prisons patronized by One-who-has-tried-them the governor was a 'Major S—, a man of no particular family, and who, in sporting parlance would have decidedly been styled a "half-bred 'un." '[108] And for a prisoner such as Captain D— S—, who was not only a gentleman but an officer as well, the indignity of serving under a governor who was neither was doubly compounded. 'This man is what is known in the army as a "Ranker" – that is, one who by merit has raised himself from the rank and file to his present position – and had apparently brought with him many of those habits which, however commendable in a turnkey, are beneath the dignity of a Governor and lower the position he ought to occupy.'[109]

The actual duties of governors were laid down in the Regulations for Prisons in England and Wales, and in the Standing Orders for the Government of Convict Prisons. The governor's duties constituted in fact a blueprint for the management of the entire institution; from the global injunction to 'see that discipline is maintained among the convicts at all times',[110] to the minutely particular, e.g. 'He will not allow any dog, poultry, pigeon, pig, or rabbit to be kept in the prison, or in any quarter of a subordinate officer.'[111] Some of the regulations were as prescriptive of the governor's private life as they were about the warders: 'He shall reside in the prison, and he shall not be absent from it for a night without permission in writing from a visiting justice.'[112]

In practice, though, many governors did not find their duties too demanding. Like Colonel Rich, Basil Thomson's first governorship was at Northampton. 'The prison was small', he said. 'One might stand in the central hall and see the whole of it; one might almost run it with one's eyes shut.'[113] Wallace Blake agreed.

Speaking generally the work of a Prison Governor is just as hard as he cares to make it. In the small Class IV prisons there is not very much to do. He will be able to make his inspection in something under the hour; there is very little office work, and if he is fortunate enough to have a reliable chief warder – and in my whole career I have not met one who was not reliable – he has plenty of time for golf and tennis or whatever his chosen recreation may be. From about 9 a.m. until noon is about all the actual time necessary for him to perform the purely routine duties of his office. A look round in the afternoon, with perhaps another in the evening.[114]

Whether they were hard-working or not, prison governors were as different in their personal styles as the warders whose work they supervised. Mrs Maybrick 'served under three governors, each of whom was an intelligent and conspicuously humane man. They knew their prisoners and tried to understand them, but there is not much a governor can do for them of his own initiative.'[115] At the same time, 'they were all advanced disciplinarians. The routine reeled itself off with mechanical precision. The rules were enforced and carried out to the letter. The deadly monotony never varied; all days are alike.'[116] According to the Reverend John Pitkin, on the other hand, 'The first Governors, appointed under this system, were a true type of the system they represented. They had a righteous contempt for the prisoners they kept in custody. They spoke to them with a harsh and unsympathetic voice. They had grown up under rigid rules, and had become rigid themselves.'[117]

But there were other governors who were pleasant and considerate to their charges. The governor of Newgate in 1841, 'whose name was Cope, was a jolly old gentleman, fond of fun, and always wore a smile upon his countenance'.[118] Mrs Fawcett, on a visit to Holloway to see a fellow suffragette in custody, thought the then governor 'a courteous old gentleman',[119] and the sister of Lady Constance Lytton, on a similar errand, 'thought him rather a nice kind man with a military manner'.[120] And following his release from Reading Gaol, Oscar Wilde spoke warmly of the last governor under whom he served as 'a man of gentle and humane character, greatly liked and respected by all the prisoners'.[121]

PARLIAMENT STREET

Above the governors of the later Victorian period there existed a short chain of unified command that led via the inspectors of prisons to the office of the Prison Commission in Parliament Street. Evelyn Ruggles-Brise was first appointed as

Sir Edmund DuCane

an ordinary member of the Commission in 1892. 'Since the Local Prisons were taken over by the Government in 1877, and all prisons, both Local and Convict, placed under the Home Secretary, the administration of both sets of Prisons was almost entirely in the hands of one man, Sir Edmund DuCane. Prior to 1877 he had been Chairman of the Board of Directors of Convict Prisons. In 1877 he was made Chairman of the new Board of Commissioners of Local Prisons. . . . There were two distinct Boards, but all under the domination of their very able and distinguished Chairman. He was also by ancient title Surveyor General of Prisons and was a distinguished officer of the Royal Engineers and a noted architect and engineer. Although he had a large body of trained experts at his command, in course of time he had completely sterilized them by absorbing all matters, great and small, into his own hands. His word was law; the Home Secretary himself bowed to his decision when any question involving expert knowledge of Prison administration was on the *tapis*.' Ruggles-Brise was an able and ambitous young man to whom this regime was stifling: 'I found that although we were a Royal Commission, where theoretically each member exercises a real authority, subject to the control of the Chairman, as a matter of fact we rarely ever met as a Commission, and then only on some petty question of patronage and never, as far as I remember, on any question of general administration.'[122] On one occasion Ruggles-Brise ventured some mild criticism of one of Sir Edmund's favourite underlings: 'He was then approaching the age for retirement; his health was failing and I cannot remember that he ever spoke to me again.'[123]

The same fate had earlier befallen the first Secretary appointed to the new Commission after 1877. He was Robert – later Sir Robert – Anderson, an Irish barrister. He was also a part-time Protestant evangelist, and had been long connected with Dublin Castle and the Home Office in undercover work against the Fenian movement. 'I threw myself *con amore* into the general work of the department', he tells us, but 'the more active and zealous I became . . . the more unpleasant did my relations become with Sir Edmund DuCane.' A colleague eventually confided to him that DuCane's resentment stemmed from Anderson's independent access – as a member of the Secret Service – to the Secretary of State. In other words, 'DuCane was jealous of me'. The remedy was simple. 'I changed fronts at once. I never visited another prison, nor did I ever do a real day's work again in prison business.' Sir Edmund, he says, 'was my firm friend ever afterwards, and helped me in many ways'.[124]

Other Commissioners were equally friendly and helpful, none more so than 'Admiral Wyndham Hornby, afterwards gazetted a KCB. "Anderson, I have something to tell you in strict confidence," he announced one morning, as he sat down in my arm-chair. And he went on to tell me, as a State secret, that the Government had a scheme on foot which was certain to benefit Turkey. He had therefore telegraphed that morning to his broker to buy some Turkish Bonds. He then went out, as I afterwards discovered, to give the same tip "in strict confidence" to a number of his special friends in the various Government offices.'[125] The sudden interest in Turkish bonds amongst government officials was soon reflected in higher prices. Sir Robert 'cleared out at £12, and the Bonds soon fell back to their normal value. I do not know whether this story is typical of Stock Exchange ways', he says, 'but it is thoroughly typical of Whitehall, and especially of my friend "the Admiral." '[126]

The personal style adopted by the chairman in his autocratic management of the department is portrayed by Arthur Griffiths who knew him well from fifteen years as an inspector of prisons. 'Sir Edmund's favourite attitude was to stand with his back to the fireplace, his tall, spare figure very erect, his head thrown back, chin in air, his eyes flashing, and his mouth grim. He was easily moved to wrath.' 'As a rule, however, Sir Edmund mostly vented his wrath on paper, when he let his pen run freely, having first dipped it in gall.'[127] The temper of the man may be gauged from the following anecdote which Griffiths tells, of a time when words, both written and spoken, utterly failed DuCane. Following the amalgamation of local and national prisons in 1877 he set off to inspect some of the further flung outposts of his newly enlarged empire. At one prison he found the gates firmly closed against him.

> The gatekeeper when summoned to admit him, refused, even after he was told who it was that claimed to enter, and replied curtly, if not rudely, that the applicant must wait until reference was made to the Governor, and his permission obtained. Sir Edmund, never slow to wrath, was not the man to be thus flouted impudently, as he believed, at the door of an establishment under his supreme authority, and he took the law, with the gatekeeper, into his own hands. It was afterwards averred by his enemies that a more or less savage assault was committed upon the warder, and when the matter came before the House the Home Secretary could not deny that an assault had been committed.[128]

Sir Robert Anderson pays his former chief this oblique tribute: 'I cannot close this chapter without paying my sincere tribute to the great ability of Sir Edmund DuCane, the Chairman of the Commission. Indeed, if only he had been a man of wider sympathies, and his care for prisoners had equalled his knowledge of prisons, he would have been a perfect prison administrator. Under his rule very great improvements were effected in prisons and prison administration; and if criminals were mere animals, nothing more need be desired in either sphere. But criminals are human beings, and they ought to be treated as such.'[129]

Public unease at the nature of Sir Edmund's regime, harsh and unremitting as it was, and devoid of any feature that might have held out hope to the people locked up in it, led to the appointment of a Departmental Committee of Inquiry, which published its findings in 1895 – the Gladstone Report. In tone and content it was a damning indictment of his entire career:

> The great and, as we consider, the proved danger of this highly centralised system has been, and is that while much attention has been

given to organisation, finance, order, health of the prisoners, and prison statistics, the prisoners have been treated too much as a hopeless or worthless element of the community, and the moral as well as the legal responsibility of the prison authorities has been held to cease when they pass outside the prison gates.[130]

So at the very moment when he might have expected to retire with the respect and gratitude of a society whose values were so faithfully reflected in the system he had created, Sir Edmund DuCane departed public life instead with a bitter rebuke as his only reward.

NOTES

1. Bethune, 222.
2. Ibid., 223.
3. Ibid., 223.
4. Nihill, 62.
5. Ibid., 63.
6. Heaton, 64.
7. Ibid., 72.
8. Convict Prison Standing Orders (1902), 101.
9. Bethune, 224.
10. Ibid., 257.
11. Orton, 29.
12. D— S—, 206
13. Barrow, 10.
14. Letter, 496
15. Wood, 29.
16. Ticket-of-leave-man, 126.
17. Ibid., 127.
18. One-who-has-tried-them, I, 252.
19. Heaton, 64–5.
20. Measor, 14.
21. G. Bidwell, 433.
22. Carnarvon Committee (1863), 331.
23. Wood, 210.
24. Measor, 11.
25. Lytton, 82.
26. Lee, 94.
27. Ticket-of-leave-man, 150.
28. Lytton, 95.
29. *Pentonville Prison from Within*, 146.
30. *Kirkdale*, 96.
31. J. Balfour, 70.
32. Holloway (1877), 30.
33. Hiener, 67.
34. One-who-has-endured-it, 295.
35. *Pentonville Prison from Within*, 178–9.
36. A. Bidwell, 396.
37. Penal Servitude Commission (1879), 350.
38. Barrow, 12.
39. Gladstone Committee (1895), 384.
40. One-who-has-suffered-it, 600.
41. Ibid., 599.
42. Wood, 28.
43. Convict Prison Standing Orders (1902) 114.
44. Ibid., 113.
45. *Prison Magazine* (6), 8.
46. B. Thomson (1925), 103.
47. *Prison Magazine* (6), 10.
48. Mayhew, 338.
49. G. Bidwell, 440.
50. WBN, 76.
51. Ibid., 81.
52. Penal Servitude Commission (1879), 511.
53. Ticket-of-leave-man, 36.
54. J. Balfour, 277.
55. Ticket-of-leave-man, 37.
56. Ibid., 74–5.
57. Penal Servitude Commission (1879), 409.
58. Ibid., 444.
59. Collett, 40.

60. Dawson, 131.
61. Penal Servitude Commission (1879), liv.
62. Ibid., 409.
63. Ticket-of-leave-man, 155.
64. One-who-has-endured-it, 121.
65. B. Thomson (1925), 104.
66. Rossa, 185.
67. A. Bidwell, 398.
68. WBN, 154.
69. Fannan, 97.
70. Ibid., 128.
71. Holyoake (1893), I, 162.
72. One-who-was-there, 11.
73. Smith, 22.
74. Hart-Davis, 272.
75. Sherard, 356.
76. Hart-Davis, 269.
77. Sherard, 363.
78. Fletcher, 331.
79. Lytton, 266.
80. Female Debtor, 5.
81. Maybrick, 200.
82. Female Debtor, 9.
83. Lytton, 73.
84. Harris (1907), 792.
85. S. Pankhurst, 448.
86. Lytton, 111.
87. Fletcher, 409.
88. Kenney, 96.
89. Richardson, 76.
90. Chesterton (1853), I, frontispiece.
91. Ibid. (1856), I, 38.
92. Ibid., I, 34.
93. Ibid., (1853), 243–4.
94. Blake, 10.

95. Ibid., 12.
96. Ibid., 13.
97. B. Thomson (1939), 14.
98. Ibid., (1925), 23.
99. Shepherd, ix.
100. One-who-has-tried-them, I, 98.
101. Holyoake (1850), 97.
102. Ibid., 97.
103. Rich, 58.
104. Ibid., 84.
105. Ibid., 281.
106. Ibid., 277.
107. One-who-has-tried-them, I, 293.
108. Ibid., 113.
109. D— S—, 59.
110. Convict Prison Standing Orders (1902), 150.
111. Ibid., 152.
112. Prison Regulations (1849), 7.
113. B. Thomson (1925), 149.
114. Blake, 24.
115. Maybrick, 199.
116. Ibid., 200.
117. Pitkin, 19.
118. Miller, 135.
119. Fawcett, 186.
120. B. Balfour, 189.
121. Hart-Davis, 275.
122. Leslie, 84–5.
123. Ibid., 86.
124. Anderson, 80.
125. Ibid., 82.
126. Ibid., 83.
127. Griffiths (1904), 257.
128. Ibid. (1904), 291.
129. Anderson, 83.
130. Gladstone Committee (1895), 7.

12
RELEASE

Time passed. The prison bell tolled off the days, identical in detail and distinct only in this little incident or that. The spent days counted out the weeks and then the months that added up to whole years which somehow came and went. And as they passed, the thoughts of prisoners turned towards the world beyond the walls.

It was in fact the gradual restoration of a civilian appearance – when he was allowed to grow 'hair, beard and whiskers'[1] – that first signalled to the long-term prisoner the imminence of release. Prior to that, his return journey lay through a penal terrain he last passed on his way *into* the system. The change in appearance may have been intended as an act of kindness on the part of the authorities, but it was also a convenience. Lord William Nevill thought that men were 'obliged to grow their hair so that photographs may be taken showing approximately the normal appearance. Two or three weeks before discharge they are decorated with a sort of make-up collar and tie, and double-breasted dark-blue jacket, and photographs are taken of them in this costume.' He was not convinced that the 'copies of these works of art . . . sent to Scotland Yard and the Home Office' would serve their intended purpose, 'because nine out of ten change their whole appearance when they get outside by shaving and dressing according to their own ideas, and according to their class.' 'I am sure', he adds, 'no-one would recognise me now from my official portrait.'[2]

Short-sentence prisoners who had been cropped were denied the opportunity of growing their hair again before release, but a man called Vinter hit on a cunning solution to the problem. He was 'accustomed to wear a cap with a peak to it, and this style of head-gear, whatever other advantages it might possess, had the singular disadvantage of displaying the County crop of any victim to that operation in a striking way. Vinter recognised this, so when the official barber had completed his work of disfigurement, he collected the locks and cleverly sewed them round the inside of his hat, so that when he emerged from gaol, no one could tell but that he still possessed his curls as usual.'[3]

Long-sentence prisoners, whose clothes had been confiscated on reception, were also measured for a new suit. A Merchant, whose leg had been amputated in prison, was 'measured for *a shoe*, the only decent and honest article of clothing' he ever received from the authorities.[4] At a later date the prisoner was able to have 'his own clothes, which have been sent him by his friends'.[5] Oscar Wilde asked his friend More Adey to buy him some toiletries: 'some nice French soap, Houbigant's if you can get it: Pritchard of King Street, St. James's, used to have it for me: either 'Peau d'Espagne' or 'Sac de Laitue' would do: a case of three. Also some scent; Canterbury Wood Violet I would like, and some 'Eau de Lubin' for the toilet, a large bottle. Also some of Pritchard's tooth-powder, and a medium toothbrush'.[6] A sense of occasion clings to Wilde's list: of washing off the prison smells in a downpour of perfume and of dressing up. But for many prisoners the period immediately preceding release from a long sentence was one not of pleasurable anticipation but of anxiety and uncertainty. Jabez Balfour had 'inevitable doubts as to the possibility of finding creditable employment, and of earning an honourable livelihood'. 'And to all of these', he continues, 'was added a strange sense of the precariousness of the impending termination of my prison life.'[7] He knew that he was to be released soon, but even in the ending of its dealings with prisoners, the administration remained wedded to a policy of deliberate uncertainty: 'not one word was said to me as to the exact date of my release – I was left to guess that, and I guessed very often and very hard.'[8] David Fannan reached the end of a sentence, as long as Balfour's, and discovered that he was not after all to be let out on the day he had expected: 'The next day came, but no discharge. My hopes sank, and as day after day passed I became so sick at heart that I could neither eat nor sleep. Was I forgotten, and to be immured for ever; had my past deeds so come to light that I was to be shut up in these cells till death? That single week of suspense concentrated in itself more of anguish than the whole eleven years that preceded.'[9]

In the case of life-sentence prisoners the anguish may not have been so acute, but the uncertainty was a calculated part of their punishment. The convention in the nineteenth century was to release such prisoners after twenty years, but as the decision rested entirely with the Home Office, in consultation with the trial judge, release could come before that time had elapsed . . . or after. In some cases it might never arrive. But after a period of years, life sentence prisoners or their relatives might begin to agitate for their release. The Bidwell brothers conducted especially vigorous campaigns for their release, though adopting different strategies. George Bidwell had become crippled through his inability (his story), or unwillingness (the official version), to move his legs. He petitioned the Home Secretary from Woking Prison on 1 February 1887, in terms that suggested mental derangement as well:

It is beyond all dispute that from the time I came to Dartmoor they caused great quantities of mercury and glue to be put in my food expecting it would slowly kill me or cause my death from starvation through fear of eating the food after I discovered their plan.

The prison doctor had previously told the Home Office, in the April of 1886, that 'with the exception of four days at the end of February, he has persistently refused food from the end of November last until yesterday evening. During this time he was artificially fed twice daily, but has nevertheless become considerably reduced.' Dr Brayn also notes that he 'is a very determined, and exceedingly astute man, and it is somewhat doubtful as to whether these delusions are genuine, or assumed'.

In the midst of his petitionary ramblings, Bidwell does not omit to reiterate what he pleaded at the trial, almost fourteen years previously; that Austin was a minor partner in the fraud on the Bank of England, and should not be treated so harshly as himself. 'My marrow and brains are gone', says George, 'and the end so near that it is hardly worth the liberating me. But all his [Austin's] many relations and friends in America will vouch for his good conduct when freed, therefore:- Send brother Austin home, send him alone, I'll stay without a word, without a groan.'[10] As it turned out, it was George who went home alone – medically released in July 1887; and Austin who was left to groan – for another four and a half years.

By comparison with George, Austin had been a model prisoner, obedient, hard-working and uncomplaining. There was nevertheless a considerable agitation for his release; by his sister, who moved to London to devote herself to it more or less full time; by American notables – including President Cleveland, Mark Twain and Harriet Beecher Stowe who wrote to the Home Secretary on his behalf; by English political figures, e.g. John Bright and Lord Randolph Churchill who did likewise; and by Austin himself. On 18 April 1891 he petitioned the Secretary of State from Chatham Convict Prison. In the centre of the specially printed blue form he wrote the single word 'Grace!'[11] In the space provided for the purpose Vernon Harris, then governor at Chatham, marked his behaviour as 'good', but shortly afterwards failed – presumably with deliberation – to inform his masters of some even better behaviour on Austin's part. The matter came to light when George, by now in America, received a letter from Glasgow:

Dear Sir: I can best introduce myself when I tell you I have just been discharged from the Convict Prison at Chatham, where I left Austin. . . . I was also to give you particulars of a heroic act on his part in saving a prisoner from drowning, which should have been in some way recognized by the authorities; but I am sorry to say it was not, although at the time it was the whole talk of the prison and the free men on the Island.

George was an old adversary of Governor Harris from their Dartmoor days, and he immediately wrote to him threatening immediate publication of this and other facts, ending with the aggressive salutation, 'Give me some reason to remember you with gratitude regarding Austin.'[12] The receipt of this letter produced an immediate report to the Under Secretary of State at the Home Office by Mr Fagan, the visiting director for Chatham. In it was enclosed the statement of Assistant Warder Alford that on 11 June, when 'prisoner George Jones was lifting a pump out of the barge he accidentally slipped over the barge and fell into the water, and it being ebb tide at the time he was rapidly drifting away, when prisoner Z891 A. Bidwell jumped overboard and rescued him'. Commissioner Fagan, in presenting this evidence to the Home Office, expressed the directors' 'regret that this praiseworthy action was not sooner brought under their notice' – an administrative reprimand to Governor Harris – and ventured 'to hope that the Secretary of State will feel able to afford Bidwell some substantial recognition of his prompt and effective bravery, but for which there is little doubt Jones would have lost his life'. Mr Henry Matthews, then Under Secretary at the Home Office in Gladstone's second administration, pencilled on the papers:

> Bidwell does not deserve any consideration on the merits; but it is important to recognize such conduct as his in rescuing his fellow prisoner. Let him have his licence 18 months earlier than in the usual course. 10. Sept. '91.[13]

Austin was finally released in February 1892, although his twenty years would not have elapsed until August 1893.

His fellow American, Mrs Florence Maybrick, served fifteen years in English gaols and her last hours before release were tense ones. The last Sunday she spent in prison, she 'felt like one in a dream. I could not realize that tomorrow, the glad tomorrow, would bring with it freedom and life.'[14] When *his* time came, Balfour 'did not sleep much that Good Friday night. . . . The door was opened, and an assistant warder said to me quite naturally: "Balfour, you are wanted at the Governor's office. You are to bring your kit with you." I obeyed mechanically. I should like to have shouted, screamed, or danced. With a great effort I controlled myself and tried to assume an air of composure.'[15]

Then through the gate to freedom. 'The morning was perfectly lovely', on the day Susan Willis Fletcher was released, 'and the route from Westminster to my friend's house in South Kensington lay through Paradise. None but those who have been immured for months in a gloomy prison can ever know the ectasy of freedom. The sensation goes far towards compensating for the deprivation.'[16] Michael Davitt's sentiments echoed and amplified those of Mrs Fletcher.

I was liberated once – unexpectedly set free, after seven and a half years of close imprisonment, and I am almost inclined to say, that the punishment involved in a penal servitude of that duration would be worth enduring again to enjoy the wild, ecstatic, soul-filling happiness of the first day of freedom. It is a sensation of delight akin to that which Adam must have experienced upon waking to life and consciousness in the Garden of Eden.[17]

During his imprisonment, Thomas Cooper, the Chartist leader, had lost his religious faith and flirted with atheism, but release restored his belief. 'When

Liberation from Cold Bath Fields

the railway train began to bear me towards London, on that beautiful May morning of my release, I burst into tears, and sobbed with a feeling I could not easily subdue, as I once more saw the fields and flowers and God's glorious sun. The world was so beautiful, I dared not say there was no God in it; and the old long-practised feeling of worship welled up in my heart, in spite of myself.'[18] George Bidwell found beauty too after all his suffering: 'Though I began those years a black-haired, robust young man, at the end I found myself a gray-haired cripple; yet, on this first opening of the world anew before my ravished eyes, how beautiful everything appeared! Even dull-looking old London seemed glorious. And the throngs of people in the streets! . . . I could not tire of looking at them.'[19]

But his fellow conspirator in the Bank of England fraud, Edwin Noyes, was more phlegmatic. 'I was far less excited than I thought I would be. It seemed as though I were in my natural element, that the hideous past was a nightmare, the memory of which fresh scenes were already beginning to weaken.'[20] Oscar Wilde was 'nervous – dazed with the wonder of the wonderful world: I feel as if I had been raised from the dead. The sun and the sea seem strange to me.'[21] And John Lee 'felt like a man who is suddenly brought out of a pitchy darkness into blinding light. I was confused. I was lost. . . . For twenty three years I seem to have been asleep. I have woke up in a world that flies round in a whirlwind. Everybody and everything is in a hurry.'[22] The speed may have been a sort of optical illusion; a contrast to the measured tread of the convict's day; but his adaptation to that slower tempo, and the hibernation of his mental faculties, had left him relatively defenceless to meet the hurly-burly of everyday life.

I had neither courage nor confidence sufficient to enable me to act alone. I think I would have seen happier if, instead of the kind plain-clothes officer who accompanied me, a uniformed warder had walked behind me and said: 'Lee! go to the station!' and 'Lee! get your ticket!' I missed the 'Come here!' and 'Go there!' existence of the prison. In plain language I wanted to be ordered about.[23]

He would have been happier perhaps, had he been released from Dartmoor, where the practice was for the convict to proceed 'to the railway station at Horrabridge. . . . An officer goes with him, and at the station takes a *special* convict's ticket for him to his destination, whither he is bound.'[24] 'Once or twice' during Basil Thomson's time, by way of contrast, 'a convict would order a carriage and pair of his own and go down to Tavistock in state, with clothes specially ordered for him from a London tailor.'[25]

The clothes in which most men left prison were the cause of some distress to them. Ticket-of-leave-man complained that 'on my advent to Pentonville, the authorities took possession of a suit of clothes adapted to my position in life, and which had shortly before cost me twelve or fourteen pounds. On my release I was turned loose in a suit, the shoddiness of which is itself a lesson in rascality, and in which I should have been been quite ashamed to seek employment in my own profession.'[26] 'The contract price of the material may have been ten shillings, and it was botched together as only prison tailors can botch. Its value was *nil*; a good sharp shower would reduce it to a rag: no not even a rag, for it was shoddy.'[27] One author thought his suit of shoddy 'stamped him as a convict as much as a broad arrow could have done'.[28] And One-who-has-endured-it agreed: 'A man may just as well wear his ticket-of-leave in the front of his hat as the clothes given to him on leaving prison.'[29] There was, he thought, only one consolation in the whole business. 'I have been told that, providing a man goes straight from prison to Monmouth Street, Soho, or to Rosemary Lane, Minories, and is lucky enough not to be caught in the rain on his way, the clothes dealers will allow him 6s. for the whole turn-out.'[30]

To help the newly discharged convict with his difficulties there had sprung up in many localities specialized bodies of a charitable nature. 'It was for the purpose of carrying out some system by which such persons, on leaving prison, could, if they really desired it, be assisted to return to or commence a life of honesty that in the year 1857 the Discharged Prisoners' Aid Society was established.'[31] The Society dealt only with *convicts* discharged from the government convict prisons to London. There was one principal condition attached to the offer of help: 'By undertaking, as *a rule*, no case, unless a discharged prisoner places the whole of his gratuity in the Society's hands, it holds in safe custody, and often for a considerable period, money which would otherwise probably be recklessly squandered.'[32] The reputation of these societies was not good: 'The general impression among the prisoners who have had experience with the society is that it is conducted in the interest of those who draw salaries from its funds. . . . It appears to be a mere bank in which a man can deposit the small sum allowed him by the Government and receive it back in driblets.'[33]

The gratuity money, which the societies insisted on prisoners depositing with them, was given out in 'driblets' in order to prevent its being spent in the nearest hostelry. Josh Poole, the alcoholic fiddler, was sorely tempted as he left Wakefield Gaol: 'On leaving the prison, sixpence was given to me, and I had no sooner passed outside the gates, than Satan suggested to my mind – it was as though some one had whispered the words in my ear – "Go and get a drop of gin. You haven't had any for a long while; you want something to keep you up; go and get a drop of gin".'[34] One time, Stuart Wood was released along with another man: 'Five minutes walk from the prison we came to a public house, went in for a drink, and remained there until we were a little under the weather. With beer at twopence a pint one could enjoy a fairly satisfying séance for a shilling or two. When we felt that we had washed away the taste of skilly we proceeded into the town.'[35]

A similarly short journey from the prison gate to the top of the slippery slope was observed by the Reverend F.B. Meyer as he waited outside Leicester Gaol to meet a parishioner's father due to be released that day. He turned to the men who were hanging about on the same street corner. ' "But", said I, "if a man comes out at yonder gaol door, and goes into the door of the public house, he appears to me to come out of the gaol by the front door and go into it again by the back one; for I reckon that the public-house is the back door to the gaol." "Well", said they, "what's a chap to do? When he comes out of that 'ere place, there's nowhere else for him to go but the public." '[36] Meyer was so distressed by what he saw that he at once set about establishing a prison gate mission. With the permission of the governor he addressed a small audience of men about to be released from the gaol. 'My lads, I have come to give you an invitation to breakfast. When a man gets out of this place he often goes straight to the public-house, and gets back among his old pals, and they pull him down. But if you will come with me to a coffee house, which is a step down the road, I will see that you have a good breakfast, and will do what I can to give you a fresh start.'[37]

TICKET OF LEAVE

All penal-servitude prisoners were subject after release to the conditions of what was known as the 'ticket of leave'. The ticket of leave originated in Australian practice, permitting long-sentence men to complete their sentences working as labourers outside prison, but subject to recall if they should break the terms of their conditional release. The most onerous of these was the requirement that periodic visits be paid to the nearest police station.

Despite the penalties attached to not reporting – it could mean several more years in prison – convicts were not over-scrupulous in keeping to these conditions. 'Major Greig, the Chief Constable of Liverpool stated that whilst twenty-five male convicts reported regularly during the year ended February 28th, 1878, seven who had reported at some period during the year were afterwards missing, and eight who stated their intention of going to Liverpool when released never reported.'[38] A few former prisoners found legal ways of evading their licence conditions. 'The next month,' says Lord William Nevill, 'I petitioned the Secretary of State to have my ticket remitted, which he very kindly consented to. I was then once more absolutely free.'[39] One-who-has-endured-it, who was wealthier than many of his fellow ex-convicts, simply took French leave of the whole system. 'In a few days the Channel was crossed, and when my twelvemonths ticket was expired I had the satisfaction of tearing it up and dropping it overboard as I returned again to England to endeavour to resume my place among friends and society. A monthly report to the police in my case meant absolute ruin, and I took good care to avoid it.'[40]

But the principal objection to police surveillance came from more modestly placed former prisoners in search of honest work for themselves. This was difficult enough in the switchback conditions of the Victorian economy, but for the ex-prisoner it was doubly difficult: 'You dare not tell an employer you are just out of prison. They tried to get me on at Palmer's place at Reading, but there was no chance. Some prisoners had gone there and they had turned out badly, and consequently it made it bad for everybody else.'[41] A Norfolk poacher considered that it was not just other former prisoners who queered your pitch with employers. 'It is not the Punishment that hurt you, it is the dark looks and jeers of other People that hurt wen they know that you have been there. Once done it cannot be undone, for the Police are ever on your track. Many a man

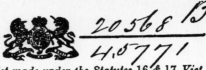

20568 B
4,577/

Order of Licence to a Convict made under the Statutes 16 & 17 Vict.,
c. 99, s. 9, and 27 & 28 Vict., c. 47, s. 4.

WHITEHALL,
18th day of *July*   188*7.*
HER MAJESTY is graciously pleased to

grant to *George Bidwell*

who was convicted of *Forgery*
at the *Central Criminal Court*
~~for the~~
on the *18th.* day of *August,* 18*73*, and was
then and there sentenced to be kept in Penal Servitude for ~~the term of~~
Life
and is now confined in the *Woking*   Convict Prison,

Her Royal Licence to be at large from the day of his liberation
under this order, during the remaining portion of his said term of Penal
Servitude, unless the said *George Bidwell*

shall, before the expiration of the said term, be convicted of some
indictable offence within the United Kingdom, in which case, such
Licence will be immediately forfeited by law, or unless it shall please
Her Majesty sooner to revoke or alter such Licence.

This Licence is given subject to the conditions endorsed upon the
same, upon the breach of any of which it will be liable to be revoked
whether such breach is followed by a conviction or not.

And Her Majesty hereby orders that the said *George*
Bidwell   be set at liberty within Thirty Days
from the date of this Order.

Given under my hand and Seal,

Signed *Henry Matthews.*

TRUE COPY.

Licence to be at large.   }   *Stanford*

for   *Chairman of the Directors* }
of Convict Prisons.   }

B & S (23,576a) 500 4—87

Ticket of leave, for George Bidwell, 1887

would have pulled up if it had not been for them – they wisper to a Master "He have been in Prisson" and blite all his good resilutions.'[42] Accusations like these were frequently made by prisoners, and just as often denied. Canon Horsley insists it 'is usually quite baseless; but where work has been lost it has usually been by the man himself opening his mouth'.[43]

Desperation for work drove ex-prisoners to desperate expedients. An employee of Henry Mayhew interviewed three hundred ticket-of-leave-men and 'found the great majority of them engaged in certain street pursuits; generally selling certain things'.[44] A young man known to Sarah Martin came to inform her 'that he had entered on board a man-of-war, as there seemed no prospect of his getting work, it appeared the only opening to obtain an honest living.'[45]

People like Mayhew and Sarah Martin did what they could to help in individual cases, but for many others, the only alternative to starvation, the workhouse or renewed crime, was emigration. Its attraction to the Discharged Prisoners Aid Society can be seen from the fact that in the three years 1860, 1861 and 1862 no less than 655 out of a total of 2217 men who were helped by the society were 'assisted to emigrate'.[46] Within these totals were individuals like those enumerated by Reverend Horsley: 'a laundry woman, who had done well in the Streatham Refuge, to America, £3: two others from the same place and for the same destination, £4 and £5; a man to Boston, where he got constant work and good wages directly as a carpenter, £9 2s. 11d.; W.R., to America, at a cost (to give the items instead of lump sums, as above) of £1 18s. 6d. for sustenance and outfit; £4 10s. for passage; expenses and pocket-money, £1 15s.; total £8 3s. 6d. True he returned in 1886, but this was in 1882, and he has kept himself, and appears in every way bettered now, while had he remained in England unbefriended it is not £8 or £80 either that he would have cost us.'[47]

This thriving export trade was a phenomenon that came to the attention of Austin Bidwell. 'Throughout twenty years I conversed with several thousand men who joined the society avowing they were going to America, and were never heard of again in England.'[48] In other words, economic conditions and the attentions of the police re-created in the later Victorian period a voluntary form of transportation, the very practice whose abolition had led directly to the creation of the sentence of penal servitude. And it provided American citizen Austin Bidwell with an opportunity to comment, apparently without irony: 'This flow of moral sewage to our shores is constant and unceasing.'[49]

There was no crowd present to see Austin off to America at the end of his sentence; public interest in the Bank of England fraud had not survived the serving of so many years in prison. Not much more than half the haul from the fraud was ever recovered by the Bank, and the assumption must be, as Austin boasted in the awful letter to his wife, that 'a fortune' was indeed his, and that his after years were spent in some comfort. Whether he thought it was worth it is a question he never chose to answer in his memoirs. The Bidwells were responsible for one of the most sensational crimes of the nineteenth century, and their prison experience – that of George in particular – was out of the ordinary. We will leave the Victorian prison in the company of a more typical small-time crook, and subsequent Christian convert – Stuart Wood:

> With a shilling from the Society and four shillings of my own, and an injunction not to do it again, the prison gate swung open and I stepped into freedom, filled with bitterness and hatred of the forces that had made me suffer, homeless, friendless, workless, with just five shillings with which to face the world.[50]

NOTES

1. One-who-has-endured-it, 359.
2. WBN, 46.
3. Bird, 43.
4. Henderson, 245.
5. WBN, 47.
6. Hart-Davis, 250.
7. J. Balfour, 232.
8. Ibid., 234.
9. Fannan, 137.
10. PRO HO 144/7 20568B
11. PRO HO 144/7 20568C
12. A. Bidwell, Appendix.
13. PRO HO 144/7 20568C
14. Maybrick, 216.
15. J. Balfour, 235.
16. Fletcher 408.
17. Davitt (1885), II, 168.
18. Cooper, 262.
19. G. Bidwell, 19.
20. A. Bidwell, 520.
21. Hart-Davis, 268.
22. Lee, 103–6.
23. Ibid., 103.
24. One-who-has-endured-it, 357.
25. B. Thomson (1925), 100.
26. Ticket-of-leave-man, 210.
27. Ibid., 211.
28. One-who-has-just-left-prison, 40.
29. One-who-has-endured-it, 352.
30. Ibid., 355.
31. Ranken, 10.
32. Ibid., 11.
33. Ticket-of-leave-man, 212.
34. Poole, 73.
35. Wood, 201.
36. Meyer, 31.
37. Ibid., 33.
38. Penal Servitude Commission (1879), xxxiv.
39. WBN, 50.
40. One-who-has-endured-it, 362.
41. Gladstone Committee (1895), 285.
42. Rider Haggard, 45.
43. Horsley (1911), 107.
44. Committee on Transportation (1856), 93.
45. Martin, 129.
46. Ranken, 13.
47. Horsley (1887), 126.
48. A. Bidwell, 429.
49. Ibid., 427.
50. Wood, 37.

LIBERTY

It was a lovely morning in the autumn of 1881, and the infirmary garden in Portland Prison was aglow with the bloom of the late summer flowers which the governor had kindly permitted me to sow in the early portion of the year. The English Channel, which often lulls the weary Portland prisoner to sleep by the storm-chorus of its waves as they dash against the rocks underneath the walls, lay in unruffled calm. From the headland upon which the great convict establishment stands could be seen the picturesque shadows which the Dorsetshire cliffs fling out upon the bosom of the sea. Away beyond the coast-line appeared harvest-fields and homesteads, melting into the distance, and so sadly suggestive of what imprisonment was not – liberty, home, and friends – conjuring up that contrast between the manacled and the free which constitutes the keenest mental pain in the punishment of penal servitude.

It was a day which would fill one's whole being with a yearning to be liberated – a day of sunshine and warmth and beauty, and the moment had arrived when my resolution to give freedom to my little feathered 'chum' could no longer be selfishly postponed. I opened his door with a trembling hand, when quick as a flash of lightning he rushed from the cage with a wild scream of delight, and in a moment was beyond the walls of the prison! The instinct of freedom was too powerful to be resisted, though I had indulged the fond hope that he would have remained with me. But he taught me the lesson, which can never be unlearned by either country, prisoner or bird, that Nature will not be denied, and that Liberty is more to be desired than fetters of gold.

Davitt (1885), 255–6

APPENDIX I

ABSTRACT OF THE REGULATIONS RELATING TO THE TREATMENT AND CONDUCT OF CONVICTED CRIMINAL PRISONERS

1. Prisoners shall not disobey the orders of the Governor or of any officer of the prison, nor treat them with disrespect.
2. They shall preserve silence, and are not to cause annoyance or disturbance by making unnecessary noise.
3. They shall not communicate or attempt to do so with one another, or with any strangers or others who may visit the prison.
4. They shall not disfigure any part of their cells or damage any property, or deface, erase, destroy, or pull down any rules or other papers hung up therein, or commit any nuisance, or have in their cells or possession any article not sanctioned by the orders and regulations.
5. They shall not be idle, nor feign sickness to evade their work.
6. They shall not be guilty of profane language, of indecent or irreverent conduct, nor shall they use threats towards or commit assaults upon officers or one another.
7. They shall obey such regulations as regards washing, bathing, hair-cutting, and shaving as may from time to time be established, with a view to the proper maintenance of health and cleanliness.
8. They shall keep their cells, utensils, clothing, and bedding clean and neatly arranged, and shall when required clean and sweep the yards, passages, and other parts of the prison.
9. If any prisoner has any complaint to make regarding the diet, it must be

made immediately after a meal is served and before any portion of it is eaten. Frivolous and groundless complaints, repeatedly made, will be dealt with as a breach of prison discipline.

10. A prisoner may, if required for the purposes of justice, be photographed.

11. Prisoners shall attend divine service on Sundays, and on other days when such service is performed, unless they receive permission to be absent. No prisoner shall be compelled to attend the religious service of a church to which he does not belong.

12. The following offences committed by male prisoners convicted of felony or sentenced to hard labour will render them liable to corporal punishment:-

1st.   Mutiny or open incitement to mutiny in the prison, personal violence to any officer of the prison, aggravated or repeated assaults on a fellow-prisoner, repetition of insulting or threatening language to any officer or prisoner.

2nd.   Wilfully and maliciously breaking the prison windows, or otherwise destroying the prison property.

3rd.   When under punishment, wilfully making a disturbance tending to interrupt the order and discipline of the prison, and any other act of gross misconduct or insubordination requiring to be suppressed by extraordinary means.

13. A prisoner committing a breach of any of the regulations is liable to be sentenced to confinement in a punishment cell, and such dietary and other punishments as the rules allow.

14. Any gratuity granted to a prisoner may be paid to him through a Prisoners' Aid Society, or in such way as the Commissioners may direct.

15. Prisoners may, if they desire it, have an interview with the Governor or superior authority to make complaints or prefer requests; and the Governor shall redress any grievance or take such steps as may seem necessary.

16. Any prisoner wishing to see a member of the Visiting Committee shall be allowed to do so on the occasion of his next occurring visit to the prison.

Printed at H.M. Convict Prison, Millbank.

(D— S—, 152)

APPENDIX II

ENGLISH PENAL HISTORY: A SELECT CALENDAR

1775   Transportation to the American colonies ceases on the outbreak of the War of Independence. Surplus convicts kept instead in converted warships moored in the Thames and elsewhere – the 'hulks'.

1777   John Howard, sheriff of Bedfordshire, publishes *The State of the Prisons* – a comprehensive survey of conditions in English prisons, which inspired a wave of reformist sentiment and activity.

1779   The Penitentiary Act, drafted with Howard's advice to permit the erection of a national penitentiary incorporating his ideas for the reform of prisons.

1788   Arrival of the first fleet of transported convicts sent to Botany Bay; the first European settlement in Australia.

1791   Jeremy Bentham, utilitarian philosopher, publishes his *Panopticon*, a proposal for a circular penitentiary.

1792   Sir George Onesiphorous Paul, a Gloucestershire magistrate, reorganizes all the prisons in the county, opening a new penitentiary at Gloucester and five houses of correction elsewhere.

1794   Penitentiary for Convicts Act: legislative permission for the construction of Bentham's national penitentiary, to be managed by him under a government contract. Bentham acquired a site at Millbank but the money to build the prison was never forthcoming from the Treasury.

1810-11   Select Committee on Penitentiary Houses (Holford Committee) rejects Bentham's scheme, but recommends that government take direct responsiblity for building and managing a national penitentiary at Millbank. Prisoners to be held there prior to transportation.

1813   Elizabeth Fry pays her first visit to the women prisoners of Newgate.

1816   Elizabeth Fry forms a Ladies Committee at Newgate, the model for many more at home and abroad.

1816   National Penitentiary at Millbank opens.

1816   Treadwheel invented by William Cubitt, civil engineer and contractor.

1820   Flogging of women discontinued.

1821   John Clay appointed chaplain to the Lancashire House of Correction at Preston.

1826   Edward Gibbon Wakefield imprisoned in Newgate.

1829   Appointment of William Calcraft as hangman.

1832   James Cook hanged at Leicester; the last occasion in English legal history when the body of the murderer was hung in chains after execution.

1834   William Crawford, secretary of the Society for the Improvement of Prison Discipline, visits the United States of America to see for himself and report to the Home Secretary, on the rival 'silent' and 'separate' systems of prison discipline.

1834   The 'silent' system introduced at Wakefield prison, and later at Cold Bath Fields.

1835   Select Committee of the House of Lords on Gaols and Houses of Correction in England and Wales reviews the state of the prisons controlled by the local justices. Recommends the national adoption of 'a uniform system of discipline' along 'silent' rather than 'separate' lines. Proposes the appointment of government inspectors of prisons.

1835   Prisons Act: implements the conclusions and recommendations of the Select Committee. The first prison inspectors to be appointed included William Crawford and a former Millbank chaplain, Whitworth Russell.

1837   Victoria succeeds to the throne.

1838   Parkhurst Prison opens for juvenile offenders.

1839   Captain Joshua Jebb RE appointed technical adviser to the Home Office on the construction of prisons.

1839   William Lovett, Chartist, sentenced to one year for 'seditious libel'.

1842   Pentonville Prison, designed by Jebb, is opened as a new National Penitentiary.

1842   George Jacob Holyoake sentenced to six months' imprisonment for 'blasphemy'.

1843   Thomas Cooper, Chartist, sentenced to two years for conspiracy and sedition.

1843   Millbank closes as the National Penitentiary.

1843   Sir James Graham, Home Secretary, issues 'exemplary' diet tables for use in local gaols.

1848   Portland Convict Prison opened.

1850   Portsmouth Convict Prison opened; also Dartmoor, intended for invalid convicts, on account of its bracing climate.

1850   Select Committee on Prison Discipline (Grey Committee) deplores the continuing lack of uniformity in local gaols administered by the justices. Urges the general adoption of the 'separate' system, on the Pentonville model.

1852   Chatham Convict Prison opens.

1853   Penal Servitude Act marks the end of transportation to Van Diemen's Land. Western Australia becomes a penal colony. Sentences of penal servitude to be served in England. Prisoners to be released under the conditions of a 'ticket of leave'.

1854   Royal Commission Appointed to Enquire into the Condition and Treatment of the Prisoners Confined to Birmingham Borough Prison: investigation of alleged cruelties and illegal restraints leading to the suicide of a young prisoner, Edward Andrew. The governor, Captain Austin RN, dismissed; the medical officer resigns.

1854   Royal Commission on the Condition and Treatment of Prisoners Confined in Leicester County Gaol and House of Correction: investigation into the high rate of floggings, and the linking of food to performance on the crank. Condemns the latter practice but absolves the governor and his regime of the charge of excessive severity.

1856   Report of the Select Committee of the House of Lords Appointed to Enquire into the Provisions and Operation of the Act 16 & 17 Vict: Enquiry into hanging. Recommends that it take place privately rather than in public.

1857   Reverend John Clay dies.

1857   Hulks discontinued.

1859   Convict Prison at Woking opens for invalid prisoners.

1861   Riot at Chatham Convict Prison suppressed by troops.

1863   Major-General Sir Joshua Jebb, Director of Convict Prisons, dies. Edmund DuCane appointed as an assistant director.

1863   Report of the Commissioners Appointed to Enquire into the Operation of the Acts Relating to Transportation and Penal Servitude, set up in response to public disquiet over a wave of 'garottings' or street robberies, popularly ascribed to ticket-of-leave men. Recommends stricter penal discipline in the convict prisons, and the surveillance of ticket-of-leave men by the police.

1863   Select Committee of the House of Lords on Gaol Discipline (Carnarvon Committee); pivotal report in the development of Victorian prison discipline, insisting on uniformity in local gaols to

be imposed by Act of Parliament, and recommending a more punitive regime in place of the failed experiment of the penitentiary.

1864   Report of a Committee Appointed by the Home Office to Enquire
into the Dietaries of County and Borough Gaols recommends a more
uniform dietary in local prisons, and a reduction in meat content.

1865   Prisons Act implements recommendations of the Carnarvon Committee, including a mandatory duty for local justices to maintain a
centrally determined mode of penal discipline.

1865   Jeremiah O'Donovan Rossa sentenced to penal servitude for life on
charges of 'treason-felony' arising out of the Irish nationalist
struggle.

1866   Report of the Capital Punishment Commission: enquiry into hanging. Recommends that it take place privately, rather than in public.

1867   Last transport sails for Australia.

1867   One-who-has-endured-it sentenced to five years' penal servitude.

1867   Prison wall at Clerkenwell dynamited in an unsuccessful bid to
rescue Colonel Ricard Burke, a Fenian. Six civilians killed in the
street outside.

1868   Michael Barrett hanged in public after being convicted of com-
plicity in the Clerkenwell explosion. The last public hanging.

1873   George and Austin Bidwell, and two others, sentenced to life
imprisonment for fraud against the Bank of England.

1870   Michael Davitt sentenced to fifteen years' penal servitude for
'treason-felony' – dealing in arms for the Fenian cause.

1874   The 'Tichborne Claimant' sentenced to fourteen years' penal servitude for perjury.

1874   William Calcraft retires from his hangmanship.

1877   Prison Act: local gaols brought under central government control in
the person of Sir Edmund DuCane.

1877   Michael Davitt released from Dartmoor under the terms of an
amnesty.

1878   Report of the Committee Appointed to Enquire into the Dietaries of
the Prisons in England and Wales recommends the substitution of
meat with vegetable items.

1883   James Berry appointed hangman.

1883   Berry's attempt to hang John Lee.

1889   Mrs Maybrick sentenced to death; and reprieved.

1892   James Berry retires as hangman.

1895   Jabez Balfour sentenced to fourteen years' penal servitude on
charges of fraud.

1895   Report from the Departmental Committee on Prisons (Gladstone
Report): another turning point in English penal policy; rejects the
sterile punitiveness of the DuCane regime; recommends more
reformative and 'hopeful' measures.

1895   DuCane retires; succeeded by Evelyn Ruggles-Brise.

1898	Prison Act gives legislative expression to the Gladstone reforms. Treadwheel and crank discontinued.
1898	Lord William Nevill sentenced to five years' penal servitude for fraud.
1903	Queen Victoria dies.
1905	Imprisonment of militant suffragettes begins.
1908	Borstal Act sanctions the Ruggles-Brise experiment with male offenders between the ages of sixteen and twenty-one.

BIBLIOGRAPHY

SELECT COMMITTEES AND ROYAL COMMISSIONS

Select Committee on Inquiry into Drunkenness. *PP* 1834 (559), VIII, 315.

Select Committee of the House of Lords on Gaols and Houses of Correction in England and Wales. First Report, *PP* 1835 (438), XI, 1. Second Report, *PP* 1835 (439), XI, 495. Third Report, *PP* 1835 (440), XII, 1. Fourth and Fifth Reports, *PP* 1835 (441), XII, 157.

Royal Commission Appointed to Inquire into the Condition and Treatment of the Prisoners Confined to Birmingham Borough Prison. *PP* 1854 (1809), XXXI, 1.

Royal Commission Appointed to Inquire into the Condition and Treatment of the Prisoners Confined in Leicester County Gaol and House of Correction. *PP* 1854 (1808), XXXIV, 197.

Report from the Select Committee of the House of Lords to Look into the Present Mode of Carrying into Effect Capital Punishments. *PP* 1856 (336), VII, 1.

Select Committee on Transportation. *PP* 1856 (244), XVII, 1.

Report of the Commissioners Appointed to Inquire into the Operation of the Acts Relating to Transportation and Penal Servitude. *PP* 1863 (3190), XXI, 1 (Carnarvon Committee).

Report from the Select Committee of the House of Lords on the Present State of Discipline in Gaols and Houses of Correction. *PP* 1863 (499), IX, 1.

Report of A Committee Appointed by the Home Office to Inquire into the Dietaries of County and Borough Gaols. *PP* 1864 (467), XLIX, 9.

Report of the Capital Punishment Commission. *PP* 1866 (3590), XXI, 1.

Report of the Committee Appointed to Inquire into the Dietaries of the Prisons of England and Wales. *PP* 1878 (95), XLII, 53.

Report of the Committee Appointed to Inquire into the Working of the Penal Servitude Acts. *PP* 1878–9 (*c*. 2368), XXXVII, 1.

Report from the Departmental Committee on Prisons. *PP* 1895 (C. 7702), LVI, 1 (Gladstone Committee).
Report from the Departmental Committee on the Education and Moral Instruction of Prisoners in Local and Convict Prisons. *PP* 1896 (C. 8154, C. 8155), XLIV, 1.
Report of the Departmental Committee on Prison Dietaries. *PP* 1899 (C. 9166), XLIII, 1.

REPORTS AND REGULATIONS

Second Report of the Inspectors. *PP* 1837 (89), XXXII, 1.
Third Report of the Inspectors. *PP* 1838.
Fourth Report of the Inspectors. *PP* 1839 (210), XXI, 1.
Reports Relating to Parkhurst Prison. *PP* 1839 (197), XXII, 643.
Seventh Report of the Inspectors. *PP* 1842 (422), XX, 1.
Circular Letter addressed by Sir J.R.G. Graham, Bart, to Chairman of Quarter Sessions accompanying copy of Prison Rules, *PP* 1843, XXVI, pt 1.
First report from the Commissioners on Pentonville Prison. *PP* 1843 (449), XXIX, 377.
Report of the Surveyor General of Prisons on Pentonville; with various plans. *PP* 1844 (594) XXVII, 127.
Sixth Report from the Commissioners on Pentonville Prison. *PP* 1847–8 (972), XXXIV, 59.
Regulations for Prisons in England and Wales. *PP* 1849.
Report of the Directors of Convict Prisons. *PP* 1852–3 (1656), LI, 385.
Report of the Directors of Convict Prisons. *PP* 1862. 1863 (3208), XXIV, 1.
Standing Orders . . . for the Government of Convict Prisons. 1902.

PUBLIC RECORD OFFICE

PRO. HO. 144/7 20568B. (George Bidwell).
PRO. HO. 144/7 20568C. (Austin Bidwell).

STAFFORDSHIRE RECORD OFFICE

D661/2/3/1/11. Dyott's Diary. Vol. II. 4th October. 1828.

OTHER SOURCES

Adam, Hargrave Lee (1907) *The Story of Crime*, London, T. Werner Laurie.
Allday, Joseph (1853) *Truth is Stranger than Fiction*, London, J. Pitman.
Allen, Mary S. (1936) *Lady in Blue*, London, Stanley Paul.
Anderson, Sir Robert (1910) *The Lighter Side of my Official Life*, London, Hodder & Stoughton.

Andrew, Llewellyn (1930) 'A chaplain's journal, 1825'. *Transactions of the Lancashire and Cheshire Antiquarian Society*, XLV, 21–31.

Bacchus, F. (ed.) (1911) *Essays*, London, Longmans Green.

Balfour, Betty (1925) *Letters of Constance Lytton*, London, Heinemann.

Balfour, Jabez Spencer (1901) *My Prison Life*, London, Chapman & Hall.

Barrow, Thomas Pateman (1881) *A Month in Her Majesty's Prison, Leicester – And How I Got It*, Leicester.

Becke, Louis (ed.) (1899) *Old Convict Days*, London, T. Fisher Unwin.

Beecham, Sir Thomas (1944) *A Mingled Chime*, London, Hutchinson.

Bent, James (1891) *Criminal Life: Reminiscences of Forty Two Years as a Police Officer*, Manchester, J. Heywood.

Berry, James (1902) *My Experiences as an Executioner*, London, Percy Lund.

Bethune, Alexander (1845) *Memoirs of Alexander Bethune*, ed. William McCombie, Aberdeen, George & Robert King.

Bidwell, Austin (1895) *From Wall Street to Newgate*, Hartford, Conn., Bidwell Publishing Co.

Bidwell, George (1888) *Forging his Chains. The Autobiography of George Bidwell*, Hartford, Conn., S.S. Scranton.

Biggs, Annie S. (1907) *My Prison Life; And Why I Am a Suffragette*, Croydon, Citizens Press.

Bird's Memorials of Godmanchester (1911), Peterborough.

Blagg, H.M. and Wilson, G. (1912) *Women and Prisons*, London, Fabian Tract 163.

Blake, Wallace (1927) *Reminiscences of a Prison Governor*, London, Hodder & Stoughton.

Bleackley, H (1929) *The Hangmen of England*, London, Chapman & Hall.

Bowen-Rowlands, Ernest (1924) *Seventy-two Years at the Bar. A Memoir*, London, Macmillan.

Brocklehurst, Frederick (1898) *I Was in Prison*, London, T. Fisher-Unwin.

Burnside, D.R. (n.d.) *Sidelights on Prison Life*, Glasgow.

Campbell, John (1884) *Thirty Years Experience of a Medical Officer in the English Convict Service*, London, T. Nelson & Sons.

Carlyle, Thomas (1850) 'Model prisons' in *Latter-day Pamphlets*', Thomas Carlyle, London, Chapman & Hall.

Carlyle, Thomas (1850a) 'Pet prisoners', *Household Words*, 27 April.

Cecil, Lord Eustace (1865) *Impressions of Life at Home and Abroad*, London, Hurst & Blackett.

Chesterton, George Laval (1853) *Peace, War and Adventure*, London, Longman, Brown & Green.

Chesterton, George Laval (1856) *Revelations of Prison Life*, 2 vols, London, Hurst & Blackett.

Clarke, J. Robert (1913) *Prison Songs and Poems*, London, Erskine Macdonald.

Clarke, Thomas J. (1922) *Glimpses of an Irish Felon's Prison Life*, Dublin, Maunsel & Roberts.

Clay, Walter Lowe (1861) *The Prison Chaplain – A Memoir of the Rev. John Clay*, London, Macmillan.

Collett, J.T. (1883) *Prison Reminiscences of the Drink Curse*, London, Marshall Bros.

Commonweal, The (1892) 'A peep into Newgate', vol. 1, no. 1, Sheffield.

Convict, A (1864) 'A convict's view of prison discipline', *Cornhill Magazine*, December.

Convict 77 (1903) *The Mark of the Broad Arrow or The Life of a Convict*, London, R. A. Everett.

Cozens, Charles (1848) *Adventures of a Guardsman*, London, Richard Bentley.

Daly, John (1876) *Our Penal 'Dead-Houses'*, pamphlet.

Davitt, Michael (1885) *Leaves from a Prison Diary*, 2 vols, London, Chapman & Hall.

Davitt, Michael (1886) *The Prison Life of Michael Davitt*, Dublin, Lalor.

Davitt, Michael (1894) 'Criminal and prison reform,' *Nineteenth Century*, 36, December.

Dawson, John (1887) *Imprisoned in the House of Detention for Libel*, London, John & Robert Maxwell.

Dent, Digby Henry (1899) *Two Commissions*, London, Marshall Bros.

Devoy, John (n.d.) *English and American Prisons*.

Dilnot, George (n.d.) *The Bank of England Forgery*, London, Geoffrey Bles.

DuCane, Sir Edmund F. (1882) *Account of the Manner in Which Sentences of Penal Servitude are Carried Out*, printed at Her Majesty's Convict Prison, Millbank.

DuCane, Sir Edmund (1885) *The Punishment and Prevention of Crime*, London, Macmillan.

DuCane, Sir Edmund (1896) 'The unavoidable uselessness of prison labour,' *Nineteenth Century*, 40, Jul.–Dec.

East, Sir W. Norwood (1936) *Medical Aspects of Crime*, Philadelphia, P. Blakiston's.

Fannan, David (1897) *A Burglar's Life Story in Glasgow, Edinburgh, London, Crimea etc.*, ed. J. Wallace, Glasgow, D. Bryce.

Fawcett, Mrs M.G. (1924) *What I Remember*, London, T. Fisher-Unwin.

Female Debtor (1909) *A Summer Holiday in Holloway Gaol by A. . .*

Field, Rev. John (1848) *Prison Discipline–the Advantages of the Separate System*, 2 vols, London, Longman.

Fletcher, Susan Willis (1884) *Twelve Months in an English Prison*, Boston, Lee & Shephard.

Foote, George William (1886) *Prisoner for Blasphemy*, London, Progressive Publishing Co.

Fry, Elizabeth (1827) *Observations on the Visiting, Superintendence, and Government of Female Prisoners*, London, John & Arthur Arch.

Fry, Elizabeth (1847) *Memoir of the Life of Elizabeth Fry with Extracts from her Journal and Letters*, edited by two of her daughters, London, John Hatchard & Son.

Fry, Rev. Henry Phibbs (1850) *A System of Penal Discipline*, London, Longman, Brown & Green.

Fulford, Captain (1852) 'On prison discipline', in *Meliora*, ed. Viscount Ingestre, London, J.W. Parks.

Gibson, Charles Bernard (1863) *Life among Convicts*, 2 vols, London, Hurst & Blackett.

Good, John Mason (1824) 'A letter . . . on the mischiefs incidental to the treadwheel', *The Pamphleteer*, 23, no. 45.

Gordon, Helen (1911) *The Prisoner – a Sketch*, Letchworth, Garden City Press.

Gordon, M.L. (1922) *Penal Discipline*, London, Routledge.

Governor, A (1852) 'Gaol revelations' in *Meliora*, ed. Viscount Ingestre, London, J.W. Parks.

Graham, Robert Bontine Cunningham (1902) *Success*, London, Duckworth.

Griffiths, Arthur (1875) *Memorials of Millbank*, 2 vols, London, Henry S. King.

Griffiths, Arthur (1904) *Fifty years of Public Service*, London, Cassell.

Guerin, Eddie (1928) *Crime – the Autobiography of a Crook*, London, John Murray.

Half-Timer (1917) *Prison Reminiscences*, London, Eliot Stock.

Halkett, Samuel and Laing, John (1962) *Dictionary of Anonymous and Pseudonymous Authors*, ed. D.E. Rhodes and A.E.C. Simon, Edinburgh and London, Oliver & Boyd.

Hall, J. (1843) *Lancaster Castle: Its History and Associations*, Lancaster, W. Ireland.

Hall, L. (1896) 'For one calendar month', *The Clarion*, 18 July.

Harcourt, Henry (n.d.) *My Twelve Years Awful Torture in Our Convict Prisons*.

Harcourt, Henry (n.d.) *Prison Horrors*, London, Social Salvation Office.

Harris, Vernon (1907) 'The female prisoner', *Nineteenth Century*, 61, May.

Harris, Captain Vernon (n.d.) *Dartmoor Prison: Past and Present*, Plymouth, William Brendon & Son.

Hart-Davis, Rupert (1979) *Selected Letters of Oscar Wilde*, Oxford, Oxford University Press.

Hay, John (1894) *A Gross Miscarriage of Justice. Seven Years Penal Servitude or the Value of a Royal Pardon*, London, The Literary Revision Society Ltd.

Heaton, George (1847) *The Clergyman in the Gaol: An Essay on Prison Discipline*, London, Houlston & Stoneman.

Henderson, Frank (ed.) (1869) *Six Years in the Prisons of England by 'A Merchant'*, London, R. Bentley.

Hepworth Dixon, William (1850) *The London Prisons*, London, Murray.

Hiener, W. and J. (eds) (1968) *A Burglar's Life*, London, Angus & Robertson.

Hill, Frederic (1853) *Crime: Its Amount, Causes and Remedies*, London, John Murray.

Hill, Frederic (1896) *Hill: An Autobiography of Fifty Years*, London, R. Bentley & Son.

Hindle, Robert (n.d.) *Salford's Prison*, Salford Local History Society.

Hobhouse, Stephen and Fenner Brockway, A. (1922) *English Prisons Today*, London, Longman, Green & Co.

Hogan, James Francis (1891) *The Convict King. Being the Life and Adventures of Jorgen Jorgensen*, London, Ward & Downey.

Holloway, Henry (1877) *A Voice from the Convict Cell*, Manchester, J. Heywood.

Holloway, Henry (1877a) *An Echo from Prison; Or, My Mother and I*, Manchester, J. Heywood.

Holyoake, George Jacob (1850) *History of the last Trial for Atheism*, London, James Watson.

Holyoake, George Jacob (1864) *Public Lessons of the Hangman*, London, F. Farrah.

Holyoake, George Jacob (1893) *Sixty Years of an Agitator's Life*, 2 vols, London, T. Fisher-Unwin.

Hood, Thomas (1846) *Poems*, 2 vols, London, Edward Moxon.

Hooley, Ernest Terah (1924) *Hooley's Confessions*, London, Simpkin, Marshall, Hamilton, Kent & Co.

Horsley, Canon J.W. (1887) *Jottings from Jail*, London, T. Fisher-Unwin.

Horsley, Canon J.W. (1898) *Prisons and Prisoners*, London, C. Arthur Pearson.

Horsley, Canon J.W. (1911) *'I remember'. Memories of a Sky Pilot in the Prison and the Slum*, London, Wells Gardner.

Howard Association (1872) *Defects in the Criminal Administration and Penal Legislation of Great Britain and Ireland with Remedial Suggestions*.

Huxley, Ann (1969) *Four Against the Bank of England*, London, John Long.

Jebb, Colonel J. (1844) *Modern Prisons: Their Construction and Ventilation*, London, John Weale.

Jervis, Rev. Eustace (1925) *24 years in 6 Prisons*, London, T. Fisher-Unwin.

Joseph, Rev. Henry Samuel (1853) *Memoirs of Convicted Prisoners*, London, Wertheim & Co.

Kebbel, William Henry (1853) *A Letter, etc. . . . .*, Leicester, Crossley & Clarke.

Kenney, Annie (1924) *Memoirs of a Militant*, London, Edwin Arnold.

Kerr's Exposition of Legislative Tyranny (1834), Belfast.

Kingsmill, Rev. Joseph (1854) *Chapters on Prisons and Prisoners*, 3rd edn, London, Longmans.

Kingsmill, Rev. Joseph (1854a) *Roman Catholic Chaplains to Gaols*, London, Longmans.

Kingsmill, Rev. Joseph (n.d.) *The Prisoner's Manual of Prayer*, London, Reed & Pardon.

Kirkdale Gaol; Twelve Months Imprisonment of a Manchester Merchant (1880) Manchester, Heywood & Son.

Lachlan, Mrs (1832) *Narrative of the Conversion (By the Instrumentality of Two Ladies) of James Cook, the Murderer of Mr. Paas: in Letters addressed to a Clergyman of the Church*, London, Simpkin & Marshall.

Laurie, Sir Peter (1846) *Killing no Murder*, London, John Murray.

Lee, John (n.d.) *The Man They Could Not Hang. The Life Story of John Lee*, London, Arthur Pearson.

Leslie, Shane (1938) *Sir Evelyn Ruggles-Brise*, London, John Murray.

'Letter from a convict in Australia to a brother in England' (1866), *Cornhill Magazine, 13*.

Linton, W.J. (n.d.) *James Watson. A memoir*, Manchester, Abel Heywood.

Llewellin, Rev. G.F. (n.d.) *Lighter Side of a Parson's Life*, Hereford, Adams & Sons.

Lloyd, M.A. (1903) *Susanna Meredith; A Record of a Vigorous Life*, London, Hodder & Stoughton.

Lovett, William (1876) *The Life and Struggles of William Lovett*, London, Trubner.

Lytton, Constance (1914) *Prisons and Prisoners*, London, Heinemann.

McCook Weir, Dr (1885) *Prison Despotism. A Personal Narrative*, London, The National Publishing Co.

Mackenzie, Compton (1963) *My Life and Times, Octave One: 1883-1891*, London, Chatto & Windus.

Martin, Sarah (n.d.) *The Prison Visitor*, London, The Religious Tract Society.

Martyn, Frederick (1911) *A Holiday in Gaol*, London, Methuen.

Maybrick, Mrs F.E. (1905) *Mrs Maybrick's Own Story - My Fifteen Lost Years*, New York and London, Funk & Wagnall.

Mayhew, Henry and Binney, John (1862) *The Criminal Prisons of London and Scenes of Prison Life*, London, Griffin.

Measor, Charles Pannell (1861) *The Convict Service*, London, Robert Hardwick.

Merrick, Rev. G.P. (1891) *Work Among the 'Fallen' as Seen in the Prison Cell*, London, Ward Lock.

Merry, William (1843) *Transportation etc.*, Reading, George Lovejoy.

Meyer, Rev. F.B. (n.d.) *The Bells of Is: or Voices of Human Need and Sorrow*, London, Morgan & Scott.

Miller, Linus Wilson (1846) *Notes of an Exile to Van Diemen Land . . .* New York, Freedonia.

Mitchell, Hannah (1968) *The Hard Way Up*, London, Faber & Faber.

Moreau-Christophe, M.L. (1839) *Rapport . . . sur les Prisons de l'Angleterre, de l'Ecosse, de la Hollande, de la Belgique et de la Suisse*, Paris, Imprimerie Royale.

Newlake, Henry (1858) *The Convict Converted*, London, Partridge.

Nicoll, David J. (1897) 'The ghosts of Chelmsford gaol', Sheffield, *The Commonweal.*

Nihill, Rev. Daniel (1839) *Prison Discipline in its Relations to Society and Individuals.* London, J. Hatchard.

'No. 7' (1903) *Twenty-five Years in Seventeen Prisons. The Life story of an Ex-Convict*, London, F.E. Robinson & Co.

Old Bailey Experience . . . by the Author of 'The Schoolmaster's Experience in Newgate' (1833), London, James Fraser.

Old Warder (1847) *Importance of Prison Discipline . . .*, Dumfries.

One-who-has-endured-it (1877) *Five Years Penal Servitude by . . .*, London, Richard Bentley.

One-who-has-just-left-prison (1878) *Twelve Months' Imprisonment with Hard Labour*, London, Curtice & Co.

One-who-has-suffered (1882) *Revelations of Prison Life by . . .*, London, Potter.

One-who-has-suffered-it (1910) 'Concerning imprisonment,' *Hibbert Journal*, April.

One-who-has-tried-them (1881) *Her Majesty's Prisons and their Effects and Defects by . . .*, London, Sampson, Low.

One-who-was-there (1878) *Startling Disclosures! Six Months of Hard Labour in the City Prison, Holloway by . . .*, London, Curtice & Co.

Orton, Arthur (1895) *Entire Life and full Confession. . . .* repr. from 'People'.

Pankhurst, Emmeline (1914) *My Own Story*, London, Eveleigh Nash.

Pankhurst, Sylvia (1911) *The Suffragette Movement*, London, Longmans Green.

Paterson, Arthur (1911) *Our Prisons*, London, Hugh Rees.

Payne, W. (1887) *Stafford Gaol and its Associations*, Hanley, J. Hutchings.

Pentonville Prison from Within (With an Actress in the Background) (1902), London, Greening & Co.

Pethick Lawrence, Emmeline (1938) *My Part in a Changing World*, London, Gollancz.

Pitkin, Rev. John (1918) *The Prison Cell in its Lights and Shadows*, London, Sampson, Low.

Poole, Joshua (1867) *The Life of Joshua Poole*, London, Morgan & Chase.

Practical Hand (1866) *Convicts by A . . .*, Edinburgh, Edmonston & Douglas.

Prison Magazine, The (1876) nos 5 and 6, London.

Quinton, Dr R.F. (1910) *Crime and Criminals*, London, Longmans Green.

Ranken, William Bayne (1863) *English Convicts Before and After Their Discharge*, London, Longmans Green.

'Reminiscences of prison life' (1881) *Blackwoods Magazine*, July.

Reynolds, Rev. R.V. (1850) *The Outcasts of England, or the Prison Question Considered Theoretically and Practically*, Wakefield, John Stanfield.

Rhondda, The Viscountess (1933) *This Was My World*, London, Macmillan.

Rich, Lieut-Col. C.E.F. (1932) *Recollections of a Prison Governor*, London, Hurst & Blackett.

Richardson, Mary (1953) *Laugh a Defiance*, London, Weidenfeld & Nicolson.

Rickards, Rev. Clifford (1920) *A Prison Chaplain on Dartmoor*, London, A. Arnold.

Rider Haggard, Lilias (ed.) (1935) *I Walked By Night*, Dutton.

Ritchie, Dr Daniel (1854) *The Voice of Our Exiles; or Stray Leaves from a Convict Ship*, Edinburgh, John Menzies.

Roche, James Jeffrey (1891) *Life of John Boyle O'Reilly*, London, T. Fisher-Unwin.

Rossa, Jeremiah O'Donovan (1882) *Irish Rebels in English Prisons*, New York, D.J. Sadleir & Co.

Row, Frederick (1876) *Prison Discipline with Especial Reference to Devonport Gaol*, Devonport, T.W. Good.

Ruck, S.K. (ed.) (1951) *Paterson on Prisons. Being the collected papers of Sir Alexander Paterson. M.C.M.A.*, London, Frederick Muller.

S—, D— (Donald Shaw) (1883) *Eighteen Months Imprisonment*, London, Routledge & Sons.

Samuel, Raphael (1981) *East End Underworld*, London, Routledge & Kegan Paul.

'Schoolmaster's experience in Newgate, The' (1832), *Frasers Magazine*, 5. 6. 7.

Scougal, Francis (F.M. Skene) (1889) *Scenes from a Silent World*, Edinburgh, Blackwood.

Sharpe, May Churchill (1929) *Chicago May - Her Story*, London, Sampson, Low.

Shepherd, Maria (1857) *Leaves from a Journal of Prison Visits Torn Out and Tied Together*, London, Ward.

Sherard, Robert Harborough (1906) *The Life of Oscar Wilde*, London, T. Werner Laurie.

Smith, Isaac (n.d.) *A Warder's Experience in Lancaster Castle*, Blackburn, Thos. Johnson.

Society for the Improvement of Prison Discipline (1820) *Rules Proposed for the Government of Gaols, Houses of Correction and Penitentiaries*.

Stead, W.T. (1886) *My First Imprisonment*, London, E. Marlborough & Co.

Student of the Inner Temple (1824) *Thoughts on Prison Labour*, London, Rodwell & Martin.

Such, Augustus (1841) *Remarks on Prison Discipline and the Model Prison*, London, Shaw & Sons.

Sykes, Bill (pseud.) (1881) *Prison Life and Prison Poetry*, vol. I, London, Newman & Co.

Tayler, Rev. C.B. (1849) *Facts in a Clergyman's Life*, London, Seeleys.

Thackeray, William Makepeace (1840) 'Going to see a man hanged', *Frasers Magazine*, 200.

Thomson, Basil (1907) *The Story of Dartmoor Prison*, London, Heinemann.

Thomson, Basil (1925) *The Criminal*, London, Hodder & Stoughton.

Thomson, Basil (1939) *The Scene Changes*, London, Collins.

Thomson, R.D. (1934) *Journal of a Jail Chaplain*, Dumbarton, Bennet & Thomson.

Ticket-of-leave-man (1879) *Convict Life; or Revelations Concerning Convicts and Convict Prisons*, London, Wyman & Sons.

Timewell, James (1914) *The Prison Life of Steinie Morrison*, Police and Public Vigilance Society.

Tschiffely, A.F. (1937) *Don Roberto*, London, Heinemann.

Turner, Joseph Horsfall (1904) *The Annals of Wakefield House of Correction*, Bradford, Harrison & Son.

'Twenty years penal servitude' (1867) *Chambers Journal*, October.

Twyford, Capt. A.W. (1880) *York and York Castle: An Appendix to the Records of York Castle*, London, Griffith & Farran.

Wait, Benjamin (1843) *Letters from Van Diemen's Land, Written during Four Years Imprisonment*, Buffalo, A.W. Wilgus.

Wakefield, Edward Gibbon (1831) *Facts Relating to the Punishment of Death in the Metropolis*, London, Wilson.

Warden (1929) *His Majesty's Guests. Secrets of the Cells*, London, Jarrolds.

WBN (Lord William Nevill) (1903) *Penal Servitude*, London, Heinemann.

Willmott Dobbie, B.M. (1979) *Pounds or Pinfolds, and Lockups*, Bath University Library.

Wood, Stuart (1932) *Shades of the Prison House*, London, Williams & Norgate.
Woodruff, Douglas (1957) *The Tichborne Claimant*, London, Hollis & Carter.
Wrench, Matilda (1852) *Visits to Female Prisoners at Home and Abroad*, London, Wertheim.

WORKS CONSULTED BUT NOT REFERENCED IN THE TEXT

Bailey, Victor (ed.) (1981) *Policing and Punishment in the Nineteenth Century*, London, Croom Helm.
Beddoes, Deirdre (1979) *Welsh Convict Women*, Barry, Stewart Williams.
Bennett, James (1981) *Oral History and Delinquency. The Rhetoric of Criminology*, Chicago, University of Chicago Press.
Calvert, E. Roy (1927) *Capital Punishment in the 20th Century*, London, Putnam.
Cooper, David (1974) *The Lesson of the Scaffold*, London, Allen Lane.
Evans, Robin (1982) *The Fabrication of Virtue. English Prison Architecture 1750-1840*, Cambridge, Cambridge University Press.
Foucault, Michel (1975) *Surveiller et punir*, Paris, Gallimard.
Fox, Lionel (1952) *The English Prison and Borstal Systems*, London, Routledge & Kegan Paul.
Gatrell, V.A.C. *et al.* (eds) (1980) *Crime and the Law. The Social History of Crime in Western Europe since 1500*, London, Europa Publications.
Henriques, Ursula (1972) 'The rise and decline of the separate system of prison discipline', *Past and Present*, vol 54.
Hinde, R.S.E. (1951) *The British Penal System. 1773-1950*, London, Duckworth.
Ignatieff, Michael (1978) *A Just Measure of Pain. The Penitentiary in the Industrial Revolution*, London, Macmillan.
McConville, Sean (1981) *A History of English Penal Administration*, vol 1, 1750-1877, London, Routledge & Kegan Paul.
Melling, Elizabeth (ed.) (1969) *Kentish Sources*, vol. VI, *Crime and Punishment*, Maidstone, Kent County Council.
Rose, June (1980) *Elizabeth Fry. A Biography*, London, Macmillan.
Rusche, Georg and Kirchheimer, Otto (1939) *Punishment and Social Structure*, New York, Columbia University Press.
Thomas, J.E. (1972) *The English Prison Officer since 1850. A Study in Conflict*, London, Routledge & Kegan Paul.
Tomlinson, M. Heather (1978) ' "Not an instrument of punishment." Prison diet in the mid-nineteenth century', *Journal of Consumer Studies and Home Economics*, vol 2, no. 1, March.
Webb, Sidney and Beatrice (1922) *English Prisons under Local Government*, London, Longmans Green.

INDEX